W9-CID-786

LOST SON

ALSO BY BRETT FORREST

Long Bomb: How the XFL Became TV's Biggest Fiasco
The Big Fix: The Hunt for the Match-Fixers Bringing Down Soccer

LOST
SON

AN AMERICAN FAMILY TRAPPED

INSIDE THE FBI'S SECRET WARS

Brett Forrest

Little, Brown and Company

New York Boston London

Copyright © 2023 by Brett Forrest

Hachette Book Group supports the right to free expression and the value of copyright. The purpose of copyright is to encourage writers and artists to produce the creative works that enrich our culture.

The scanning, uploading, and distribution of this book without permission is a theft of the author's intellectual property. If you would like permission to use material from the book (other than for review purposes), please contact permissions@hbgusa.com. Thank you for your support of the author's rights.

Little, Brown and Company
Hachette Book Group
1290 Avenue of the Americas, New York, NY 10104
littlebrown.com

First Edition: May 2023

Little, Brown and Company is a division of Hachette Book Group, Inc. The Little, Brown name and logo are trademarks of Hachette Book Group, Inc.

The publisher is not responsible for websites (or their content) that are not owned by the publisher.

The Hachette Speakers Bureau provides a wide range of authors for speaking events. To find out more, go to hachettespeakersbureau.com or call (866) 376-6591.

Maps by Florin Safner

ISBN 9780316591614
Library of Congress Control Number: 2023931946

Printing 1, 2023

LSC-C

Printed in the United States of America

For my brother

Contents

Contents

BOOK TWO

Contents

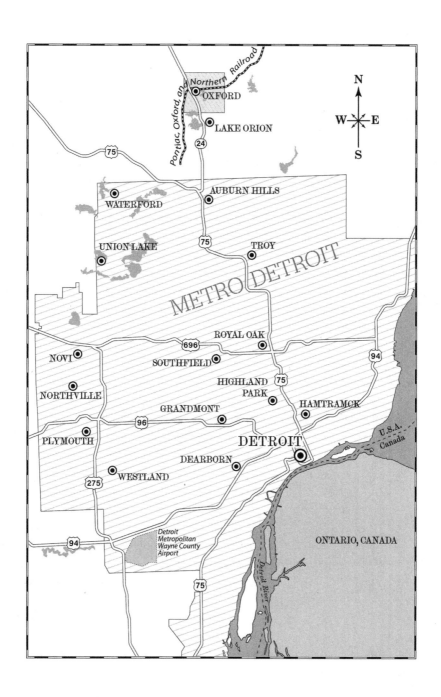

Author's Note

I was waiting in an airport immigration line departing Rostov-on-Don when a man ordered me to follow him. It was the summer of 2019. I had been practicing journalism in Russia.

I'd become embroiled in a case that was unlike any other I'd previously explored. It concerned the Federal Bureau of Investigation, Russian military and domestic intelligence, terrorism, espionage, September 11, the war in Ukraine, and a disappearance that rival agencies were concealing.

I followed the man in the direction of a duty-free shop. He was wearing street clothes, not the uniform of a border guard. This gave me to believe that he worked in the Russian intelligence services.

He approached a wall varnished with an ad for a perfume. Waving a card key, he unlocked a door. We entered an administrative sector of the airport. I followed him down a long hallway of offices and into one of them. Sitting across a desk from me, he paged through my passport.

I had spent many years living or working as a reporter in Russia, and there was no unknown for me to fear. One often heard stories of drama and intrigue, but official encounters were invariably dull. While Russians I knew liked to joke that I was a spy, the professionals understood that I wasn't worth their time.

Yet I now perceived that I could be at risk. I'd learned that the case I had been pursuing reached into both the Russian and US governments. I didn't know how high.

I was aware also that Russian authorities had recently seized two Americans on dubious charges and were holding them, I believed, to swap for a pair of Russians in US prisons. I considered that I might be facing difficulties more serious than missing my flight home.

Looking up from my passport, the man asked why I had come to Russia.

In my line of work, it's best not to dance around but instead tell the truth. Leveling with people usually appeals to them. Sometimes they can even help you.

I welcomed any help on this case. I had discovered plenty, but a definite conclusion eluded me. I began to tell the Russian security officer what I knew.

There was a young man named Billy Reilly. He lived in a town north of Detroit. The terrorist attacks of September 11 had deeply affected him, sparking an interest in people who pursued struggles in foreign countries. The FBI had come into Billy's life. Later, in 2014, after Russia annexed the Ukrainian peninsula of Crimea and fomented war in the eastern part of that country, he became personally involved. I explained that I worked for the *Wall Street Journal* and that I was searching for Billy.

Billy's story showed me how 9/11 had forced the FBI to change and how change is not always for the better. He was an example of how social media thrust issues of global importance upon regular folks in small American towns in surprising, personal ways. Through Billy, I learned how easily an amateur could penetrate the world of professional intelligence in our age of expanding threats.

Immediately upon learning of Billy's case in 2017, I realized that his personal realization through technology and adventure amid a transformation in US intelligence had the makings of a modern American fable. This story began as an investigative proposition for me. It took life later as an article for the *Journal*. It demanded further time and study, and a richer telling. This book is the result of that deeper consideration.

For the book, I interviewed more than a hundred sources, including current and former officials of the FBI, State Department, Central Intelligence Agency, and Obama, Trump, and Biden administrations, officials and militants in Russia and Ukraine, counterterrorism experts, hackers, spies, private investigators, and Billy Reilly's friends and family. I read hundreds of files from the FBI, CIA, and the Department of Justice and scoured thousands more pages from Russian, Ukrainian, and US investigative reports and court records. I combed through thousands of social media postings and text messages in several different languages.

This book is composed of two parts. The first tells the story of Billy Reilly and his family and the evolution of the national security complex that would entangle them. The book's second half picks up with my involvement in the case. It's the account of my own search for Billy in the United States and Russia and the pitfalls and dangers of probing for guarded secrets.

Billy's story has been with me now for five years. I've never been more integral to a mystery's resolution, nor more personally engaged and exposed.

I sometimes think about the 2019 encounter in the Rostov-on-Don airport. I told the intelligence services officer what I had discovered about Billy, leaving him to make what he could of the story's many pieces. I saw that he could do no better than I.

Instead, he reached for something to which he could relate. Billy was from Detroit? he asked. Together we recalled the Russians who had once skated as a unit for the Red Wings.

The man returned me to the airport's immigration line and facilitated my passage through it, doing so even with a smile. Such an easy release layered Billy's case with yet more mystery. Who was manipulating his story from beyond what could be seen?

In the succeeding pages, I've endeavored to provide answers. May the reader find more.

Phnom Penh
December 2022

LOST SON

BOOK ONE

CHAPTER ONE

The Station

May 2015

A year of shooting pictures in eastern Ukraine led Elena Gorbacheva to believe she had encountered every sort of person who goes to war. Their many types had swaggered across her photojournalist's viewfinder and into one Russian publication or another. They had emerged from across Russia and beyond and joined informal volunteer-fighter brigades pursuing Kremlin aims in the war that began in Ukraine in 2014. Some of these men were answering a call to history, others adventure or the chance to kill without earthly penalty. Some men preferred the war to the wife. Plenty of men in Russia were willing to wager their lives. As long as the experience would be diverting.

Gorbacheva commuted between the war in eastern Ukraine's Donbas region and her life in Moscow. She was in the Russian capital now and hurrying across it to a rendezvous. A contact had summoned her to meet a man who had arrived in Russia to join the war. The man was American, which Gorbacheva found thrilling and bizarre, since she knew the problems his nationality would bring.

Gorbacheva understood the volunteer-fighter class as well as anyone did, these men who undertook to cross the border into Ukraine and join up with militias. They waged war against Kiev's army and irregulars, but it was the United States the men reviled.[1]

The US had been the foe of the Soviet Union, a country that expired in the nineties and gave the Americans clear access to Eastern Europe, where they contested long-standing though troubled ties between Russia and its neighbors. *Without American interference, Moscow and Kiev could have managed their hard feelings. There would be no war in Ukraine. There'd be no Ukraine. There'd be only Russia, as before.* That's what these volunteer fighters said, and some part of it might have been true, this war reviving the Cold War, which in their way they were attempting to re-arbitrate.[2]

Gorbacheva knew that an American would likely find trouble among the rough and belligerent volunteer-fighter class. Many of these men were of ready violence, heavy drinkers, dark thinkers, given to suspicion. An American would be suspect among them. Yet she believed there was a way. Russia wasn't the only place that bred tough people and veterans of misguided wars who were too troubled to return to the comparative triviality of their former lives. Maybe this American was one of those, plagued by echoing battles. An intention to enter the war had carried him this far, to central Moscow's intrigue and disorder.

Komsomolskaya Square stood at one o'clock on the circular dial that defined interior Moscow. Three of the city's nine rail stations yoked the square, each bearing the name of a principal destination: Kazan, Leningrad (St. Petersburg), Yaroslavl. Overgrown through a century into one of the largest of Moscow's depots, the Kazan station was crafted in Russian-Byzantine style, its corner hall sustaining a six-tiered, ever-slimming wedding-cake tower, crowned by a gilded, winged dragon. The station's asymmetry of influences was its inadvertent brilliance, like a certain country.[3]

The interior of the station was no less perplexing and invigorating. Murals of blimps and electrical towers covered a ceiling of blue tempera and gold-leaf frescoes. Colored bulbs twinkled on kiosks selling cigarettes, potato chips, sketch pads bearing cameos of Vladimir Lenin, and other rudiments of Russian travel. Porters steered sharp-cornered steel carriages past people huddled on benches, the station a place of transience. With evening approaching, the sun's fading beams filtered through the soot on the station's windows. Gorbacheva's contact, a Russian named Mikhail Polynkov, was waiting for her.[4]

Polynkov was a recruiter. He attracted volunteer fighters from Russia and beyond and dispatched them to a transit camp in a city in the Russian south, Rostov-on-Don. From there, Polynkov and his aides eased men across the

Ukrainian border to join fighting brigades.[5] In the Kazan station, he dressed as he often did, like a paramilitary fighter in a faded army cap and loose infantry-man's coat. Gorbacheva was accustomed to his style. Her photographer's gaze instead fell with instinctive curiosity upon the figure standing beside Polynkov.

The man stood five-foot-eight, wore glasses, and appeared to be roughly thirty years old. He wore black sneakers, faded blue jeans, and a black fleece pullover, unzipped. A modest belly shaped his gray T-shirt. His haircut, conventional in shape and length, gave no indication of his personality. He had a spotty dark beard and an indoor complexion. At his hand was a blocky, waist-high black suitcase on wheels. It was so large that he might have fit inside of it.[6]

Gorbacheva was confused, and a little let down. This was the American? The man projected none of the fatalistic bravura of the volunteer fighters she was accustomed to photographing. Here was no romantic image. Here was a tourist. Gorbacheva envisioned the Donbas battlefields, bodies strewn and motionless, tanks afire, the artillery cruel and recalibrating, and the American moving amid the action tugging his suitcase.

Their conversation was complicated. The American used a Russian name, Vasily. This confused Gorbacheva, especially since the man faltered as he expressed himself in the local tongue. He was no native Russian speaker, nor a practiced one, unable to carry much of a spoken conversation in the language.

The talk switched to English, and Gorbacheva interpreted as well as she could for Polynkov, who knew less English than she. Their dialogue turned to the war in Donbas.

"You're sure you want to go?" Polynkov asked Vasily.

"Yes," Vasily answered. "I really want to go."

"You know, it's very dangerous."

"I'm ready."[7]

Vasily failed to mention any military experience he might have had. There were no identifying patches sewn onto his clothes. He bore no visible scars or tattoos that might have attested to relevant experience. Gorbacheva thought she had met every sort of man bound for war, but here was a new type, one who didn't belong there.

The station's loudspeakers stirred, and the American followed Polynkov and

Gorbacheva through the depot's rear doors. They walked onto an expanse of blacktop. There, a dozen bullish and lengthy trains huddled on tracks beneath a high roof. The departures board listed the track for the train to Rostov-on-Don, nearly seven hundred miles to the south, and the group of three walked down the platform, leaving the station's enclosure for open sky.

The Russian Railways train, number 19/20, was painted red and gray. Counting the wagon numbers, the group reached the car that Vasily's ticket had assigned to him. The train had a name, "Quiet Don," lifted from the novel and also the river that evoked Russia's Cossack southwest.[8]

The three paused in awkward silence. Vasily turned to the door of the train car. Gorbacheva stayed him. She had a camera. She raised her lens.

Vasily stood by the wagon, its destination stenciled on a signboard behind him and pressed against a window of the train. Looking through the camera's eyepiece, Gorbacheva strained to focus on her subject, for Vasily had no expression. She clicked several frames.

Vasily heaved his big bag into the wagon. Conductors made last calls and sealed the doors. The train edged from the station. The American dissolved into the car's interior, passing by curtained windows, a shadow bound for war.

*   *   *

June 2015

A sedan drove north, away from Detroit. The car sequenced through the deforested spray of suburbs that radiated from downtown, past Highland Park, Royal Oak, and farther up Troy, parcels that the Fords and Dodges had cleared a century ago to make room for auto plants and the people who would work in them.[9] At the northern edge of Metro Detroit, the sedan sped through Auburn Hills. The Palace, once a modern arena, now crouched there dark and derelict, fated for demolition.

The car turned off the interstate and entered a modest world. State Highway 24, slimming to two lanes, etched into the blue atlas of lake region. At the roadside appeared a car lot, a gym, and a few fast-food franchises, the vanguard of a town: Oxford, Michigan.

To people in Detroit, Oxford had always been "up north." Forty miles was little distance in a state so taken with how the car could move you. There were reasons why Oxford felt far away. Detroit's fortunes had depended on auto manufacturing, yet Oxford had hewed more surely to the land. The people there had known farming, fishing, mining, and boating. A perfect square, six miles per side, Oxford was still thick with lakes and trees, its northeastern quadrant left mostly for horses. The town's prevailing mood was conservative. Oxford's people were, broadly, unimpressed by change and did not seek it.[10]

The sedan drove toward Oxford's brick-building town center and its American grill and old movie house, then turned off Highway 24 and onto a local road bound west, where the surface turned to earth and gravel. The car approached a series of lakes, oblong in contour and sparkling with summer light. From an aerial view, the land amid this Stringy Lakes Chain formed a handprint, its digits pressing into cobalt waters.

Across one of these slender fingers of land, the road slipped past a dozen homes snugly arranged. The green leafy branches of an oak tree, taller than a giraffe, swayed in the lake breeze, shading a brown home with a peaked roof. Waist-high hedgerows drew the home's property lines, and a cluster of bushes engorged a picket fence at the road. There, pinned to a post, a blue receptacle awaited delivery of *The Oakland Press*. The sedan drew near.

Inside the house, the prospect of news unsettled Theresa Reilly. She looked through a back window, scanning the lake for an ethereal sign, a solution to the dilemma that had just now descended upon her.

Theresa was sixty-one years old and wore large eyeglasses, and her graying hair fell to her shoulders. She was a Michigander of Polish stock, a Catholic. She had grown up in Detroit amid a Polish American circle. When she was a girl, her parents were busy with auto-industry work and were seldom around to raise her, leaving an everlasting influence, like all episodes early and fundamental. Theresa had tried some college and a few jobs but in place of a career had chosen to spend her adult life caring for her two children, who were now adults themselves.[11]

Theresa liked people to call her Terry. She dressed in roomy jeans and T-shirts, tending to informality, and was possessed of a sardonic wit. Terry was partial to fast food and enjoyed watching reruns of *Seinfeld*, a TV sitcom from the 1990s, whose farce appealed to her.

Terry's husband, Bill Reilly, was a truck driver, long since retired and on disability. Eight months younger than Terry, Bill still answered to Curly, a handle from long ago, even though his white hair now sprouted in wisps, which he gathered into a ponytail. He had a snowy beard and a tranquil spirit. He looked like he might be on his way to a music festival.

Bill had also come of age in the Detroit area and was of Irish and Norwegian background, the hippie son of a demanding military father whom Bill could never please.

Terry and Bill had each felt adrift when they'd found each other in young adulthood. Newly married in their twenties, they had moved up to the lake country in 1980. They were fleeing Detroit's social and economic troubles in the decade following the city's race riots. They were also withdrawing into the shelter of their own company amid the deliberate pace of life up north.

Bill and Terry determined to raise children with the support and understanding they had been denied, encircled by Oxford's tranquil waters. Yet as Terry now shifted her focus from the lake's gentle quiet to the smartphone in her hand, she knew that no one in our modern world is beyond the reach of tempting dangers.

Their firstborn was the eighth William Reilly in succession, yet he would veer sharply from the course of this family line. As a teen, Billy, as his parents called him, developed a fascination for international conflicts, attaching himself via the expanding phenomenon of social media to the people who were fighting them. His parents strained to understand Billy yet loved him no less.

The Reillys' second child, a daughter, Catie, would become a physician. She shared many of her brother's iconoclastic views and interests and would make choices similar to his own. Yet this would estrange her from her parents, intensifying their attachment to their son.[12]

Like all families, the Reillys had their hard feelings and paradoxes, but in June 2015 they suddenly set all that aside. Billy, the son, was in peril. In May of that year, he had embarked on an ambitious international trip. Now five thousand miles from home, Billy had abruptly fallen out of touch.

Terry had slept little the night before, rolling over in bed to find no gratification in her phone's lit screen. No messages from her son. No missed calls. "Don't worry," Billy had told her at the airport in Detroit. "Don't worry, I'll be fine." He had promised to call or text every day. For six weeks, he had done just that, sharing details of his travels. Then, without warning, Billy's calls and texts ceased.

In a fog and despairing, Bill and Terry now heard the sedan pull up outside the house. A knock rattled their front door.

The Reillys received few visitors, and in their mounting distress over Billy they were unprepared for one now. Steeling themselves, they opened the door. Facing them on their front porch were two men in dark suits. The taller of the two, standing well over six feet, handed them a business card. Embossed on its upper-left corner was the seal of the Federal Bureau of Investigation.

The man introduced himself as Tim Reintjes (pronounced "Rine-chez"), and Terry Reilly stifled a gasp as she watched him duck his head and advance down the home's low entry hallway. The Reillys had a lengthy backstory with the FBI, but they had never met Reintjes or his colleague, and their unannounced visit, so soon after Billy's communications had lapsed, filled Terry and Bill with dread. The family's small terrier yapped at the guests before scampering to a corner of the living room and hiding under a rolltop desk that supported a computer.

The parlor was cozy. Reintjes and his associate eased into a sofa. Mounted above them on a wall and overpowering the room was a cast of the marlin that Billy had caught on a visit to Hawaii years earlier, before his life had taken fateful turns.

Sitting across from Reintjes, Terry and Bill took his measure. If they were to imagine what an FBI agent might look like, they might have envisioned him. Reintjes was square-jawed. Buttoned-up. He looked educated. His posture was erect. His dark hair was cut short, though not as short as a soldier's. He looked like someone who would follow through on what he said.

Agent Reintjes worked in the FBI's counterterrorism division. There was no department that the Bureau valued more highly. This outfit was most responsible for preventing and investigating terrorist attacks in the US and against American people and property abroad. By the nature of this mission, FBI counterterrorism agents were aggressive, secretive, and bound by voluminous codes and protocols that they safeguarded behind a stony reticence.

The Reillys were certain that Reintjes had arrived at their home to share news about Billy. They could imagine no other reason for the visit, especially given its timing. From the movies and TV shows they had seen, they knew that no FBI agent ever came calling to ease anyone's concern. Bill and Terry feared what Reintjes was about to tell them.

Yet when Reintjes spoke, he surprised them. He asked, "Is Billy home?"

Terry and Bill traded a curious look. "Well, no," Bill said.

Terry fixed on agent Reintjes. "Do you know where he is?" she asked.

"What do you mean?" Reintjes said.

"Have you heard from him?" Terry rejoined.

"Has he gone someplace?" Reintjes asked.

Bill exchanged another glance with his wife. They were confused. Surely the FBI possessed information about Billy's whereabouts. What else could have prompted Reintjes's visit? The Reillys thought they had misunderstood, or that Reintjes had a reason to toy with them. It was time to come to the point. "Well, yeah," Bill responded. "He's in Russia."

Reintjes looked startled. His eyes shifted from Bill to Terry and back again, as though he was trying to read them. "Russia?" he asked. "What's he doing in Russia?"

"We don't know," Terry said. "We thought *you* knew."

"I didn't know that," Reintjes said, shaking his head. "We're trying to get ahold of him."

Reintjes asked Bill and Terry if they were in touch with their son. They explained that Billy had recently fallen silent. Reintjes's interest grew. Who were Billy's companions in Russia, Reintjes wanted to know, and which cities had he visited? What was he planning to do? To the Reillys, this felt like the beginning of an inquiry.

Terry's heart pounded. She had thought that the FBI agents had come to tell her that her son had been arrested in Russia or been the victim of an accident, or worse. The fact that Reintjes appeared to have no information at all about Billy compounded her uncertainty.

Terry's gaze strayed to a mantel across the living room, where a photo of Billy stood in a frame. He was wearing a red-and-white Little League uniform, holding a baseball bat against one shoulder, smiling, ten years old. Images and emotions from those years, richer than memories, flooded Terry with feeling. Never had she been as frightened as she was now.

"Why did Billy go to Russia?" Reintjes asked.

"For the humanitarian convoy," Terry said. She and Bill shared what they knew about their son's travels, at least what he had told them. As they heard themselves talk, they realized it did not amount to much. They little understood the reasons Billy had given for his Russia trip. They regretted not having asked him more questions.

Reintjes said he'd find out all he could and on his way to the door paused. "One more thing," he said. "What side is Billy on?"[13]

CHAPTER TWO

Winging It

B ill and Terry Reilly grew up in the Detroit area in the 1950s, in the bakeries, taverns, and churches that redeemed the tedium of work on the auto-plant assembly lines. The car companies underwrote the way of life in Detroit. They demanded much from their workers and in exchange provided ample pay and pensions. Blacks, Irish, Italians, Poles, those divided from the upper class, made lives of their labor.

Terry Reilly's maternal grandparents had immigrated separately to the United States from Poland in 1913 and met each other in Detroit. They were part of a wave of Europeans drawn to Michigan's auto industry and Henry Ford's five-dollar workday.

Terry's parents, Marvin and Irene O'Kray, met in a Detroit bowling alley in the mid-forties and had five children. One died at birth. Terry was next to last. The O'Krays lived on Southfield Road in the Grandmont neighborhood. Counting grandparents, parents, uncles, and little ones, they housed ten people in a brick bungalow that measured 1,200 square feet. A finished basement made a second living room.

In such quarters a child could go overlooked, and Terry often did. Her parents didn't push the kids in school or browbeat them at home. Marvin and Irene were hands-off, often busy earning a living. Terry's mother had stayed on at Ford's River Rouge plant after the war, clocking long hours making piston rings. Marvin held down two jobs, one sorting letters at the post office, the other building a waste-oil business with his wife's brother.

Terry's Polish-speaking grandmother packed the kids' school lunches and otherwise looked after them, an in-home example of the sacrifices and benefits of immigration. Terry's grandmother had left Poland when she was sixteen years old and had learned English and the American ways, assimilating to life in the new country.[1]

In the 1940s and '50s, Detroit was still attracting people from far away. European immigration to the United States had increased after World War II, with Europe partially destroyed and American manufacturing soaring. More than 200,000 Poles immigrated to the US after the war, with about 38,000 settling in Michigan.[2] Immigrant parents and first-generation children clung to their ethnic identities.

A Polish community clustered on Detroit's east side. Houses there were modest, yet their owners took pride in appearances. In the warmer months, one might see housewives in their front yards, brooms in hand, sweeping leaves and twigs off their lawns. In the winter, if a man failed to shovel the snow from his family drive, a neighbor might do it for him, providing a lesson in what was expected.[3] On Saturdays, men would gather at the barbershop and watch baseball or boxing on a black-and-white TV. On Sundays, nearly everyone in Detroit's Polish, Irish, and Italian neighborhoods would gather for Mass at a local Catholic church.

Time, a US car slump, and social unrest pulled these communities apart. Detroit ignited in race riots in 1967, and ensuing years of economic downturn plagued the city. Many whites fled, with blacks taking their place and shifting Detroit's demographics.[4]

In 1973, the O'Krays relocated to Metro Detroit's far northwest to a village named Union Lake. They did what many of Detroit's Poles had already done, scattering to suburban limits.

Emerging from this fraying fabric was Terry O'Kray. She had no interest in following her mother into the River Rouge plant. Terry took classes at Eastern Michigan University and Oakland University but didn't last in these schools and wound up working the books at her father's business.

Bill Reilly grew up in Northville, in western Metro Detroit, and also in Battle Creek, a hundred miles to the west, where the Post and Kellogg's smokestacks disgorged the scent of toasted breakfast cereals. Bill later remembered that "it was like being inside a box of cornflakes as soon as you got around there."

Bill's father had a drive to succeed and a zeal for challenges. He had piloted Marine fighters in World War II, in the Pacific Theater, and later became an insurance man, earning a law degree in middle age. He applied discipline to his only child, but it had little effect. Bill was drawn instead to the music scene and the counterculture of the Vietnam era. He grew his hair long and cultivated a beard. His father rarely squandered an opportunity to underscore the differences between himself and the son who disappointed him.[5]

Bill's mother's roots were Norwegian, but he'd say that it was his Irish Traveller pedigree that led him to drifting. A grandfather had once roamed the country selling elixirs. Bill eventually picked up a job at a grocery store, finding communion on the loading dock with the truckers bringing in goods.

In 1979, a friend took Terry to Bill's place. Terry had heard of him. She knew his nickname, Riled, and the nature it suggested. Her first thought when she saw him at the apartment with his wild, curly hair and beard: he's too short. She left the party, and Bill left her mind.

Bill could think of no one else. He called nearly every O'Kray in Metro Detroit's white pages before getting her on the phone. Terry was dating someone else, but Bill bided time in his car outside her apartment in Westland. Before long, Terry found her thoughts turning to him. Few people had ever directed such sustained energy to her. The courtship of Bill and Terry took place in a Metro Detroit where ethnic enclaves yet remained, and in a tattoo parlor: a butterfly for her and for him a falling star.

Bill had found his girl, and in the continuing rush of impulse, he also picked up a Cadillac, a blue '75 Eldorado with a white ragtop. "I did a lot of winging it," Bill later said, characterizing his approach to life. He wound up on an O'Kray family trip to Las Vegas in 1979 and spirited Terry away once they had arrived. Meeting Terry's parents that evening for a show headlined by Tony Orlando and Pia Zadora at the Riviera casino, Terry and Bill announced they had eloped at a Vegas courthouse.

The union and its modest prospects delighted few. Back in Michigan, Bill and Terry explored the Detroit area for a place to be together, believing that life on the water would be for them.[6]

Winging It

*   *   *

In 1837, the year President Andrew Jackson signed the bill declaring Michigan the union's twenty-sixth state, a group of settlers met north of Detroit. A farmer called Thompson suggested a name for their colony: Oxford. A record of the meeting noted that "a patriotic Yankee strenuously opposed the adoption of any name so strongly savored with British life and customs." It was not the university town that had inspired Thompson, but the oxen whose labor made frontier life endurable.

The Erie Canal drew settlers from eastern states to Michigan's Native American hunting grounds. Pioneers availed themselves of oak, pine, and white cedar forests. They trudged through marshlands and drained and cultivated them. They stalked brown bear and collected three-dollar bounties per wolf scalp. On plots of a hundred acres and more, they seeded orchards and crops. They fell to disease. Generations turned. Oxford's bark-roofed log homes gave way to farmhouses with summer porches. A vinegar factory opened in town. A wainwright, a cooperage, a library of 175 volumes. In 1859, Sunday school began inculcating children at a Baptist church.[7]

A rail line, the P. O. & N (Pontiac, Oxford, and Northern), pierced the woods of Michigan's thumb. Locals called the railroad the Polly Ann, and it moved wheat, sugar beet, and rutabaga, the crop giving Oxford a turn-of-the-century nickname, Bagatown.

A man named Smith discovered a richer harvest. Ice-age glaciers had torn through the local bedrock, churning a mass of chipped granite. Farmers in their fields encountered great stone impediments and summoned Smith to haul them away. By the 1920s, five million tons of gravel shipped from Oxford each year, more than from any other origin in the world. The Polly Ann ran the Gravel Extra, a special cargo train to and from Detroit.[8]

Gravel formed the substance of the roads now threading the country in service to the cars coming off the line at Ford's River Rouge and other Metro Detroit plants. The car business boomed, and new towns appeared around Detroit, and they boomed, too. Oxford's population, though, never exceeded 4,000. Life changed by increments.

Most of the gravel pits in time gave up their last, and the Gravel Extra stopped running on the Polly Ann. The miners had dug their pits deeply enough to hit water, which seeped from below to fill the great holes they'd made. New lakes formed. Houses rose up around their perimeters.

High times never came to Oxford, and neither was there anything left to pioneer. As the 1970s concluded, Oxford remained remote. One might drive up there from Detroit with a fishing rod or to visit a cousin, but rarely on a lark.

Terry and Bill slipped into this quiet in the Carter years. They found a quadrangular piece of land less than a quarter acre, with water on two sides. Standing on the lot was a single-room cabin, two hundred feet square. It was a shack, really, meant for changing into a swimsuit for a dip in the lake, not for the life the Reillys hoped to build. Even such a modest possession lay beyond the grasp of the young couple. They owned a single asset, Bill's Eldorado, which he relinquished in lieu of money down.

In the Oxford shed, Bill and Terry lived life as in the age of the Jackson-era pioneers. Bill installed a Franklin stove, and for two winters its heat and the cabin's reedy walls were all that resisted the winds coming off the lake. Life was no more modern in the other homes along this finger of land, which Terry took to calling Hillbilly Row. She and Bill didn't complain. Life in Oxford, never hasty, was comprehensible and appealing. They gathered enough in cash and loans to build a house on their lot in 1982.

The home felt nest-like, and the Reillys sought to fill it. For four years, five, they tried. Terry submitted to rounds of in vitro fertilization, experimental for the day yet fruitless for them.[9]

Their futility suited an era of decline. Foreign carmakers had caught their American counterparts flat-footed, and the Detroit auto industry pitched toward downfall. The Big Three laid off labor and shuttered plants. Banks foreclosed on the homes of workers who no longer claimed wages. Many went on welfare, some turned to crime. Fowl reclaimed the land.[10]

Witnessing the stable world around them falter, Bill and Terry received news they had long ago stopped hoping would ever come: a natural pregnancy. Bill's grocery had succumbed to the spreading economic malaise, stripping the family of health insurance as Terry gave birth to Billy in 1986. The Reillys were saddled with hospital bills but swore they'd find a way to cover them. Two summers later, a daughter, Catherine, or Catie, was born. Bill picked up a job through friends from the grocery store's loading dock, driving a Teamsters route for Coca-Cola.[11]

Winging It

The Detroit-area ethnic European neighborhoods he and Terry had known were now gone, vanished through generations of assimilation, intermarriage, and departure to the suburbs. The grandkids of earlier immigrants were all now, simply, Michiganders, having lost hold of their ethnic roots.

In the 1980s and '90s, a new type of immigrant community was gathering. These people had escaped the Lebanese Civil War. They had fled the first US war in Iraq, the Gulf War. Arab Muslims, they had come to the United States not so much by choice but more from desperation, and they were suspicious of America's freedoms and immoral temptations. They safeguarded their identity, religion, and rituals.[12]

South of Oxford, in and near Dearborn, west of downtown, store signs were written in an alphabet strange to many people whose families had been in Detroit for generations. Muslim mosques had sprung up in place of Christian churches whose believers no longer lived nearby. Dearborn, the lion heart of auto-making and the US economy, where Henry Ford had forged a deal with labor and put it to work in his city-like plant, had become an Arab enclave.

This Middle Eastern origin and language, this habit of dressing in robes and head coverings and inscrutable beards, many people in Metro Detroit found it unsettling. This new wave of immigrants appeared to make little effort to blend in and belong, leaving many in the area to wonder why such people had come to the US in the first place.

Yet there was a precedent. Many Detroit-area Polish immigrant families at the turn of the previous century had likewise resisted assimilation, declining to send their children to English-speaking public schools that offered little to no instruction in Polish culture, history, and language.[13] Even into the second half of the century, one could enjoy a meal at a Polish cafe in Hamtramck and never hear a word of English spoken there.[14] "No matter what nationality you were, you knew there was a little area you can go, where they're all talking your language, just as if you're back in the old country," Terry later remembered. "All the little areas, they're all gone. There's no Irish neighborhood. There's no Polish neighborhood. There's no German neighborhood." In their places, Arab neighborhoods had formed.

The phenomenon that many in Detroit sentimentalized, clannish communities, was the very privilege they would deny others who had arrived in the United States from someplace other than Europe. The Arab Muslims

19

who clung to their ways in and around Dearborn felt like an affront to the assimilation that European immigrants had been unable to resist. To some, it felt like outside influences were closing in.

These changes affecting Dearborn and other sections of Metro Detroit, distinctive though they were in the '90s, were for the Reillys a world away. Oxford remained its own sort of enclave. Bill and Terry were determined to guide their children away from puzzling influences, toward conventional lives.

CHAPTER THREE

Disaffection

I n the years that would unfold, the Reillys' son, Billy, took to school, sports, and church, indistinguishable from other boys his age in Oxford. In time, though, he would conceive a path toward a different purpose, making choices that would confound Terry and Bill. In his own way, Billy would decline to assimilate to the life his parents wished for him.

At first, Billy knew rejection. In the early 1990s, Terry and Bill sought to enroll their son at a local grade school. But teachers at St. Joseph Catholic School declined Billy's admission on the grounds that his speech needed remediation. All he really needed was a pair of glasses, which clarified the world around him, allowing for self-expression. With glasses, he could see the writing on the chalkboard once he ultimately started at St. Joe's. He could see well enough to hit a baseball.

Billy was sharp-witted, if quiet, and protective of his sister. People outside the family often mistook the children for twins due to their resemblance and closeness, and since Catie was tall for her age. Billy had school friends, and at summer camp on the lake, he took to fishing, developing a lasting attachment. He was a Cub Scout.

Billy was close to his grandfather Marvin, Terry's father, a World War II veteran. Marvin O'Kray had deployed with the 116th Infantry Regiment as a replacement soldier two weeks after the Normandy landing.[1] But instead of sharing war stories with his grandson, Marvin preferred to discuss the Detroit Tigers, baseball stats and arcana revealing Billy's talent for remembering.

Billy went down the road of the American boy, his promise hovering beyond him past the ice creams and the reruns, toward a horizon that to his parents had no limits. There was a TV sitcom drama that was then popular, *Family Ties*, which followed a family of five, including a whip-smart son who wore suits and carried a briefcase. The show amused Bill and Terry, for they saw a resemblance to their own boy, while also identifying a possible model. They thought that Billy would one day carry his own briefcase, wear his own suits to the office, or maybe to a lecture hall. He might one day be a college professor. He might be something more. Encouraged by how Billy was getting on in school and also recognizing how his developing intellect distinguished him from other kids, they visualized all he would achieve.[2]

These visions would dissolve. In the midst of his time at St. Joe's, Billy began expressing a desire to stay home from school. Terry chalked it up to a conflict he'd had with a friend. But when she pressed Billy further, he recounted an incident from years earlier, from perhaps second grade. A priest at St. Joe's had summoned him to his office, along with another boy. Small for his age, and wearing his glasses, Billy generally kept quiet and avoided trouble. He wasn't the sort of student on which a principal or teacher would ordinarily focus. But Billy had indeed come to the notice of this religious authority. Once Billy and the other boy had entered the office, the priest flipped the lock on the door. He turned toward Billy and exposed himself.[3]

A societal reckoning with the Church's epidemic abetting of sexually abusive priests was yet to come. Abuse in the church was difficult for families to reconcile with the clergy's role as an ethical guide. St. Joe's, like many churches and parochial schools, had experienced its troubles, having already removed an abusive priest.[4] Terry had been volunteering at the school as a teacher's aide but learned of the incident involving Billy only years later, when he felt confident enough to share it.

On Sunday mornings, he bristled when Terry told him to wear something nice for Mass.[5] Catie later said that her brother "definitely did not want anything to do with the Catholic Church." Eventually, he quit going altogether. When the extended family would drive off to church, Billy would stay behind at home.

Each summer, once the kids were out of school, the Reillys would hit the road in an RV for lengthy drives, fortnight vacations. With Bill at the wheel, they would make for New England, or California, or Florida. Terry and Bill took their kids through the lower forty-eight along hot summertime roads. Catie took to calling such trips "quantity time," presaging conflict and an urge to break away. Billy and Catie found allies in each other on the long and dusty drives.[6]

Billy wasn't drawn to activities that most other kids enjoyed, like swimming in a lake or a hotel pool, or climbing into a roller coaster. He had given up baseball and preferred to avoid crowds. He didn't care for parties. For him, it was all right to be alone. On vacations, when the family would head out to play a round of miniature golf, Billy would watch the TV news in the motel room.[7]

Billy had his own escape, but that too was solitary. He often landed a spot on a fishing boat on a small-town lake or river or even on the ocean. "The beauty and intricacies of the natural world have always amazed and fascinated me," he later wrote in a college-application essay. "Even as a child, I would love to investigate the world around me."[8]

Once the school year resumed, Billy would begin to feel boxed in. He wanted out of St. Joe's, and in 1999 Terry and Bill obliged him.

Billy and Catie enrolled in Oxford Middle School, the public school in town. Gone were the uniforms of Catholic school, along with its regimentation and religious instruction. Public school provided a freer environment that Terry and Bill hoped would encourage Billy to develop new interests and friendships. They found instead that it hadn't been the structure of St. Joe's that had frustrated Billy's development, but perhaps the sting of abuse. In the liberality of public school, Billy found a truant crowd. A teacher discovered him smoking pot in a school bathroom. Billy received a suspension.[9]

Terry and Bill were dismayed. They knew Billy was intelligent, and they had to arrest his slide. Forget advanced degrees and visions of esteem. They just wanted to get Billy to eighteen. Their thoughts returned to Catholic school, fixing on Our Lady of the Lakes Parish School, in Waterford, a sixteen-mile drive south of Oxford.

When a student enrolls in a high school in the middle of a term, there is a reason why. Billy arrived at Our Lady of the Lakes in January 2001, halfway through his freshman year, with his hair dyed orange. This was an unacceptable form of expression at an institution that required students to wear uniforms and attend Mass. The school principal suggested that Billy make time for a barber. With his head freshly shaven and Catie likewise enrolling in the school, Billy did not avail himself of the clean start. He clashed with teachers and administrators. One teacher later said that Billy came to his new school "kicking and screaming."[10]

Billy was an outsider, especially at Lakes (as students called it). The school's lowest grade was kindergarten, and many of the students of high school age had known each other since they had learned to read. Into this closed social system came someone new who didn't play sports or an instrument or make much effort to belong. In every high school class, there's a Billy Reilly, bright but shiftless, friendly but friendless, sensitive but so withdrawn that one would never know he had any feelings at all.

Into the fall term of his sophomore year at Lakes, his third school in as many years, Billy, now fifteen, was adrift, failing to connect with those around him. Inside of him, imperceptible to his parents, his energy and acumen were entwined and coiled, poised for release upon some fascination, if only he could find it.

One morning in the fall of 2001, he was attending Mass at Lakes with his class, in the small church that stood in front of the main school building. It was the sort of compulsory activity that Billy loathed but endured. In the midst of the service, a teacher's aide scurried into the chapel, drawing the students' attention. The aide was agitated. She announced to the students that an airplane had just struck the World Trade Center in New York City.[11]

CHAPTER FOUR

Cataclysm

In the immediate aftermath of the terrorist attacks of September 11, 2001, a single question gripped the country: Who had directed the 19 hijackers, all of whom were dead and beyond retribution? Once the American people had the answer to that question, they demanded to know where Osama bin Laden and the rest of the Islamic fundamentalist terror group al Qaeda were hiding.[1] In short order, the country focused its revenge, as US troops funneled into Afghanistan.[2] The Global War on Terror had begun.

Its smoldering battlefield, Manhattan, was emotionally devastated, a destination that most any American avoided. Yet the Reillys had never needed much of a reason to hit the road. Like everyone else, they were trying to make sense of 9/11. In January 2002, Terry and Bill packed up the kids and the camper. It was a half-day drive east on I-80 and through the Holland Tunnel to the edge of the 9/11 wreckage. "We wanted to see it for ourselves," Terry said.

At Ground Zero, Billy viewed the result of the terrorist act with his own eyes. He peered through the fencing that encircled the debris where the World Trade Center towers had once blocked out the sky, having no inkling of the role he would play in the story that was changing the world.[3]

Billy had been unable to find anything that stirred him in Oxford or at Lakes. But now, as he stood on the edge of the attacks' epicenter, he was engaged.

Billy didn't formulate the same questions that most Americans were asking. He didn't care to learn who was responsible for the attacks or where these people were now. He wasn't interested in revenge. Staring at the gnarled result of 9/11, Billy didn't ask who had done it. He asked *why* they had done it. Why did so many people have to die? "He wanted to understand what would make someone angry enough to do this," his sister Catie would say later.[4]

"Who?" and "Where?" were the immediate questions. "Why?" was the ultimate question. If you could answer why, you could distinguish motive. You could unlock understanding. You could begin to explain how countries behaved as they did, and how religious and political groups arose to commit brutal deeds. You could assign sense to acts that appeared senseless, maybe even to the 9/11 attacks. "Why?" was the rational question, and the most difficult one to answer. With "why" as his guide, Billy would begin to question everything about 9/11 and the events spiraling from it. His adolescent searching for meaning now had focus.

Back in Michigan, the TV newscasters and the teachers and kids at Lakes and even Billy's parents all seemed too certain: Islam was to blame for 9/11. Arabs were to blame. Billy found the explanation pat. "Billy just didn't believe that all the things people were saying on TV about Islam were true," Catie later said.

No one Billy encountered appeared to take into account how possible mistakes of US policy might have filled in a fuller picture of the attacks. Billy knew little of the history of US activity in the Middle East, but he sensed a field of inquiry. Seeking his own conclusions about what had assaulted the world, he realized that a ready tool was at hand.[5] On the rolltop desk in the corner of the Reillys' living room sat a bulky computer and monitor that Terry and Bill had bought a few years before.

The family used the computer to send and receive emails and to roam the Web. Billy and Catie sometimes used it for homework assignments. The family computer, like the family dog and car, had settled into its place in the Reillys' lives, a comfort and a utility. The ungainly block of gray plastic, in aesthetic disharmony with the antiquarian rolltop, would be Billy's vehicle to understanding worlds beyond Oxford.

Like Billy, the Internet was in adolescence. The squelch and beep of his dial-up connection prefigured his scrolling through web pages of rudimentary design. Amazon wasn't far removed from simply selling books. "Social media" wasn't yet a term.

September 11 triggered a new stage of digital growth. The event gave purpose to the bloggers who staked out positions beyond traditional news outlets. The Internet enabled anyone to publish, and publish anything. There was no filter, nor any professional standard required, allowing bloggers to sidestep the gatekeepers of the old-guard news media. Some bloggers unearthed facts and broke news and pressured the established press to match their pace and revelations. Others, untroubled by ethics, spread doubt and confusion, their material feeling illicit and alive. September 11 theories proliferated, raising questions instead of verifying facts, some postulating that the attacks had been an inside job. The Internet provided more information with less supervision, sometimes mingling fact with fancy.

The Internet supplied Billy with a counterpoint to the uniformity of the conclusions around him. He found a gateway to new answers.

"Some people may find that their most memorable childhood experiences include the birth of a sibling, the first day of school, or an exciting vacation," he wrote years later in an essay. "But for me, the day I will always remember was when my family got our first computer. The computer brought the whole world into our living room."[6]

*   *   *

At Our Lady of the Lakes, the cliques were loosening. The cataclysm had united the students of high school age, who now tried to come to terms with 9/11 and its aftermath. Within the radius of the attacks, Billy shared something with the other kids.

A football player at school found something curious in Billy, appreciated the dry wit that Billy was developing, and began inviting him to hang out. Other friends came along. Billy started joining them before school for a cigarette beyond the view of teachers. One of their group later said that "anyone who was a smartass seemed interesting."[7] Billy and his new friends slouched at the back of the class, doing the minimum.

Even as he was becoming one of the guys, Billy was developing views that held him apart from them. His new friends weren't online delving into the terrorist attacks to learn why they had occurred. They viewed 9/11 as a starting point, not one with antecedents. Several of Billy's friends talked about enlisting in the US military to fight al Qaeda.

Billy told his friends that they might want to learn more about the war on terror before consigning their lives to it. He wasn't shy in telling kids at Lakes that 9/11 was a comeuppance for foolish US policies. "Wherever he was getting his information," one classmate later said, "it was different from the rest of us."[8]

Other guys in school chased girls or grades or found or lost themselves in sports or music or drugs, but Billy withdrew after class, retreating to the home computer. He immersed himself in online readings on global affairs, yearning to understand the post-cataclysmic world. He read books for a provocative mind, *The Communist Manifesto*, *Mein Kampf*, the Koran, selecting from the aspirant iconoclast's bookshelf. The Internet allowed him to follow his own directed study. There, he found something real and immediate, different from his lessons at Lakes, which he believed impractical.

He perceived the school's insularity. Lakes wasn't known to be broadminded. Islam, Arabism, one was as the other, un-American. The largest Arab community in the United States was located just thirty miles south, in Dearborn, and Billy asked himself how many kids from Lakes had ever been there. How were they in position to judge a whole people? How many had even met an Arab or Muslim? Billy felt like he was the only curious person in school.

Yet even he had to admit that his knowledge was incomplete.[9] A difference between Billy and others he knew was his willingness to make an effort to learn. In order to refute the allegations about Islam, or to accept them, he had to study the religion. Many people in the new Internet age had picked up the habit of repeating unfounded claims they encountered online. Billy hadn't achieved much in school, but he would distinguish himself through online scholarship.

There was no one to show him the way, no professor, no imam. Billy never thought to venture to Dearborn or to visit a mosque. He had only the Internet, and this was all he would need to discover a vivid Muslim world. He learned about Islam's roots in the seventh century, its customs and observances. From Islam's supposedly supernatural beginnings, the angel Jibril whispering divinely to Muhammad, the religion took shape through Muhammad's preachings in Mecca. Billy learned how in the Middle Ages Islam grew from a creed to a way of life to a political structure, the caliphate system developing into the Ottoman Empire.[10] A religion that Billy had barely noticed before 9/11 quickly came to command his attention. When he contrasted Islam to the religion he knew, he found Catholicism wanting. The Church had let him down.[11]

Billy hadn't expected his research into the reasons for 9/11 to lead him to a personal conclusion, but it had done so. In the Lakes cafeteria during lunchtime one afternoon in the fall of 2002, a year after the terrorist attacks, a friend asked Billy why his plate was empty. Billy replied that he was observing Ramadan, the Muslim commemoration of Muhammad's initial divine revelation, marked by a month of fasting. Billy hadn't undergone any formal study or ceremony. But he now told a select few friends that he had converted to Islam.[12]

CHAPTER FIVE

Conversion

How genuine was Billy's conversion? For someone of his background, and so soon after 9/11, Islam was a means of adolescent rebellion. Accepting the religion, or at least telling people he had done so, allowed Billy to declare that he was different from the other students in his Catholic school. He made a choice characteristic of his age, bold, without counsel or regard for consequence, a revolution all his own.

As the end of 2002 neared, and Lakes was strung with Christmas decorations, a friend told Catie Reilly that her brother had converted to Islam. "I freaked out," she said later. Billy was two years older than Catie, and eventually his forbidden knowledge would exert a paternal hold over her. She followed her brother's lead, with 9/11 likewise focusing her intellectual curiosity.

Billy delved further into Islam and provocative concepts, and Catie pored over the books he'd finish and lay down, books by Marx and Nietzsche, others by Islamic scholars obscure to kids in their Lakes circles. Eager for knowledge and attracted to the ideas that Billy was unveiling for her, Catie waded with her brother into the political issues of the day.[1]

In 2004, Catie and Billy, along with their parents, attended a political rally for President George W. Bush at the Silverdome in Pontiac.[2] The United States had invaded Iraq the previous year, falsely claiming that Iraq possessed weapons of mass destruction. Bush sought to topple Iraq's president Saddam Hussein and remake the country as a democratic, pro-American regional ally. The invasion was a gross overstep, a flagrant violation of international law, and a naïve miscalculation of both US capabilities and local customs.[3] Billy and Catie saw the Iraq War as an opportunistic hustle. When Bush took the stage at the Silverdome, Billy rose from his seat and yelled, "Heil Hitler!" This drew the ire of a man seated nearby. The two began shoving each other before Billy reared back and landed a punch, sending the man's glasses flying.[4]

Billy had discovered a subject that enflamed his passion, and he drifted further from schoolwork. He found school dull and irrelevant, a place that society assigned him to go. In class, oblivious to lectures, he would read a Koran propped up on his desk. He didn't attend football games or dances or parties, immune to their pull. His school friends watched him leave at the end of classes each day, puzzling over why he never accepted their invitations to get together. A single topic thrilled Billy: the world beyond Michigan.[5]

Online, Billy began to encounter more than information. In online forums, he discovered people like himself, the alienated and underdog. They pursued political struggles in troubled regions of the world. In Michigan, Billy was beginning to understand that he could pass through life without ever having done something that counted. His sympathies settled on the world's disenfranchised. In his bedroom, he hung the flags of Chechnya, the turbulent Muslim region in the Russian Caucasus, and Palestine, the nation of people who chafed under Israeli rule.[6]

Terry and Bill Reilly didn't know what to make of Billy's views. They didn't recognize the flags of Palestine or Chechnya. They didn't even really know where these places were located. The 9/11 attacks and the Internet had conspired to lead Billy to interests beyond his parents' knowledge of the world.

Terry and Bill hoped that the influences Billy had accepted would leave no lasting marks. Yet the parents were also impressed by Billy's ability to absorb new information. When he sermonized on faraway countries, he sounded like an expert, like a professor giving a lecture, as they had once thought he might do. They had struggled over their son's waywardness but now marveled at the person he was becoming. Even if they didn't share or understand his interests, Bill and Terry would encourage them.

In 2003, Bill's father passed away and left the Reillys a modest inheritance. Terry and Bill suggested that the family use a portion of the windfall to finance a vacation. This time, they wanted to reach far beyond places their camper had taken them. The family chose a cruise on the Baltic Sea. When the ship came to port in Saint Petersburg in the summer of 2004, the Reillys saw Russia for the first time.

The city before them was unlike any other, an open-air museum, its many Italian-designed palaces newly re-painted in pink and pistachio for the 300th anniversary of its founding in the swampy marshes of the Neva River estuary. Russia's naval access to the Baltic, Europe's fourth-largest city, Saint Petersburg was a relic of Russia's imperial age. Now far beyond Oxford, Billy took to the opportunity. On a street corner, he struck up a conversation with an elderly man, intrigued by the resonance of his speech. Buying a newspaper, Billy puzzled over its Cyrillic symbols as though they were a code.[7]

Once back home in Oxford, Billy, online again, looked up the Russian alphabet. He learned Russian words and phrases. Applying himself further, he was soon reading and understanding the Russian language, and he wanted to know more. He read Russian and Soviet history. He read about Ukraine. He learned about World War II, the Nazi–Soviet pact that partitioned Poland, about the Battle of Stalingrad. He contacted native speakers online to test his developing skill.

Encouraged by his Russian studies, Billy thought to explore another language, Arabic, which he had dabbled in previously, as it dovetailed with his interest in Islam. Here, too, he found his brain willing. In a short span of time, Billy, the C-student at Lakes,[8] had gained a working knowledge of two demanding foreign languages.

Billy used his new skills as keys to unlock still more information, accessing provocative areas of the Internet. He told his parents he had received a password to an online forum where Islamic terrorist sympathizers gathered. Billy told his mother that it felt like playing a video game, faced with the challenge of reaching incrementally higher levels.[9] Terry said he was being naïve. She cautioned him to abandon online contact with anyone who discussed terrorism. "You keep doing that," she told him, "we're going to have FBI agents on the porch yet."

In 2004, Billy graduated from Lakes, ranking thirty-ninth in his class of fifty students.[10] That fall, at Oakland University in nearby Auburn Hills, Billy formalized his Arabic studies and found that he had managed to teach himself adequately. The A's earned in four classes of Arabic elevated his academic standing, helping him find himself as a student and manage an overall B average. In the evenings at home, Terry would watch Billy copy Arabic letters into a notebook and shake her head over the path her son had discovered.[11]

The following year, the Reillys took another trip abroad. The parents suggested that Billy select the destination this time, supporting the expansion of his knowledge by giving him the opportunity to plot the family course. The Reillys would leave behind the shelter of a cruise ship and strike out on a bold adventure, with Billy escorting Catie and his parents deeply into the world of his fascination, out there, on their own, in Syria.

The Reillys toured open-air markets in Damascus. They drove through the desert to Palmyra's Roman ruins. They savored the people and the food years before civil war would come to Syria, tearing apart the country and making way for a new terrorist group, the Islamic State. *Sham* to Arabic speakers, a cradle of seventh-century Islam with desert and a Mediterranean coastline, Syria was still a place where a visitor might feel welcome.

Terry and Bill were surprised at how they were enjoying the trip. They had derided the changes that Arab Muslim immigration had brought to Metro Detroit. But the family dynamic was shifting, the child now guiding the parents. Bill and Terry felt their minds and hearts opening, and they related to those whose ways were strange to them. When the Reillys' rental car suffered a flat tire, a man passing by helped them change it. He offered to host the Reillys for the night at his home, suggesting even that they sleep in his own bed. Terry and Bill, on an unlikely adventure, eating roasted corn on a street corner in Aleppo, felt their views broaden.

Billy hoped to stay behind in Syria after his family had gone home. Now drawn to scholarship, he wanted to study language and religion in Syria. He met with a Damascus professor to arrange a slot in a university. But Billy wavered from taking such an ambitious step, from satisfying an urge to make his Internet interests tangible.[12]

Back in Michigan, at meetings for Oakland University's Muslim Student Association, Billy asked others to call him Bilal.[13] He was beginning to fashion a dual identity just as a wave of innovation came again to the Internet, social media, allowing for the possibility of disguise.

While Billy was attending college, Facebook, Instagram, Twitter, YouTube, and the iPhone appeared, transforming the ways in which he would connect with the world. He established numerous accounts on these platforms and began formulating a social circle of people he would never meet in person. People who knew the Koran. Would-be revolutionaries. People who justified terror. The wayward or dedicated or misguided, desperate that their lives should find meaning.

Who could say if these people on social media, or even Billy, were as they appeared? The new technology encouraged him and others to try on disguises. With its fiction of human interaction, social media enabled Billy to pass himself off as anyone he liked. He talked dangerous ideas with dangerous people, took chances without risk. He said anything he wanted to say and never had to back it up. He didn't ever have to look someone level in the eye.

*　　*　　*

Terry and Bill declined to believe that Billy had formally converted to Islam. They told each other that their son would be reasonable in the end, that his interest in the religion would subside as he matured. Avoiding the issue by denying that it existed, they had no such luxury with their daughter.

In 2005, Catie was a junior at Lakes and feeling isolated at home. She believed she had little in common with her parents and that they favored her brother while marginalizing her, even though she excelled in school.[14] She wanted out. Catie had been studying Islam alongside Billy and warmed to the religion on her own terms. Islam was something her parents couldn't understand. In 2005, Catie converted.[15]

Catie's conversion shook Terry and Bill. Unlike Billy, who as a man looked no different after he had accepted Islam, Catie took to wearing a head covering. To the parents, Catie's conversion, made visible in this way, was real. In Syria, Terry and Bill had found themselves tolerant of people. But accepting the assistance of an Arab Muslim man on a road outside Damascus was not the same to them as supporting their daughter's wish to join a group to which they felt she didn't belong. They took Catie's choice as a rejection of everything they'd taught and given her. She would continue to live under their roof for several years, but nothing between them would ever be the same.[16]

As Catie approached her high school graduation, she intended to apply to nursing school. Billy convinced her that she had the grades to become a doctor instead. With his encouragement, Catie enrolled in Wayne State University, in

Detroit, with plans for medical school. That first college fall, in 2009, Catie volunteered to work at a health clinic in Detroit that served Muslim patients. The experience gave her an unvarnished look at their lives.[17]

Her first days at the clinic were consumed with talk of a violent episode that had erupted in nearby Dearborn. In a federal criminal complaint, an FBI agent alleged that a Detroit imam, Luqman Abdullah, was preparing for jihad. The FBI presented evidence that Abdullah's group was engaged in theft and fraud, accumulating an arsenal to wage war against federal agents. One morning that October, Abdullah and several other men were stacking boxes in a Dearborn warehouse when nearly two dozen FBI agents in riot gear confronted them. A standoff ensued, recorded on FBI surveillance video. An agent loosed a dog. Abdullah pulled a gun. Shots rang out. When the skirmish ended, four FBI agents had shot Abdullah twenty times. The FBI's dog had taken a bullet. Agents rushed the dog to a hospital by helicopter, while Abdullah died at the scene.[18]

Abdullah's death rattled the Detroit-area Muslims whom Catie was beginning to know. A fellow volunteer at the health clinic where Catie worked was eloquent in his opinions of the FBI and the government's post-9/11 attitude toward American Muslims.

Mohammed Cherri was Lebanese, a naturalized US citizen with a degree from the University of Michigan's Dearborn campus. He had lived in both the Middle East and the United States, and he understood these environments as though he was native to each. Arabic was his first language, but he spoke English like an American. His family was academically inclined. His father taught electrical engineering at a university in Kuwait. Mohammed was studying medicine and blogged about Arab American issues.

Catie had never met anyone like Mohammed. She noted his expressive vocabulary and realized that for years, in Oxford and at Lakes, she had been simplifying her own speech for fear of appearing eager to impress. She knew she was intelligent, but she had learned not to let it show. Speaking with Mohammed encouraged and rewarded her instincts and intellect.

One afternoon that fall, Catie gave Mohammed a lift from the clinic to the Wayne State campus. They shared dinner that evening at a Middle Eastern café and recognized a spark between them.[19]

Mohammed lived in Dearborn, and Catie began visiting him there. To

Bill and Terry Reilly, Dearborn represented a rejection of American life, but Dearborn for Catie was an oasis from what she felt was the aridity of her environment. Living there were people who spoke multiple languages and who had traveled extensively. They understood the world because they had seen a great deal of it. In Dearborn, Catie encountered people who were interested in politics, religion, and foreign affairs, people who held invigorating opinions. Catie began spending more time in Dearborn with Mohammed than she did with her parents in Oxford, having found someone who understood her mind and her views.[20]

As Christmas 2009 approached, the conflicts that had been simmering in the Reilly household came to a boil. Catie had been dating Mohammed for just a few months, but they had grown close. It was natural to Catie to invite him further into her life. She wanted to bring Mohammed home for Christmas.

Terry and Bill bristled at the idea, saying that Christmas was reserved for family.[21] The usual group convened at the Reilly house, Terry's sister Kathie and brother Jim, Grandpa Marvin. Catie stewed but could do little else.

All families deal in denial, and this was the Reillys'. Islam, 9/11, the Internet, Billy's seductive interests, Catie's religious conversion: Terry and Bill hoped that these challenges to their way of life would simply dissolve. They missed the old neighborhoods and certainties. They fought change by ignoring it. In Oxford, they believed they could shut the door, refusing to assimilate to the world's changes. But the changing world would come knocking.

The following spring, an FBI agent would pay the Reillys a visit.

CHAPTER SIX

Siege

A man ducked into a coach-class bathroom on a plane in flight from Amsterdam. He was Nigerian, in his twenties. He washed his face in the bathroom's small sink. He brushed his teeth. He sprayed cologne on himself then returned to his seat. It was Christmas Day 2009, and Umar Abdulmutallab was preparing to die.

The plane was bound for Detroit, but Abdulmutallab had a plan to ensure that it would not land. A syringe was sewn into his underwear. He depressed the plunger of the syringe, releasing a fluid into a packet affixed to his waistband. Inside the packet was a mix of pentaerythritol tetranitrate and triacetone triperoxide, powdered explosives.

A passenger seated nearby heard what sounded like a firecracker exploding inside of a pillowcase. Others smelled smoke. Abdulmutallab's crotch burst into flames, and someone yelled, "Fire! Fire!" A man leapt across a row of seats and landed atop Abdulmutallab, subduing him. Abdulmutallab's plan had failed.[1]

In the Detroit suburb of Southfield that day, Andy Arena watched his three young daughters open their presents and was hauling the wrapping paper to the curb when his cellphone rang. Arena was accustomed to interruptions, even on Christmas morning. They came with the job: he was the special agent in charge of the FBI's main Detroit office.[2]

On the phone, a colleague described the attempted bombing of the airplane. Arena sped to Ann Arbor. He parked at a hospital on the University of Michigan's north campus, where doctors were treating Abdulmutallab for burns. Arena's operations chief, Timothy Waters, was already there. In touch from headquarters in Washington was Andrew McCabe, an FBI official who would later come to national notice as a Bureau interim director who clashed with President Donald Trump in 2017.[3]

In 2009, McCabe was the director of the FBI's High-Value Detainee Interrogation Group. This was a new initiative, developed in response to a revelation that the Central Intelligence Agency, in the wake of 9/11, had been torturing suspected terrorists and jihadi sympathizers at undocumented prisons around the world. The CIA had been employing a tactic known as waterboarding, in which water was poured through a towel placed over a person's mouth and nose, inducing the sensation of drowning. Waterboarding was not only inhumane, it was ineffective, eliciting false confessions and information. The men subjected to it would say anything to make it stop.[4]

In the outcry over the public disclosure of this CIA tactic, and with Barack Obama having succeeded George W. Bush in the White House, the FBI instituted the High-Value Detainee Interrogation Group, which advocated questioning over torture. Umar Abdulmutallab, the underwear bomber, would be the first suspect subjected to these methods. Arena, Waters, and colleagues persuaded him to talk.[5]

September 11 was more than eight years in the past, but the terrorist threat remained ever-present. With US troops in Afghanistan and Iraq, terrorist groups and bases had relocated, morphed, even grown. The United States was engaged in a broad governmental effort to map these movements and the figures who, inspired by bin Laden, had arisen to lead a renewed effort to attack Americans.

In Michigan, Abdulmutallab told the FBI that he had spent much of the previous year in Yemeni training camps associated with Anwar al-Awlaki, a leader of a bin Laden offshoot called al Qaeda in the Arab Peninsula. Al-Awlaki was of particular importance, since he held a US passport. He had known three of the 9/11 hijackers and had inspired subsequent attacks in Britain, Canada, and the US.[6] The US wanted to locate and eliminate him.

Abdulmutallab, the underwear bomber, provided the FBI with a sketch of al Qaeda in the Arab Peninsula and a layout of the Yemeni camps he had attended. This was valuable counterterrorism intelligence. It gave Obama and the FBI an opportunity to turn the page on the CIA's waterboarding program, proving that it was unnecessary to torture suspects in order to gain useful information from them.[7] In 2011, Obama authorized an attack on al-Awlaki in Yemen, making him the first US citizen killed by a US drone strike.

Despite the intelligence that the FBI was able to gather, the underwear bombing was disturbing. Abdulmutallab's failed operation made major headlines. If he had succeeded, an airplane carrying hundreds of Americans would have disintegrated midair, the plane's many fragments raining down over Michigan. The strike, carried out on an airplane, would have been a terrifying echo of the 9/11 attacks and revived the mass hysteria that many Americans were still struggling to forget. The underwear-bombing plot proved that the threat to the United States endured, that the FBI had to remain alert.

It was the FBI's responsibility to prevent terrorist attacks against Americans. The Bureau worked in concert with the CIA, the Department of Homeland Security, and hundreds of other federal and local investigative and intelligence agencies, but the FBI was the primary organization in charge of such domestic investigations and operations.[8] September 11 had dramatically exposed the Bureau's inability to perform this basic function. In the event's aftermath, Congress had threatened the agency with closure. The FBI had spent the ensuing years transforming from an investigative body into one that also collected international intelligence in support of operations beyond the courtroom. Since 9/11, the FBI had been working extensively domestically and overseas, pumping resources into penetrating terrorist groups and gathering counterterrorism intelligence, endeavoring to short-circuit attacks before they could succeed.

Abdulmutallab exposed an FBI failure. His incompetence alone, his inability to ignite the bomb effectively, had preserved the lives of the people on the plane bound for Detroit. Despite his ineptitude, he had penetrated the FBI's defenses, eluding the billions of dollars and countless men and women directed at finding and stopping Islamic terrorists like him. A demoralizing *déjà vu* eight years after September 11, the underwear-bombing incident demonstrated that the FBI was still struggling to gain access to terrorist cells in order to develop foreknowledge of attack plots. If the FBI had known about Abdulmutallab's plans, it would have prevented the underwear bomber from boarding the flight to Detroit.

An FBI agent's duty was to collect information that the Bureau didn't possess. The agent had to venture outside the agency and bring information and intelligence into it. The fundamental means employed to achieve this aim was informants.[9]

Traditionally, there are two types of FBI informants. One, a confidential informant, belongs to a criminal enterprise and agrees to work with the Bureau to develop information about the group's activities in exchange for the mitigation of criminal charges or sentencing.

A confidential informant is typically someone who has been charged with or convicted of a crime. Such a person, legally vulnerable and eager to avoid confinement or reduce a sentence, is often open to an FBI agent's approach. The agent, sometimes in concert with a prosecutor, will make a deal, a proffer, offering to confer with a judge on the person's behalf in order to condense or void a prison term. The confidential informant will work for the FBI, sharing information about crimes or meeting with criminal associates while carrying a recording device to capture evidence of offenses or conspiracies, which can be used in court to implicate senior members of the criminal group. Criminal groups detest confidential informants. They're known as snitches, people who trade their associates' liberty for their own. Police have been combing jailhouses for such people and opportunities for centuries.[10]

The second type of informant is the cooperating witness. This person isn't sitting in jail and isn't in legal jeopardy. This person is not a member of a criminal enterprise but someone who has agreed to penetrate such a group on behalf of the FBI or another agency, often for pay. A cooperating witness might know someone associated with a criminal organization or be of an ethnic, social, or geographic background that will ease entry to a crime group. A cooperating witness is motivated not by fear of prison time but by financial gain, or, in some cases, by patriotism, ego, or the thrill of covert work.

Cooperators and informants have been a part of the Bureau's mission since President Theodore Roosevelt bypassed Congress in 1908 to establish the FBI, a collection of agents designated as "special," since they reported to the attorney general.[11] FBI director J. Edgar Hoover used informants and cooperators as early as 1919, in the first red scare in the United States, in the Palmer Raids. FBI informants penetrated American leftist groups that were inspired by the Russian Revolution and collected the identities and whereabouts of their members. The US deported scores of alleged communists and anarchists aboard a World War I troop transport ship that the press dubbed "The Soviet Ark."[12]

During World War II, anxious about Axis saboteurs, President Franklin Roosevelt authorized Hoover to direct informants to break into homes and businesses to collect information and install listening devices.[13] Later, the FBI's Counterintelligence Program (COINTELPRO) made positive achievements but suffered from mission creep, as agents enlisted informants and cooperators to encourage targets to commit felonies that would enable prosecutors to take them out of circulation.[14] Informants have often done the FBI's dirty work, and there has sometimes been little regulation of them.

In 1961, Hoover instructed agents to develop "particularly qualified, live sources within the upper echelon of the organized hoodlum element." This initiative, the Top Echelon Criminal Informant Program,[15] proved that a single informant or cooperator with proper access and motivation could make an FBI agent's career. Some top-echelon informants, on the other hand, have achieved the opposite effect, destroying an agent's reputation and threatening the agency.

In the 1990s, years before he would take charge of the Detroit office, Andy Arena was working as a supervisory special agent in the organized-crime section at FBI headquarters in Washington.[16] His bosses sent him to Boston to investigate a Bureau scandal. James "Whitey" Bulger, the leader of Boston's Irish mob, was the most striking affiliate of the FBI's top-echelon program. Over more than a dozen years, Bulger had used information his FBI handlers had given him to eliminate rivals and commit a host of felonies, including several murders. His primary FBI handler had been an accessory to one of the killings. Bulger had subverted the relationship's dynamic. As a court unsealed his federal indictment, Bulger disappeared from Boston in 1994, becoming a fugitive beyond control of the agency he had maligned. He was arrested six-teen years later and was murdered by fellow inmates in federal prison in 2018, beaten to death with a padlock wrapped in a sock.[17]

In 1998, amid the fallout of the Bulger revelations, FBI management dispatched Andy Arena on a tour of the agency's regional offices, and to the FBI's training ground in Quantico, Virginia, where he lectured agents on the Bureau's adjusted policy for handling informants and cooperators. Bulger's activities had changed the FBI's attitude about informants and cooperators. Arena told agents that if they began to lose control of an informant or cooperator, they were to terminate the informant relationship. Walk away. The risk of doing otherwise was intolerable.[18]

FBI agents had often played fast and loose with informants and cooperators. This was the nature of dealing with people who operated in the criminal world, but the practice had also drawn rebuke. In response to COINTELPRO's over-reach, Congress and the Department of Justice restricted the FBI's usage of informants and cooperators. However, the FBI sidestepped these regulations when the advent of the War on Drugs, in the 1980s, necessitated the penetration of trafficking gangs.[19, 20]

The FBI often shed limitations and oversight when national emergencies emerged, but the Whitey Bulger case appeared to be different. It suggested to the public that FBI agents were hiding behind the badge to facilitate crimes in order to advance their careers. The Department of Justice established the Confidential Informant Review Committee, a mechanism designed to approve and monitor high-level and long-term assets, severely limiting the latitude that FBI agents and their supervisors had enjoyed.[21] A House of Representatives Committee on Government Reform report on the Bulger case, "Everything Secret Degenerates," urged a curb on the FBI's use of informants and cooperators.[22]

The rise of global terrorism short-circuited ethical concerns. The September 11 attacks inspired Congress to pass the Patriot Act, which allowed the FBI to collect data on anyone it suspected of terrorist links.[23] DOJ authorized the deployment of informants and cooperators at the earliest stages of investigations and directed the FBI and other agencies to use them to monitor mosques across the United States, liberating agents from establishing legal predicates of suspicious conduct.[24]

Enacting DOJ's directives was a new FBI director, Robert Mueller, a longtime federal prosecutor and former Marine officer who had served with distinction in combat in the Vietnam War.[25] Mueller had assumed the FBI job seven days before the 9/11 attacks. Sixteen years later, he would take on another challenge as the Department of Justice's special counsel investigating the Russian government's alleged effort to influence the 2016 US presidential election. But it was this immediate aftermath of September 11 and Mueller's management of the FBI's adaptation to a new international security environment that would constitute the central contribution of his long career of public service.

In the wake of 9/11, Congress considered dissolving the FBI and founding a new office patterned on the United Kingdom's domestic intelligence agency, MI-5.[26] A principal failing identified by the congressional 9/11 Commission was the FBI's use of counterterrorism informants and cooperators. Unlike during previous inquests, Congress this time directed the FBI to make more, not less, of these assets.[27] The commission resolved that the Bureau could survive, dependent "on an assessment that the FBI—if it makes an all-out effort to institutionalize change—can do the job."[28] Part of that change would be the expansion and modernization of the FBI's informant program. The FBI's greatest failure, the September 11 attacks, awarded the Bureau with its broadest mandate.

After 9/11, Andy Arena, like many FBI agents and supervisors, transferred to the counterterrorism division, and in 2007, Mueller chose Arena to run the Bureau's Detroit office. Arena was a native, born in Dearborn, raised in Detroit. He had a degree from the University of Detroit School of Law.[29] He understood what made Detroit important to the FBI's counterterrorism strategy. Immediately to the city's east was an international border through which plotters might enter the country from Canada. And to Detroit's southwest was Dearborn and the largest Arab-Muslim community in the Western Hemisphere.

This population, like other Arab and Muslim communities in the country, became a focus of FBI attention because of its connection to the Middle East. Agents from the FBI and other federal agencies would secure warrants to monitor phone and email traffic, clock international travel, designate "people of interest" for questioning and delays at US borders, and employ a host of additional investigative and harassment schemes to frustrate possible terror plots.[30] The tactics also snapped up innocent people along the way. Together with the 2002 formation of the Department of Homeland Security, the FBI's counterterrorism expansion, focused on the prevention of another 9/11, marked a new era in US national security.

In Detroit, the FBI had one of its largest field offices, with roughly 200 agents, 300 support staff, and three counterterrorism squads organized by target and geographic focus. In 2009, Detroit would rank in the top five by caseload among field offices in every FBI investigative category.[31]

Held to account for not having done enough to avert 9/11, the FBI countenanced reproach for overreaching in working to prevent a sequel. Arena would approve the October 2009 raid on the Detroit warehouse that resulted in Luqman Abdullah's death,[32] the event that had nudged Catie Reilly and Mohammed Cherri together.

The Whitey Bulger affair seemed trivial after September 11. But the case still held lessons for FBI agents who were now cultivating more counterterrorism cooperators and informants than ever before.

FBI agents feared informants but needed them. In counterterrorism, few agents possessed skills that one might consider essential to the task. In 2006, just 33 out of roughly 12,000 FBI agents, or less than 1 percent, spoke Arabic.[33] Most agents and staff lacked a solid understanding of the Muslim world, having no pre-9/11 interest in it. Agents could paper over their deficiencies by bringing on informants and cooperators who had necessary abilities. After 9/11, the FBI standard for enlisting such people loosened, as Bureau counterterrorism budgets surged.[34] In addition to signing up high-level sources, the FBI recruited scores of people whose tenuous relationships and knowledge had only the minutest chance of generating anything useful.[35]

Developing an informant or cooperator who might possess or acquire knowledge of terrorist plots was risky. An informant could be a plant, dispatched by a foreign intelligence agency or terror group. An informant could fall out of touch on a visit home to the Middle East, disappear into a terrorist training camp. In the years following 9/11, as the FBI ramped up recruitment of these assets, such events did happen. Agents lost track of informants who were traveling abroad and were left to worry that the people they had cultivated would come back to haunt them.[36] Lost informants could inspire others with their knowledge of FBI dealings, then slip back into the United States with a plan.

In the world after 9/11, the FBI had to accept new, heightened risks. But agents didn't like it. They dealt regularly with foreign nationals, permanent resident card ("green card") holders, and naturalized US citizens, but they questioned the allegiance of these people. While developing assets, agents were always on shaky ground, never sure which person in their stable of informants could be the one to betray their trust.[37]

There was no perfect informant or cooperator. But if agents could conceive of one, this person wouldn't be from the Persian Gulf or from Dearborn, but from a place and background that any FBI agent could easily understand.

CHAPTER SEVEN

Factotum

I n the spring of 2010, Billy Reilly was finishing his final college classes at Oakland University. He had spent the previous few years accumulating credits in biology, yet as he prepared to graduate, he was unsure how he would use a biology degree in professional life. His interest in fishing inspired him to consider a career in marine biology. He also mentioned applying to law school, but such talk waned. He and Catie grumbled over Michigan's depressed employment market and concluded that they had few prospects.[1]

"Living in Michigan, the job market is one of the worst in the country and unemployment is very high," Billy wrote in an essay. "This is true even for college graduates." He mentioned "the difficult economic times we are experiencing, many job seekers and not as many jobs."[2]

Billy knew what interested him, what drove him to work hard, distinguish himself, and develop a specialty. But devoting himself to the computer and the reach it gave him beyond the house in Oxford hardly seemed like a career path. It felt like a hobby.

Billy's parents were powerless to guide him, since his interests and education had already outdistanced their own. They couldn't provide him with any fitting example. Billy's mother, Terry, had been working piecemeal as something called a "mystery shopper," earning freelance fees for reporting on the quality of service at area businesses and restaurants. She posed as an ordinary customer while discreetly keeping tabs on the staff and later submitting reports to those who owned the companies. Terry took the assignments as much for their covert thrill as for the chance to indulge her fondness for fast food. This sort of work provided no inspiration for Billy, and neither did he consider following the professional line of his father, who had retired from truck driving on a workmen's compensation claim after dual hip replacements.[3] Terry worried over Billy and consoled him, acknowledging that at his age she had also struggled to find direction.

As the weeks elapsed to Billy's college graduation, he was so removed from the achievement that he would end up skipping the ceremony.[4] He huddled at home, trying to figure out what to do next.

*   *   *

One afternoon in April 2010, a knock rattled the Reillys' front door. Terry and Bill found a man in a dark suit standing on the landing. He said he was a special agent from the FBI. His name was David Kotal.[5]

Bill and Terry didn't know what to say, and as they took in Kotal, they noticed a folder in his hand. Protruding from it was a printout of the identification page of Bill's passport. The Reillys were perplexed, unaware of what Bill could have done to draw the FBI to the house.

Kotal told a story that Terry and Bill could scarcely believe. Kotal said the US military had recently overrun an enemy position in the Middle East and recovered a laptop. The computer's drive contained communications with a user in the United States.

Years earlier, when Billy was in high school, he had told his parents that he was using his newfound ability in Arabic to access forums that harbored terrorist sympathizers. To Billy, persuading people online to give him passwords that unlocked prohibited areas of the Internet was an entertaining challenge. But Terry had cautioned him. She had gathered enough from news reports since 9/11 to understand that when it came to Islamic terrorism, the US government wasn't playing games. She had warned Billy that his online life would turn serious. Now, it appeared, that moment had arrived.

A protocol that the government had developed after 9/11 dictated that any time a battlefield retrieval of evidence, known as a "sensitive site exploitation," revealed a US connection suggesting criminal activity back home, the material was transferred from the military or an intelligence agency to the FBI.[6] It was the Bureau's job to check out the tip. FBI director Mueller had ordered his agents to run down every terrorism lead, no matter how slight it might appear to be.[7]

Missed leads, careless investigations, and mismanagement had helped to enable the 9/11 attacks. In 2001, an FBI agent in Phoenix had alerted headquarters and the New York office about the possibility that bin Laden had sent operatives to the United States to attend "civil aviation universities and colleges." The lead had withered.[8]

In the immediate aftermath of September 11, FBI agents and supervisors didn't require much of a lead to dispatch assault teams in the hope of over-powering terrorist cells. Such cells, as it turned out, were hard to find in the US. As years passed and memories of 9/11 began to fade, counterterrorism agents realized that there was rarely cause to put on riot gear. The FBI generated or received an endless flood of terrorism leads, nearly 220,000 from the public alone in 2006.[9] Leads rarely checked out. Agents tired of making house calls.[10] They didn't see the point of them. Running down every lead chewed up time and energy. Mueller's command, as well intentioned as it was, fatigued his agents.

Case agents were also bogged down in increasing amounts of regulations and paperwork that encroached on the time they could spend doing investigative work. Agents joked that the FBI was the world's greatest bureaucracy, since "Bureau" was its middle name. In counterterrorism, agents struggled to gather enough intelligence to craft a coherent picture. In place of quantifiable investigative results, FBI managers were left to evaluate agents by other measures. Managers often pressed agents with an FBI term known as TURK ("time utilization and record keeping") and often demanded of agents, "What did you TURK that to?"

Nine years after 9/11, feeling that their jobs were increasingly secretarial, some agents had grown cynical about Mueller's mandate to chase down every lead. But they followed the order all the same. No counterterrorism agent wanted to be on the hook in retrospect for having fumbled a lead that did turn out to be worthwhile.[11]

There was a potential benefit, however, behind even the flimsiest lead. Counterterrorism agents were meant always to be fishing for suspects and fellow travelers in the world of terror whom they could turn to their side.

Running down a lead might seldom result in a formal investigation. But it could produce an informant. The ability to recruit and run informants had become a metric that FBI managers used to evaluate an agent's job performance. Not every case agent was skilled at handling sources, but they all had to do it. The anxiety over being downgraded on a performance review led some agents to open informants they might better have left alone.[12]

Standing on the porch of the house in Oxford, agent Kotal told the Reillys that he had studied the messages on the computer drive recovered in the Middle East. On the hard drive, the FBI had discovered that the person corresponding from the US had done so via an Internet service provider in Oxford, Michigan. This was a fingerprint for the modern age, implying accessory to terrorist conspiracy. Kotal said the FBI's research revealed that the Oxford IP address was registered to William Reilly. Billy was the one making terror connections, but his father's name was on the Internet bill. Kotal had printed out the passport page of the wrong William Reilly.[13]

Bill and Terry looked at each other in surprise, but they knew. Terry was amazed that her prophecy from years ago had come to pass.

The parents called for their son. Billy joined agent Kotal on the porch and started explaining how and why he had been trading messages with terror suspects. Billy described his interest in foreign languages and cultures, how he enjoyed memorizing political maps and learning the ways in which conflict could alter them. He illustrated his social media explorations and the people he had encountered, how he had used guile and pretense to gain a password to a jihadi forum. Billy was even a little proud of the access he had achieved to illicit worlds and conversations.

Once Billy had painted the full picture of his activities, Kotal explained that Billy might well have committed a crime.[14] The comment set Billy on his heels, but Kotal himself might have been more surprised.

What Billy had described was the sort of work that the FBI did, using aliases and false personal histories, building out what is known as a legend in order to work undercover to develop investigative contacts and targets. This wasn't easy, especially in counterterrorism. The work often demanded language skills that the FBI still lacked to an adequate degree and also a feel for cultural signals that you couldn't pick up from an Arabic course. Not just anyone could travel where Billy had gone in the digital world. Gaining access to jihadi forums and befriending international terror suspects on social media was evidence of talent and proficiency. Billy had achieved this out of simple personal interest.

Billy Reilly's appearance didn't betray his ability for navigating global intrigues. Twenty-three years old, he stood five-foot-eight and weighed 160 pounds. The frames of his metal glasses were rectangular, giving his appearance a dash of practical acumen. He often wore an expression of impassivity, which some mistook for indifference. He might have been an engineer, or a store clerk reading graphic novels and dreaming of places he'd never go.

To the FBI, Billy presented a different profile. He knew foreign languages and was adept at new technologies. He understood how Islamic radicals were using social media. He was interested in the wider world yet was also reliably American. He had been born in the United States, raised a Christian. He could trace his line to Eastern Europe and the British Isles. One grandfather had fought in Europe during World War II, the other flown missions in the Pacific theater.

Billy's race and background might well have marked him for special treatment. The FBI was monitoring, investigating, and harassing Arabs and Muslims around the country, some of whom had engaged in behavior that appeared no more threatening than Billy's Internet travels. To agent Kotal, Billy, born and bred in the US, appeared to pose little risk.

The FBI remained eager for outside assistance. Only four months before Kotal's visit, the underwear bomber had nearly brought down the airliner approaching Detroit. Agents and managers in the FBI's Detroit office needed to cultivate people who could help them penetrate Arab circles in Dearborn and identify potential ties between international terrorists and the locals who might help them realize their schemes.

It seemed unreasonable, but Billy Reilly, in the context of the Bureau's existing resources and its need for information, was a viable candidate for FBI work. Standing on the Reillys' porch, Kotal asked Billy, "What would you think about doing some volunteer work for the FBI?"[15]

FBI agents were trained to use people's vulnerabilities against them. In drug cases, counterintelligence, and now in counterterrorism especially, agents pressured immigrant citizens who were often ignorant of their rights, lawful permanent residents who wanted to retain their green cards, and people who were visiting the US legally on a visa or illegally without one. Threatening these people with deportation or worse was a standard FBI tactic to encourage them to become a cooperator. If such people didn't agree to sign up, FBI agents could and did place them on a terrorism watch list, which restricted their liberties.[16]

Coercing a person to become an informant could be even easier if the target had committed a crime or was believed to have done so. For many people like Billy, who weren't experts in the law, FBI pressure was difficult to resist.

Billy took in Kotal's proposal. Rather than a threat, it seemed too good to be true. The FBI? The world-famous investigative agency? J. Edgar Hoover, the Ten Most Wanted Fugitives list, national secrets, the war on terror? Billy wasn't sure what the Bureau saw in him, but what he saw in the FBI was an opportunity. Working with the FBI could offer the direction he was seeking.

Later in 2010, after his talk with Kotal, Billy drove from Oxford to the FBI office in Troy, twenty miles south.[17] He sat through interviews and polygraph tests. An FBI policy guide said the tests were designed to determine Billy's "core personality." They would reveal the level of his social and emotional maturity, his ability to handle stress and adapt to change, and his sympathies and vulnerabilities.[18]

Such tests might have laid bare Billy's inadequacies. Although his zeal for Islam had softened in the eight years since he'd accepted the religion and he didn't voice terrorist sympathies, how solid was his allegiance in the War on Terror? With no close friends to speak of, he was not as socially mature as he might have been. Billy had always lived with his parents. He hadn't yet been forced to find an apartment, earn a living, feed himself, or figure out how to overcome life's quotidian challenges.

Yet, in these tests, Billy had an advantage over numerous candidates who had come before him. Many of the people whom the FBI invited to take the exams had been born abroad. Since 9/11, as the expanding counterterrorism division recruited great numbers of new FBI informants, many such people originated in countries where the FBI analog, a given country's domestic security agency, operated like a secret police. It was routine for these foreign security squads to suppress dissent and to line the pockets of those in power. Such agencies could commit any crime. They could even make someone disappear. In the United States, public confidence in the FBI waxed and waned, but most Americans believed that FBI agents were on their side. However, many green card holders and naturalized US citizens from the Middle East couldn't avoid viewing the FBI through the lens of their own knowledge of domestic security agencies in their home countries. For the Middle Easterners whom the Bureau recruited as counterterrorism informants, being probed with ominous questions in an FBI office was often too much to bear. An FBI staffer told Billy that several people before him had broken down under the strain of the exams and had soiled themselves.[19]

Billy applied a different perspective to the process. He had seen countless movies and TV shows that depicted FBI agents in a positive light. The Bureau exerted great energy in projecting a good image. In addition to its press offices that interfaced with reporters to disseminate news of indictments and investigations, the FBI employed staffers who worked with movie and TV producers and writers to influence portrayals of agents and operations. Billy wasn't immune to such media. He trusted the FBI.

Through the exams in Troy, he proved steadier than others and passed the tests. And like that, he was on board with the FBI.

The function that Billy would fulfill for the Bureau was difficult to categorize. He wasn't a confidential informant, a member of a crime outfit. Nor would he necessarily perform the role of a cooperating witness, agreeing to penetrate a terrorist cell. After 9/11, the FBI adjusted the way it handled informants and cooperators, using them not only as windows into criminal conspiracy but also as sources of intelligence. In 2004, the FBI had initiated what it called the Confidential Human Source Reengineering Project. This expanded the Bureau's usage of informants and cooperators, while also reclassifying them. From that point forward, this disparate group of people, which Billy was now joining, would be categorized under a single designation: confidential human source, or CHS.[20]

There was no typical CHS, nor any typical CHS duty. What a CHS did, at least in the initial stages of the relationship, depended on what a CHS *could* do, contingent on the knowledge and abilities the person brought to the role. The nature of the FBI's relationships with CHSs varied, depending on the urgency of particular investigations and the style of a handling agent. Some CHS relationships quickly outlived their utility. Others lasted for years. The longevity and intensity of the connection relied on the quality of information a CHS could consistently generate. High-level CHSs who provided direct access to terror groups or information of major value could earn a serious wage, up to $100,000 or more per year.[21] But the enticing prospect of working with the FBI, or the threat of an FBI agent's negatively impacting one's life, was often enough to persuade a person to sign up. For people like Billy, there was no steady pay.

His inculcation came with standard admonitions and pledges to secrecy. Staffers told him he should never presume to behave like an FBI agent or tell people that he was one. He must report all international travel ahead of time, even if it was, in the FBI's terminology, "nonoperational," or personal. Agents would log the record of his trips into an internal software system, Delta, which tracked CHSs.[22]

Despite the FBI's reputation for competency and vigilance, it provided CHSs with negligible training. Agents instructed their charges how to file paperwork to receive reimbursement for routine expenses, and they might discuss the best ways to record conversations or communicate (via encrypted applications or virtual private networks). Aside from these directives, there was little guidance, and no course in tradecraft.[23] The FBI was like a construction company operating in the developing world, able to throw cheap, abundant labor at its problems. If a CHS soured on the arrangement, committed crimes, or came to a bad end, the FBI could discard the person and plug in another.

Billy didn't know about other volunteers like him. The active CHS population rivaled the enrollment of a large state university.[24] Yet there was no school brochure. There was no yearbook, no alumni club. And there was no recourse. All such people were unaware of their peers in this clandestine world and unacquainted with the risks of an association with the FBI. The FBI's Confidential Human Source Policy Guide stated that a CHS's relationship with the FBI would "forever affect the life of that individual." The guide said, portentously, that this person would always be known as "either an 'FBI source' or a 'former FBI source.'"[25]

If there had been a warning, would Billy Reilly have heeded it? This was his chance to learn secrets of national security. A student of languages, Billy would pick up another one, the FBI's counterterrorism vocabulary. He would learn how the Bureau collected, processed, and utilized information, a valuable skill, no doubt, for a future profession. No longer on his own, Billy would work within a group under the guidance of FBI agents, finally getting a chance to belong to something.

Billy's relationship with the FBI seemed a stretch, given his lack of professional experience. But like a marriage that appears ill conceived to those outside of it, the union between Billy and the Bureau had its own intimate rationale. The FBI needed the skills he had.

Withdrawing into his bedroom, Billy started with Internet research. He monitored Islamic fundamentalist websites. Agents directed him to research topics or events or people that caught their attention. He translated Internet postings from Arabic or Russian into English, adding context to them. He identified Americans who joined jihadi groups. He mapped the leadership of terror organizations, reporting which group had pledged allegiance, or *bayat*, to whom.[26]

Billy filed regular reports, but the FBI didn't require him to clock in at an office. There were only irregular meetings. Agents didn't mind if Billy picked up side work, pursued an unrelated career, or studied for advanced degrees, as long as he was available to take their calls and do their bidding.[27]

The informality of the arrangement obscured its stakes. Billy was now subordinate to Andy Arena, who in the wake of the Whitey Bulger affair had directed agents to abandon a source when necessary, no matter the consequences for that person. And FBI manuals were explicit about the need to manipulate and coerce CHSs, advising agents to use "natural actions" when cultivating a CHS to create a "seemingly personal relationship." Guidelines instructed agents how to "inspire an individual to do something that they may not otherwise do."[28]

Billy's excitement over this new relationship led him down a path he was unable to read for the shadows cast upon it.

CHAPTER EIGHT

Falcon

Before World War II, the FBI stationed agents abroad. They worked with foreign governments to track suspects and collect evidence but also sometimes conducted the sorts of operations one would associate with spies.[1] The CIA did not exist in those prewar years before the United States attained true global range. The war hastened the expansion of the Office of Strategic Services, the OSS, a skunkworks intended to sabotage the Axis powers. Once the Allies had achieved peace in 1945, President Harry Truman confronted a quandary, with the FBI and the OSS vying for power in a new American age.

FBI director J. Edgar Hoover made a play for expansion, advocating for the Bureau's formal role in foreign operations. With Hoover holding immense, almost unchecked influence, Truman feared that the FBI, if granted the mandate its director sought, would deform into an American analog of the Gestapo, the Nazi secret police, and operate beyond oversight to undermine the US Constitution.[2]

Truman devised a method of power sharing. The OSS disbanded, but he gathered what remained of its know-how and structure and in 1947 established the CIA, assigning it foreign intelligence responsibilities. Humbling Hoover, Truman restricted FBI duties to domestic law enforcement and counter-intelligence.[3] If the FBI couldn't work outside the country, the CIA, for its part, was prohibited from operating against US citizens inside the the country.

By bifurcating national security responsibility, Truman believed he would foster a beneficial rivalry between the two agencies. This competition would safeguard American citizens both from threats to US interests abroad and from harassment at home.

The rivalry that Truman had envisioned indeed came to life but not entirely to the national benefit. CIA officers, many of them drawn from exclusive schools and via privileged family connections, fostered an elitist ethos and maligned FBI agents as glorified gumshoes. FBI agents worked to produce evidence that prosecutors could use in court and regarded their CIA counterparts, who sometimes violated the laws of foreign countries, as deceptive, even criminal.[4] Inevitably, the FBI and CIA became contemptuous of one another. They nevertheless had to find ways to work together. With technological advancements in air travel and banking fudging international boundaries, the interests of each agency often bled into the territory of the other.

In pursuit of investigations, the FBI sometimes had cause to send informants and cooperators to foreign countries. The Department of Justice forbade FBI agents from handling informants who traveled outside the United States. Agents were prohibited even from speaking with their operatives while they were abroad. Regulations required the FBI to hand off traveling informants to CIA officers in relevant regions. Likewise, the CIA had to request FBI assistance for some domestic tasks.[5]

Such an imperfect arrangement generated opportunities for misunderstanding. Bureau agents groused over the chores they had to execute on behalf of CIA officers. CIA officers were unenthusiastic about carrying the FBI's water and feared that FBI agents would share details of classified operations with prosecutors.[6] The CIA was often engaged in the recruitment and management of military and political assets in foreign countries, people who could be jailed or killed if their association with the United States were revealed. CIA officers could find themselves in physical jeopardy depending on how involved they were in foreign operations. Given these stakes, the CIA didn't always welcome the arrival of FBI informants to foreign areas of operation. Who had vetted them? How reliable were they, and what were they after? CIA officers couldn't be sure.[7] It came to pass that when FBI agents dispatched informants and cooperators abroad, CIA officers would sometimes lose track of them.[8]

In the 1980s, the FBI did manage to carve out its small slice of the international pie. After FBI agents and lawyers realized that the Bureau occasionally directed informants to violate laws in foreign countries, they modified their policy to allow for extraterritorial informant operations. A Department of Justice memorandum stated that "the President, acting through the Attorney General, has the inherent constitutional authority to deploy the FBI to investigate and arrest individuals for violating United States law, even if those actions contravene customary international law."[9] This allowed handling agents to communicate with sources in other countries.

This new standard was narrowly applied, and the natural tensions between the CIA and FBI intensified over time. The agencies' mutual suspicion encouraged them to withhold information and intelligence from one another. They distorted the spirit of Truman's bifurcation, sometimes working opposite ends of the same case or operation and declining to fuse their knowledge, compromising US national security.

The representative example of this obstinacy was September 11. The CIA and FBI had each been investigating al Qaeda for years but failed to provide each other with full disclosure. CIA officers tracked an eventual 9/11 hijacker through his entry to the United States in California, yet they declined to share this information with FBI agents who possessed other pieces of intelligence that might have exposed the September 11 plot.[10]

This omission and others, once the terrorists had murdered thousands of Americans in the attacks, made it easy for Congress and the administration to identify how the flawed US counterterrorism apparatus had unintentionally enabled 9/11. In its 600-page report, the 9/11 Commission zeroed in on the agencies' troubles in cooperating with one another. The commission demanded that the FBI and the CIA set aside their differences and forge an earnest working relationship.[11]

The CIA and FBI joined other intelligence and law-enforcement agencies under the purview of the new Office of the Director of National Intelligence. The agency would coordinate efforts where the CIA and FBI had failed, subordinating both agencies to the wider intelligence effort. At least, that was the goal. FBI director Robert Mueller built ties with CIA director George Tenet, the two officials attempting to overcome the interagency mistrust that had confounded the pooling of intelligence.[12]

The 9/11 Commission criticized the Bureau's inability to penetrate Islamic terrorist organizations. Considering that these groups were almost uniformly located and run outside the US, the commission directed the FBI to expand its operations abroad, mandating an increased use of CHSs domestically and overseas.[13] Truman's reasoned separation of power, which had held for more than fifty years, was undone, as the FBI began operating broadly outside the United States.

Mueller placed FBI agents on the front lines in Afghanistan and Iraq,[14] where they conducted what the FBI called sensitive site exploitations, gathering the type of frontline evidence that would lead an FBI agent to visit the Reillys in Oxford in 2010 and extend an invitation to Billy.

Since the FBI's founding, its central mission had been the retrospective investigation of crimes. Agents were bound by the law and couldn't act until a crime had been committed. However, over the years during national crises such as the Dustbowl-era scourge of bank robbers and kidnappers like John Dillinger and Alvin Karpis, agents had grown proactive, less interested in solving crimes than in capturing or eliminating known criminals before they could commit a new outrage. More recently, as bin Laden and al Qaeda grew emboldened, bombing US embassies in Kenya and Tanzania in 1998 and hitting an American warship, the USS *Cole*, in the port of Aden in 2000, the FBI worked abroad on specific assignments, trying to get ahead of new attacks.

The 9/11 Commission endorsed more of this sort of work, directing the FBI to prevent terrorist attacks before they could take shape, transforming the Bureau's fundamental mission. The FBI would have to identify, frustrate, arrest, and even participate in the government's elimination of terror suspects.[15] Continuing to operate as something of a national police force, the FBI also began to mutate into an international intelligence agency, operating in ways similar to the CIA. Institutionalizing the change, the FBI in 2005 established a directorate of intelligence, a compartmentalized "service within a service."[16]

Some CIA officers bristled at the Bureau's encroachment onto the international field, but they had to play ball. And they were required to assist the FBI with its new directive. The FBI knew how to wrangle an informant in a federal lockup, but cultivating international counterterrorism sources required a set of deft new skills. This sort of work was similar to the CIA's specialty, recruiting foreign political and military assets. As a sign of new cooperation between the agencies, CIA officers began instructing FBI agents at Quantico in the art of developing and handling counterterrorism sources.[17]

The field of intelligence categorized information in one of three ways:

human, open-source, and signals. Open-source intelligence, or OSINT, for short, is information that is readily available to the public in news reports, published documents, speeches, and the like. Signals intelligence, SIGINT, comes from, for example, foreign military and diplomatic correspondence, and is often captured in clandestine fashion. Human intelligence, or HUMINT, describes information derived from people. For the FBI, this was the sort of intelligence that a CHS often produced. The new designation, confidential human source, signaled the FBI's philosophical shift.

Informant, cooperator: that's how cops often talked, directly and descriptively. It was easy to understand what an informant was. *Confidential human source* was a perplexing term. It was both self-evident (it could be assumed that the person in question was human) and inexact. What did a source do? A source of information could be anyone at all, performing any sort of service. CHS, the term, seemed as though it was meant to conceal and confuse. And who normally concealed in order to confuse? *Confidential human source* was the language of spies. The FBI was shedding its courthouse nomenclature for the ambiguous terminology of espionage. The Bureau was beginning to sound like the CIA.

In the world after 9/11, the FBI's reach grew through the multiagency Joint Terrorism Task Force. JTTF offices were situated in cities around the country and allowed the FBI to pool resources with local police, the Drug Enforcement Administration, the Internal Revenue Service, the Bureau of Alcohol, Tobacco, and Firearms, and other agencies. The JTTF existed before 9/11, but after the attacks, Mueller authorized their proliferation, and roughly a hundred new centers sprang up around the country and expanded in size and mandate.[18]

The JTTF allowed the FBI to access documents, evidence, and intelligence via partner agencies. It was difficult, for example, for FBI agents to gain approval for mail cover, an age-old investigative technique by which postal inspectors recorded the return addresses of the letters and packages delivered to a certain recipient, enabling the mapping of correspondence. FBI regulations required agents to navigate a Byzantine approval process for mail cover. DEA agents, on the other hand, could simply write a memo and get started. In a JTTF, FBI agents would often run a mail cover request through their DEA colleagues.[19]

Agencies in a JTTF also shared informants. Anytime a CHS generated useful material, the handling FBI agent filled out an intelligence information report and filed it to a computer system that colleagues in other agencies could access. The more reports a CHS generated, the more valuable that CHS and the FBI handling agent appeared to be. If a CHS developed intelligence germane to operations outside of the FBI, a relevant agency might find that CHS worth getting to know.[20]

An FBI CHS was not exclusive to the FBI. The Bureau could farm out a CHS to other agencies. When a CHS like Billy Reilly embarked on a working relationship with the FBI, agents weren't required to disclose this fact.

The process of sharing could be formalized, with a CHS documented in the systems of multiple agencies, which would then co-handle the CHS and pursue joint operations with the FBI. But poaching also occurred. As in any office environment, some agents and officers in a JTTF were collegial, while others requisitioned CHSs summarily.[21]

It was by this process and others that the CIA enjoyed access to CHSs.

CIA officers were still prohibited from conducting domestic operations against Americans. However, after September 11 especially, and in the spirit of the interagency information sharing that the 9/11 Commission imposed, CIA officers were assigned to FBI offices and JTTFs around the country.[22] Notionally, CIA officers observed the work of their colleagues in other agencies without participating in operations. But that line, especially after 9/11, blurred.

Since the 1960s, the CIA had operated a little-known office, the National Resources Division, a department within the agency's clandestine service that recruited foreign nationals, such as diplomats and professors, who were in the United States temporarily. These people, once they returned home, could be valuable assets. There had been nearly thirty-five National Resources Division offices in the US in the 1980s, though that number later diminished. After 9/11, the CIA received additional funding to revive the department and recruit people to its cause.[23]

All such tools and contacts were brought to bear in the post-9/11 atmosphere of intelligence sharing. In a JTTF, CIA officers might ask colleagues in other agencies to share passenger manifests of flights entering the US, for example, or similar information that the CIA was barred from collecting domestically.[24] In a JTTF and in FBI field offices, CIA officers developed relationships with FBI agents, with each agency now having a hand in what the other was doing.

That's not what Truman had envisioned, but it is what the new security age and the 9/11 Commission demanded.

FBI agents had an incentive to farm out their CHSs. The more often other agencies used a CHS, the greater the luster on the FBI handler and the Bureau's ability to recruit and develop sources of intelligence. And because FBI agents and CIA officers worked together within JTTFs, it was easy to facilitate contact with CHSs. CIA officers often asked FBI colleagues to arrange meetings with CHSs. As long as the FBI handlers were present at these sit-downs, CIA officers could deny having been there. Meetings would enter FBI logs as routine sourcing conferences.[25]

Sometimes these meetings led to more. CIA officers, from time to time, appropriated CHSs from the FBI and sent them on missions abroad in support of agency operations. And if something went wrong on these overseas trips, and an FBI supervisor or internal inspector explored the CHS file for culpability, it was possible that the CIA wouldn't be listed in the paperwork. Officially, the FBI had handled all contact with the CHS. Yet the CHS's handling agent could at the same time in good faith state that he or she hadn't directed the source beyond the US border. Lacking clarity, the matter could be closed.[26]

*   *   *

Billy Reilly was in over his head, yet he had only just begun.

As 2010 turned to 2011, social and political upheaval consumed the Middle East. The Arab Spring, sparked by a street vendor's self-immolation in Tunisia, swelled across the region into mass public protests against corruption, inflation, unemployment, and constraints on civil rights. It was a political awakening. But as unrest consumed Bahrain, Egypt, Yemen, and other countries, it also released dark forces, especially in Syria, which the Reilly family had visited several years before. The country plunged into a civil war that would divide and obliterate large parts of it, the instability unleashing a new scourge, as bewildering as a sandstorm, the Islamic State of Iraq and Syria, or ISIS.[27]

At the computer, Billy devoured news of these developments. These were just the sort of world-altering events that gripped him, and he drew up reports for the FBI about what he was learning, his assessments sparkling across the pages.

In a typical report from later in the Syrian conflict, Billy wrote: "I think that after IS consolidates their control of Raqqa, Deir Zowr, East Aleppo and Hasaka (division 17 and brigade 93 in Raqqa, the bases around Hasaka, the airport in Deir Zowr and Keweris air base in Aleppo), their target will be the Homs area..." His prediction proved accurate.

As ISIS won territory and plied its hand farther into Iraq, Billy's scope widened. One of his reports analyzed assaults carried out against the Iraqi military in the city of Al-Awja by ISIS and a tribal military council. "These were not claimed as joint attacks, but shows both groups have combat areas that overlap and they dont [*sic*] fight against each other," Billy wrote. "It will be interesting to see if IS and the tribal alliance will clash further south, or if the truces will hold."

Billy's FBI reports would deepen and mature. In another, he wrote: "JN [Jabhat al-Nusra] and IS [ISIS] seem to be not hostile with each other in Qalamoun unlike other areas, though the trend is JN defecting to IS. This is emphasized by Abu Ali al-Shishani who said that he is neutral in the dispute between JN and IS and hopes it will be resolved. He also called on FSA [Free Syrian Army] to join IS. The most significant situation will be what JN emir of Qalamoun Abu Malik al-Tali decides to do."[28]

The reports evidenced how distinctions between the FBI and CIA had substantially dissolved. It was difficult now to know where the Bureau's boundaries were drawn, or if there were any, or if Billy, like other CHSs before him, was now working for other agencies in addition to the FBI.

Billy's handlers urged him to get involved in social media, where ISIS was staking out territory and pressing a recruitment drive.[29] He established an array of accounts on various platforms. There were the majors, Facebook, Skype, and Twitter, and others more obscure to Americans, such as Kik, Nimbuzz, and VKontakte, a Russian social media app. The names Billy chose for his accounts, Bilal for the Arabic world, Vasily for the Russian, weren't so different from his own. He hewed to legends that felt comfortable. On social media, he told people he was a Russian raised in the United States, a recent convert to Islam seeking interpretation of the Koran. A Facebook profile under the name Bilal Al Rusi gave his birthplace as Kazan, a Muslim center of Russia, and his residence as Windsor, Ontario, across the Detroit River into Canada.[30] For the FBI, Billy assembled a portfolio of social media jihad.

Agents praised his dexterity in the digital world, and he developed a close working relationship with his eventual FBI handler, agent Timothy Reintjes. The two had a few things in common. Agent Reintjes was from the Midwest, too, from Kansas City, Missouri. Like Billy, he'd gone to a Catholic high school. Reintjes had picked up two degrees at a Catholic university in Philadelphia, Villanova. It was Reintjes who would appear at the Reillys' door in Oxford in the summer of 2015, after Billy had gone dark in Russia, and had told Terry and Bill that the FBI had no knowledge of their son's travels.[31]

Billy began meeting with his handler and other agents in the parking lots of Detroit-area restaurants and stores, places such as Panera Bread, Tim Horton's, and Home Depot.[32] Sometimes Billy and the agents would meet inside a restaurant, piling into a booth for lunch. Billy told his parents that it must have seemed odd to the people seated around them, with the FBI men dressed in suits and ties while the rest of the clientele wore casual clothes. Billy started referring to his FBI contacts as "the men."

He took to whispering around the house, as though he was full of secrets on which the nation's security depended. Bill and Terry teased him. Sitting on the couch at home, watching TV, they would point at the screen when a spy movie came on, one about Jason Bourne or James Bond. "Look, there's Billy." Terry and Bill were proud of Billy and the work he was doing, proud enough to joke about it, and he played along, the parents and the son oblivious to the stakes.[33]

After 9/11, with his high school friends, Billy had talked about the US role in its comeuppance. Now he had taken a post on the American side of the terror war. The FBI validated his instincts. What interested him was no longer obscure. He was sharing secrets with agents who worked the front lines of the nation's concern. Feeling as though he belonged, Billy thought he might one day become one of "the men" himself. He asked them if they would help him find a staff job with the FBI, and they said that they would.[34] They gave him a code name to sign property slips: Falcon.[35]

Billy's relationship with the Bureau, a beguilement, rendered him defenseless to suggestion as "the men" prepared to send him into the field.

CHAPTER NINE

Operational

I n mid-2012, Billy drove south from Oxford to Westland, in Wayne County between Detroit and Ann Arbor. He parked at a home that was like others on the block, a single-story brick house with slit windows and a strip of lawn, built for auto workers in the 1950s, now worth seventy grand. The cars on Warren Road's four lanes whipped past without a break.[1]

A man stepped out of the house. Aws Naser, twenty-four, was five-foot-eight and had curly dark hair. He slid into the front passenger seat of Billy's car.[2]

Naser believed that the man at the wheel was named Mikhail. This was the name Billy had used when he had sent a message to Naser's YouTube channel days earlier. Naser had been posting videos about the FBI's handling of Arab Muslim émigrés, asserting that they were victims of bias. Writing to Naser as Mikhail, Billy said that he himself was an immigrant, too, from Eastern Europe, and that he lived in Ann Arbor. Billy said he had recently converted to Islam.

With Naser seated beside him, Billy drove a mile east on Warren Road to a mosque named Dar al Salam.[3] This was not a visually arresting building, with a dome and minarets, but instead looked like a careworn community center. Inside were thin paneled walls, frayed rugs, and corridors darkened by the impression that the owner worried over the electric bill. Billy and Naser found a spot at the back of the mosque's large main hall. A crowded Friday prayer session was underway. Men knelt, bent at the waist, and pressed their foreheads to the floor in prayer. Naser took Billy's measure.[4]

Operational

*   *   *

Aws Naser loved being American. Born in Baghdad, he and his family immigrated to the United States in 2001, months before the September 11 attacks, settling in Utica, New York. Then twelve years old, Naser took to his new life in the freewheeling way that distinguishes immigrant children from their parents, who often carry into exile a fear of the unknown and regrets over what they've left behind them. Naser quickly learned to speak English with depth and idiom, and he made friends at his middle school, which was named for John F. Kennedy. Naser felt like he was fitting in.

It was the cataclysm of 9/11 that revealed to Naser a darker shade to his surroundings. One afternoon, a woman approached Naser and his mother outside a Utica grocery store. "This is America," the woman said, gesturing to the hijab Naser's mother wore. "You can take that off. You're free now." At school, boys blamed Naser for the fall of the towers. One classmate punched him in the head while Naser was waiting in line for food in the cafeteria. Another boy tackled Naser as he rode a bike in his neighborhood. Naser's father decided to make a change.

He moved the family to Michigan, to Dearborn, but there Fordson High School was no more peaceful. There was more fighting. Naser was now ready to throw the first punch, and this earned him detentions. His grades fell. He dropped out of school. He listened when his father recommended that he stop by Dearborn's Parklane Towers.[5]

At the office complex on Parklane Boulevard, a Pentagon contractor was recruiting people who were fluent in both Arabic and English.[6] The contractor flew Naser to San Diego for six months of desert training at Camp Pendleton: IED detection, artillery spotting, field dressage. He was learning battlefield skills, but not so he could be a soldier. In 2007, Naser joined a Marines unit as an interpreter out of Habbaniya base, Iraq. He had returned to his origin in the uniform of the United States.

Naser's pride in being an American swelled. He accompanied the Marines on missions, interpreting dialogues between squad leaders and locals. Sometimes there was shooting. Sometimes Naser carried a shotgun.

On night patrols, Marine units entered private homes, rousting families from sleep and rifling through their possessions. The wives and children were afraid, the fathers were shamed by their weakness. All they could do was ask Naser why. He watched a young Marine pocket meager belongings from a family that had little. When Naser asked the Marine why he had stolen, the man replied, "Because I can."

Naser stood by as US military officers and clerks dishonored deals they'd made with locals, taking advantage of powerless people, sullying the flag on the uniform. In his native Arabic, Naser apologized and explained to the Iraqis who pleaded with him for help. In time, he no longer believed what he was saying.

Naser's uniform couldn't conceal the person beneath it, an Iraqi, a Muslim. This identity flowered within him. In an Iraqi market, he bought a *shemagh*, a patterned head covering, and wore it beneath his helmet. A Marine officer snuck up behind Naser one day and grabbed hold of the garment, choking Naser with it until he passed out.[7]

Naser broke one of his legs in Iraq and left the Marines for home, where he began to understand that the experience had changed him. He had never been religious, but he began attending a mosque in Dearborn. He sometimes wore a *dishdasha*, a long white robe. He enrolled at Henry Ford Community College, in Dearborn, and planned for a medical degree, but new thoughts clouded his priorities.

Naser's family had fled Iraq and life under Saddam Hussein's regime for better prospects in America. But Naser's wartime experiences caused him to question the US mission in the fight against terror, convinced that America was betraying its ideals.[8]

He kept close watch on news reports, documenting a rise in FBI terrorism cases, which seemed to focus on young men who shared Naser's background. In 2003, when the US military invaded Iraq, the White House had ordered the FBI to question more than ten thousand Iraqi émigrés living in the United States in search of ties to Muslim extremism. FBI director Mueller said that such people were one of the Bureau's greatest challenges.[9] The FBI's leadership feared that Iraqis would conspire to strike from within the US, as though it were their duty to retaliate for the invasion.

An internal FBI intelligence report stated that attending a mosque was cause enough for scrutiny.[10] So was wearing a beard or Muslim clothing. The 9/11 Commission Report said that the FBI's new role would be a "domestic equivalent" to the "job of the CIA's operations officers abroad."[11] Naser read about cases in which FBI CHSs had engineered false terror plots that ensnared unwitting suspects, cases that sounded to Naser like entrapment.

Naser believed that the FBI blamed every Muslim for that tragic day in September. Like Billy, he wanted to find the truth. Online, he studied the details of terrorism cases, and he perceived a pattern. Just as the military had passed judgment on Arab Muslims abroad, so, too, had the FBI at home. Naser believed that the armed forces and the Bureau, potent tools of government, were afflicted with an identical prejudice against people like himself. He concluded that the FBI was hounding Muslim men without cause, violating their rights, framing them, inducing courts to lock them away forever on faulty grounds.

On a YouTube account, Naser began airing his views. He produced simple videos, with text and voice-over tracks, explaining in his own unpolished manner how he believed the United States was betraying its ethos. On the campus of Henry Ford Community College, he began speaking out.

On campus one day in the spring of 2011, Naser was sharing his views and distributing pamphlets when security guards told him that he didn't have permission to hold a rally. Naser pointed out that campus Christian students had freely promoted Bible study. After a talk with a college vice president, Naser was expelled. (Henry Ford Community College said Naser had not been enrolled at the time of the incident.)

The episode confirmed what Naser already believed. He had served his adopted country in a war. But what really mattered was his religion and ethnic makeup, which marked him for extralegal treatment, at minimum the violation of his right to free speech. Shortly after the incident at the college, two FBI agents arrived unannounced at Naser's house in Westland. The agents showed Naser printouts of comments he had made on his YouTube channel, unnerving him, though he wasn't dissuaded from his course.

YouTube allowed Naser to speak his mind and connect with people who valued his point of view. His videos, as rudimentary as they were, attracted a like-minded crowd. Through the channel, Naser struck up a correspondence with a man from Florida.[12]

Russell Dennison had grown up in Pennsylvania. Like Billy Reilly, he was a Catholic of European descent who had gravitated to Islam in the wake of 9/11. He had grown a long red beard. Dennison wrote to Naser on YouTube and said he had converted to Islam. The two traded messages, and Dennison flew to Detroit, staying with Naser in Westland.[13]

The two men engaged in lengthy discussions about the US government and its attitude toward Islam. Dennison sought to draw out his host. Naser felt that Dennison was encouraging him to develop practical plans to address their shared grievances, to punish the United States for its hypocrisies.[14]

Dennison said he was thinking about traveling to Iraq. Naser knew the country well and suggested places to visit. With Naser's help, Dennison was working through these plans when the FBI agents returned to the house in Westland. Naser began to believe that he had been added to an FBI watch list, like the many American Muslim men about whom he had been reading.

Naser didn't know what a CHS was, or how FBI agents did their jobs, but he feared that Dennison was doing the Bureau's bidding, attempting to goad him into developing a plan of attack that the FBI could easily foil. In 2012, Naser traveled to Iraq. Dennison was already there. The two met. The rendezvous sharpened Naser's fears about Dennison and the FBI. But Naser was mistaken.

Dennison was in the midst of an Islamic radicalization and would never see the United States again. He would travel to Egypt, Iraq, Jordan, and Lebanon before crossing into Syria in 2012. There he would join ISIS and fight for radical Islam. The FBI, CIA, and other security agencies worried that home-grown American sympathizers of fundamentalist Islamic terror would inspire others to head overseas, as Dennison had done, or to carry out attacks on US soil. Dennison would last seven years in the ISIS army before dying in battle in a village in eastern Syria in 2019. Naser was wrong about Dennison, but not about the FBI's interest in him.[15]

In Michigan, Naser, married and facing financial pressures, took a job at a gas station. In 2012, when he received a message through his YouTube account from a user identified as Mikhail, Naser was certain that the man was another FBI plant sent to entrap him.[16]

*   *   *

Agents routinely encouraged CHSs to forge personal relationships with investigative targets in order to help the FBI map connections, predict behavior, and figure out whether Bureau suspects were genuine threats to national security and worth the time to pursue. Billy's FBI handlers had directed him to contact Naser, marking a significant expansion of his FBI role.

Billy wasn't prepared for it.

A portion of instruction at the FBI academy in Quantico concerned field operations, how to navigate relations with armed suspects and the dangers of working under the cover of a legend. Throughout their careers, depending on the duties they would assume, FBI agents received additional coaching meant to enhance their work and safety.[17]

A CHS received no such formal guidance. Before sending a CHS into the field, agents tested a CHS operationally. They would direct a CHS to a mosque, for example, to gather material that agents already knew, such as names and phone numbers of people who worshipped there. If the CHS succeeded in such tasks, the handling agent would shift to a live operation, instructing the CHS to engage in what was called a collection activity. FBI agents knew how tricky this work was, yet they dispatched inexpert CHSs to engage suspects and targets in person using legends that were challenging to maintain in convincing fashion.[18]

It was possible that Aws Naser had become radicalized. His YouTube videos made a convincing argument for it. He had made trips between Iraq and the US, and his association with Russell Dennison was provocative. Naser was the type of person whom Mueller had said represented the FBI's greatest challenge. It didn't help Billy that Naser was immediately suspicious of him.

Over YouTube, Billy and Naser agreed to get together. In their first meeting, Billy did himself no favors. His goal was to induce Naser to relax, to let down his guard and begin to confide. But it was Billy who couldn't relax. He was nervous and fidgety. This set Naser more firmly on edge, solidifying his suspicion that "Mikhail" was working for the Bureau. When Billy contacted Naser to schedule a second meeting, Naser was determined to avoid the fate of other Muslim American men he thought the legal system had sidelined.

Naser was secretly creating a YouTube video asserting that Russell Dennison was an FBI plant. Making a public stand was the only way Naser felt he could combat the FBI. He decided to create a second video, this one exposing Billy on YouTube as an FBI operative.

Naser was waiting at a 7-Eleven store in Westland when Billy pulled into the lot and parked. He stepped out of the car and found Naser pointing a video camera at him. Billy froze. He knew that several FBI agents were observing the interaction from cars parked nearby.

Naser took control. He swiped the keys from Billy's hand and climbed into the car, sliding behind the steering wheel. Billy had little choice but to join him, and the two drove off the 7-Eleven lot.

Naser made small talk as he drove, but Billy grew anxious. His face was tight, and his words were clipped. He pulled a phone from a pocket and tried to type out a message, but Naser kept him talking.

Naser steered the car off the main road and into a public park. The two found themselves secluded in a cul-de-sac, and Naser brought the car to a stop. He told Billy to get out, directing him to a park bench. Naser lifted his camera.

Naser's use of the video camera was unsettling. Billy understood how ISIS and other jihadist groups had taken to social media, attracting followers with visceral images of their exploits. They posted videos of gun battles, torture, and even beheadings. The FBI routinely picked up chatter between terrorist recruiters and targets in the United States, young men who were eager to make their mark in the name of jihad.

With the camera trained on Billy, Naser lobbed questions about Islam, eager to make Billy slip up and contradict his legend. Billy searched for the answers that would maintain his cover.

Billy and Naser were two amateurs feeling their way along an imaginary line of contact in the boundless war on terror, ignorant of how powerless they were. They could have been friends. Instead, Naser was pursuing a remedy for his grievances, believing that he could outsmart the FBI, while Billy was eager to do his duty but unsure exactly what it was. Cops and FBI agents working cases in counterterrorism, organized crime, and narcotics routinely sent CHSs into field operations they didn't survive, though the public rarely learned of it.[19]

Whatever plan Naser had for Billy, the sound of several approaching cars interrupted it. Billy's FBI tail had arrived.

Naser directed Billy back into the car and wheeled out of the park and onto Warren Road. Naser pushed the car to eighty-five miles per hour, and the tail cars weaved through traffic to keep up. Laughing to himself, Naser watched in the rearview mirror as the chase proved that "Mikhail" was no simple seeker.

Naser believed he now had enough material to produce his video about Billy. Unrelated troubles would intercede.

Naser had left his gas station job believing that the owner owed him a final paycheck. On New Year's Eve, 2013, Naser arrived at the station to collect it.[20] The cashier said there was no paycheck, and Naser grabbed a can of pepper spray from a store shelf. He sprayed the clerk in the face and scooped $180 from the cashbox.[21] Discounting the gravity of what he had done, or perhaps emboldened by it, Naser released his Russell Dennison video on YouTube days after the filling-station theft.

On the morning of January 4, 2013, the front door of Naser's house flew open. The glass door at the back of the house shattered. West Bloomfield policemen flooded into the living room, tossed Naser to the floor, and pummeled him as his wife looked on. Naser had once accompanied Marines on home invasions in Iraq, but now he was the target.[22]

As police led Naser away, two FBI agents observed in the driveway. Agents were also in court for Naser's arraignment, when a judge read out a charge of armed robbery. The judge set the bond at $100,000, a reasonable amount since Naser had no previous criminal record. He might have managed to pay the bond with his house as collateral.

But one of the FBI agents conferred with the prosecutor, who lobbied the judge for a sterner bond. The judge reset the bond at $2 million, ensuring that Naser would remain confined until his case was resolved.[23]

Naser went to trial, serving as his own counsel. "The men" told Billy about the sessions. One agent laughed when describing how Naser, as defense attorney, fell into repeated procedural tangles.[24] Convicted of armed robbery, Naser received three to twenty years in prison, in line with Michigan's sentencing guidelines. "You should have been there," one of "the men" told Billy. "It was so funny."[25]

Billy failed to see the humor. He understood that Naser had to be called to account for the gas station crime. And Billy realized that he didn't understand the nature or extent of Naser's travels to Iraq, nor of his relationship with Dennison. Surely "the men" knew more than Billy did about Naser.

What Billy did know was that Naser's crime had no connection to terrorism. It was the result of an irrational, spontaneous decision, not a devious scheme.

Billy found Naser naïve. Naser's progression, from a proud immigrant aspiring to be American to an object of ridicule bound for federal prison, struck Billy as pointless and sad. He didn't have all the details, and he was consumed by questions he couldn't answer. Why were FBI agents present at Naser's arrest? Was the arrest an opportunistic ruse, a chance for the FBI to bag evidence from Naser's house without having to apply for a terrorism warrant? How were agents able to influence the judge, via the prosecutor, to escalate Naser's bond? Had the FBI steered the course of justice? Billy suspected that agents had stacked the deck because they couldn't get Naser on a terror offense.

Billy struggled with his role in the case. He had been contributing to the FBI's counterterrorism mission from the computer and smartphone at a distance from the people and events he was cataloguing. He had made no genuine personal connections. There had been be no confusing emotions, no feelings of betrayal when a suspect, led into custody, realized that Billy had engaged in deceit.

Stepping onto the field of play changed Billy's perception of the work he was doing. He hadn't calculated the cost of getting to know counterterrorism targets. Naser wasn't a cipher from the digital world, a name on a report that Billy filed to Dropbox. Billy knew Aws Naser. He even liked him. Now he had helped put him away.

Billy wasn't a cop. He wasn't a spy. He wasn't tough and calculating, as an FBI counterterrorism agent had to be. He hadn't signed up to participate in the manipulation of justice. He felt like the FBI had used and deceived him. Billy told his parents that when he'd learned what had happened to Naser, he had nearly vomited.[26]

CHAPTER TEN

The Secret

C atie Reilly grew more determined to follow a path independent from her parents' wishes the more strongly Terry and Bill sought to impose them. In 2013, four years after Catie and Mohammed had met, they took what even by then Terry and Bill recognized was an inevitable step. Catie and Mohammed married. A year later, they had a son.

Catie's interest in Islam had brought her to Dearborn and into the society of Metro Detroit's Arab Muslims. She felt she belonged there more than at home, that Muslims in Dearborn accepted her even though she was a convert. The hijab she wore signaled her observance of the religion, but it also exposed her to the post-9/11 troubles from which her Christian, European origin had formerly exempted her.[1]

Catie occasionally drove to Canada to visit friends. Crossing the border was routine for people in Detroit. In high school or college, one could drive to Ontario and drink legally at the bars in Windsor. Before 9/11, there was no riddle to these outings. US border agents often waved people back into the country after a few routine questions. Following the terror attacks, with control of airports, seaports, and the roads into the US tightening, the government enhanced its scrutiny of the traffic entering Detroit from Canada.[2]

After Catie had accepted Islam, border guards routinely pulled her aside for questioning upon her approach to the US. In her hijab, she looked like any other Dearborn Muslim, possibly a threat. Border guards never arrested Catie, or seized her belongings, or demanded to examine her phone. But the inconveniences felt like an affront, giving her a taste of life on the other side of the ethno-religious divide.[3]

Of all the US security agencies that enforced the shift in policy after September 11, it was the FBI that Catie came to despise. The FBI often instigated enhanced searches at the border, using guards from the US Customs and Border Protection as *gendarmerie*.[4] The FBI also maintained a lengthy no-fly list of people, mostly Arabs or Muslims, whom it prohibited from traveling by air.[5] The list was not public or subject to independent oversight. Many of those on the list didn't know how they had wound up on it or how they could have their names expunged. The FBI's work was essential for national security, but it was imperfect, drawing Catie's sympathies for blameless people enmeshed in the machine.

During George W. Bush's final days as president in late 2008, the Department of Justice had liberalized FBI guidelines, allowing agents to open evidentiary files on people after establishing only a "clearly defined objective," which fostered ambiguity and gave the Bureau greater license. In the two years that followed, the FBI initiated almost 43,000 of these counterterrorism investigations.[6]

Many such inquiries grew out of the post-9/11 spirit of interagency cooperation. The CIA sometimes collected intelligence abroad about terrorist recruiters who worked refugee camps that sheltered Middle Easterners. Some of these refugees subsequently immigrated to the United States. When they did, FBI agents would pay them house calls, trying to determine if they were under the influence of recruiters they might have come across in the camps.

Agents interviewed these new arrivals and didn't stop there. Running down the leads, agents questioned immigrants' family members and their friends and others in their neighborhoods. This was the sort of thorough work that the job and the issue demanded. But people in these communities lived under sustained fear, unsure of who among them had agreed to become an FBI informant.[7]

Catie and Mohammed regarded the Bureau with suspicion and dread. Mohammed's older brother, Abdulrahman Cherri, was waging a personal battle with the FBI. Agents had once visited the Cherri home to question Abdul about a digital posting he had written about the metaphysical world, which could have been interpreted as an advocation for martyrdom.[8] Whenever

Abdul returned to the US from international trips, border agents would pull him aside. They asked where he prayed, how often he attended mosque. They asked for the name of his imam. The sessions often lasted for hours. As a US citizen, Abdul was outraged, concluding that the FBI had profiled him for his religion and ethnicity.

In 2012, Abdul and several other Muslim men filed a lawsuit against the FBI, the Department of Homeland Security, the US Customs and Border Protection, and the Transportation Security Administration, alleging harassment and discrimination. The suit named FBI director Mueller as a defendant. It would drag on for years.[9]

Catie identified with Abdul's fight against the FBI, having endured her own questions and delays at the border. His plight cinched her closer to her new Muslim identity.

*   *   *

Mohammed Cherri was not the husband Bill and Terry had imagined their daughter would select. He had become an indication to the parents that either they or Catie, despite her academic achievements, had somehow failed one another. The Reillys believed that Mohammed pursued knowledge with greater zeal than he sought employment. With Catie in the midst of her physician's residency and logging sixty hours per week at a clinic, Mohammed taught part-time language classes.[10]

Billy saw something more in Mohammed. Since he had come from beyond Detroit, Mohammed was one of the few people in Billy's small circle who understood his global interests. The two found common ground discussing the Arab Spring, the war in Syria, the rise of ISIS. As an endorsement of Mohammed, Billy took him fishing.

Mohammed thought he knew as much as anyone about events unfolding in the Middle East, but he had to admit that Billy's knowledge exceeded his own. Anyone could read the news. Billy understood the personalities of terror-group leaders. He knew how dogmas interwove or clashed, and he predicted the path of these undercurrents. It was a marvel to Mohammed that his brother-in-law could speak modern standard Arabic better than many native Arabic speakers in Dearborn, who employed regional dialects.

With Mohammed, Billy shared his views about US policy in Syria, Russia's intervention there, and Turkish opportunism. "He would give you volumes and volumes," Mohammed said later. Billy didn't push a group or a position. There was no emotion, only analysis. It wasn't the ascendance of a group or dogma that fascinated him but the spasm of history in the making.

For Billy, these deep geopolitical interests didn't amount to enough of a life, however. The time he spent in the company of his sister and brother-in-law intensified Billy's impulse to belong in the way that they belonged to each other. He told them he wanted to start a family of his own.[11]

Catie never asked, and she wasn't sure if her brother, now in his mid-twenties, had ever known a woman in an intimate way. Billy had mentioned a Syrian woman in college, but no one in the family had met her.[12]

Mohammed knew a woman who worked as a librarian, a profession that attracted the sort of studious person who might match Billy's disposition. Mohammed took his brother-in-law to an Islamic library in Dearborn, where the woman worked, and introduced the two. The time Billy had devoted to the computer and phone little aided his attempt to charm. The meeting was awkward and uncomfortable.[13]

Billy found himself involuntarily celibate. But his inability to appeal or relate to women romantically did not turn him against them. Billy was attracted to women, but they made him nervous. He had never learned how to speak with them with an easy manner. He didn't go to parties or other events and places where people gathered and relaxed, where he could run across someone in a casual way. Billy believed that a woman for him was out there. He just couldn't figure out how to make a connection.

He wasn't going to spend too much time trying. He instead directed his energy down a path his sister had forged. Her interest in medicine had led her to a career. As Catie had done, Billy decided to try for an advanced degree.

He couldn't decide between high tech, hard science, and the law. He took a software class at Oakland Community College.[14] At Walsh College, a business school in Troy, he studied cyber security.[15] He took classes at Cooley Law School, in Detroit. Added together, software, cyber security, and the law made a complementary package of disciplines. Yet Billy also filled out an application for a degree in industrial hygiene at Montana Tech and would eventually focus on a biology master's degree at the Illinois Institute of Technology in Chicago.[16]

He was jumping from one topic to another perhaps in avoidance of the one field of concentration that truly interested him. "My ideal position five years after obtaining my Master's degree would being [*sic*] working in the field of national security," he wrote in a personal statement. "I would especially like to continue academic work and pursue a PhD, as well. This way I will have the knowledge and skills to pursue the work that I have dreamed of doing."[17]

There was a reason that Billy's dream had failed to take practical form: his dream job, the work he did for the FBI, was already his. But it wasn't really a job. He worked long hours in his role as a CHS and received little compensation for it, and no offer of permanent employment. He couldn't even mention his valuable FBI experience on a resume. He had been working in secret for an organization that by regulation would deny that he had ever been associated with it. The FBI had reeled Billy in on the cheap, preying on his interest in the subject matter, and on his aimlessness.

Billy knew that the FBI was holding him back, but he didn't know how to move on. He needed to talk things through. His younger sister, married with children and on her way to becoming a doctor, was a source for him of practical advice. Eager to unload some of the weight he was carrying, Billy confided in his sister, sharing the secret of his FBI involvement.

Catie was staggered. To her, the FBI was the enemy. She couldn't understand how Billy, the person who had guided her to Islam, was working for the agency she believed was oppressing people for this very religious belief.

Catie realized that Billy's secret would have to be hers, too. She couldn't tell anyone about her brother's FBI affiliation, least of all Mohammed or Abdul Cherri. Catie worried that her new Muslim circle might think that she also worked for the FBI.[18]

*   *   *

On April 15, 2013, two bombs detonated near the finish line of the Boston Marathon, expelling shrapnel into the crowd, killing three people, and leaving scores more with ghastly injuries. Nearly a dozen years after the September 11 attacks, the panic of the marathon events underscored terrorism's fixed role in American life.

A host of security agencies sprang into action. The FBI, CIA, ATF, DEA, and local police scoured security-camera footage and social media accounts to identify who had committed the bombing. The agencies zeroed in on two brothers.[19] Tamerlan and Dzhokhar Tsarnaev, ethnic Chechens, had immigrated to the United States with their family in 2002 from the Russian province of Dagestan, which was nestled in the mountainous North Caucasus. The older brother, Tamerlan, twenty-six at the time of the bombing, had pursued a career in boxing in the Boston area but felt detached from life in the US. He returned several times to the Caucasus and met there with Islamic fighters who were challenging Russian control. The FBI began keeping tabs on Tamerlan. In Boston, agents visited the Tsarnaev home several times to speak with him and his family.[20]

Tamerlan was already radicalized. Dzhokhar, seven years younger, was under his sway. Following instructions in an Islamic terror magazine, the two made rudimentary bombs packed in stovetop pressure cookers. They carried the bombs in backpacks and laid them on the sidewalk amid the marathon crowd. Like the underwear bomber before them, the Tsarnaevs pierced the FBI's defense. They escaped the scene, igniting a manhunt.[21]

The FBI reached out to Russia, the Tsarnaevs' place of origin, to learn if the Boston bombing might be part of a larger plan. The inquiry would mark a new stage of cooperation between Russia and the United States.

For years, the FBI had maintained a legal attaché, colloquially known as a "legat," at the US embassy in Moscow, as it did in scores of other missions abroad. A law-enforcement liaison to Russian counterparts, the legat interfaced primarily with the Federal Security Service, or FSB, Russia's main domestic intelligence agency. In countries that were friendlier to the US, in Australia and the UK, for instance, FBI legats and staff enjoyed close collaborative partnerships with local law enforcement. Not in Russia. The FSB compartmentalized the relationship, restricting the FBI's access to information. The legat submitted requests to the FSB's international affairs department, which served as a filter between the FBI and the FSB's operational divisions. While the two sides sometimes helped one another, typically on counterterrorism cases, FBI officials believed that the FSB viewed the relationship as transactional.[22]

That changed after the Boston bombings. For the first time in many years, the FSB permitted the FBI legat and his staff to meet with high-ranking counterterrorism officials, including General Dmitri Minaev, a veteran of the

FSB's Caucasus operations. FBI staff in Moscow met with investigators from the Ministry of the Interior, which was usually off limits. Russia even permitted a group of FBI agents who were working the marathon case to fly in from Boston. They followed an escort to Dagestan, the Tsarnaevs' place of origin, where FSB agents identified people the FBI sought to interview.[23]

Since its push southward in the first half of the nineteenth century, Moscow had encountered fierce resistance to its rule in the Caucasus. After the fall of the Soviet Union, Russia had fought two bitter wars in Chechnya, which spawned a years-long scourge of terror attacks across Russia that targeted airliners, concerts, and schools.[24] Now that two men from the Caucasus had sprung an attack on the United States, Russia was eager to prove that it had played no part in it. FBI officials suspected an ulterior motive behind Russia's collegiality but took advantage of the access while it lasted.

With the Tsarnaevs still on the run, Billy received a call from his FBI handler, Tim Reintjes. The urgency of the moment clouded the misgivings Billy had experienced working the Aws Naser case. It was gratifying to feel wanted. Reintjes needed Billy's help. The FBI was enlisting anyone who could assist the effort to locate, arrest, and prosecute the Tsarnaevs. Billy's knowledge of Islamic terror and the Russian world converged in a search of the brothers' digital lives. Billy told his parents that he sat in on a meeting with "the men" and people from Russia who were assisting the case. When the Tsarnaevs' spree in Boston ended with Tamerlan dead and Dzhokhar in custody, Billy felt he had contributed to taking them down.[25]

After the marathon bombing, FBI managers discussed the prospect that the Tsarnaevs would inspire others to commit similar acts. An intelligence report suggested that an al Qaeda member was communicating with a terror cell in California, again two brothers. In Washington, at the FBI's International Terrorism Operations Section, Andrew McCabe, who had worked with Andy Arena on the underwear-bomber case, was determined to locate these men.[26]

The Detroit office picked up McCabe's directive, and Billy's handler set him on the task. Billy locked onto brothers from Russia, Alexey and Anatoliy Trofimov, who were living in the United States. Like Tamerlan Tsarnaev, the Trofimovs were involved in martial arts.[27] Billy's inquiry stalled when he discovered that the Trofimovs had returned home. Andy McCabe later said the California brothers investigation had squandered valuable time and resources.[28]

It was another instance of an empty counterterrorism lead, yet it demonstrated how Billy served FBI priorities.

When the rush of the Boston bombing investigation subsided, Billy took stock of his situation. He told his Uncle Jim, Terry's brother, that the FBI had paid him $4,000 for his work on the marathon case,[29] but this wasn't the sort of recognition Billy was after. He told his parents he had learned that management had praised Reintjes for work on the Tsarnaev case that Billy believed was his own. Billy groused that he wasn't getting the credit he deserved.[30]

Three years into his relationship with the FBI, Billy thought he had demonstrated his value. He wanted a job. Again, he asked "the men" if they thought he was FBI material. They said that he was, but they did little for him. They never would. FBI agents frequently dangled opportunities in front of CHSs with no obligation to fulfill them. Telling Billy that he belonged was a common FBI lure.

FBI agents didn't respect CHSs. Agents often called their sources snitches, just as criminals did, despite the critical value that CHSs brought to the Bureau. For someone like Billy, FBI agents reserved a special nickname, "keyboard commando," which suggested a computer-bound CHS who had an inflated notion of his role.[31]

Mistrust was a principal reason for this disdain. As part of operational instruction, agents encouraged CHSs to lead double lives, to deceive. A CHS was meant to shield the truth from FBI targets, while revealing the truth to FBI agents. The more adept a CHS was at lying, the more effective a CHS could be. But FBI agents could never be sure where the lying ended. CHSs sometimes broke the law, or passed themselves off as FBI agents, or cut financial deals to work with other agencies.[32] The very qualities—duplicity, access to crime or terror—that made people worthy CHSs also effectively disqualified them from consideration for full-time FBI employment.

It was unlikely that Billy could have passed a basic FBI background check. The online connections he had pursued and the provocative notions about US foreign policy he had entertained as far back as high school made him a risk. It was one thing to be a CHS, vested to do "the men's" shadow work, and quite another to be an FBI employee representing the Bureau in the light of day.[33]

"The men" had done such an effective job of praising and encouraging Billy that he misjudged his standing. He wasn't one of "the men." He was one of thousands of alpha-numeric designations in the Delta system, a tool of "the men."

On a federal employment site, Billy found a listing for an FBI intelligence analyst job. In a cover letter, he wrote that he was "hardworking and committed," concluding, "based on my travels and my experience I think I would be a good candidate for this job. My language skills in Russian and Arabic languages and my knowledge and familiarity with cultures from the middle east and my own family's eastern European cultural background would be beneficial in this field."[34]

Billy chased this hopeless vision unaware that his fate was formulating elsewhere, far from Oxford. The Tsarnaev brothers had linked the two worlds that interested Billy, Islamic terror and Russia. In early 2014, he would cross that bridge to its other side. Conflict between Russia and Ukraine was coming.

CHAPTER ELEVEN

Origins

I t began in the Middle Ages as a search for plunder. Vikings in their marauding travels learned of Constantinople, in Byzantium, the seat of the Eastern Roman Empire. A stronghold of treasure, the city straddled the Bosporus Strait, linking the Black and Mediterranean Seas. The European Plain separated Constantinople from the Scandinavian Vikings. The task was finding a way to reach the city.[1]

The Vikings rowed modest rivers southward, portaging their boats from one waterway to another. Near the present border between Belarus and Ukraine, the Vikings discovered the place where the Dnieper River widened and quickened. The river flowed nearly 700 miles in a southeasterly hook, with whitewater rapids animating its final sections. The Dnieper estuary released into the Black Sea. From there for the Vikings was open-water sailing to Constantinople and a chance to raid.[2]

Once the Norse oarsmen had established this route to Byzantium, they regularly used it. The Dnieper carried the Vikings past Slavic settlements, including Kiev, on the river's right bank. The Vikings came to tarry there, and to intermarry and rule.[3]

A host of principalities emerged between the Black and Baltic Seas. In the eleventh century, a Kiev prince, Yaroslav the Wise, consolidated these citadels into the region's first centralized state, a realm later known as Kievan Rus.[4]

It was a tribal name that some sources traced to an ancient Swedish word, *rus*, meaning "to row," evoking the Viking boats that swept down the Dnieper. While Kiev, Novgorod, and other Kievan Rus cities flourished, a great-grandson of Yaroslav's, Yuri Dolgorukiy, ventured northeast in the twelfth century to strengthen the fortification in an outpost known as Moscow.[5]

The thirteenth-century Mongol invasion of Europe transformed the political landscape. Batu Khan sacked towns and fortresses in what is now southern Russia before arriving at Kiev's city gates in the year 1240. Kiev's splendor awed the Mongols, and they laid siege. Breaching the gates, they set fire to Kiev and slew most of the 50,000 or so people who were there.[6]

Kievan Rus disintegrated under the Mongols, but Moscow survived, emerging as the region's principal tax collector for the Golden Horde khans. By the time Moscow threw off the khanate, in 1480, the city had become a political and military power. In the sixteenth century, as Western European monarchies began colonizing the New World, Moscow did likewise to its south and east, through battle and annexation expanding its possessions. The name Russia, taken from the old Viking tribes, first appeared.[7]

The large parcel of land that would become Ukraine was formless. The name itself, Ukraine, was a contraction of two words translating to "on the edge," or "on the frontier." Its meaning depended on one's choice of historical narrative. Russians preferred to believe that this land marked Moscow's own southwestern frontier. Ukrainians cited a supposed first mention of the name, when those living within Kievan Rus in the Dark Ages regarded as borderland anything beyond their own realm. For centuries, there was no political state in Ukraine, but something like an ethnic polity. Ukraine was a territory. Portions of it fell under the Polish-Lithuanian Commonwealth and later Russian tsardom and imperium.[8]

A sovereign nation with Kiev as its capital was a phenomenon of the twentieth century. This country emerged in the Russian Civil War, with the Communist Bolsheviks occupied fighting White armies loyal to the slain tsar. While this war lasted, so did independent Ukraine. In 1922, the Bolsheviks, having prevailed in the fighting, incorporated Ukraine into the new Soviet Union.

Ukraine had been more a sense than a country, more a people than a state, yet nationalist sentiment endured. In 1991, the year that the Soviet Union's leaders dissolved the country, Ukraine declared its independence.

For the next two decades, Ukraine suffered from violence, corruption, and social turbulence, just as Russia did, but Kiev was at last governing itself. Along Ukraine's western border were countries that enjoyed European laws and prosperity, which many Ukrainians began to believe they were also entitled to have. Russia took a different view. Moscow held that Ukraine was not a country but a province, that Ukraine was its lost possession, nothing more than a Russian island.[9]

The current chapter of Russian–Ukrainian troubles began in 2013. In that year, Ukrainian president Viktor Yanukovych pledged to sign a political and trade agreement with the European Union, which many Ukrainians favored as a step toward stability and prosperity. Russia pressured Yanukovych to walk back his pledge, and when he did so, Ukrainians took to the streets.

Thousands of people gathered in the center of Kiev to protest, demanding European integration. The rally stretched on for months and grew violent. Demonstrators clashed with riot police. In February 2014, snipers positioned above the city's central avenue targeted protesters, killing more than 100 people. Yanukovych fled to Russia, and the Ukrainian parliament voted to remove him from office. The Kremlin took advantage.

Russian troops seized the Ukrainian peninsula of Crimea, and Moscow swiftly annexed it. The ease of Crimea's capture inspired Russia to further designs.

Ukraine's southeastern region took its name from a river, the Seversky Donets, which drained from a lake in the Russian city of Belgorod, looped south into Ukraine past Kharkiv and then southeast to Luhansk before crossing the border once more and joining the Don River near Rostov-on-Don. The Seversky Donets described a region rich in sedimentary rock and coal seams, the Donets basin, or simply Donbas.[10]

In April 2014, militiamen, criminal groups, and Russian special-operations troops declared an autonomous state there, the Donetsk People's Republic (that is, the *Donetskaya Narodnaya Respublika,* or DNR), and then another, the Luhansk People's Republic (LNR). Kiev dispatched its army. Tanks faced each other on the Ukrainian plains for the first time since World War II. The war for Donbas had begun.[11]

*   *   *

In the summer of 2014, at home in Oxford, Billy Reilly received a text message from his FBI handler, agent Tim Reintjes: "Can you look into this group...People's Republic of Donetsk."[12]

Earlier that morning, July 17, a passenger airplane leased by Malaysian Airlines had been flying eastward over Ukraine from Amsterdam on its way to Kuala Lumpur. A missile launched from the ground and burst into shrapnel in front of the plane's cockpit. The plane flew into these projectiles at a speed of more than 500 miles an hour. The shrapnel and aerodynamic forces destroyed the cockpit, which fell away. The remainder of the plane continued to fly for five miles before it disintegrated, expelling passengers to the sky at 33,000 feet. Their bodies and luggage, along with the plane's engines and lumps of the fuselage, plunged to earth in and around a Donbas village called Hrabove. All 298 people aboard flight MH17 had been murdered.[13]

At Reintjes's direction, Billy located, as others would, a posting on VKontakte, a Russian equivalent to Facebook, that appeared to assign responsibility for the tragedy. Billy shared a translation with his handler: "We warn you that there will be no flying through our skies. Here is a confirmation of the plane being shot down."[14]

The VKontakte post was tied to a Russian military figure named Igor Girkin. Early in his career, in the 1980s, Girkin had cycled through the Soviet army and special-operations schools. When Communism had fallen, he'd fought for Russian interests in the Baltics, the Caucasus, and the Dniester region of Moldova. Girkin assumed a *nom de guerre*, Strelok, which translated roughly to "shooter." In time, he was known as Strelkov, similar to the name, Strelnikov, which Boris Pasternak had given to Pasha Antipov, the aspirant-revolutionary in the novel *Doctor Zhivago*. It was Girkin who had ignited the war in Donbas in 2014 by seizing a regional government building with a team of commandos. At the time of the MH17 downing, Girkin was the so-called defense minister of the Donetsk People's Republic.[15]

Some said Strelkov was an FSB colonel. The European Union identified him as an officer in the FSB's military equivalent, Russia's Main Intelligence Agency, or GRU. Strelkov's VKontakte post, deleted shortly after its publication, appeared to show that he had participated in an atrocity. He would deny it. Russian-backed separatists in Donbas had been downing Ukrainian warplanes in recent weeks and months and had apparently mistaken a passenger plane for a military jet. The destruction of MH17 and the killing of all aboard it underlined the heartlessness of the Donbas war.[16]

For Billy, the MH17 tragedy and the broader advent of war in Donbas, four years into his work with the FBI, reinvigorated his interest in global conflict. In October that year, 2014, Billy looked on from afar as fighting in Donbas was at its most intense, a battle for control of the Donetsk airport wasting many young lives.[17] Men like Billy were sacrificing themselves for their beliefs. He began to imagine himself among them, pursuing a life of real stakes.

The more vivid Billy's imagination, the farther he traveled in his mind from Oxford. Only a dispatch of immediacy wrenched him back to his own surroundings. He learned that his grandfather Marvin had passed away.[18]

Dementia had dimmed Marvin's final years, but for Billy vivid memories remained.[19] He wanted to give his grandfather in death what he had never had in life. Marvin had lived in ignorance of his roots, his father having died while Marvin was still an infant. Marvin never knew for sure where his father's parents had come from before arriving in the United States, assuming that his origin was Polish.

Billy researched the O'Kray family history through genealogy websites, on-line search tools, and immigration records. He told his parents he had made a fascinating discovery. An ancestor of Marvin's had not been Polish but had originated in the Donbas region of Ukraine. Billy said that this man had worked in the mines as a coal miner, the iconic profession and identity of the region.[20]

For Billy, the information was more than family history. It might have explained his own present: the connection to the old man on the street in Saint Petersburg, the pull to the Russian language, Billy's interest in the history of Kievan Rus.

It appeared that Marvin's surname and Terry's maiden name, O'Kray, might have been not Polish, but instead an Anglicization of the Russian and Ukrainian *u krai*, "on the edge," the root of the name of Ukraine itself. Billy believed that he had stumbled upon an origin more fundamental than his link to Oxford, a personal tie to the war in Donbas.

The November 2014 morning of Marvin's funeral was unseasonably warm. Bright yellow and orange leaves remained on the trees amid the groomed lawns at Holy Sepulchre Cemetery, in Southfield. American flags, edged in gold brocade, were pinned to the front posts of the hearse and flapped in the wind as the car slowed by the gravesite. Billy served as a pallbearer. He helped set his grandfather's coffin beneath a green tent above a cavity in the ground. An enlisted man in Army dress, his right hand at salute, stood guard over the burial place, honoring Marvin's time in uniform.[21] Billy joined family at the gravesite. Watching her brother, Catie thought that he was the saddest of them all.

CHAPTER TWELVE

Entanglement

Agent Reintjes directed Billy to ingratiate himself into a circle of people, "nodes," who were using social media to promote global jihad. A node could ferry cash and supplies to terror cells or collect information to pass up a chain of command. Nodes could recruit. They found soft targets on social media, young men looking for purpose. ISIS-affiliated nodes instructed recruits how to cross into Syria, where they would find people waiting to receive them in territory held by the terror group.[1]

Using aliases and legends, Billy connected with nodes over social media. He spoke directly with people on the other side of the terror war, trying to learn their secrets.[2]

Nodes were often women. They could be men posing as women, hiding in social media's weeds. It was easy to conjure feelings of intimacy, especially among disaffected young men who were searching for a connection. The FBI itself employed such tactics, romance another Bureau tool used to exploit vulnerabilities in search of information and intelligence.[3]

Affairs of the heart were tricky and sometimes backfired. In 2014, a translator in the FBI's Detroit office with a top-secret clearance, Daniela Greene, was cultivating a German terror suspect, Denis Cuspert, over Skype. Cuspert lived in Syria and recruited German speakers to join ISIS. In June that year, Greene told an FBI supervisor that she was traveling to Germany to visit family. She didn't go there. Greene instead flew to Turkey and crossed the Syrian border into ISIS territory. There she united with Cuspert. They married.[4]

Greene quickly soured on the relationship and fled ISIS. Back in the United States, she accepted a plea deal on a terrorism-related charge and served two years in federal prison. The State Department designated Cuspert a terrorist; he died in Syria in 2018.[5]

Greene was a problem for the new special agent in charge of the Detroit office, Paul Abbate, an ambitious official with designs on higher management. He had joined the Bureau in 1996 and like many other agents had transferred to counter-terrorism after 9/11. He'd worked in FBI headquarters in Washington, focusing on Iraq, and later served in that country as a liaison to the Pentagon. For Abbate and other senior FBI officials, despite the risks that Greene's case illustrated, sending FBI staff and CHSs after terror targets of the opposite sex remained a fertile route.[6]

*   *   *

Five years Billy's junior, Amera Lomangcolob had grown up in the poverty of the Philippine south. The region had for years been in the grip of Abu Sayyaf, a Wahhabist terrorist group waging war against the state. In 2014, the group had sworn *bayat* to ISIS, placing the Philippines in the heart of the war on terror. Amera Lomangcolob began appearing in intelligence files, designated as a node for Abu Sayyaf and by extension for ISIS.

Lomangcolob was one of several nodes Billy contacted on behalf of the FBI. She surfaced in his social media correspondence and provided information about other targets. She and Billy talked frequently. Lomangcolob was person-able and shared information about her life, telling Billy that she held an IT degree and worked as a graphic designer. She texted him photos of her ID cards from work and school and shared a nickname, AMZ.[7] Billy reported his contacts with Lomangcolob to agent Reintjes, but a divide would open between the FBI's needs and Billy's desires.

In November 2014, Billy informed Reintjes via text that Lomangcolob had asked him to wire her money, $200. Persuading targets to send cash was a basic device employed by terror and criminal organizations. Giving money, even a little, displayed a willingness that a terrorist or criminal could further exploit, working toward a significant sum. Terrorist groups were always in need of funding, especially since governments and law enforcement closed off their avenues to money through sanctions and account seizures.

Reintjes replied in an unequivocal manner: "Were not going to send her money." He instructed Billy in a text message to "leave AMZ alone." Billy did, for a time.[8]

As Billy had learned through his work on the Aws Naser case, a CHS had to get to know targets, even develop a degree of intimacy with them, in order to obtain information and intelligence. As Billy built a rapport with Lomangcolob, she became less a node to him and more a person. Billy was meant to cultivate Lomangcolob for the FBI, but his need for female connection began to turn his head.

Lomangcolob was young and attractive, and she exploited her sensual shape. The photos she sent Billy at first were vaudevillian, cast in arousing shadow, taken from the front, taken from the rear. The images eventually progressed to nudes. Callow and eager, Billy had little defense.[9]

Lomangcolob again asked for money. She told Billy that she planned to use the funds to travel to Manila for a job interview. She wanted to get out of the Philippines, she said, to go to Kuwait, to work as a maid, as many Filipinas did, and make a new life.[10]

In November 2014, Lomangcolob sent Billy photos from Mindanao's Laguindingan Airport, near where she lived in Illigan City. Later, from Manila, she sent him shots from an employment agency, as she appeared to pursue her plan to work in Kuwait.

Lomangcolob texted Billy more photos. The first was an image of a typical Filipino street scene, with a bustle of people and well-used motorcycles and scooters. In the background of the image was the storefront of a currency exchange. In another photo, there was a row of teller windows with wiring instructions affixed to them. The last picture in the series showed a fan of Filipino-peso bills. Lying atop the money was a snapshot of Lomangcolob, looking willowy and severe in a black abaya.[11]

With money in hand, she explained to Billy that her travel plans had changed. She would still go to Kuwait. But after securing her maid's job there, she said she would travel into Syria, to the front line of the terror war. She told Billy that she planned to become a martyr for ISIS.[12]

*　　*　　*

December 16, 2014, was gray and rainy in Detroit, with a late-afternoon temperature in the mid-forties. Billy, his parents, and his sister and brother-in-law drove south in a single car from Oxford, bound for the airport. Billy was embarking on an international trip. As required, he had told Reintjes about his upcoming travels. "My parents got me a Christmas present of a Asian tour," Billy texted his handler. "I don't know if am excited or not about it lol." But Billy concealed a central fact.

In fact, there had been no gift from Bill and Terry. Billy had used a credit card to book his own trip: five days in Manila, then four in Kuala Lumpur, Malaysia, for a rendezvous with Lomangcolob, a suspected ISIS node.[13] Billy had planned his first solo international adventure without telling the FBI what he was really doing.

Bill Reilly parked curbside at Detroit Metro Airport. Billy heaved his suitcase onto the sidewalk and said his goodbyes. He slipped into the terminal.

Inside the airport, Billy checked his bag at the Delta Airlines desk. He readied for a flight to New York's John F. Kennedy International Airport, from there to Seoul, then onto Manila. The flights would take Billy into adventure, in pursuit of Lomangcolob's promises.

What were Billy and Lomangcolob planning? Which one of them was manipulating the other? Was Lomangcolob even a woman at all, and was Billy being lured into a trap?

Terry and Bill had questions of their own, unsure if their son was traveling for the FBI or charting a personal course. He had become impossible to read. Many parents might have pressed a son in his late twenties to find a salaried job, to move out of the house and embark on an independent life. But Terry was thankful that Billy still wanted to live with her and Bill. In return, the parents granted the son great latitude, which often left them ignorant of Billy's intentions. All Terry and Bill knew for certain was that Oxford couldn't contain Billy. Still, his mother worried. Bill drove back toward Oxford, but Terry's heart remained at the airport.

Her phone rang. It was Billy calling. He said he wanted to come home.

Bill returned to the airport and found Billy standing by the curb at the departures hall, looking chagrined. He climbed into the car. The Reillys drove homeward with a new mystery, why had Billy abandoned his plan on the very cusp of realizing it.

He told his mother that "the men" had nixed his travels. Yet as with nearly everything Billy now said and did, the truth was buried. Returning home, Billy texted Reintjes. "I ended up canceling trip," he wrote. "Too much trouble to go alone."[14]

*   *   *

When Lomangcolob learned that Billy had abandoned his trip, she lashed out at him, but days later felt better about it and apologized to him over Twitter. "Don't ignore me please," she wrote. "I beg you. Lets make it work again...Please i regret wat i said. . . . Forgiv me, please Dont abandon me."[15]

Billy responded by wiring her 4,341 Filipino pesos, or about $100, but he'd already begun playing the digital field.[16]

He was talking to a woman from Indonesia. They had met on a South Asian dating site for Muslim singles and exchanged messages and photos. Her name was Suratni, and she was many things that Lomangcolob was not. Suratni voiced no dangerous ideas about religion. She pursued no cross-border schemes. Suratni was modest, and she held a degree in biology, as Billy did. For Suratni, it was a big step to remove the veil that covered her face, in order to post a profile picture on the dating site. When she did so, she revealed a heartbreaking trait, a harelip.

Billy told her that the imperfection was immaterial to him. "InshAllah no disability will not bother me," he wrote, "because looks do not make a marriage last but compatibility and intellect and iman do." Suratni was kind and bright, and Billy sought to connect with her. In a chat that winter, Suratni marveled at the idea of cold weather, since she had known only a tropical climate. Billy stepped outside of the house, made a snowball, and sent her a picture of it in his palm. The gesture stirred her heart.[17]

Billy liked Suratni well enough to mention her to his parents, but Lomangcolob remained difficult to ignore. She had developed a connection to him and wouldn't let it wither. The two traded Valentines, one in the form of a locket holding a picture of each of them. Another image labeled them a "Happy couple." In one photo, Lomangcolob looked suggestively into the lens, an infant in her arms.[18] Billy explored the requirements of a Muslim marriage in the Philippines. By early 2015, he was researching residential properties in Manila. His link to the suspected ISIS node appeared only to solidify.

Entanglement

In early 2015, Lomangcolob shared photos with Billy from Manila of a rented room with a suitcase. She sent Billy images from a shopping center, Manila's Mall of Asia, photos of strangers, people of European origin. The images made it appear as though she had been conducting advance surveillance. This was the kind of target Abu Sayaf had hit before.[19]

CHAPTER THIRTEEN

The Falcon Flies

Regretting his indecision over the trip to see Lomangcolob, Billy was now overcome with the urge *to do something*. Twenty-eight years old, he fixated on an approaching milestone. He told his parents he needed to embark on an adventure before his twenties were over.[1]

He had received no reply to his FBI job application. "The men" advised him to wait until Obama's successor took office, which was still two years away, when they said it would be easier for them to recommend Billy for full-time work. Billy at last caught on to "the men's" sustained avoidance, accepting the fact that they were stringing him along. He felt foolish for having trusted them. And he began to worry for his safety as his FBI work took grave turns.

Billy met agent Reintjes one evening for dinner at a hotel near the FBI office in Troy. Joining them was a man who had been wounded in war. His face and hands were mottled in burn scars. Another man at the table said he was Russian. Billy returned home that evening and told his parents about the encounter, referring to the Russian man as "the professor" and "the biologist."[2]

Billy grew nervous about events and operations that he was beginning to have trouble understanding. His FBI work now appeared to place him in more direct danger.

In December 2014, Billy told Reintjes that one of the nodes in his sphere of ongoing chats was pressuring him to conduct a suicide bombing in Detroit. The node had sent him a list of proposed operations. Billy said another node encouraged him to use his car as a weapon. She told him to run down pedestrians in Detroit, then shoot into the crowd that would gather. Reintjes asked Billy how the nodes proposed that these attacks would be planned and funded and who would assist in their execution.[3]

In the course of his FBI work that year, Billy sent Reintjes an issue of *Inspire*, an online magazine published by al Qaeda in the Arab Peninsula. The Tsarnaev brothers had followed instructions in an earlier issue of *Inspire* to make the pressure-cooker bombs they had planted at the finish line of the Boston Marathon in 2013.[4] The cover of the issue Billy shared with his handler depicted a passenger jet in the clouds, with "cutting the nerves & isolating the head" written beneath it. Inside was a forty-four-page manual for making a potassium chlorate bomb, a nonmetallic explosive that could defeat airport security measures.[5] Billy was also reading *The Mujahideen Book of Explosives and Weapons*. Reintjes told him to share bomb-making instructions with an FBI target. Billy worried where his handler was leading him.[6]

Billy had been working with the FBI for nearly five years and knew how the Bureau operated in ambiguity. He understood that agents could use and discard him. He knew that the Bureau possessed a voluminous record of his conversations with terror suspects, which could be interpreted in various ways. Billy realized that "the men" had been leading him on about FBI employment, and now he believed that they were encouraging him to participate in illegal acts.

Billy told his parents about Reintjes's order to share the bomb-making instructions, which could be grounds for a terrorist conspiracy charge. "There's no way in hell I'm doing this," Billy said. "This is a setup."[7]

Billy handed his mother a document. It was a property sheet, a record of a memory card the agents had given him. Billy had signed at the bottom of the paper, using his code name, Falcon.[8] "If they ever try to deny that I'm working for them, you'll have some kind of proof," he said. "Because there is no other proof."

Terry urged Billy to sever his relationship with the FBI.

"I'd like to," Billy said.

"Then do it," Bill said.

"It's not so easy," Billy replied. "I can't just walk away." In fact, he could have. A CHS could leave the Bureau at any time. But Billy worried over the consequences of ending the relationship on bad terms. FBI manuals described the everlasting connection that CHSs would have to the Bureau. And the Aws Naser case had convinced Billy that the FBI could influence the judiciary, and that he himself wasn't immune. He became irritable. He let his beard go. One afternoon, while Billy was watching TV with his parents, a missing person's notice appeared on the screen. "My picture's going to be up there one day," Billy said. Terry bolted upright, alarmed by his fatalistic tone.[9]

Winter 2015 slipped into spring. The war in Ukraine was in its second year, and it increasingly gripped Billy. He watched videos of shellings on separatist positions in Donbas, of wounded civilians who wanted the region to secede from Ukraine, to join Russia as Crimea had done, or to become a country of its own. Mindful of the family connection he believed he had to Donbas, Billy now called these people his.[10]

He took notice of the truck convoys that Russia had been running into eastern Ukraine since August 2014. Russian officials said the trucks contained baby food, cereal, and other supplies meant to help civilians in Donbas. Ukraine, on the other hand, said the convoys included weapons and soldiers.[11]

Catie became worried about her brother and where his interests were taking him. His visits with her dwindled, then ceased altogether. During a drive to Oxford, she noticed a white van in her rearview mirror. The van tailed her to her parents' house, then it wheeled around and drove away. Catie pressed Billy for a full accounting, demanding to know what he was planning. "What if you're working," she asked, "and you have to go away somewhere and disappear for a while?"

"You gotta do what you gotta do," he said. "I can't waste my life here."

On the coffee table in the living room in Oxford, Catie found the printout of a conversation written in an alphabet that was unfamiliar to her. Billy said the printout was an exchange with a person who was linked to the Russian security services. Billy said that there were people in Russia who were "interested in me going there." Catie thought he was putting her on and joked that he was planning to become a double agent. Billy just shrugged.[12]

Billy's disillusionment with the FBI had solidified through a years' long chain of events: the Naser case, the Boston Marathon bombing, the Detroit terror plots, the nodes' bomb plans, "the men's" effort to keep Billy at bay while feeding him what he wanted to hear. Billy knew he would never belong with the FBI. He was nearly thirty and still adrift. All he had were the phantoms on his screens. He needed them to become real. *He* needed to become real. He broke free in pursuit of dramatic change.

One evening at the house in Oxford, Billy told his parents he had booked a flight to Moscow. Terry and Bill were alarmed. They asked what he planned to do there. Billy said he would travel to the southwestern part of Russia, to a city named Rostov-on-Don. He told them that it was a staging point for the war in Ukraine.

"That just doesn't make any sense," Terry insisted. "You've never been in the army. You're not any fighter. That's nuts."

"Oh no," Billy said. "What I'm gonna do, I don't have to be." He explained that he was going to Russia as a volunteer aid worker, to assist with the truck convoys that the Kremlin was sending over the border, the so-called humanitarian convoys.

Terry couldn't accept it. In the five years that Billy had worked with the FBI, his mother had never been able to locate the line between reality and fantasy, where the truth of Billy's actions eased into his self-mythology. Now she needed to cut through the games. "This whole thing seems really crazy," she told him. "I don't know exactly what you're doing."

"There's nothing to worry about," he said.

"What about 'the men'?"

"They don't know I'm leaving."

Bill and Terry had heard enough of Billy's gripes about "the men" to conclude that it might, in fact, be better if their son was indeed traveling on his own. Terry and Bill didn't understand how dangerous Russia could be. They had enjoyed their own visit to the country years before. Plus, they remembered how wayward Billy had been in school, before he had discovered the interests that focused his intellectual energy. The parents understood that they were powerless to dissuade Billy, and, fearing to lose him, as they felt they had lost their daughter, they chose not to try. Even after Billy, on the eve of his departure, said he was going to meet "the men" one last time, Terry and Bill couldn't think how to persuade him to abandon his plans while also remaining in his corner.

On the afternoon of May 14, 2015, they treated Billy to lunch at Culver's, a diner in Lake Orion, south of Oxford.[13] His aunt and uncle, Kathie and Jim O'Kray, were there, but Catie and Mohammed were absent, estranged.[14]

Terry extracted a promise from Billy to text or call her every day from Russia. When Uncle Jim wished his nephew well and shook his hand, Billy was trembling.[15]

At the airport, the family got out of the car in an odd replay of Billy's aborted trip to the Far East months earlier. Terry had trouble saying goodbye. Billy hugged his mother. "Don't worry," he told her. "I'll be okay."

The car was silent on the drive back to Oxford. Terry felt sunken inside and tried not to cry. She had known that her son would one day take the steps to becoming his own person. Billy was pursuing his interests. It was what he needed to do. Still, Terry stared at her phone, willing it to ring.[16]

This time, Billy didn't call. He wouldn't let himself down. He passed through the airport's security checkpoint, located his gate, and boarded the flight. He settled into a seat on a plane bound for a connecting flight in Washington, DC, its engines warming.

Billy carried with him many secrets. Three days earlier, he had completed a Russian visa application. It was not for himself but for Amera Lomangcolob, indicating her arrival date a week after his.[17] Adventure, romance, maybe even a wife: these many goals that he might have achieved over several years, Billy wanted to burn through them in the span of a month, when his return ticket would bring him back to Detroit.

Nothing stood in Billy's way now. His bold gamble had taken shape. The plane eased out to the runway. The engines surged, consuming the cabin in rumble and echo, pitching the plane forward. It lifted into the air.

Billy had made his leap, but had the motivation for the trip been his own? His lust for the world was powerful enough. There was a still-greater force, the grip the FBI had once held over Billy, and how "the men" might recover it. They knew how to suggest an idea, a goal, a chance for glory.

Billy Reilly was an expert in global conflict but otherwise an amateur, on his way to a place of grave stakes. He had never spent a night away from home on his own.[18] As the airplane pierced the clouds above Detroit, there would be no turning back. Billy had witnessed conflict online for years. Now it was his turn to experience it. He was taking himself to the edge of war.

CHAPTER FOURTEEN

The Base

Billy's plane landed in Washington, where he connected to a second flight bound for Geneva. Hours later, after arriving in Europe, he wrote to a family WhatsApp group: "Im in geneva and no problems."

"I'm getting really nervous now," Terry replied.

"Dont be too nervous," Billy wrote. "I havent had any airport problems."

"Let me know when you get there. Love you." Billy returned his mother's affection and said he would call when he arrived in Russia. "Ok be careful," Terry wrote. "Getting scary."

"Dont be sad," Billy replied. "Im not gonna do anything risky or dangerous."

"I'm worried but I know your doing something you really want."

Billy's father chimed into the chat. "I was watching you on flight tracker, there are ton of planes in the air," Bill wrote. "Can't wait to here about how every goes when you there." Billy wrote to say that his flight to Moscow was ready to board.

More than eight hours later, he resurfaced on the group chat. "I got there," he wrote.[1]

Fifteen hundred miles northeast of Geneva, the Russian capital was a loud, busy city of twelve million people. At Domodedovo International Airport, one of Moscow's three major hubs, Billy encountered a commotion of humanity coming and going across the eleven time zones of the world's largest country.

Billy had only just arrived in Russia, and his mother's apprehension was quickly upon him. "Do you know where your going and what's happening?" Terry asked on the chat.

"Yeah its ok and its something that wouldn't make u worry too much." He failed to elaborate, maintaining the ambiguity that shrouded the trip.

From Domodedovo, Billy transited into Moscow's inner city, to Komsomolskaya Square and its cluster of train stations. It was there at the Kazan station, employing the alias Vasily, that Billy met with Elena Gorbacheva, the photojournalist, and Mikhail Polynkov, the volunteer-fighter recruiter. They escorted him to the train bound for Rostov-on-Don.[2]

The train left the Kazan station and attained speed. It breached the city's outlines. It slipped past villages. Alongside the tracks were houses made of wood. They were single story and slanting. The houses looked like they had stood there since before the revolution, and that they might not stand for much longer. Their wood was weather-worn, dried-out and gray. The train carried into the green of trees and brush and near creeks that bent away. The train sped through places where life slows, where this country began to look like others. Billy felt the vibration of steel wheels rolling and heard their hum and dull clacking.

He was heading into the provinces, known in Russian as the regions. Few Westerners cared or dared to go there. Billy would stand out even more starkly than in Moscow. On the train, he declined sausage and beer from people who shared his cabin. He took the tea the train attendant poured into a glass cup encased in an etched metal holder, a *podstakannik*.[3]

Night drew in. Billy found his bunk. The train pushed southward to Rostov-on-Don.

Sunlight seeped through the curtains. Billy realized he had never been on such a long ride, not even on the Reilly family drives to Florida or out West. Through the train-cabin window, he took in the sights of the country. He told his family in the chat that he thought he had seen poor people in Detroit but here recognized deeper despair.

Over WhatsApp, he shared pictures of leafy trees blurred by the train's movement. A World War II Victory Day poster tacked to a door at the end of a train-wagon hallway. Kasha in a metal bowl. He said that his trip to Russia would be brief. "If i see that area," he wrote, "i think ill be content."

"If possible, try to at least text every now and then so we know everything's going good," Terry wrote.

"Really you dont have much to worry about," Billy replied.

On the morning of May 16, 2015, with the local temperature reaching 70 degrees and the clouds straining sunlight, Billy texted his family a snapshot of an urban scene. A river ran along the foreground and was placid. A bridge crossed high above the water toward a clock-faced tower. Billy had arrived in Rostov-on-Don, at the volunteer-fighter base where Mikhail Polynkov, the recruiter, collected his charges.

The base was a single-story rectangular building on the southern bank of the Don River, thirty yards long, whitewashed, with a flat roof and green doors. It sat on stilts above the sand fifty yards from the water. There was a café behind the camp on a local road and beyond that a rope of highway. On the river's opposite bank, city dwellings rose along a bluff.

Billy sent his family another picture. Daylight filtered through a window into a room with a linoleum floor. There was a set of bunk beds, and Billy's black suitcase sat nearby it. "I get my own bed at least," he wrote. Terry suggested that he eat the granola bars she had packed for him in case he grew hungry. Her motherly note seemed out of tune, with Billy now situated near the Ukrainian border and the war that lay just beyond it.[4]

Volunteering to fight for the Russian and separatist cause in Donbas had at first been an informal process. In 2014, ad hoc units accepted almost anyone who arrived eager to oppose Kiev. Many men and a few women came from Russia. Foreigners also arrived, nearly all of them from former Soviet republics or the pan-Slavic world.[5]

By the time Billy reached Rostov-on-Don, the situation had changed. The volunteer-fighter units were formalizing. Moscow had mandated that they adhere to a central command. There were new rules at the Polynkov camp. Men with criminal records or significant debts were banned, hindering them from slipping into the anonymity of the war zone. And volunteers had to prove prior military experience to gain entry. Those under twenty-two were required to produce a note of consent from their parents.[6]

Foreigners, on the other hand, remained apart, welcome under any condition. Yet fears were growing among militia leaders and their Russian overlords that spies were infiltrating their ranks, collecting information and transmitting it to the other side.[7]

The guard was up at the Rostov camp. Its boss was a man who went by the name Bronya Kalmyk. He had the look of the Mongols who had swept westward across the steppes in the thirteenth century and settled in Central Asia, Crimea, and Kalmykia, Russia's Buddhist province and Bronya's origin, its capital lying 250 miles east of Rostov. Bronya was a veteran of the Russian military, a beefy figure that year turning forty. His real name was Sanal Viktorov, Bronya his call sign. A call sign was earned in battle or in carousing, or it described a physical trait or the way a man carried himself. Bronya was the Russian word for armor, and the man who bore this nickname was known for his zeal for maintaining discipline in the camp.[8]

There were drunks and drug abusers among the volunteer fighters at the base. Many of the men, though, were serious about what awaited them. The Rostov camp was the final stop on their migration to the war zone. They stayed briefly at the base, never more than a few days. Mikhail Polynkov maintained a list of the Donbas units that were accepting fighters, who needed what and how many. He, Bronya, and others shuttled volunteers across the Ukrainian border, where commanders armed them and led them to battle.[9]

Billy was the only American at the Rostov base, and an instant curiosity. To himself, he was much more, a man on the move, a true adventurer. But he didn't know what lay in store. Terry seemed to know or to fear it, and she right away began texting Billy about more than just keeping well fed. She wanted her son to see what he had come for and then hurry home. This was hardly a place for Billy to be, surrounded by men who had signed up to kill and die. For all of the knowledge he had gained online and with the FBI, Billy wasn't their kind. Now, offline, he would struggle to manage any sort of disguise.

CHAPTER FIFTEEN

Volga Sojourn

O n May 18, 2015, Billy had been in Rostov-on-Don for only two days when he texted his parents with news that he was leaving the volunteer-fighter base. He sent a photo, in it a set of rail lines. "Im going on tour of russia with them," Billy wrote, failing to identify his companions or his purpose.[1]

The train followed the course of the Volga River along its eastern bank from Volgograd. The river carried its great flow in the opposite direction, two thousand and more miles through locks and reservoirs and past hydroelectric stations of Soviet industry. Europe's largest river watered a mass of Russian cities before dispersing at the Astrakhan delta across more than seven thousand square miles, swelling the Caspian Sea.[2]

The train took more than twenty-two hours to reach Saratov, a city of nearly a million people where the Lower Volga narrowed. In Soviet times, the state had restricted access to Saratov, a defense center that manufactured Yakovlev fighter planes, giving the city a strategic importance. Westerners remained a novelty there even now. Billy disembarked at Saratov and texted his parents pictures of churches, memorials, and statues.[3]

"We're both glad you did this," Bill wrote. "Don't give it second thought you just enjoy the experience."

Billy carried on from Saratov and through the Volga region. On May 21, he rode a bus to Ulyanovsk, the hometown of Vladimir Lenin. Here, in 1887, Lenin's family mourned his brother, hanged for plotting to assassinate Alexander III. Radicalized by this event and others, Lenin later avenged his brother, eliminating Alexander III's successor, Nicholas II, concluding the Romanov dynasty. Billy visited Lenin's childhood home, now a museum, and texted his mother a picture of it. On the family chat, he wrote, "Lenins parents house."[4]

"Just make sure u aren't going the way of tsar nicholas," Catie joked.

"Hopefully not that," Billy replied.

In the days since Billy had arrived in Russia, his messages home had provided little more than a travelogue. Now, in Ulyanovsk, he made reference to the work he had previously done for the FBI in Detroit. He wrote to his mother that it would be "interesting to meet with that russian biologist."[5]

This was the man whom agent Reintjes had introduced to Billy during a dinner in Auburn Hills. Billy had never elaborated on the Russian biologist's identity, though the man's basic profile was enough to interest the CIA's National Resources Division, the office charged with recruiting foreigners who were in the US temporarily.

The following day, Terry, savvy enough to realize that a rendezvous with the biologist would reveal a possible link between US security agencies and her son's trip to Russia, asked Billy if he had met with the man.

"Not yet," Billy replied by text. "He teaching at another school. And when i get to that city." Billy's thought trailed off, incomplete, leaving Terry to question once more why her son had traveled so far and under whose auspices.

Billy texted home his first Russian portrait. It showed him standing at the base of a statue. A female form reached into the sky, a sword in her right hand, her mouth slashed in a roar of defiance. The picture had been taken in Volgograd, the former Stalingrad, where the Soviets in World War II had devastated the Nazi advance and taken their first steps westward toward Berlin, turning the tide of the war. Terry and Bill worried over the hand at the controls of the Volgograd pictures, who had taken their son to that place and why.

There was a second picture from within the Volgograd monument. The wall of a rotunda was gold-flaked. Light descended from a gap in the ceiling. Billy looked shaggy from the road, his hair tousled. Behind him, in the open center of the hall, a white-marble hand held a flickering flame. Ringed along the gallery's perimeter were the words: "Yes, we were mere mortals, and few of us survived, but we all fulfilled our patriotic duty to the sacred Motherland!"[6]

Billy's gaze was fixed on the lens, his only indication of sentiment a creased brow. At Stalingrad, men and women living in their time had written their history. But more than 300 miles to the west, history was being made in Donbas, Billy's intent.[7]

*　　*　　*

On May 28, 2015, in the midst of his Volga sojourn, Billy texted his mother a snapshot from Ulyanovsk. In it was a bust of Ho Chi Minh, the late Vietnamese leader who had opposed the United States in the Vietnam War, with the backing of China and the Soviet Union. Ho Chi Minh was memorialized in Russia as a symbol of resistance to American designs. There was another monument to him in Moscow, in the city's southern Gagarinsky District, a large bronze disk with his bearded face emerging from its center.[8] For any American, even for Billy, such public tribute to an adversary of the US was striking, evidence of a Russian perspective.

"Isn't he from Vietnam?" Terry asked in a message.

"Yeah vietnam," Billy replied. "But im not there. U should worry if its was a bust of one of the marcos."

Ferdinand Marcos was Ho Chi Minh's Cold War obverse. Marcos had ruled the Philippines for two decades, from the 1960s to the 1980s, a US-backed anticommunist bulwark in the region who came to abuse his power. Billy's allusion to Marcos signaled the direction of his thoughts. Amera Lomangcolob, the alleged ISIS node, was from the Philippines.

Before Billy had left the United States, he had completed a Russian visa application in Lomangcolob's name. The arrival date on the document had come and gone. She hadn't appeared.

"Oh I'm catching on," Terry wrote. "Is she planning on popping in there?" Billy said he had been chatting with Lomangcolob. Terry cautioned him against encouraging her to travel to Russia. "If you bring here there, what will you do with her when you leave?"

"I dont even know yet what to do," Billy wrote.[9]

A few days before, Billy had wired Lomangcolob $72, maintaining the financial link he had earlier established with her.[10] Now he was conceiving a new plan. "If u want to worry, u can worry about side trip," he texted his mother.

Billy had taken a bold step in traveling to Russia and was now ready to take another. He wanted to atone for his indecision six months earlier, his humiliating retreat from the airport in Detroit. Billy no longer wanted to bring Lomangcolob to Russia. He would go to her.

Billy had succeeded in removing himself from the computer, tearing himself away from his parents. He was out in the world, free and open to experience. While he was still beyond Oxford, Billy had one chance to achieve every goal, to see war up close in Donbas and also to be with Lomangcolob in Asia. He told Terry that he intended to fly to the Far East.

Here he hit a snag. When Billy tried to buy the flight online, the purchase wouldn't go through. His credit cards were down.[11] Billy needed his mother's helping hand. He asked Terry to buy the ticket, a one-way flight from Moscow to Bangkok.

Terry resisted. "Why don't you want a return ticket?" she wrote in a text message. "I don't get it why?" She worried that once he was in the Far East with Lomangcolob, Billy might never come home.

Billy evaded his mother's question.

"This has me completely 100% spooked and nervous," Terry wrote. "It doesn't make any sense. There will be a large red flag for a one way tic to Thailand." Terry sensed that her son was keeping a secret. Over the period of his association with the FBI he had confided in his parents, but often just enough to cause them concern. "What are you planning?" she asked.

Terry balked at buying the plane ticket, and Billy grew upset. "Its fine," he wrote. "I wont go there then."

"Why are you acting like this?" Terry asked.

"Just really frustrated."

"But you won't tell me what's going on. I could just cry."

"Really its fine," Billy wrote. "U don't want me to see her, its fine."

"Something's up and I'm terrified," Terry replied. "Why won't you tell me? What are you keeping secret? What do you have planned? You're not even acting like yourself. I'm so worried."

Billy craved independence and now felt humiliated, reduced to asking for his mother's permission to chase a romatic liaison. He wanted to pursue his base desire and was eager to travel halfway around the world to fulfill it. He couldn't explain that to his mother. Instead, Billy withdrew. "You win," he wrote. "I give up."

Terry panicked. She feared for Billy's safety but also for her connection to him. Caught between competing motives, she made a choice. On May 30, she texted Billy: "Qatar air. 17770 rubles." Terry had bought Billy's one-way ticket to Bangkok.

He was elated. Now he wanted more. He asked for another ticket, and Terry agreed. She booked a second reservation, this one in Lomangcolob's name, along with four nights for two people at a Bangkok hotel. Billy wrote back: "She will be excited."[12]

*   *   *

Energized by the Far East side trip that now was set, Billy completed his Volga sojourn. He rode a train south, returning to Rostov-on-Don. There at the volunteer-fighter base, he encountered a violent scene. Bronya Kalmyk, the camp boss, was disciplining a volunteer. Billy wrote home that the volunteer had been "misbehaving when drunk. He was bloodied."

Billy rose early at the base most mornings for training and instruction. He took runs on the beach with the others. An instructor led them through urban combat drills. They simulated evacuating wounded comrades. It was hot by midday when the mosquitoes came alive.[13]

Bronya swaggered around the camp in fatigues and a beret, cinching a belt over his belly. "I don't love you all," he sometimes told the men, "but I respect you for your choice." Periodically, Bronya would sound the alarm, commanding volunteers to abandon the camp and make for the bushes at the edge of the beach, hiding from surprise visits paid by agents of the Russian security services. Shifting allegiances within the hierarchies of the Donbas brigades made it hard to predict where Polynkov's group of volunteers stood with authorities in Russia from one day to the next.[14]

The men at the base were curious about Billy and peppered him with questions. They wanted to know why he had come. They flooded him with queries about American habits and perceptions. Billy obliged, but it was hard to keep up. Only one other man who passed through the base spoke competent English. The rest knew only words or phrases. Billy discovered that reading and writing Russian had taken him only so far. With its speed and slang, conversational Russian eluded him. The men at the base could speak openly about him, make jokes or say more, and Billy could do little more than smile and try to get along.

He joined other volunteers at the café behind the camp, Smirnov, which served simple Russian food, grilled fish and chicken and beef noodle soup. Sometimes the men at the base had a barbecue, *shashlik*, grilling squares of pork on metal skewers and passing around bottles of beer or vodka. Billy told his mother he wouldn't like to live in Rostov-on-Don but that he was glad he had made the trip there. He shaved his head to stubble like some of the other men, amidst the air of camp life and adventure.

One by one and in groups, men gathered their belongings and left the base nearly each day, heading west to the Ukrainian border. But for Billy, and for him alone, the plan was different. He stayed behind. Three weeks into his trip, while dozens of others had made for the battle lines in Ukraine, Billy wrote his mother to say that he was "just sitting around."

Terry and Bill, deep into a Michigan summer but concerned for their son and unable to savor the pleasures of lake life, could only wonder what barrier Billy had encountered. They were glad he was far from the fighting and had said he had no intention of joining it. But the fact he'd been singled out indicated something perhaps more fearful about his condition. Again they asked themselves why he had gone to Russia, why he'd become involved with mercenaries and Russian nationalists and how he would wriggle free from them. With Billy remaining cagey over texts and phone calls, Bill and Terry could think only of the FBI and mysteries beyond reach. Terry amplified the frequency and appeal of her text messages, urging Billy to come home.

He considered it. He realized that he had misjudged the difficulty of his undertaking. Making his way into Donbas wasn't the formality that he had imagined it would be. Billy had conceived of his Russian adventure as a one-month bargain. With unexplained delays holding him on the Russian side of the border, the investment he had made to gain a view on the war appeared to be in jeopardy. Billy told his mother that "not going at all is throwing the money completely away."[15]

CHAPTER SIXTEEN

Blood

I n the US that summer, the TV news was taken up with Donald Trump, a New York City businessman and TV personality who had declared his candidacy for the Republican presidential nomination. Terry paid little attention to it. Every exchange with Billy accentuated her fears. He had been gone from Oxford for less than a month, but the time was passing slowly. "I can't wait for you to get home," Terry wrote on June 11, 2015. "This is way to long."

Terry offered to buy him a flight home if Billy would just ask for it. She wrote that she wanted him "to come back alive." Billy resorted to gallows humor. "Ill be back soon," he wrote. "Hopefully not dead."

Billy again expressed his frustrations. If he left the country before realizing his goal of crossing into Donbas, he wrote, "this whole trip would just be a bad memory." Terry sensed an opening. If she could convince Billy that he had already achieved plenty, he might be inclined to leave Russia now with his pride still intact. "You had fun didn't you?" she asked. "And excitement. I want you to be happy . . . and alive."

But the pull of Donbas was stronger than that. On June 17, 2015, as Billy began a second month in Russia, his mood suddenly revived. "I want to do that a activity tonirrow," he wrote to his mother.

"Can you say anything about it?" Terry asked.

"Humanitarian convoy going there."

"Isn't that really dangerous?" Terry asked. "Please don't."

"Aid convoy. Not dangerous."[1]

A path for Billy into Donbas had appeared to open. By joining a so-called humanitarian convoy traveling into Ukraine, he would get a taste of war without fighting it. His original goal achieved, he could train back to Moscow and then fly to Bangkok for his side trip with Lomangcolob. He'd have his adventure, and he'd seek his romance.

In the early hours of June 18, 2015, Billy's opportunity materialized. At 7:05 a.m., a forty-three-truck convoy from the Russian Ministry of Emergency Situations rumbled through Rostov and arrived at the Ukrainian border under the banner of humanitarian aid. Russian border guards waved the trucks into Donbas.[2]

But Billy didn't make the convoy. Like "the men," those who administered the volunteer-fighter base were promising Billy that his turn would come. "I asked when and they said soon," Billy wrote to Terry on June 22. "Ill go home if much longer." He stuck around at the camp for a week more, fixed on the goal that he wanted to believe remained within reach.

"If it's not this week, I'm gonna go," Billy texted. By the following day, June 24, there was still no movement. He wrote that he would leave Rostov in "probably [a] day or two." Bill and Terry sensed that their son was nearly out of danger.[3]

In Oxford that evening, the Reillys set off for a bike ride as the sun fell. The Gravel Extra that had once run along the "Polly Ann" railroad through Oxford on its way to Detroit had lain inactive since the eighties. The path it had carved remained, its route now a leafy escape for hikers and bikers, the Polly Ann Trail.

Before the Reillys had pedaled far along the trail, Terry's phone pulsed with a text-message alert. She and Bill pulled to the side of the trail. Terry saw that Billy had written, "Any thing else interesting happening there?" he wanted to know.

"We're on our bikes," Terry replied.

Then Billy called. His words were quick and spirited. "There's been a change in plans," he said. He sounded excited.

Terry and Bill were so engrossed by what Billy was saying that they failed to notice a small dog that was approaching them on the trail. The dog lunged at Terry's ankle, nipping her. Only when the call with Billy had ended did Terry look down at her heel. The dog had drawn blood.

Terry was too anxious to tend to her wound. Billy's enthusiasm alarmed her. She and Bill had presumed that their son was on the verge of abandoning his goal of Donbas, that he was returning home. Now they understood that he wouldn't give it up.

Terry and Bill had been following the news. They knew that people were still dying in the Donbas war. Now that the obstacles that had been preventing Billy's movements into Ukraine appeared to be lifting, the parents visualized their son taking a fateful step.

Terry wasn't going to leave anything unsaid. She wanted Billy to reconsider crossing the border. Standing on the edge of the Polly Ann, with blood trickling from her ankle, Terry tapped out a few words on the phone with her fingers. "I think you should leave," she wrote to Billy. "Why stay there any longer?"[4]

CHAPTER SEVENTEEN

The Computer

In late June 2015, Catie Cherri was preparing for a trip to Mackinac Island on Michigan's Upper Peninsula with Mohammed and their son. It would be their first vacation as a family. The trip meant all the more to Catie because of the feelings that had hardened between her and her parents. Catie held a grudge over their rejection of her choices but now had her own family.

Relations with her parents were endangered but intact, bonded somewhat by the arrival of Catie's son. Bill and Terry enjoyed being grandparents. Terry still sometimes sought her daughter's counsel.

In the last week of June, as Catie was setting out for the vacation, Terry phoned in a panic. She said Billy had gone silent. After he had phoned on June 24 about the change in plans at the base in Rostov, he had stopped answering his parents' calls and text messages. Terry was frantic. She told Catie that her brother had disappeared.

Catie thought her mother was overreacting. She knew how involved Terry liked to be and reminded her that Billy was an adult in pursuit of his own life. It wasn't reasonable to expect him to maintain a tether to his mother. He would be twenty-nine years old in a couple of months. Catie understood that her brother was out in the world on an adventure. She was even a little jealous.

Catie was also upset. She had learned that the family had driven Billy past her clinic on the way to the airport for his trip, without stopping. She'd had no chance to say goodbye. Catie felt guilty for having moved away from home years before. She thought she had abandoned her brother. Even though Billy's

Russia trip stimulated her, she understood that it carried dangers. She believed she might have talked him out of going to Russia, if only she had spent more time with him.

After a few days of vacation on Lake Huron's northwestern rim, Catie and Mohammed bought a platter of smoked salmon at a Mackinac Island shop, then drove south. Oxford was on the way home to Dearborn. Catie and Mohammed decided to stop and see her parents. The salmon was meant for them, a peace offering.

On July 3, Catie and Mohammed pulled up to the Reillys' house on the lake. Inside, Mohammed handed his in-laws the salmon platter. Terry and Bill showed little interest. They were in distress.

They told Catie and Mohammed that Billy still hadn't turned up. It was now a week since he had been in touch. FBI agent Tim Reintjes had recently visited the house and shared his puzzling questions and denials.

Catie froze. A week was a significant period. As a physician, she knew the urgency of time. The longer that someone was in crisis, the less likely were the chances of recovery. Catie felt the complicated emotions she had for her parents suddenly recede. She realized that her mother had been right. Billy was in trouble in Russia.

Catie quickly considered the available options to remedy her brother's condition. Her eye fell to the family's desktop computer on the rolltop desk in the parlor. The four adults who now gathered in the living room knew how attached Billy was to the Internet and social media. His life was tied up in it. Now that he had fallen silent, it was imperative to scour the computer for relevant clues.[1]

Terry and Bill had already done just that. But their understanding of Billy's interests was limited. By contrast, there was someone now beside them who knew a great deal about social media, extremism, and global conflict. Mohammed, the son-in-law who exasperated the Reillys, had unexpectedly become indispensable.

Mohammed took a seat at the computer and began searching it for information. On the screen, he found several Internet browser windows that were opened to web pages that Billy had been using seven weeks earlier, before he had left for Russia. It was a promising discovery. Mohammed clicked through these pages, looking for leads.

One page was opened to VKontakte, the social media site used primarily by Russian speakers. The page was logged into an account with the name, in Russian, Vasily the Foreigner. This was the alias, Vasily, that Billy had been using during his trip in Russia.

The account showed dozens of friend accounts. There was a recent direct-message conversation with Mikhail Polynkov, the man who recruited fighters for Igor Strelkov, the Russian security-services officer who had allegedly been involved in the MH17 downing and had served as the DNR's so-called defense minister. A translation tool revealed that Polynkov and Billy had been discussing Billy's arrival at Moscow's Domodedovo Airport nearly two months earlier.[2]

Watching the screen over Mohammed's shoulder, Terry and Bill grew uneasy. They had already found the messages Billy had traded with Polynkov. They knew how important this connection could be. They also knew that there was more on the computer. But they weren't sure that learning more about Billy's digital life was worth involving their son-in-law. Mohammed's sudden insertion into their effort to locate Billy unnerved them. Mohammed was unaware of Billy's FBI connection. To them, Mohammed was still an outsider. They feared what he might find.

Mohammed discovered a web page logged onto a Twitter account. The profile depicted a man with an unruly dark beard, military fatigues, and a lion cub in his lap. The account's banner photo showed a group of men in orange jumpsuits of the sort worn by inmates at the US prison in Guantánamo Bay and also by ISIS captives. Mohammed read aloud the account holder's postings and direct messages. The words suggested Islamic extremist sympathies.[3]

Terry and Bill stepped in. They pleaded with Mohammed to stop. They said he had no right to dig through Billy's affairs. They themselves didn't know how sensitive Billy's FBI documents were and if it was safe for Mohammed to access them.

Catie was caught in the middle, still keeping Billy's FBI secret. But she knew that this was no time for her parents to restrict access. Everything had to be examined. If Billy was in danger, she said, the information on the computer could be essential in aiding him.

Mohammed continued. He shifted his attention away from social media to materials that Billy had saved on the computer's hard drive, opening a series of folders. He discovered more than a thousand files. Dossiers, photos, screen grabs. There were snapshots of Iranian passports, documents promoting global jihad, and terrorist recruitment videos. There were directions for making a bomb. One document, titled "isisusa," hinted at terror plots on US soil. There was a video of a beheading.

Mohammed blanched. He couldn't believe what he was reading. He pushed away from the computer and turned to Catie. "Oh my God," Mohammed said. "Billy's a friggin' terrorist."[4]

Bill snapped. So did Terry. Billy wasn't a terrorist. He was serving his country as an FBI CHS. The antipathy Terry and Bill felt for Mohammed combusted with their fears, and Bill lost control. "Get out of our house!" he yelled.

Mohammed had only just discovered useful leads and wanted to dig further through the computer's files and accounts. But he understood from his father-in-law's tone that Bill wasn't messing around. Mohammed shot up from the rolltop desk and backpedaled toward the front door of the house. Catie followed with her son in her arms. They made it outside to the driveway and climbed into their car.

Bill stood on the porch, shaking with rage. Global forces beyond his control and understanding had pulled apart his family. He believed he had lost a daughter and now maybe a son.[5]

CHAPTER EIGHTEEN

Agents Again

B ill and Terry sidelined Catie and Mohammed from the effort to locate
Billy and began feeling their way on the Internet for people in Russia
who could help them. Google searches pumped out scrolls in Cyrillic, cities
and police stations and government officials that were impossible to character-
ize or evaluate. Bill and Terry quickly felt overwhelmed. They weren't
investigators and had no relevant training or tools.

Terry chastised herself. Over the six weeks of Billy's travels, she had failed
to extract the name of anyone he'd met in Russia. She didn't have a phone
number or an email address of a single Russian person. All she knew was that
Mikhail Polynkov had made plans to meet Billy at the airport in Moscow. But
that was nearly two months earlier and a day's train ride away from Billy's last
known location. How useful could Polynkov be? Now that Billy had fallen
silent, Terry and Bill felt paralyzed.

Their fear led them to limitless theories. Bill and Terry thought that the
Russian security services might have arrested Billy. They were holding him in a
cell, torturing him for information. Or maybe Billy had offered his counterterrorism services to Russia. His parents knew he had always enjoyed such work,
if not so much "the men." The Reillys also thought it possible that Billy, in
search of adventure and stymied at the Rostov base, had found his way to Syria
to study Arabic and Islam, as he had once planned to do. Then again, maybe
he'd met a woman who interested him in Russia and was engrossed in pursuit
of her. And what about the side trip to Bangkok? Had he taken it? Terry and

116

Bill even thought that this whole affair could be chalked up to Billy's love of fishing. Maybe his phone had fallen into a river. Terry imagined the call that would come any moment now. There'd be Billy's voice, casual, saying he was boarding the plane bound for home.

Beneath their theorizing and hoping, a single factor complicated the possibilities. The Reillys could not discount the idea that Billy had gone to Russia on behalf of the FBI or another US agency. They discussed Billy's mention of the Russian biologist. Had he met the man during his Volga sojourn, and, if so, did that prove anything? Billy had become secretive in recent years, layering his stories in ambiguity and half-truths. Searching for answers, Bill and Terry found their thoughts turning to the Bureau.

Only days before, so soon after Billy's disappearance, FBI agent Tim Reintjes had paid his curious visit to the house. The Reillys had known about Reintjes, one of "the men," from Billy's FBI stories, but until then had never met their son's handler. Reintjes had never been to the house before. Terry and Bill questioned why Reintjes had arrived at just that moment, when Billy's communications had halted. They doubted that the visit had been a coincidence of timing.

In early July, Reintjes phoned the Reillys and arranged a second visit. In fact, he came several times more. Other agents joined him, a woman and a man. The increased manpower convinced Terry and Bill that the search for Billy was an FBI priority.

The additional agents ran the Reillys through a battery of questions, many of which Reintjes had already asked. Bill and Terry felt like they were being interrogated. They told themselves to be patient and kept their doubts private. They wanted the FBI, the world's leading investigative body, to apply its resources to locate one of its own, a CHS lost abroad.

Reintjes assured the Reillys that he would find out all he could. One of the agents who accompanied Reintjes, Christine Taylor, hugged Terry and consoled her. Taylor told Terry to rely on her, to be sure to call her anytime.

Reintjes asked to see Billy's latest phone bill, and Terry handed it over. The billing cycle predated Billy's Russia trip. Reintjes said that he wanted to get hold of the bill yet to come. Clues were bound to be hidden among the record of the communications Billy had made from inside Russia.

The agents made another request of the parents. They said the Bureau had lent Billy cell phones and a laptop and that they now needed to reclaim these devices and scan them for leads. Bill and Terry handed over the devices, believing that their contents would bring the agents closer to Billy's location.

Bill and Terry were private people, and the FBI's scrutiny unsettled them. During one visit, Taylor asked Reintjes if it made sense to tap the Reillys' phones. Reintjes shot Taylor a look as though she'd spoken out of turn.

Reintjes and his colleagues continued with their visits and their questions. "Even after we gave them the laptop and phones, they still were coming," Terry said later. "And he kept calling and coming."

On one visit, Reintjes explained to the Reillys that the FBI had stationed a legat at the US embassy in Moscow, and he suggested that this person could provide critical assistance in the search for Billy. This sounded to the Reillys like a promising resource, and involving the legat was a sign of the FBI's commitment to their cause. Yet as quickly as Reintjes shared this detail, he puzzled the Reillys by asking them for information to provide the legat. Terry and Bill knew little about their son's Russian adventure. Surely, they thought, an FBI agent in Moscow had access to better leads than theirs.[1] This request and the agents' continuing questions seemed to Bill and Terry designed to probe the depth of their knowledge rather than service an investigation.

The Reillys didn't realize it, but they had encountered a conflict between the FBI's goals and their own. Billy's disappearance was a provocation to Reintjes and his colleagues. It was a threat to their careers, something they would have to explain to their superiors. Where had Billy gone? What was he planning? The Bureau instructed agents to expect the worst from a CHS. When in doubt, agents had to look after themselves and the FBI. That was the lesson of Whitey Bulger. The Reillys would soon learn it themselves.

*　　*　　*

In the summer of 2015, Bill discovered his son's T-Mobile bill in the mailbox at the end of the drive. This was the document Reintjes had been requesting. In the house, scanning the bill, Terry and Bill found their own phone numbers, a record of conversations they'd had with their son. There was also a block of phone numbers carrying the Russian international prefix, 7, indicating local calls Billy had made and received while in the country.

The Reillys studied the bill but could make little of it. They thought Reintjes would be able to decipher more. They called him with the news, and Reintjes drove up to the house straightaway. He left just as quickly with the bill in hand.

The FBI agents now knew whom Billy had spoken with by phone from Russia. Reintjes and his colleagues could also see if their own numbers were among those listed. From the day when Reintjes received Billy's final phone bill, the nature of the FBI's interaction with the Reillys fundamentally shifted.

The FBI's visits to the house in Oxford ceased. Bill and Terry phoned Reintjes, but he wasn't available. They left messages for him that he failed to return. The Reillys didn't know what to do, with the FBI still the keystone of their hopes.

After weeks of worry, Terry and Bill did manage to reach Reintjes by phone. They asked him what he had discovered on Billy's final phone bill. Reintjes's tone was no longer solicitous, but now short, as though the Reillys had become an imposition. He was dismissive of the phone bill, saying that the numbers on it held no investigative value. The Reillys asked what further steps the FBI planned to take in the search for their son.

Reintjes balked. He said he had no information about Billy, and he told the Reillys that there was no cause for worry. "He's probably just wandering around Russia," he said. Billy would reappear someday soon, Reintjes maintained, as though Billy was a runaway, not a CHS lost on the edge of Russia's war in Ukraine. Reintjes told the Reillys that he saw no point in speaking with them again.[2]

The Reillys were confounded. For five years, Billy had been on constant call for the FBI. Now, when Billy needed the FBI's help, the Bureau had no time for him. The FBI could have enlisted the State Department to press Russian authorities to search for Billy. The Moscow legat could have requested assistance from FSB counterparts. The Reillys felt like the Bureau had abandoned them.

Searching for an explanation, they found it in a cellphone they'd held back from the FBI. On that phone, they discovered a text-message dialogue between Billy and a contact named Tim, whom they presumed was agent Reintjes.

The conversation was a lengthy one, comprising thousands of messages. It had begun in the summer of 2014 and extended until Billy's departure for Russia in May the following year. The final messages were sent on May 15, 2015, the very day the Reillys had driven Billy to the airport in Detroit to begin his trip to Moscow.

At first, the text messages made little sense to the Reillys. Many of the messages were in the service of arranging meetings. Tim or Billy would suggest a time and place to get together, and the other party would agree. Other messages referenced topics Billy and Tim appeared to have been discussing outside of the texts, in person or on phone calls. The messages included names and references to documents and plans. Without greater context to plug the gaps in their understanding, Terry and Bill struggled to gauge whether the phone would prove useful.

Quickly, though, they realized how devastating their son's predicament truly was.

Two weeks before Billy's departure to Russia in May 2015, Tim had written a message that would fundamentally alter the Reillys' thinking about their son's purpose in Russia. "Do you have your trip itinerary yet?" Tim asked in the text.

Billy replied: "I'm still waiting on visa."

Reading these two sentences, Terry and Bill were stunned. They remembered the first time agent Reintjes had visited their home. He had denied knowledge of Billy's Russia trip.

This text-message exchange proved otherwise. Its significance was undeniable. It established the fact that before Billy had left for Russia, he and Reintjes had been discussing the imminent trip.

For the Reillys, it was plain: Reintjes knew. The FBI knew. The FBI had known about Billy's trip to Russia all along.

Also in the texts, two days before Billy flew to Moscow, Tim had arranged a meeting for the following day. He had sent a message: "Bring your travel info." The two had met hours before Billy boarded his flight for Russia.[3]

Here it was, unmistakable, an indelible indictment of the FBI. The text messages didn't prove that the Bureau had dispatched Billy to Russia, since he might have been notifying his handler of a personal international trip, per FBI guidelines. But the messages did prove that Reintjes had deceived the Reillys by feigning ignorance of Billy's plans and whereabouts.

Reintjes had concealed the FBI's foreknowledge of Billy's travel. The FBI had lied. And every lie had a motive.

It hardly seemed possible now to Bill and Terry that their son had gone to Russia as a tourist. Lost, Billy might never come home again.

CHAPTER NINETEEN

300

Reading the text messages caused the Reillys to reassess Billy's final days at home. Terry recalled the day before Billy had left for Russia in May 2015. He'd said he was going to meet "the men" that evening. Terry had thought it odd that Billy would leave the house just then, with arrangements still to solidify before such a significant trip. She had cornered him. "What's going on?" she'd asked. "Don't tell me they don't know you're leaving." Billy had wriggled free without explaining.[1]

That evening, after he'd returned home, Billy had received a text message from Reintjes: "Whatsapp, skype, viber?"

"Once I load the apps," Billy had replied, "I'll msg u the info."

Past midnight, Billy had texted Reintjes again: "The number I got for those is the new phone number."[2]

Terry and Bill puzzled over these text messages. The dialogue made it appear to them that the FBI had been arranging to communicate with Billy once he had arrived in Russia. The Reillys wondered if Reintjes was talking to Billy even now.

The discovery of the text messages reordered the Reillys' thinking about the FBI. They now understood that it would be pointless to expect anything from the Bureau. If they were going to find Billy, they would have to do it themselves. Terry and Bill were on their own.

That felt impossible. The only thing resembling investigative experience the Reillys had was Terry's role as a mystery shopper. Bill and Terry didn't speak Russian. They knew no one in that country, nor in Ukraine. They knew nothing about digital forensics. Their knowledge of the Internet went little further than email and Google. They had no contacts in Washington, and they had no subpoena power. But they understood that if they didn't start looking for Billy, no one else would.

They turned again to the computer in the parlor. On it, one of Billy's VKontakte accounts was still open to the discussion he had been having with Mikhail Polynkov, the recruiter, before the trip had begun. Polynkov was the only person the Reillys knew had met with Billy in Russia. They set out to learn all they could about Polynkov. He had made it easy.

*   *   *

Mikhail Polynkov maintained an account on LiveJournal, a blogging site favored by Russian speakers. He had titled his page *A Soldier's Truth* and had published nine years' worth of postings. He wrote profusely about his upbringing in the 1970s and '80s in a Far Eastern village named Moy-Urusta.[3]

The town was located in the Magadan region, which was the site of an infamous Stalinist labor camp where few inmates survived the exposure to winter conditions and a scarcity of basic provisions. The "zeks," as inmates were known, were perpetually starving. The preface to the first volume of *The Gulag Archipelago*, Aleksandr Solzhenitsyn's account of the Soviet penal-camp system, told of prisoners in Magadan who made a strange discovery while slaving in a winter's landscape. By chance, they unearthed a prehistoric creature, "whether fish or salamander," Solzhenitsyn wrote, which was preserved in a frozen stream. The men were so desperate, forever hungry, that they devoured the ancient fauna.[4]

The Soviet state largely restricted zeks who survived their terms to living out their remaining years in the local area. Some raised families. Many ended up working in mines.[5]

Polynkov, born in Magadan in the 1970s, was conscripted into the army in 1990, the waning days of the Soviet Union. The USSR officially ceased to exist on Christmas Day 1991, and Polynkov was demobilized the following year into a new country, the Russian Federation, amid the great uncertainty of the era. The early nineties were a time of hardship and decline as Russia lurched from a command economy to capitalism, leaving many people behind.[6]

Polynkov wrote on LiveJournal that he was the fifth in a line of miners and followed his father, Vladimir, a blast master, into the Forty Years of October gold mine in Kolyma. Polynkov piloted a bulldozer in an underground shaft. The mining company, newly privatized, drew up a contract that pegged the Magadan miners' pay not to the volume of rock they mined, the way things had been before, but to the gold content within the mined stone. When the miners blasted a new shaft and found little gold within it, paychecks zeroed out.[7]

Similar episodes played out across the country. A chaotic new way of life in Russia rattled generations of former Soviet citizens and confirmed for them what the state and the schools had long taught them about capitalism and its rapaciousness. These people hadn't asked for the Soviet Union to fall. It had simply done so, leaving them in a world to which they struggled to adapt. The economy degenerated. Self-worth crumbled. Confused, powerless, the people had to carry on.

Devoid of options, the miners and their families suffered, and Polynkov's father decided to do something about it. He led the Magadan miners in a strike. It swelled into an uprising, a reaction to the loss of working-class guarantees, an emotional outcry over the loss of Soviet identity.

Polynkov's father urged his son to leave the mine and enter the law, the better to battle this new world's iniquities. But Polynkov failed a college entrance exam. He did leave the mine, though, and Magadan too. In 1998, he fled nine time zones westward, following the whispers of quick and easy fortune that were drawing many Russians to the capital.[8]

It was true: people were getting rich in Moscow. The wholesale sell-off of Soviet industry was underway.

Until the final years of the Soviet Union, the command system had prohibited the private holding of property. The state owned everything: your home, the concern that employed you, your car if you could get your hands on one.

A central proviso of Russia's adoption of capitalism was the privatization of industrial entities that the state still controlled. There was much to privatize. Even after the other fourteen Soviet republics declared their independence from the USSR, Russia remained the largest country in the world. At about six and a half million square miles, it covered roughly one-eighth of the Earth's livable area, and it was rich in natural resources and industrial syndicates that suddenly had to be sold to someone. Soviet oil. The state natural gas concern.

The world's largest aluminum extractor. Diamonds, potash, metals, minerals. One by one, the Russian government held auctions to sell off the state firms. Sealing the freewheeling and cynical flavor of the country for decades to come, many of the auctions were rigged, with Russian president Boris Yeltsin and his government coterie pocketing bribes to sell chunks of massive formerly Soviet companies to approved bidders at a fraction of the properties' values. It was theft and corruption on a grand scale.

At first, these privatizations and the oligarchic class they created gave many Russians the sense that easy wealth could be theirs, too, and people tried on new identities as Russian capitalism rumbled to life. In time, however, dreams of prosperity turned to scorn. Most Russian people could scarcely keep pace with the changes to society, let alone thrive amid them. In 1998, the year Mikhail Polynkov arrived in Moscow, Russia defaulted on sovereign-debt payments and devalued its ruble. As the decade drew to a close, many Russians saw through Yeltsin and his circle, who had enriched themselves while the country fell into economic and social decline.[9]

In Moscow, Polynkov lurched from one profession to another, his story typical of the time. He worked as a janitor, then found a job as a copywriter. Moscow's windfalls eluded him.[10]

Like many Russians who had initially thrilled to the mobility and opportunity of the new social and economic system, Polynkov by the year 2000 had begun to lose faith in the country's direction. The liberal-minded Russian government officials who had overseen the Yeltsin years had discredited the free market, the free press, democracy. Few in Russia wanted to live any longer in the period of transition that the country couldn't seem to escape. Many people were willing, even eager, to relinquish tarnished liberal ideals in exchange for stability.

Vladimir Putin had been a mid-ranking KGB officer and then a bureaucrat. He was hardly someone qualified to lead a nuclear power. But Yeltsin was ailing, and he and his circle needed to install a successor they could be sure wouldn't throw them all in jail. When Putin became Russia's president in 2000, he was an instant upgrade over his predecessor, if only because Putin was sober. Buttressed by rising oil and gas prices for Russian exports, the economy steadied. A Russian middle class began to emerge. Putin would establish firm control. Within several years, he neutered the oligarchs, all but abolished independent journalism, sidelined political opposition, gifted industries to his friends, and forged a lasting grip on power. As the period of Putin's rule lengthened, the rowdiness of the Russian nineties became a fading memory.[11]

Many in Russia supported Putin's methods in exchange for what felt like a better life. "The country is once again independent and has earned respect for itself," Polynkov wrote on his LiveJournal account, in 2007. "Undoubtedly, Russia's mysterious president, Vladimir Putin, is leading this resurgence of Russia. I need a Strong Country. Fuck the liberals. I'd rather have a Tyrant."

In that year, 2007, Putin, speaking at an international security conference in Munich, defined a new Russian attitude toward the West. He railed against US dominance of international relations. He said that the North Atlantic Treaty Organization had broken a promise by expanding eastward to include several former Soviet and Warsaw Pact states, though no such deal had ever been made. Putin's speech reflected frustrations that he had shared privately with other leaders, and it marked his first cogent, forceful public formulation of a new Russian posture. The speech was a turning point. Russia had attained the stability to address what Putin viewed as the losses the country had sustained while it had been on its knees.[12]

From this point onward, Putin would no longer go along to get along with the growing number of countries that were skeptical of his rule. The Kremlin wouldn't be shy about pursuing what many Russians believed was theirs.

A central issue for Putin was NATO's encouragement of Georgia and Ukraine, former Soviet republics that had previously been in thrall to the Russian Empire, along a road to eventual membership. In 2008, NATO and Russia held a bilateral meeting in Bucharest, and on the question of Georgian and Ukrainian membership, Putin cautioned NATO to act "very carefully."[13]

Four months later, in August, Russia violated what had been nearly two decades of military circumspection beyond its borders, launching an attack on Georgia. Prevailing in the twelve-day war, Russia gained control of two Georgian regions, Abkhazia and South Ossetia, and granted them diplomatic recognition. Moscow placed military bases in these regions, shutting down talk of NATO's expansion to the country.[14]

The 2008 Bucharest speech, like Putin's remarks in Munich the year before, would come to be seen as a landmark address. At the Bucharest NATO meeting, Putin spoke at length about Ukraine, sketching out a skeptical Russian view of Kiev's statehood. These were the formal beginnings of a policy that would ripen over time into military action.

Putin said that roughly a third of Ukraine's population was ethnically Russian and that there were people of no other type in Ukraine's east and south. He was effectively laying claim to these lands, stating that the placement of the border that separated them from Russia was a fluke of history, a reckless Soviet administrative reworking of the map. And Western Ukraine, Putin said, was a construct cobbled together with fragments of Czechoslovakia, Poland, and Romania seized after World War II.

"Ukraine is a very complicated state," Putin said in the Bucharest speech. "We have our interests there as well." Addressing the topic of Ukraine's potential accession to NATO, Putin went further, leveling what sounded like a threat. "If we introduce it into NATO," he said, "it may put the state on the verge of its existence."[15]

Western political leaders failed to take Putin at his word. Enjoying its victory in the Cold War, the United States had directed diplomatic and military resources to other parts of the world that now meant more. By the time Putin took power in 2000 and especially after 9/11, the principal American security concerns had shifted to the Middle East, Islamic fundamentalist terrorism, and China. Senior State Department diplomats who had dedicated themselves to the Cold War remained in their posts, but with reduced duties. The department's middle ranks were nearly devoid of Russia specialists. And among people entering the State Department in junior roles, almost none spoke Russian or had any acquaintance with the country. A plurality of new staffers spoke Arabic, Farsi, Cantonese, or Mandarin, reflecting the regions of chief concern. Russia had fallen out of fashion.

For the Russian president, conversely, the United States remained the focus. Many Russians felt the same. Russian people were fascinated by the US. It was a standard, a norm to which Russians aspired and compared themselves. With time and some heartbreak, however, Russians, including Putin, discovered that the US felt no reciprocal attachment.

The US government, even the remaining Russia experts, failed to judge Putin's landmark speeches for what they were, the dawning of a new period. US officials couldn't be blamed for neglect. Russia retained the world's largest nuclear arsenal, but its economy and military were not world-class. Some Russian infantrymen still wore felt boots. When Putin articulated the beginnings of his new policy toward the West, Russian specialists in the State

Department didn't view his remarks as a strategic shift. They didn't believe Putin could back up the tough talk.[16]

In Russia, on the other hand, most people were listening closely to what Putin had to say, aching to hear these words. Living through the 1990s in Russia had been humiliating, painful. It had been easy to intimidate Russia. Now Putin was demanding respect.

The topic of Ukrainian sovereignty would become a vehicle for the resumption of Russian pride. Putin initially suggested and would later explicitly state: How could Western Europe and the United States understand, much less claim jurisdiction over, the intimate and regional history that Russia shared with Ukraine? It would be like Russia telling the US to reverse the Trail of Tears.

Beginning with his Munich speech and carrying on through periodic addresses and published treatises, Putin would strengthen and sharpen his case for Russian designs on Ukraine. Ukraine, as it existed, was the result of a Western set of rules, he said, the country's boundaries artificial. The very existence of modern Ukraine was an insult to Russia. If the US-backed European order didn't grant a newly assertive Moscow concessions in Ukraine, Russia would formulate remedies.

Putin's bellicosity pleased many ordinary Russians. It was gratifying to talk tough. It felt good to be taken into account again, feared. The issue of Ukraine allowed Russians to work out long-standing frustrations.

Mikhail Polynkov would seek his self-value in the recovery of national purpose. Polynkov believed Russia could regain its direction by retaking territory it had long ago possessed.

When the 2014 violence on Kiev's streets led to Russia's annexation of Crimea and fomentation of war in Donbas, Polynkov was eager to do his part.

Donbas had been the heart of Soviet mining, and the new war there touched Polynkov in a personal way, given his family's attachment to the mines in Kolyma, in the Russian Far East. On his LiveJournal account, Polynkov recalled the Donbas miners who had mobilized in response to the German invasion of 1941, in World War II. "More than seventy years later, when hordes of Nazis again stepped onto the land of Donbas to reap a bloody harvest, the miners did not stand aside," he wrote. "They responded to [Igor] Strelkov's call and on June 18, 2014, the legendary 'Miners Division' was re-formed."[17]

One month later, in mid-July 2014, Igor Strelkov's social media messages would suggest Russian involvement in the downing of the MH17 flight. This was the incident that agent Tim Reintjes had singled out, setting Billy on his path to Russia.

In the early stages of the Donbas war, Strelkov revived an old name, Novorossiya, or New Russia. This was a mid-eighteenth-century governorate of the Russian Empire, which had extended north of the Black and Azov Seas.[18] Volunteering to join Strelkov in 2014, Polynkov compared him to Alexander Suvorov, the general who had captured Bessarabia for Catherine the Great, and Mikhail Kutuzov, who had chased Napoleon from Russia to defeat at Borodino. "In my life, there are only two indisputable authorities," Polynkov wrote. "My father and Strelkov." On LiveJournal, Polynkov posted a photo of a business card listing him as Strelkov's "Chief of Mobilization."

Polynkov's writings assumed new focus and vigor. He styled himself as an anti-Western geopolitical seer in fatigues and a khaki cap, railing against the United States and the European Union. He referenced the Americans and the Ukrainian "Nazis" who had taken liberties with Russia while the country was down and would now get theirs, with Moscow rising.

At Strelkov's direction, Polynkov helped formulate an apparatus by which volunteer fighters could join the battle in eastern Ukraine. Polynkov managed a coterie of coordinators. In Rostov-on-Don, he helped establish two bases, one a city apartment for experienced military specialists, the other an infantrymen's camp along the Don River, where Billy Reilly would lodge.

Polynkov helped populate a unit in Donbas for foreign fighters, the 1st International Brigade of the South-East. His LiveJournal account included scores of photos of him and other men holding automatic rifles in Donbas villages and weed-choked fields. There were images of separatist parades in Donbas cities and towns. For his LiveJournal avatar, Polynkov used a quarter-profile headshot of himself wearing a tan cap above a knuckle's length of sideburn, scruff dusting his jaw. When he picked up a tattoo, he posted a photo of it, a snake curling down his spine carrying an inscription in Spanish: "Defenda me Dios de mi."

*   *   *

At the family computer in Oxford, Bill and Terry Reilly scrolled through Polynkov's LiveJournal writings, looking for anything that might indicate where Billy had gone. On May 15, 2015, Polynkov had posted a photo of two $100 bills. Above the image, he had written: "Greenies already aren't the thing." This was a reference to Russia's frustration with American economic might, a desire to topple US currency from the global standard.

There was another picture. In its background was a train car painted white, red, and gray. Fitted into a window of the train, a placard contained writing in Cyrillic: "Rostov-Moscow." The Reillys had come upon photos Elena Gorbacheva had taken on the platform at Moscow's Kazan railway station.[19]

The foreground of the image was a close-up of a left arm clad in a black sleeve, with several fingers clutching a US passport. Terry recognized her son's hand. Tucked inside the passport was a train ticket to Rostov-on-Don. The posting's date, May 15, was the day Billy had arrived in Russia. Polynkov had captioned the photo: "Not all Americans are equally useful to Ukraine," betraying pride, it seemed, in snapping up an American for the Russian side.[20]

For Bill and Terry, this was proof that Billy and Polynkov had met. The Reillys recognized a first step in their investigation. Bill sent Polynkov a friend request over Facebook. Polynkov accepted it.

On August 17, nearly two months after Billy's last contact, Bill wrote to Polynkov, using an online translation tool: "Hello Mikhail, my wife and I are desperately searching for our son, William Reilly. We simply want to know if he's safe. Any information you can give me will be accepted with appreciation."

Polynkov replied in short order: "He is totally safe."

The Reillys were overwhelmed. They had made contact, and it appeared that Billy was okay.

"If there's anything else you can tell us, please do it," Bill wrote. "You've made us very happy."

"Nothing is threatening his life," Polynkov wrote. This was a puzzling message. It suggested that Billy was in good condition, though somehow removed from contact.

"If you speak with him," Bill replied, "please tell him that we love him and are proud of him."

The Reillys were careful not to jeopardize their contact with Polynkov by flooding him with messages. A week went by before they tried Polynkov again. "Sept. 4 is William's birthday," Bill wrote. "We would like to speak with him. We haven't spoken with him the last two months. Can we do that?"

Polynkov wrote that he would try to learn how to contact Billy. Another week elapsed. "We still haven't heard from our son, William," Bill wrote. "His birthday Sept. 4 will we hear from him? Thank you for your help."

"Don't mention it for now," Polynkov replied. "I still haven't helped yet." The Reillys sensed humanity in this response, and an opening to share more of themselves, enhancing the appeal for their son.

"William's mother cries for him every day," Bill wrote. "We don't know what to do. I hope he's not suffering."

Two days before Billy's twenty-ninth birthday, Polynkov wrote: "One thing I know for sure is that his objectives are harmless." Bill and Terry puzzled over the message. Billy's objectives? For the Reillys, this again raised doubts about their son's motives in Russia.[21] The Reillys were grateful for Polynkov's sustained correspondence, but time was elapsing.

Bill and Terry realized the need to develop additional leads. They turned their attention to Billy's cell phone bill, hoping to learn what agent Tim Reintjes had been so eager to find there. The bill showed that while Billy had been on his Volga sojourn, he had made no fewer than two dozen calls to Russian numbers. Only a third of these calls had lasted more than a minute.[22] Nevertheless, with the help of a Russian interpreter they had found in the Detroit area, Bill and Terry phoned each number. One by one, the calls rang through without answer, before someone finally picked up.

The man on the other end of the line projected a rough and cavalier demeanor. The Reillys listened on speakerphone as the interpreter explained that she was calling on behalf of a family looking for a son who had phoned this particular number in the spring. The man gave his name as Bronya; he was the manager of the Rostov-on-Don volunteer-fighter camp where Billy had been living.

The interpreter asked Bronya if he knew a Billy, or a Vasya or Vasily, an American traveling in Russia. Bronya answered without hesitation. "He's 300," he said. This was a military code assigned to a soldier wounded in battle.[23]

When the interpreter asked Bronya to elaborate, he complained that his phone had been bugged by Ukrainian intelligence agents and that there might be unwelcome listeners on the call. Bronya launched into a lecture on the Obama administration and US foreign policy.

Returning to Billy, Bronya changed his tune, saying that Billy, in fact, wasn't 300, and that he was perfectly healthy. When Bronya ended the call, the Reillys were so confused by what he had said that they didn't know if they should credit any of it.[24]

Yet the Reillys were also encouraged. From thousands of miles away and with no contacts or relationships in Russia, they had scored two quick victories, speaking with Bronya and Polynkov. These men knew Billy and had admitted to it. But what had these conversations yielded? The Reillys believed that Bronya and Polynkov were hiding something.

The Reillys again turned to Polynkov, reaching out to him via VKontakte in September 2015, writing now in English. "We remain very concerned about my son, William," Bill wrote. "His mother and I have not heard from him for 90 days."

Polynkov's reply startled the Reillys. "Strange," Polynkov wrote, in Russian. "I thought he was already home."

Terry and Bill couldn't imagine that their son had returned to the United States without letting them know. "He is not," Bill responded. "Please help us."

"They told me they sent him home," Polynkov wrote. "I'll try again to find out."

Bill and Terry could only wait, unsure where Polynkov was getting his information and how reliable it would be. The Reillys' ignorance of the Donbas field of play restricted them from important facts. As knowledgeable as Polynkov might have been, he was only a cog in a machine. He had ties to intelligence officers in eastern Ukraine's so-called republics. These people took their orders from Moscow. Many of them were, in fact, Russian military intelligence officers.[25] They possessed the preponderance of sensitive information in the sphere of the war and regulated its dissemination, propagandization, or suppression.

As active and dedicated as Polynkov was in the volunteer-fighter movement, he had limits. He wasn't a member of the GRU, Russia's military intelligence division, or the FSB. He knew only what he was allowed to know. Polynkov wasn't at the core, but only on the middle rings of the Kremlin-administered operation in Donbas. His knowledge of Billy's location and condition might well have been limited.

Bill replied to Polynkov, attempting to place a time-frame on Billy's theoretical deportation. "Do you know when? I am so afraid. Mikhail, have you found out anything? Where is he? Have you found him?"

Polynkov lost patience. "Don't you fucking understand Russian?" he wrote.

The Reillys' correspondence with him was now in jeopardy, but Bill didn't pick up on the tension, and he pressed his inquiry. "What do you mean?" he wrote. "Is William OK? do you know where he is located?"

"I advise you to find out through the CIA," Polynkov replied.

Terry and Bill froze. Their son had worked for the FBI, not the CIA. To the Reillys, the FBI was similar to the police. FBI agents had business cards. They appeared in court and gave testimony. They were part of the judicial system. The CIA, to the Reillys, was a collection of spies. "I do not know what you mean," Bill wrote. "We are not CIA."

Polynkov shared a link to the CIA's homepage and advised Bill to "send a statement there about a lost son."

Bill issued a string of desperate pleas. "Please we are his parents. How can we prove we are his parents? . . . Please, please help us. . . . When did he leave?"

Polynkov wrote: "It seems he's alive."

The Reillys felt that Polynkov was toying them. From one message to the next, he was tossing them from hope to despair and back again. "It seems he's alive": Polynkov's imprecision and informality made the message feel glib.

Yet Bill was happy to latch onto any hint of hope. "Thank God," he replied. "Do you have any idea where? Who was he with?"

"In the FSB," Polynkov wrote. The FSB, Russia's domestic intelligence agency, was no welcoming committee. Polynkov's message drove the Reillys into still further confusion.

Polynkov was contradicting himself. He wrote that Billy was in the custody of the FSB yet only moments before had said that Russian authorities had deported him to the US. The Reillys felt that Polynkov was embroidering his account to confuse them, and they didn't know why.

"Can he call us?" Bill asked.

Polynkov answered, flatly, "No."

"His mother is crying," Bill wrote. "She is so worried not [sic] see William again. I know he wants to do this, but is there any way he could write or email? Any contact with his mother. She is very very sad."

Bill tried once more: "I am sorry if I am disturbing you. Please, if you can tell us what day he left your organization. Is there someone he talked to that we can communicate with. We are heartbroken." Polynkov didn't respond. Like Billy before him, he had suspended communications with the Reillys.[26]

CHAPTER TWENTY

Beowulf

W hen it came time to name his Moscow private-investigative agency, in 2003, Dmitri Tyurin recalled a book he had read as a child, *Beowulf*. "I wanted to be tough enough, just like in Anglo-Saxon mythology," he said. "A man who is not afraid to go underneath, even to meet the devil, if necessary."

Raised on Moscow's outskirts by a Belorussian mother and Russian father, Tyurin had served in the Soviet army in the 1980s. He later picked up a degree at the Moscow State Institute of International Relations, the Soviet Union's elite foreign affairs academy, which molded many diplomats and more than a few spies.

During the 1990s, Tyurin worked in Russia's Ministry of Foreign Affairs. He took advantage of society's new freedoms and traveled the world. He cycled in Europe. He camped in Iceland, New Zealand, and other places to which the Soviet Union had long forbidden its citizens to travel. He spent time in the United States. He made friends in Boston and Virginia and like many Russians in those years felt an easy closeness with American people.

Exposed to the world, Tyurin grew tired of handling ministry paperwork. He felt no pull to advancement within the state and instead found purpose in adventure. He left the diplomatic corps in search of work suited to his temperament and the new era of possibility.

He read books about Russian prisons, fascinated by the psychology they bred, the criminal outfits and their rituals and hierarchy. Observing how crime big and small had overtaken Russian society, Tyurin imagined dabbling in the world of thieves and thwarting their designs. He remembered the fable he had loved as a child, conceiving of himself as a Beowulfian slayer of demons. He picked up a private investigator's license.

Not long after entering the profession, Tyurin felt his idealism fade. Money lay not in catching Russian crooks and serving society but in courting Western clients. They alone paid enough to provide a comfortable living. Russia had recovered from the ruble devaluation of 1998, and by the mid-2000s business and financial bonds were once again strengthening with the West. Tyurin found clients from London and New York who enjoyed Moscow's fast money but were unsure about their fast-talking local partners. He fashioned a business by helping foreign customers determine if their Russian affiliates were working for themselves or for the state or for criminal enterprise, or in some measure for all three.[1]

It was easy for a man of Soviet resourcefulness to find pathways to information. At Gorbushka, a block-long electronics bazaar on Moscow's west side, Tyurin met with merchants who traded not only in TVs and cellphones, but also information databases of many kinds. For as little as $20, Tyurin could buy federal tax registries, phone records, Interior Ministry arrest files. Vendors at Gorbushka and other Moscow markets paid off government clerks who earned less than a living wage and had embraced entrepreneurialism.[2] These raw data sets assisted Tyurin in finding useful information and connections. In time, he developed his own contacts in ministries, police precincts, and state agencies.

Tyurin acquired a second professional specialty, since money wasn't Moscow's only temptation. Credulous foreigners also hired Tyurin to disentangle them in matters of the heart. He tailed errant wives and girlfriends to compromising positions.

After years working as a private investigator, Tyurin realized that he had fallen short of his mythological ideal. Yet he experienced no moral dilemma. Life was made of disappointment. Survival was hard enough. In movies and TV shows, he observed American private eyes and how they challenged power, and he knew that he was unlike them. Pushing too hard for truth in Russia could lead to misfortune.

A dozen years into his line of work, Tyurin approached midlife recognizing how good he had it. Friends of his had failed to adapt to society's changes and had fallen on hard times, but his income was steady. His original sense of purpose did not tug at him.

In November 2015, Tyurin received an email via his Beowulf website. Bill Reilly was asking for assistance in finding his lost son.[3]

In Tyurin's experience, when a person disappeared, there was seldom a mystery to it. People had reasons for wanting to be left alone, choosing in their own time to reappear, or to remain out of reach. But Bill's mention of his son's FBI connection made Tyurin reconsider. He noted Bill's lack of guile in sharing a detail that could endanger the son. Maybe this case was different. Tyurin understood that solving the mystery of Billy's disappearance could mean more than his previous cases. Beowulf took the commission.

Tyurin spoke English, which facilitated his discussions with the Reillys. He studied the documents they shared with him, and his first target was easy to identify. Tyurin believed he would draw more from Mikhail Polynkov than Bill had retrieved via social media. One Russian man could level with another.

When Polynkov answered his phone, it was clear to Tyurin from the echoes and hum on the line that Polynkov was riding a subway train. Polynkov told Tyurin that he indeed remembered the American and said that Russian officials had expelled him from the country. Tyurin knew this version of the story from his talks with the Reillys. When Polynkov proposed that they speak later, Tyurin didn't pressure him. Experience had shown that gradual cultivation was the method to induce Polynkov to unburden himself.

Tyurin relayed a summary of the call, and Bill and Terry were confident they had made the right hire. Tyurin also told them he had spoken with an FSB contact who located Billy's flight and train records in agency databases.

Tyurin considered another possibility. Bill's mention of the FBI connection caused Tyurin to speculate that Billy had been caught out in Russia while working in secret for his government.[4]

For decades, Soviet and Russian authorities had rounded up suspected spies and collected them in prisons in or near Moscow. For two years in the early 1960s, a Soviet prison held Gary Powers, an American pilot who had flown the high-altitude U-2 reconnaissance plane across the Soviet Union as its cameras snapped pictures of military sites. The U-2 traveled too high for Soviet antiaircraft batteries, allowing US president Dwight

Eisenhower to deny that the sorties were taking place. Soviet premier Nikita Khrushchev knew about them, though, and was infuriated. When Soviet missile technology caught up to the U-2, downing Powers in 1960, Khrushchev stashed the pilot in prison before parading him in a show trial.[5]

The Soviets traded Powers and another American for a KGB colonel in 1962, but other American assets languished for years in both Soviet and later Russian custody. Tyurin told the Reillys said that if the FSB had arrested or interviewed Billy, the US embassy in Moscow should have received a notification.[6]

An employee at the US embassy told Tyurin that no such notice had arrived. Tyurin suggested to Bill and Terry that their son might have crossed the Ukrainian border into Donbas. Tyurin wrote to the Reillys in an email: "Let's hope that we'll find him alive and healthy in nearest time."

Tyurin concluded that the best way to pursue the search was by visiting the places Billy had been. In preparation for a trip south, Tyurin stopped by the Moscow office of Vladislav Surkov, a senior Kremlin aide. Surkov was responsible for administering the war in Donbas, orchestrating the movements and activities of armed groups in tandem with diplomatic concerns.[7] From Surkov's office, Tyurin received a letter of introduction meant to smooth passage through sensitive areas.

"We'll be really lucky if they only removed William back to Russia and drove him to some remote location and gave him sort of reeducation treatment," Tyurin emailed Bill, "possibly making him work at a farm somewhere in Krasnodar region or in the Caucasus where Cossacks have demand for labor." After WWII, Soviet leader Joseph Stalin had effectively dissolved the Cossacks, semi-autonomous groups of people on the former frontiers in Kazakhstan, Russia, and Ukraine. In recent years, groups claiming Cossack heritage had reemerged.

Reeducation or "filtration," which Russia would employ broadly to citizens of eastern and southern Ukraine after Moscow's wider invasion of the country in 2022, sounded to Terry and Bill like science fiction. But they reasoned that the private investigator knew his country in ways they did not. They encouraged him. As Tyurin departed Moscow for points south, Bill wrote: "We hope and pray this has a happy ending."[8]

*   *   *

In Oxford, there was no happiness. In the course of a day, if something on TV might amuse Bill, Terry would be quick to chasten him. "What the hell are you laughing about?" When she, in turn, dropped her guard, she would catch herself. *How dare I laugh*, she would whisper. *Nothing is funny.*

The last leaves had fallen from the trees that autumn. The sky was gray, and the air coming off the lake was cool. Billy had promised to be home by fall. Now winter was approaching. Terry and Bill knew that each passing day took with it a measure of their chance of finding Billy. With Tyurin on his way to Rostov-on-Don, they refocused their efforts at home.

The FBI had stolen part of their belief in the federal government, but the Bureau was just one component of it. The Reillys realized that they had to find someone within the system who had an inclination to help them. The Department of State in Washington assisted US citizens who were in distress in foreign countries. The Reillys could recall hearing about instances through the years in which US diplomats had gained the release of Americans held captive abroad. Terry and Bill didn't know how this process worked. They simply believed that the US government, a powerful advocate, would help find their boy.

The Reillys phoned the State Department, and an operator routed them to the Bureau of Consular Affairs, which oversaw such cases. Matthew Steele, a consular official, picked up the call. Bill explained his predicament and found Steele receptive, sympathetic even. After their experience with the FBI, Terry and Bill were relieved.

Steele told the Reillys they needed a yellow notice, a missing persons alert from Interpol, the global policing organization based in Lyon, France, which could help authorities find Billy if he had left Russia and traveled to another country. Terry and Bill contacted the sheriff of Oakland County, Michigan, who facilitated issuance of the yellow notice.

Steele contacted colleagues at the US embassy in Moscow and obtained records of Billy's train trips along the Volga. These documents confirmed information the Reillys had already received from Tyurin, and this proved to them that Steele was dealing squarely.[9] Bill and Terry regretted the time they thought they had squandered while believing that the FBI had been looking for Billy. With Steele's help, they felt they were making progress.

Steele's colleague at the US embassy in Kiev requested information about Billy from the Ukrainian government, but there was no record of his entrance to the country. The Foreign Ministry in Moscow told another State Department official that there was documentation of Billy's arrival in Russia but none of his leaving it. Steele and his State Department colleagues took many routine steps, but as information accumulated and revealed no new leads, Bill and Terry grew more convinced that there was nothing routine about Billy's disappearance. They believed that the FBI had played a role.

Bill told Steele, as he had openly shared with Tyurin, that Billy had worked with the FBI. This stopped Steele cold. He said Billy's Bureau connection would only vitalize the government effort to find him.[10]

CHAPTER TWENTY-ONE

DNR

Arriving in Rostov-on-Don in the fall of 2015, Dmitri Tyurin visited the local offices of the Investigative Committee, a stand-alone inspectorate within the Russian government.[1] Tyurin provided an officer with Billy's vitals. This information enabled the committee to initiate a search of hospitals, morgues, and databases. The officer admitted to Tyurin that the work wouldn't get started without financial inducement. Tyurin understood. He knew how paperwork could shuttle from one agency to another in Russia, with letters stuffing folders while investigations bled cold. Tyurin slipped the officer 25,000 rubles, a few hundred dollars, and the man later phoned him.

A morgue at a children's hospital in Novoshakhtinsk, a Russian town fifty miles north of Rostov, listed a male corpse corresponding to Billy's height. But the morgue had only just received the body, five months after Billy's disappearance, and Tyurin considered it a false lead. He wrote to Bill: "If Billy is not found within one–two weeks from now I'll have to go on with actually visiting the places such as morgues."

Tyurin asked around Rostov about the volunteer-fighter base and met people who had spent time there. He spoke with a local Cossack who said he'd known of an American at the riverside camp. The man told Tyurin that Billy hadn't fit in there. The Cossack said he'd heard that Billy had crossed the border and joined a Donbas battalion. The unit's commander went by the call sign Chibis.[2]

*   *   *

Tyurin made his own border crossing at Novoazovsk, near the Azov Sea, along-side Russian-flagged soldiers and matériel whose presence betrayed the Kremlin claim that its men were not involved in the Donbas war. Tyurin caught a bus. It struggled seventy miles north along road 508 to Donetsk, the regional capital under separatist control. He disembarked to a world shattered by war.

Shelling had ruptured buildings and gutted their interiors, their facades blackened by fire. People wandered Donetsk's streets in a daze, lost. Amputees begged for money. A man missing a leg asked Tyurin for a bottle of vodka. Tyurin took pictures with his phone, compiling a visual record of his work, proof for the Reillys that he was earning his pay.

At the DNR's Ministry of Internal Affairs, on Bogdan Khmelnitskogo Avenue, an officer told Tyurin that he would check for Billy in police logbooks. The officer confided that the city morgue had a backlog of John Does. Many dead people would remain unidentified, he said, since those who had known them had fled the war.[3]

Among the dead and missing, Billy was unique, or nearly so. Americans seldom found trouble in southern Russia or eastern Ukraine. Few Americans even visited these places. At the time of Billy's disappearance, only one American was known to have fallen in the Donbas conflict, while fighting in a pro-Ukrainian battalion in 2014. (Another American, serving as a conflict monitor, would die there in 2017.) Being an American in this part of the world, involved even vaguely in the war, was exceptional.[4]

Tyurin stopped outside the headquarters of the DNR's Ministry of State Security, the main intelligence and counterintelligence body known as the MGB.[5] He was snapping photos of the building when several MGB officers emerged from it. They hauled Tyurin inside and locked him in a cell. The Ukrainian military had been shelling the area, they said. They told Tyurin they'd been on the lookout for Ukrainian agents spotting for artillery and that he looked the part. The MGB officers said that Alexander Zakharchenko, the DNR's so-called prime minister,[6] was in the building along with members of his Republican Guard.

Tyurin produced the letter of passage from Vladislav Surkov's Moscow office and explained why he had come to the DNR, in search of a lost American. The MGB men explained the complexity of Tyurin's task. They said that Moscow was in the midst of consolidating the volunteer-fighter battalions, placing them under centralized command. Numerous people were now trapped in camps run by commanders who were clinging to power, resisting being absorbed into the DNR military structure. Tyurin remembered Chibis, the battalion commander he had heard about in Rostov. He knew he needed to find him in case Billy had been caught in this power struggle.

Released from the MGB office and back out on the street, Tyurin flagged down a cab. He directed the driver to road H21 out of Donetsk. The Cossack in Rostov had advised Tyurin to drive toward two neighboring villages twenty miles southeast of Donetsk, places called Starobeshovo and Ilovaysk. He'd find a military cordon. Fate would take its course from there.

The taxicab approached the checkpoint. Men there were heavily armed. In this war zone, Tyurin was growing accustomed to such scenes, and he had to make his play. He believed that Billy might be located just down this road at a camp beyond the barricade.

Tyurin stepped out of the car. He told the men he was looking for an American who went by the name Vasily. Tyurin asked to speak with Chibis. Looking Tyurin up and down, the checkpoint guards quickly soured on the encounter. They recommended that, for his safety, Tyurin had better return the way he had come. Scanning the road beyond the checkpoint, wondering if Billy was close, Tyurin acknowledged that he could go no further.

*   *   *

Tyurin recrossed the border and traveled home to Moscow. He wrote the Reillys, recounting his grilling at the hands of the DNR MGB. "If Billy was suspected of espionage then these same people who interrogated me would be holding Billy till now," Tyurin wrote. "For what reason? I am not sure. As a bargaining asset at the POW [prisoner of war] exchange talks with the UA [Ukrainian] army? Possibly yes. Then Billy is relatively safe, they do not practice torture or otherwise starve him to death."

The Ukrainian and rebel sides had indeed conducted prisoner exchanges,[7] and Billy, simply because of his nationality, would have been a valuable property. The prospect that Billy had become a commodity of war shook Terry and Bill, despite Tyurin's breezy dismissal of deprivations.

Tyurin attempted to frame Billy's situation in the context of the greater war.

He mentioned the Minsk Protocol, an international agreement implementing Donbas cease-fires that never held for long. The protocol also governed the exchange of prisoners of war. "But some field commanders may have preferred to keep their prisoners as their security," Tyurin wrote, "or because they did not get their own men or relatives from the UA army and they need a 'worthy' American to bargain."

Tyurin concluded his assessment on a positive note: "No official in the region was aware of this case, now they are supposed to move responsibly because they will not be able to hold it secret for long time." This was an optimistic appraisal, given the war's brutality, but the Reillys latched onto it.

"Please, please keep trying to find him," Bill wrote to Tyurin. "We don't know what to say or do. By God's mercy we will find him."[8]

*   *   *

On a line parallel to Tyurin's work, the Reillys continued their efforts at home. They contacted the offices of Michigan's US senators, Gary Peters and Debbie Stabenow. They called the staff of Mike Bishop, who was then the House of Representatives delegate for the Reillys' electoral district. Each member of Congress had aides charged with fielding constituent petitions.[9]

With each new contact, Bill and Terry told their story all over again. The effort was tiring, but they understood its necessity. They sent along the materials they were collecting and shared the fact of Billy's FBI connection. The staffers on the phone sounded overextended and impersonal, as though the Reilly case were unwelcome work that would merit no reward.

Christmas 2015 approached, and the Reillys were in no mood to celebrate. Billy's disappearance monopolized their emotions. They visualized him in a dark prison. They also imagined that he was working covertly for a US agency and that his plan was proceeding. They began attending Catholic Mass nearly every day, saying prayers for Billy.

"Our hearts are sad, but we have much faith," Bill wrote to Tyurin. "What a wonderful Christmas gift it would be to have Billy back home."[10]

Tyurin's contact at the Rostov Investigative Committee phoned him. He said that it would have been difficult to conceal the kidnapping or killing of an American at the Rostov fighter base, since the Interior Ministry was obliged to track the volunteers who lodged there. The man told Tyurin that committee investigators had questioned a number of volunteer fighters, but that none had provided useful leads about Billy. "Why?" Tyurin wrote to Bill. "Because Billy had left the camp and headed to DNR/LNR" (that is, to Donetsk or Luhansk, in Ukraine).

Tyurin had no hard evidence for this conclusion, but he was assembling a working picture. He said that he had "collected about 20–25 out of 100 pieces of the puzzle."

Three days before Christmas, Tyurin wrote to say that he had received a call from a senior Rostov Investigative Committee official who had asked him a series of questions about the DNR. "That's rather disquieting," Tyurin said. The call suggested to the private eye that the Investigative Committee had collected evidence showing that Billy had crossed the border and plunged into the lawlessness of Donbas.

Tyurin could only make suppositions. He was facing the difficulty of finding one person among the many gone missing in the war. Authorities had little enthusiasm, never mind the time or resources, to develop and chase leads. Billy was just another open-ended question. His only outstanding attribute was his nationality. This made him a curiosity, though not much more. Tyurin was looking for a trail to follow, but where did it begin? Someone knew what had happened to Billy . . . but who? Tyurin returned to an earlier inquiry.

Tyurin had spoken with Mikhail Polynkov, the recruiter, by phone several times, and they finally met in person. Tyurin didn't hide the fact that he was working for the Reillys. He tried to reassure Polynkov, saying that Terry and Bill wanted only one thing, to find their son. They had no interest in placing blame for Billy's disappearance or pursuing legal recourse.

Polynkov said he had canvassed his contacts after corresponding with Bill Reilly that fall and had learned of Billy's deportation. Polynkov told Tyurin that he sympathized with Terry and Bill but didn't know how he could help them.

Tyurin detected a deeper truth and aimed to get closer to his subject in order to unearth it. In one of their conversations, Polynkov had mentioned that his girlfriend was looking for work. Tyurin hired Polynkov's girlfriend as an assistant. The two men grew friendly. Polynkov confided in Tyurin, saying that Billy had, in fact, not been deported but was in the custody of the FSB.[11]

Polynkov had told Bill Reilly as much in their autumn exchange, so Tyurin was unsurprised to hear it, yet there was something in Polynkov's manner that forced Tyurin to take this version seriously. It made sense to Tyurin that the FSB would have taken an interest in an American nosing around the Russian side of the Donbas war. In charge of Russia's counterintelligence, the FSB was the lead agency for rounding up spies. It would have been a dereliction of the FSB's duty if its agents hadn't brought Billy into the office for a chat.

Tyurin again phoned his Moscow FSB contact and now pressed him to dig harder for information about Billy. Here the FSB agent lost his patience. He told Tyurin "to relax."[12]

This reaction only excited Tyurin's curiosity. Left to speculate, he wondered if Russian officials were expressly withholding information because Billy was American, at a time when the two countries had hardened into adversaries.

CHAPTER TWENTY-TWO

The List

The FBI and FSB had at one point maintained a productive relationship. It had begun early in the post-Soviet era, and in 1994 Russia accepted the FBI's proposal to install a legat at the US embassy.[1]

Russia and the United States had once shared interests in combating terrorism, organized crime, and the flow of dirty money from Eurasia into American banks and real estate. When notorious Russian outlaw, Vyacheslav Ivankov, known as Yaponchik, emigrated to New York to pursue criminal opportunities in the early 1990s, Russian officials alerted the FBI, whose agents had been unaware of the development and its significance. The Bureau's criminal division was still focused on the Mafia (known as *La Cosa Nostra*, or LCN in FBI nomenclature) and was unprepared for the coming wave of ruthless, sophisticated former Soviet ex-cons who identified the open American society as a bountiful new source of plunder. From that first Russian tip, the FBI made an organizational shift. It eventually all but shuttered its LCN unit, reallocating manpower to a new Eurasian organized-crime division.[2]

After 9/11 the FBI–FSB relationship only deepened, especially in counterterrorism, but in 2010 it began to shift. In that year, two US federal cases made political waves in Russia.

A freelance pilot from Rostov-on-Don, Konstantin Yaroshenko, had been looking for work in Africa. Through intermediaries, Yaroshenko found his way to Liberia, where a drug-trafficking syndicate needed people to fly cargo. The syndicate had hatched a plan to ship cocaine from South America to Liberia, from which the gang would distribute it internationally. Yaroshenko told the traffickers that he could handle the job. He was unaware that the DEA had been investigating the Liberian ring for years, since its leaders planned to move a portion of the drug haul into the United States. After the DEA and Liberian authorities took down the group in 2010, Yaroshenko learned that he had been indicted on trafficking conspiracy charges in the US. On Yaroshenko's first trip to the United States, a Manhattan judge sentenced him to twenty years in federal prison.[3]

The security services of the United States had never before apprehended a Russian national in a foreign country and extradited him to American soil to face federal charges.[4] Russian officials were perplexed, believing there had been a mistake. Yaroshenko had never flown drugs to the United States. He had never even been to the United States. Russian foreign minister Sergei Lavrov reasoned with Hillary Clinton, who was then the US secretary of state.[5] But US officials wouldn't budge. It didn't matter that Yaroshenko had never smuggled anything into the United States. He had schemed to do so. Conspiracy to commit a crime was its own offense in US federal law.[6]

Russian officials were outraged that the United States would apply an American legal interpretation to Russian nationals in foreign lands. Russia considered this to be judicial overreach, a symptom of how the United States used superior diplomatic and economic power to move unilaterally against Russian citizens. In a statement, the Russian Foreign Ministry said the U.S. had kidnapped Yaroshenko.[7] The DEA's reach into Liberia mirrored the extension of the FBI's own mission after September 11, as agencies sought their pieces of international action.

Months after Yaroshenko's arrest, the issue flared up again, this time in Bangkok. US officials prevailed upon their Thai counterparts to extradite Viktor Bout. A former Soviet military translator, Bout had for years allegedly moved weapons to warlords across Africa. Bout was so well known that Yaroshenko, who apparently had never met him, had dropped his name in the Liberia meetings to make himself appear more employable. Russia lost a diplomatic battle with the United States in Thailand, and Bout left the country on a plane in shackles. In 2012, the Manhattan federal court handed him a twenty-five-year sentence.[8]

Putin and Lavrov pressed for Bout's release,[9] but Russia knew that this time there had been no mistake. The United States' new approach to applying its laws internationally was self-evident.

The US wasn't the only country adjusting its international approach. Concurrent to Putin's policy speeches, the Kremlin was dispatching assassins to eliminate enemies and foreign assets in the West. Such operations had been the norm since the Cold War, on both sides of it, but Russia conducted some of these new missions with brazenness, even sloppiness, that felt intended to intimidate and terrorize. The country took still more steps to show that it was back in business, a threat to take seriously. Russia provided safe haven to cyber-criminals who fleeced American businesses and investors. And Russia's effort to influence political outcomes in the US and the European Union, through voter targeting and the direct funding of parties friendly to Kremlin policies, was well underway.

Now clocking Russia's renewed offensives, the US wasn't done. Washington was preparing to hold Russia and the Putin regime accountable for crimes allegedly committed within Russia itself.

In 2009, a Russian accountant, Sergei Magnitsky, involved in exposing a tax-fraud scheme allegedly perpetrated by Russian officials, died from abuse and neglect in a Moscow jail. In 2012, the US Congress passed a law in his name that handed the White House tools to sanction Russians that the United States alleged were involved in the fraud scheme and Magnitsky's death. Many of the people suspected of these crimes worked for Russia's Interior Ministry. They were Russian federal cops.[10]

In an initial salvo, Obama sanctioned eighteen Russians. The law also enabled the United States to target Russian individuals and companies that had no connection to Magnitsky's death but were allegedly involved, broadly, in violating human rights. Eventually, these US sanctions reached into Russian business and politics, barring influential figures and companies from the global financial system. Their accounts in the West were frozen. Western banks wouldn't touch them.[11]

The Magnitsky List, as the roster of designated people came to be called, infuriated Russian officials, evidencing its effectiveness. It also caused problems for the FBI agents who worked in the US embassy in Moscow, revealing the tension between politics and operations. With little regard for the list's effect on frontline relations, lawmakers and officials in Washington sought to expand it.[12]

On an initial quarterly basis, the Department of Justice sent its Moscow legat at the time, Don Robinson, an inventory of proposed Magnitsky additions. He then confidentially disclosed the names to his Russian counterparts, granting them an opportunity to argue for the removal of any of these people before the list would be finalized and released. The Russian side often pushed back. There was little Robinson could do.

"That was a constant irritant," Robinson said about the list. "Some of our key liaison contacts were on it." He accepted the gravity of the Magnitsky case and appreciated the utility of the list, but he needed Russian cooperation to address practical law-enforcement and national-security tasks. "Do you want to talk to these people or not? You want to put the head of the FSB on this list, and then you expect me to walk through the front doors at Lubyanka (FSB headquarters) and talk to these guys? We're trying to work together. And this is a problem."

Bout and Yaroshenko, and principally the Magnitsky List, cast a new die for relations between Russia and the United States. In 2014, when Russia annexed Crimea and filtered troops and matériel into Donbas, productive contact between the FBI and FSB had already all but ceased. "We fell off a cliff," Robinson said. "Gone were the days when you could come in and go, 'Hey, I got a hot case in Detroit. There's a Russian guy in it. Do you have anything on this guy?' I would write up a brief letter with the questions on it, and give it to them, and that would be good enough."

With the United States and its allies sanctioning and penalizing Moscow over the Crimean and Donbas events, the FSB drew down its contact with the FBI. The FSB now required FBI requests in the format of an MLAT document, meaning that they had to adhere to the formality of the countries' mutual legal assistance treaty. An MLAT request had to pass through numerous bureaucratic steps, processing through the Department of Justice and Russia's Ministry of Justice before filtering to the relevant Russian agency. Robinson and his FBI colleagues felt that the procedure was designed to go nowhere. Russian officials would often kick back the FBI's MLAT requests on clerical grounds. "It kept getting worse," Robinson said. "There was barely any contact at all."[13]

The relationship between the FBI and FSB, and between the two governments, had never been easy, but there had been a time of cooperation. Now that was over. Each country called out the other, escalating mutual reactions. Long past was the time when a chat between US and Russian law-enforcement officials could solve a problem, no matter how thorny, even if it concerned one agency's man imperiled on the territory of the other.

CHAPTER TWENTY-THREE

Inducement

B y the close of 2015, months had elapsed since Terry and Bill had hired private investigator Dmitri Tyurin, yet they couldn't understand why his reports remained speculative. He had produced no tangible results. Bill Reilly urged Tyurin to encourage the Investigative Committee in Moscow and Rostov to interview Bronya Kalmyk and Mikhail Polynkov. This appeared to be an obvious step. Tyurin agreed but explained the complications.

Russian investigators, he said, "respond properly to cases which are supervised from above." Such influence and pressure, he concluded, could come only from officials at the US embassy in Moscow. "If they present a diplomatic note asking the RU authorities to help to find Billy, that would be most effective," Tyurin wrote. "They can find virtually anybody if there is a political will at the top."

Bill and Terry remembered what their son's FBI handler, Tim Reintjes, had told them about the US embassy's FBI legat. (Don Robinson had left his post in Moscow earlier in the year.) It was worth a try.

Bill phoned the US embassy in Moscow and pleaded his case to several officials. "They keep saying they are talking to someone," Bill wrote Tyurin. "They later say they know nothing."

Tyurin called his own US embassy contact and received a determination. "They have taken somewhat interesting approach," Tyurin wrote to Bill. The embassy official had said, according to Tyurin: "We will not write a diplomatic note on this case."[1]

Terry and Bill were confounded. This was the document they needed in order to persuade Russian authorities to initiate an official search. The Reillys questioned the point of having a US embassy if it wouldn't exert its influence. The embassy's refusal demonstrated that the United States, which had limited capital in its relationship with Russia, had chosen not to spend any of it by supporting Billy.

With the embassy effectively having cast Billy aside, the Reillys redirected their search to the Russian half of the puzzle. They wrote to the Ministry of Foreign Affairs in Moscow. They tried the Red Cross there. They petitioned every agency and official they could find online. A Russian-speaking lawyer in Michigan helped them hire a Rostov private investigator, an augmentation to Tyurin's efforts. The investigator took payment yet produced nothing in return. They spoke with a retired Moscow police captain who promised much but delivered little. Bill wrote a letter, by hand, the words scrawled unevenly across the page, addressed: "To FSB."[2] The efforts produced nothing.

Bill wrote another letter, this one to the Russian embassy in Washington, and received a reply acknowledging awareness of Billy's circumstances. "As we know the Russian Ministry for Internal Affairs is working on his case trying to find out where your son is right now," the embassy note read. "It sent research requests with detailed information about William to the regional Police offices as well as asked medical facilities there to share information whether your son has ever been hospitalized."

The Reillys were stuck. Was Billy so beneath the regard of official bodies that they wouldn't waste their time trying to find him? Or was he somehow so important that his disappearance was too threatening to investigate?

Dmitri Tyurin, a seasoned investigator, took his own stock of the case. At first, it had been a novel challenge, a break from tailing unfaithful wives, a return to important investigative work. But his view of the case was evolving. Tyurin had rarely encountered a job that was beyond his abilities, and he now grew dispirited, suspecting that larger forces were in play.

In 2016, Tyurin walked up Tverskaya Street, the wide avenue that led northwest from Red Square. He hiked the street's mild hill, past the throngs collecting by the entrance to a metro station and other people along the sidewalk near shops and cafés. Tyurin turned into a theater, a venue for stage plays, and climbed the stairs to a higher floor.[3]

In an office there, he scrutinized a portrait of Felix Dzerzhinsky hanging on the wall. A Polish noble who turned to socialism, Dzerzhinsky had led the Bolsheviks' original secret police, the Cheka, beginning in 1917. During and after the Russian Civil War, he led a campaign against people maligned as "counterrevolutionaries," murdering thousands without trial and waging what he called "organized terror." Through decades and administrative changes, the Cheka would become the KGB, which in turn would retain most of its departments, in post-Soviet Russia, as the FSB.[4]

For thirty-three years, a statue of Dzerzhinsky had stood on a pedestal in front of KGB headquarters, Lubyanka, guarding a wind-swept square. As the nineties dawned, and the USSR faded, Dzerzhinsky became a symbol of the criminality of the Soviet system. In August 1991, a crowd tried to pull down the statue. Moscow officials removed it.[5] But the old attitudes remained. In 2005, the Moscow police installed a memorial to Dzerzhinsky at its main branch.[6] Dzerzhinsky had died in 1926, nearly a century ago, yet his face, with a bushy Van Dyke and a furrowed brow, was a common presence in portraits hanging in security-service offices across Russia.

A former FSB senior officer joined Dmitri Tyurin in the office above the theater. Tyurin explained that he had come seeking advice. He summarized the Reilly case. An American had vanished in the Donbas war. He had worked with the FBI in counterterrorism. FBI agents had visited the American's home in Michigan after his disappearance and had taken several of his devices.

The room fell silent, Tyurin's presentation echoing. "What would you do?" he asked.

The ex-official deliberated. He crinkled his nose. He walked out of the room without saying a word. "His reaction was explicit," Tyurin said, "that I should not take this case. But I had already taken it."[7]

Tyurin wouldn't let it go. That spring, nearly a year after Billy had come to Russia, Tyurin devised a new approach, emailing Bill Reilly that he had "arrived at a plan which we should discuss." The plan concerned Vladislav Surkov, the man whose office had issued Tyurin the letter of passage to Donbas. Surkov was responsible for the management of the exchange of POWs between Kiev and Russian forces in Donbas. Tyurin suggested that the Reillys offer Surkov an inducement.[8]

Bribes were a routine tool of business, government, and crime in Russia.

This was often how investigators like Tyurin received the raw data that under-pinned investigations, greasing the palms of government officials. Tyurin wasn't alone. In Russia, you bribed a customs officer to release your imported car for less than the import duty. You paid a bribe to excuse your son from military service, to make sure your house passed a building inspection. You could pay a bribe to a government official to change the name on a deed so that you could claim the property as your own. Bribes could be sizable and criminal, but they were often banal, negligible. They were baked into the cost of Russian life.

When a bribe was paid, an intermediary often took a cut, sometimes up to half its total. This didn't necessarily mean that the bribe was a scam. The cut was simply the price of doing business. The requested service would often still be performed.

Tyurin believed that a bribe would succeed where he had so far failed. He had cycled through his standard investigative approaches and used up all of his contacts. Tyurin had to get creative. Vladislav Surkov was part of Russia's power structure. He wasn't like Mikhail Polynkov, intimating access. Surkov advised Putin. Surkov could find Billy. He could send him home. "That will guarantee a final solution to the issue here," Tyurin wrote to Bill, suggesting that $8,000 would suffice.

Bill and Terry didn't know what to think. They would have gladly paid $8,000 or even $800,000 to regain their son. But it was unclear to them if there would be a return on the investment.

The Reillys had already paid Tyurin nearly $20,000 for his work, and they felt no closer to finding their son. How much more were they meant to pay? How long was this meant to last? Despite Tyurin's investigative notes and his photos from Donbas, the Reillys began to question if their investigator had ever left Moscow at all. "I don't think he's done one damn thing," Terry told her husband.

Bill balked at wiring $8,000, and Tyurin reduced the figure to $5,000. It felt to the Reillys like he was bargaining. "That's when we just knew, you know," Bill later said. They believed that Tyurin had joined the list of people who were using their desperation against them. The Reillys dropped Tyurin from the case.[9]

* * *

Billy Reilly wasn't the only American with intelligence ties who was lost in a country belligerent to the United States. Robert Levinson, a former DEA and FBI agent, had disappeared on Iran's Kish Island while on an errand for the CIA in 2007. In 2010, Levinson's family received a video of him in custody, and photos of him surfaced the following year. He had a long gray beard and a head of hobo's hair. When the United States conducted an internal investigation into the Levinson affair, it was clear that the CIA should never have sent him there. Iran, like Russia, was one of the most challenging environments for US personnel.

During the Obama administration, FBI director Mueller and Attorneys General Eric Holder and Loretta Lynch had spoken with the Levinson family and expressed the government's commitment to the case.[10] Trump's first attorney general, Jeff Sessions, took an opposing view. He sought no contact with the Levinsons and believed it wasn't government's responsibility to help them. Sessions told deputies that Levinson had assumed the risk of going to Iran.[11] The Trump administration later increased the reward that the US offered for information about Levinson's whereabouts and sanctioned two Iranian officials who it alleged had taken part in his abduction.[12]

The United States often washed its hands of operations gone awry. Another example was the case of Freddie Woodruff, a clandestine CIA officer murdered in Georgia in 1993, as the new country was establishing its independence from Russia. Woodruff was shot in a car outside Tbilisi, the Georgian capital. The government there engaged in a cover-up of the crime and convicted an innocent man. The US accepted Georgia's account rather than press for answers, sacrificing Woodruff on the battlefield of the post–Cold War.[13]

The Levinson and Woodruff episodes illustrated Washington's attitude toward professional operatives who were killed or abducted abroad. Billy didn't even have their status. He was a freelancer, an amateur, a CHS, and all the easier for Washington to ignore.

The Reillys faced the same frustrations that numerous other families had dealt with for years. Relatives of Americans lost or abducted abroad often didn't know where to turn for help.

Given the many US citizens who travel abroad for tourism and business, it's inevitable that some encounter trouble. Nearly every month, an American is jailed abroad under questionable pretense or abducted for ransom.

Government contractors. Energy-sector executives. Aid workers. Tourists who wander into the wrong neighborhoods. Many Americans work and live in unstable countries in Africa, Asia, and South America, where they hold value to criminal groups tied to police and governments.[14] This isn't an epidemic but a persistent concern that for decades has troubled the US.

It was never clear who in government, if anyone, was responsible for addressing the problem. Each case was different. Many cases went on for months, even years. The families of those who had been taken expected the US government to free their loved ones, but these were difficult puzzles. Some governments, like those in Italy and Spain, often paid requested ransoms, doing so confidentially and thereby helping to create a marketplace for kidnapping. But the United States, officially at least, did not. Often, it was a matter of locating an advocate beyond government who had useful relationships in a relevant country.[15]

In the 1980s, Jesse Jackson entered the picture. A charismatic civil rights leader who had made spirited plays for the Democratic presidential nomination in 1984 and 1988, Jackson was critical of US race relations. This endeared him to some international leaders, especially in countries beyond Europe. Jackson had an exalted status in many such places and traveled widely. He was a rousing speaker who knew how to utilize the press to advance his missions.

He was popular in some places where abductions of US citizens had occurred. When Americans were held for ransom or unjustly incarcerated, it was often Jackson, not a US government official, who would hop on a plane to conduct sensitive negotiations. He would often go on his own, without consulting anyone in Washington.

Over the years, Jackson gained the release of Americans in Colombia, Cuba, Gambia, Iraq, Syria, and other places. He was effective. The families of those he helped free were grateful. But for the US government, Jackson was a tricky proposition. From Ronald Reagan onward, Jackson gave presidential administrations headaches. Despots and terror groups broke bread with Jackson. They released pictures and videos of their meetings, winning PR value. It was a way for them, and also for Jackson, to needle the US establishment. It gave them and Jackson a pulpit. He was conducting freelance diplomacy, upstaging the State Department and the White House.[16]

Eventually, the United States formalized its approach to cases of Americans in captivity abroad. And it did so, coincidentally, on the very day that Billy

Reilly disappeared in Russia. On June 24, 2015, the Obama administration established the Hostage Recovery Fusion Cell.

Like the FBI's JTTF, the Fusion Cell was a task force. It comprised officials from the Departments of Defense and State, along with other agencies, formalizing the effort to bring home Americans who were in distress in other countries. Roughly fifty people worked in the cell full-time. It was headquartered at the main FBI building in Washington. The FBI led it.[17]

In 2018, three years after the cell's founding, a spokeswoman would say that it had helped free nearly 200 Americans who had been held abroad. But the cell didn't help every American who was in trouble in a foreign country. It couldn't. There were too many such cases. The officials who ran the cell had to choose. The group's resources were limited, and its focus was narrow, as its name suggested. Hostages were its aim, Americans who had been abducted. Those who had simply gone missing, as Billy appeared to have done, fell outside the Fusion Cell's purview.

There was another set of people who lay beyond the cell's concern. Americans who joined foreign movements that were opposed to the US, like Russia's volunteer battalions, such people were on their own.[18]

But Terry and Bill Reilly had no evidence that Billy had joined a battalion in Donbas. Maybe Billy wasn't, in fact, missing. He might well have been arrested without charge or taken hostage in Russia. The Hostage Recovery Fusion Cell was the sort of centralized government initiative that might have been tailor-made for the Reillys.

But Terry and Bill didn't know that the cell existed. The FBI agents who had promised the Reillys that they were searching for Billy hadn't told his parents about the US government's prime tool for doing so.

As the search for Billy extended through 2016, his parents remained alone, feeling their way in the dark. In the evenings in Oxford, Bill and Terry would go for walks in the woods. They wore headlamps to illuminate their way through the dusk. On these walks, the Reillys would reach out to Billy. They gave voice to feelings they could no longer keep inside themselves, talking to Billy as though he were there. Terry told Billy not to blame himself for whatever had happened to him. For his part, Bill said he was sorry. He said many things he hadn't told his son but had always felt. "For a brief period, you look through the trees at night and the moon's up there," Bill said later, describing the walks. "You feel like you're talking to him, and he's talking to you."

Inducement

With every new day, the Reillys ached for news of their son. One afternoon in Oxford, Bill was shuffling through the mail when he noticed an envelope bearing a familiar return address. He called out to Terry. "Hey, we got something in the mail from Bishop," he said, referring to their congressman, Mike Bishop. Bill tore open the envelope. Inside it was a campaign flyer asking for a donation. The flyer underscored the Reillys' belief that their delegates in Washington were intent on seeking and retaining power, instead of advocating for the folks back home.

The Reillys held out hope for Matt Steele at the State Department. Steele wasn't a legislator. His livelihood didn't depend on running for office and winning elections. He wasn't going to ask the Reillys for a donation. Plus, Billy had worked for the government as an FBI CHS.

Steele phoned to say that he had spoken with an FBI official but could produce no information. Steele assumed a consoling tone, telling Terry and Bill he could do nothing more for them. His phone calls dropped off, along with his practical assistance. Before long, Steele transferred to another office, one of the State Department's 25,000 employees, subsumed into the bureaucracy.[19]

The Reillys had expected something from government that Washington wasn't inclined to give. Billy's case didn't present a clear solution. Gaining the release of a priority American hostage or detainee who was in the custody of a radical group or foreign government could take months or years of delicate negotiation. Liberating such people often took into account larger issues of diplomacy and US national interest. And this applied to known cases, when it was understood where a detainee was located or with whom the United States could deliberate. Billy's case was more difficult. The Reillys didn't know where he was. There didn't appear to be anyone in Russia who cared to negotiate for his freedom.

Such nuance didn't matter to Bill and Terry. Their son had given five years to the FBI, and the Reillys believed that this had to count for something. Instead, it seemed to count against Billy.

Having exhausted their options in Washington, the Reillys felt a new emotion rising within them. They were angry.

CHAPTER TWENTY-FOUR

"Mr. Trump!"

When the Reillys failed to hang lights and decorations on the house the December after Billy's disappearance, a neighbor asked why the Christmas spirit failed to move them. They made a halfhearted excuse, instead of really explaining. They didn't want to tell the story to yet another person. Word would get around Oxford, and they'd be the object of sympathy. People would stop by the house. They'd want to know the details. They'd make well-meaning but infuriating suggestions about what the Reillys ought to do. People might even start wearing yellow ribbons. Bill and Terry wanted to handle the disappearance on their own terms, without being forced to work through it publicly.

No one else, perhaps excepting Catie, could understand what they were dealing with, the mix of misery, frustration, and rage that had overtaken them. No one could grasp how they felt Washington had let them down, or how terrified they became when they imagined where Billy was and what he was enduring.

Terry and Bill were alone, but for the TV. They would catch the odd *Seinfeld* rerun, though their TV was more squarely tuned to the Fox News Channel. They started most days with a morning talk show, *Fox & Friends*. The Reillys felt an attachment to this program and others on the network. Many Fox anchors and talking heads seemed to dislike Washington, or at least the Obama administration, as much as the Reillys now did.

Terry and Bill had never taken a great interest in politics. Lengthy discussions of policy bored them. Like most voters, they followed a gut instinct when deciding which politicians would lead best. The Reillys had spotty voting records and had never identified with one party or the other. Partisanship turned them off. The Democrats and Republicans always seemed to be reading from the same tired scripts.

But there was a new sort of candidate running for president in 2016.

The Reillys had seen Donald Trump's TV program, *The Apprentice*, a reality show in which contestants competed to win a job in his employ. For Terry and Bill, and for many other Americans, Trump's political candidacy felt at first like a reality show. He was the colorful contestant who was good for ratings but wouldn't survive the elimination rounds. Trump was unbridled. He didn't talk like a politician. The Reillys found him amusing.

Trump's campaign, the longer it went on, through 2015 and into 2016, gained steam and legitimacy. Terry and Bill watched the favorable coverage of Trump on Fox. He would even sometimes call into *Fox & Friends* and speak with the hosts in an extemporaneous way. The Reillys began taking what he said more seriously.

Trump sounded different than the professionals in Washington whom Terry and Bill had grown to despise. Trump said that the federal government had failed the American people, that the system was rigged. Run by thieves, he said, Washington had betrayed those it was meant to serve. The Reillys felt like Trump was talking to them. They had believed that no one could understand their pain, but listening to Trump changed their minds.[1] In July 2016, when Trump secured the Republican nomination for president, the Reillys rejoiced for the first time since Billy had disappeared the year before.

On September 30, Terry and Bill drove to Novi, thirty-five miles south of Oxford to see Trump in person. The chanting of several thousand people filled a Novi convention center. On a set of bleachers, people waved Trump flags and banners. Bill and Terry took a position on the floor near the stage. Standing above them behind a lectern, Trump wore a blue suit jacket and a blue-and-white striped tie. Bathed in light, he told the crowd: "I'm an outsider fighting for you."[2]

Bill and Terry felt like they were a part of something, a groundswell of people united in frustration and anger over being abandoned by the country's political class. "This will finally be the year that the American people say: 'Enough is enough,'" Trump said. "Together we are going to save this country."

The Reillys believed that Trump was going to win the general election and eliminate the red tape that had entangled them. Under Trump, Washington officials would have to respect people like the Reillys and give them straight answers. "The arrogance of Washington, DC," Trump said, "will soon come face to face with the righteous verdict of the American voter."

Concluding his speech, Trump paced the stage, whipping up the audience. He descended a set of stairs and walked along the front line of the crowd, shaking hands with supporters. As Trump approached her position, Terry sensed a chance. She had written a letter outlining Billy's case and now dug it out of her purse. She waived the letter back and forth. "Mr. Trump!" she yelled. "Help us. We've lost our son!"

Her words were lost in the clamor. She was just another fan, unable to engage Trump directly. He climbed back onto the stage and withdrew through a set of blue curtains.

The Reillys weren't discouraged. Seeing Trump in person only galvanized their belief in him. Three months later, after Trump had won the election, Bill and Terry mailed their letter to the Trump Tower on Fifth Avenue in New York City, petitioning the president-elect to help find Billy. They received no reply but were determined to get Trump's attention. In mid-January 2017, they drove east.

*　　*　　*

The Reillys spent a night in a hotel in northern New Jersey and headed into Manhattan the following morning. They waded into the city's foot traffic.

It took a few minutes for Bill and Terry to get their bearings amid the office towers on Sixth Ave. At the corner of West 48th Street, they found the News Corp Building, forty-five stories and nearly 600 feet tall, a minimalist box of limestone and glass. Inside the tower was the headquarters of the Fox News Channel.

The Reillys paced the building's perimeter before locating a ground-floor window. Through it, they saw the lights and cameras of a TV studio, the set of *Fox & Friends*. The program aired live, using the New York City street scene as a backdrop. When the show began broadcasting that morning, Terry and Bill planned to place themselves amid that setting, with a chance to help Billy.

On 48th Street, with people hustling past them on their way to work, the Reillys peeled off their coats. Underneath hers, Terry wore a white T-shirt with red letters that read, "SON MISSING IN RUSSIA." Bill's shirt was similar: "Mr Trump HELP US." Via *Fox & Friends*, the Reillys hoped to attract the attention of Trump's inner circle. An improbable plan, it was all they felt they had.[3]

Waiting for the show to begin, Bill and Terry saw someone they recognized. Anthony Scaramucci was a banker and investor. He knew Trump and people close to him and was helping select staff for the incoming presidential administration.

The Reillys knew Scaramucci's face from the TV appearances he had been making in support of the president-elect. Scaramucci had just walked a few blocks west from Trump Tower, where the presidential transition offices were headquartered. He was gathering his thoughts for another interview on Fox News when the Reillys waved him down.

Terry spoke frantically, as if fearing to lose Scaramucci's attention, and he backpedaled. "On a scale of one to ten, the mother was a twenty-five," Scaramucci said later. He tried to make sense of what Terry was telling him, her words lassoed by a Michigander accent. "There was a suggestion the kid had gone AWOL inside Russia," Scaramucci said later. "Like, he went off the grid."

Scaramucci promised to speak further with the Reillys once his interview concluded. When he reemerged from the News Corp Building, they were waiting for him. They explained in detail what had happened to their son and how the FBI and Washington officials had failed to advance the search. It had been eighteen months since they'd last heard from Billy.

Scaramucci sympathized. And after a life spent outside of politics, suddenly he was now close to power. He was in a position to help. Scaramucci told the Reillys he would raise their case at Trump Tower. Terry handed him a folder of materials she had prepared: her letter to Trump, photocopies of FBI business cards and Billy's passport page, and a sheet on Mikhail Polynkov. Scaramucci and Terry traded phone numbers.

The Reillys watched Scaramucci dissolve into Midtown's pedestrian sequence. They could scarcely believe their luck. Scaramucci was just the sort of person they had been seeking all along, someone with access to power and an impulse to help. They had forgotten about *Fox & Friends*. They didn't need it anymore. They had already accessed Trump's world. They were stunned by how easily they had achieved this. All they had done was gone to New York City and loitered outside the Fox News Channel studios.[4]

Scaramucci walked back toward Fifth Avenue. Air-traffic authorities had diverted planes from flying over Trump Tower. On the sidewalks below, police held bomb-sniffing dogs on short leashes. Men wearing combat helmets and holding automatic rifles guarded the tower's entrances. Applicants for cabinet posts and White House jobs rode elevators within the tower's smoked glass and gold-plated exterior to the twenty-fifth floor. There Trump and his staff were trying to assemble a government before inauguration day, two weeks away.[5]

Scaramucci knew it would be difficult to get anyone's attention amid these pressures. He also realized that because Billy had disappeared in Russia, of all countries, it would be challenging to muster support for his case in the coming administration. US intelligence agencies had recently determined that the Kremlin had interfered in the course of the presidential election that had just concluded. Reporters were publishing articles about meetings that Trump associates had held with Russian spies and officials, suggesting that the Kremlin had helped place Trump in the White House. It didn't aid Billy's plight that he'd gone missing in Russia.[6]

Nevertheless, Scaramucci had made a pledge to the Reillys. He waded into the Trump Tower with Terry's folder of materials in hand. He located Michael Flynn.

A former US Army general, Flynn was Trump's choice to lead the National Security Council, the group of advisers who worked in the White House and the nearby Eisenhower Executive Office Building and helped guide foreign policy. As National Security Adviser, Flynn would have the president's ear and the ability to influence government. The job was one of the most powerful positions in Washington.[7]

Inside Trump Tower, Flynn paused to give Scaramucci his attention. Scaramucci laid out the basics of Billy Reilly's case to Flynn and his deputy, K. T. McFarland.

The permeability of the incoming Trump administration was remarkable. Moments before, Terry and Bill had been standing on Sixth Avenue with little hope, dressed in homemade T-shirts, planning to stage a public spectacle.

With ease, they had placed their petition in front of the incoming National Security Adviser.

When Scaramucci concluded his pitch, he tried to read Flynn's reaction. Flynn and McFarland appeared to sympathize with the Reillys, as Scaramucci had done, but they waved him off. They said that now wasn't the time to pursue such an undertaking, in the midst of their selecting candidates to populate the administration. They could pick up the Reilly case once they were at work in the White House.

Scaramucci understood. Nonetheless, he couldn't be sure that Flynn would ever find the time for Billy's case. Feeling obligated to the Reillys, although he had just met them, Scaramucci thought of other ways to assist. He remembered a friend from the financial world.[8]

Bob Foresman was a vice chairman at the Swiss investment bank UBS. He had grown up in New York's Finger Lakes region and held a Harvard graduate degree in Soviet Studies. He spoke Russian and had lived in Moscow periodically since the early 1990s, working in the financial industry.[9]

Over the years and through many commercial deals, Foresman had made strong ties with Kremlin officials. He was also a religious man and had friendships in the Russian Orthodox Church, whose leadership was close to Putin. Foresman had become so comfortable in these circles that some people who knew him no longer speculated he was a spy. It was assumed he was just part of the game.

Foresman's knowledge of Russia and his experience there had led Trump's advisers to consider him for positions in the administration, including a seat on the National Security Council. Some in Trump's circle were discussing Foresman as the US ambassador to Russia.

In January 2017, Scaramucci contacted Foresman and passed along Terry Reilly's folder of documents. Foresman's first call was to Matt Steele at the State Department.

Steele was frank with Foresman. He said he was sympathetic to the Reillys. He told Foresman that he thought the government was stonewalling the family, but he offered no reasoning for it. Foresman understood that the State Department could do little in Russia, given the countries' poor relations. Steele said as much, suggesting that Foresman might achieve more through personal contacts, operating outside of diplomatic channels, much as Jesse Jackson had once done.

Foresman agreed. He began contacting people who he thought could develop information about Billy's whereabouts. He phoned an associate who had influence in Rostov-on-Don and another contact with relationships in Donbas. As he set these inquiries in motion, Foresman spoke with the Reillys. He was a father of five children, one of whom he and his wife had adopted from an orphanage in Rostov-on-Don, Billy's last known position. Terry's anguish touched Foresman. He understood her parental pain and fear.

Bill and Terry told themselves to be patient, but they had trouble containing their excitement. They had succeeded in an end run around FBI obstruction, State Department bureaucracy, and political calculations on Capitol Hill. The Reillys watched on Fox as Trump took the oath of office on January 20, 2017. They felt momentum gathering in their favor, with Trump forecasting imminent change.

Change did come, though not in the way the Reillys had foreseen. Shortly after the inauguration, reports surfaced that Michael Flynn had lied to the FBI and to Vice President Mike Pence about meetings he'd had with Russian officials. In addition, it emerged that the Department of Justice was investigating Flynn for lobbying that he had performed in secret on behalf of Turkey. Flynn held his post as National Security Adviser for only three weeks before Trump fired him. McFarland also left her post.[10]

Bob Foresman encountered his own obstacles in his effort to assist the Reillys. He prepared to contact Alexander Voloshin, a Russian businessman and politician who had served as Putin's first chief of staff.[11] But Foresman reconsidered. He imagined how it would appear to his influential Russian contacts if he began buttonholing them about the disappearance of an FBI CHS who had arrived in Russia with unclear aims. Foresman himself didn't know the truth of the story and sensed a risk in associating himself with it. If he pursued the Reilly case, Foresman feared he could jeopardize his chance at a senior position in government.[12]

The Reillys again found themselves alone.

*　　*　　*

Terry and Bill had followed Michael Flynn's downfall on the Fox News Channel. In 2017, they watched a new drama unfold. Trump and the FBI were at odds.

Trump suspected that the FBI's leadership had conspired to attempt to bar him from office, investigating members of his staff in search of Russian connections.[13] Trump at first courted FBI director James Comey, the successor to Robert Mueller, who had retired to private practive in 2013. When Comey declined to declare personal loyalty to the president, Trump began maligning him. On May 9, 2017, amid intensifying inquiries into Trump's possible links to Moscow, he fired Comey, rocking the US political establishment.[14]

Just eight days later, another bombshell fell. Facing political pressure to probe the Russia allegations, Deputy Attorney General Rod Rosenstein installed a special counsel, selecting Mueller to head the office.[15] The choice of Mueller encouraged Trump to step up his attacks on the Bureau, and he targeted an institution in which many Americans had placed their faith for generations.[16]

The Reillys were enjoying this show, gratified that Trump wasn't letting them down. They believed that the FBI was getting the war it deserved.[17]

They didn't realize, however, that Trump's moves initiated a Bureau shell game that would negatively impact their efforts to find Billy. After Trump fired Comey, White House advisers compiled a list of possible replacements as FBI director. On the list was Paul Abbate, who had led the FBI's Detroit office in the two years before Billy's Russia trip and during his arrival at the volunteer-fighter camp in Rostov-on-Don.[18]

A CHS like Billy resided many managerial levels beneath Abbate, in a great wash of personnel and information. Still, Abbate had been in charge in Detroit when Tim Reintjes, Billy's handler, had taken the unorthodox step of visiting the Reillys in Oxford. Reintjes had lied to Bill and Terry about his knowledge of the Russia trip and enlisted other Detroit FBI agents in the scheme. The FBI was a regimented organization that rarely took such measures without managerial knowledge and approval. No matter Billy's low rank, Reintjes's actions indicated that management, perhaps even including Abbate, understood that the disappearance of this CHS presented a problem.

Trump ultimately didn't choose Abbate as Comey's replacement but settled instead on Andy McCabe. Eight years earlier, McCabe had directed agents Andy Arena and Tim Waters in the underwear bomber case. McCabe, a Comey loyalist, clashed with Trump, and the president soon removed him also, further undermining public confidence in the FBI.

In August 2017, Trump installed Christopher Wray, a former assistant attorney general, to run the Bureau.[19] Once in the job, Wray turned to Paul Abbate, naming him the agency's associate deputy director. The FBI manager who had ultimately overseen Billy's final years of work as a CHS and the initial inquiries into his disappearance was now the third-highest-ranking official in the FBI. Abbate had landed at the core of the Bureau's decision making.[20]

Amid Trump's sustained public barrage, the FBI was closing ranks. Managers were intent on ensuring the Bureau's survival. This was no time for the FBI, or for Abbate, to unearth operations that had gone awry on their watch.

These maneuverings lay beyond the Reillys' scope of knowledge. All they could perceive was the futility of their inquiries. The summer of 2017 arrived, marking two years since they had heard their son's voice. For two years, they had been searching, hoping that Billy was locked away in a cell, held for ransom, suffering but still alive. They understood that they might soon have to accept that Billy was gone for good.

But they resisted the impulse to let him go. They knew they had to do more. They had to go out into the world and find him. On July 21, 2017, Terry and Bill boarded a plane bound for Russia.[21]

CHAPTER TWENTY-FIVE

In His Footsteps

T he Reillys left the baggage carousel at the airport in Rostov-on-Don and entered the arrivals hall, strung out from the long trip from Detroit. Their faces lit up. Russell Bentley was waiting.

Bentley, in his fifties, was dressed like a militiaman. His white hair spilled from the sides of an infantryman's cap and out its rear in a ponytail. He was far from his home in Texas and had lived a colorful life. In the 1990s, Bentley had picked up a felony conviction for pot smuggling. Paroled in 2008, Bentley blamed the US government and the Western liberal order for taking the best years of his life.[1]

When the Donbas war began, Bentley, watching online videos of the events, understood this as a battle of civilizations. He believed that Putin was the only world leader willing to stand up to the political and economic tyranny of the US. Bentley traveled to Russia, crossed into Donbas, and volunteered for military service. He had served in the US Army and was comfortable with guns. Bentley's anti-American pronouncements won over the separatists, who invited him to join the battle. They gave him the call sign Texas, or, in the way they pronounced it, "Tekhas." In its media outlets, the so-called government in Donetsk publicized Bentley as an American who'd chosen the right side.

The Reillys, in their search for people who could help them, had discovered Bentley's media appearances and contacted him. Bentley agreed to assist them. He asked around about Billy among the people he'd come to know in frontline life. He passed along Billy's information to contacts at the DNR MGB, the group that had briefly detained the Reilly's investigator, Dmitri Tyurin. Bentley didn't hear much in reply and concluded that Billy hadn't ever crossed into Donbas, that whatever had happened to Billy had transpired in Russia.[2]

For Bill and Terry, this had the weight of authority. They began to believe that the answers to Billy's disappearance remained in the vicinity of Rostov. After their disappointments in Washington and their disillusionment with the FBI, the Reillys felt like Bentley was their only honest broker.

Despite the fact that Bentley and the Reillys had never seen one another before, their airport meeting had the feel of a reunion. They had something in common that was more fundamental than their shared knowledge of Billy's case. All three mistrusted the US government, believing that their country had stolen something from them, Bentley his prime, the Reillys their only son. They were Americans exiled to a distant part of the world that now possessed their fates.

Bentley had become essential to the Reillys' search, especially after they had dismissed Tyurin. But Bentley could do only so much. He knew only a few Russian phrases. He had taken a wife in Donbas, Lyudmila, who joined him to greet the Reillys at the airport. Bentley and Lyudmila had married only days before and were meant to be on their honeymoon. Instead, they had chosen to help the Reillys navigate the Russian system. This sacrifice endeared them to Terry and Bill.[3]

The Reillys saw that Rostov-on-Don was a well-planned city of leafy parks. The Don River bordered a cluster of downtown buildings. There was heavy construction underway around town. In a year's time, Russia would host the soccer World Cup, and several matches were slated for play in Rostov. A new stadium was rising along the Don's left bank. To Bill and Terry, Rostov presented no conspicuous danger, and this gave them comfort as they imagined how Billy had lived there.[4]

The Reillys' plan of attack in Russia was vague. They didn't conceive of seeking out Mikhail Polynkov, believing they had gone as far as they could with him via social media messages in 2015. They didn't request meetings with officials at the US embassy in Moscow, since they had no faith in such people. Bill and Terry instead believed in the universal appeal of anguished parents, hoping that this would gain them access to the people and information they needed. They had no one left to trust but themselves.

With Bentley and Lyudmila, they visited a police precinct. An officer said that a case like Billy's was a matter for the Red Cross. Across town at a Red Cross office, a woman told them that the case was beyond the organization's scope. The following day, the Reillys returned to the police. An officer said he'd be in touch. To Bill and Terry, this felt like the Russian version of the runaround they'd endured with US officials.

The Reillys chose a modest hotel near a pedestrian street in the center of Rostov. The rooms were small and simple, and guests shared a bathroom on each floor. They struck up a conversation with the hotel's owner, explaining why they had come to Rostov. The owner listened to the description of the Reillys' exchange with the local cops and shook his head. His son was a policeman, he said. He told them that the police would never call them back. He said that Lyudmila, who was serving as the Reillys' interpreter, had to push the police to do something.

In order for Lyudmila to represent their interests officially, the Reillys had to assign her power of attorney. This required the translation of documents and visits to a notary. Each errand took a day or more, and additional steps in the process continued to proliferate. Terry and Bill were learning that such tasks in Russia were achieved in a haphazard way, yet also within a rigid framework, the combination seemingly designed to make them surrender.

Waiting days on end for the documents they'd need to secure meetings with officials, they ventured around Rostov. There were several stores along the pedestrian lane. A grocery. A cupcake shop. A café. A coffee stand and another for kvas, a cold drink made of fermented bread. It tasted like beer, and Bill drank his share. In stores, the Reillys pointed at things they wanted to buy and held up fingers indicating quantity. They found the language indecipherable but the people friendly and accommodating. Yet no matter how pleasant the interactions, these days were laced with uncertainty. Finding Billy in this confusing foreign place seemed impossible to them.

The Reillys spent hours walking the city, up and down its rising hills, thinking of Billy and why he had come here, what he'd done while he had been in Rostov, and if he was still somewhere nearby. They questioned why things had to be this way. Terry frequently broke down in tears, often at night as she and Bill bedded down at the hotel, when sound and activity faded and reflection was all that remained.

Bill argued that this should be a happy time, too. Whatever had befallen Billy, he had achieved the unexpected. He'd had the courage to follow his fascinations. Terry and Bill imagined how thrilling it must have been for their son to live this distant dream. Such comforting conclusions stood in for the gaps of the Reillys' knowledge of Billy's fate, allowing them to stave off the darkness of their emotional despair.

One afternoon, Bentley, Lyudmila, and the Reillys packed into a small elevator in an office tower in the city's southeastern quadrant, ascending to the offices of the Rostov Investigative Committee. There they met with investigators. With Lyudmila interpreting, Bill and Terry told their story once again, how Billy had come to Russia and disappeared. They opened the folder of documents they had brought to Russia: the vitals page of Billy's passport, his Russian visa, snapshots of him from home, his phone bills and selections of text messages he had sent before vanishing. The investigators were more interested in Dmitri Tyurin, the Moscow private eye, and how much the Reillys had paid him. When the investigators heard the figure, roughly $20,000, they laughed, since they were experts in the financial value of such services.[5]

Bill and Terry again thought that Tyurin had scammed them, though the interchange revealed a more worrisome truth. The investigators were part of the system of entrepreneurialism in Russian ranks, in which cops and investigators used their positions to elicit side payments. The investigators, recognizing the Reillys' ignorance of local customs, now leveled with them. The investigators had received no payment, and there was no active case on Billy, they said. Indeed, there had never been one. Two years had gone by, and the Rostov Investigative Committee had done nothing.

The Reillys were crestfallen. Lyudmila tongue-lashed the investigators for failing in their duties, but they said it wasn't so easy. Evidence suggested that Billy had crossed the border into Donbas, and that was another country, beyond their jurisdiction. Lyudmila pressed the investigators, and in the end, they filled out paperwork for a missing person case. When Bentley, Lyudmila, and the Reillys left the building and walked out onto the street, evening had fallen, and Bill and Terry felt like they had scored a victory, however minor. The Reillys understood that even in Russia they would have to develop their own leads.

Terry and Bill had been speaking with Suratni, the Indonesian woman Billy had met on a Muslim dating site. She told the Reillys that she had been texting with Billy on the day of his disappearance, when he had sent her a photo of a wound he had suffered to one of his legs. An abrasion, it had been splashed in iodine. When Suratni asked Billy what had happened, he'd said he had been involved in a motorcycle accident. The timing of the injury led Terry and Bill to believe that someone had treated their son roughly, presaging his disappearance. Another clue, where did it lead?

The Reillys ventured further around Rostov, seeking evidence of people who bore responsibility. On one of their walks, they and the Bentleys reached the left bank of the river coursing through town, the artery of Mikhail Sholokhov's Cossack elegy, *And Quiet Flows the Don*. Windsurfers collected there. The squalls that gusted eastwardly across the southern steppe filled their sails, propelling them across the water's surface.

Along the sandy riverside beach, Bill stopped short. He felt like he had been in this place before. On his phone, he called up the batch of photos that Billy had texted home from Rostov in 2015. One image was taken from the riverbank. It showed the Voroshilovskiy Bridge, which spanned the river at great height, and a residential tower with a large clock.

Looking up from the image on the phone, Bill and Terry saw an identical tableau in front of them. A new bridge, an addition for the World Cup, was being built next to the old one. Aside from this, the images were the same. Bill and Terry realized that they were standing where Billy had positioned himself two years earlier when he had taken the picture. Their heels pressing into the sand, the Reillys felt nearer to their goal than they'd ever been. Billy had been here.

The Reillys took in their surroundings. Behind them loomed the half-finished World Cup stadium. Closer was a tumbledown, single-story building, rectangular in shape. Washing hung over its walkway railing. Boots sat against a wall, set out to air-dry. Men were loitering in front of the building and along the beach. Many of them were drinking beer, and several looked drunk as they glared at the outsiders who had wandered into their midst.

Russell Bentley spoke in a low voice to the Reillys. He knew where they were. He knew this place. Bentley said they had stumbled into Mikhail Polynkov's Rostov volunteer-fighter camp.

Terry and Bill blanched. But they sensed an opportunity. Among the people gathered here, they thought, there must be someone who knew something about what had happened to Billy. A man descended the stairs from the building to the beach. He had East Asian features and wore a beret and military fatigues. Only later would the Reillys deduce that this was Bronya Kalmyk, the man who had managed the base while Billy had lived there. The Reillys had spoken to Bronya by phone with an interpreter in 2015.

Bill took a step toward the base. Bentley gripped him by the shoulder. He knew something Bill did not. Bentley understood that the base was liable to be stocked with firearms and that these men had little to lose. He understood that the only thing that would compel these men to talk was a force stronger than their own. Lyudmila broke free, and Terry followed her. They marched directly to Bronya and asked him what he knew of Billy. Bronya was noncommittal, professing ignorance. Outnumbered and outgunned, surrounded and vulnerable on that beach, Terry, Bill, Bentley, and Lyudmila tactically retreated. Bentley told Bill that there would come another day.

*   *   *

The plane home reached altitude, and the lights dimmed. A sleepy lull engulfed the cabin. Terry peered into the darkness of the sky through a window and thought of the last time she had heard Billy's voice. It had been during the bike ride along the Polly Ann Trail. He had called. He'd said, "Plans have changed."

Grief bottled up Terry. She and Bill had tried everything they could imagine to find their son. They had traveled across the world and come up empty. It felt like their search was over.[6]

BOOK TWO

CHAPTER TWENTY-SIX

Contact

In 2017, each weekday around quitting time in Washington, a motorcade departed the Eisenhower Executive Office Building, west of the White House, and eased north on 17th Street NW. Vice President Mike Pence sat in the back seat of one of the convoy's limousines on the way to his residence at the US Naval Observatory. Policemen in sedans and on motorcycles cleared the road. Their lights flashed and their sirens arrested the senses as the cars slid past Farragut Square and joined Connecticut Avenue where it skimmed by the Mayflower Hotel.

On one darkening winter afternoon, on the eighth floor of an office building off the square, several newspaper reporters and editors, roused by these sirens, rushed to the windows to watch the motorcade pass by on the street below them. The Washington office of the *Wall Street Journal* had occupied the eighth floor of this building for more than thirty years.

The office had a settled-in look. The carpet was well-walked and gray. The desks and cabinets were gray. On the walls hung placards from political campaigns of the past. One poster read, "Reagan Country," and pictured the former president beaming beneath a cowboy hat. There were posters of FDR, JFK, and RFK, and another that read, "Goldwater for President." There was an invitation to "bring your family and see" Richard Nixon's 1973 inaugural parade. Just inside the office's front door was a pinball machine bearing the faces of Hillary Clinton and Donald Trump, opponents in the 2016 presidential election.

A series of front pages from previous *Journal* editions also hung on the walls. One was dated September 12, 2001. Printed across the top of the page were the words: "TERRORISTS DESTROY WORLD TRADE CENTER, HIT PENTAGON IN RAID WITH HIJACKED JETS." Nearby this was a small square plaque of metal and wood memorializing someone who had once worked in the office. In 2002, Daniel Pearl was reporting for the *Journal* in Pakistan when terrorists connected to al Qaeda abducted and murdered him.[1]

Each day, as *Journal* reporters and editors entered the office, they passed by these two markers, one to 9/11 and the other to Pearl, reminders of the importance and potential perils of the work that was meant to happen here.

The newsroom was open-plan, with a few editors privileged with glassed-in offices. More than a hundred people worked there. After the New York office, the Washington bureau was the *Journal*'s largest, signaling the consequence of its location.

From the office, it was a ten-minute walk south through Lafayette Park to the White House. In 2017, the first year of the Trump administration, this proximity mattered. Under Trump, a scandal or emergency or deviation from protocol seemed to materialize every week. The *Journal*'s reporters and editors struggled to keep pace with events and compete with rival news outlets. Deadlines overlapped and there was no end to them.

Reclined in a chair in the office, I faced different pressures. I belonged to the *Journal*'s national-security group. I didn't have a beat, like colleagues of mine who covered the Pentagon, the State Department, or the CIA. I was meant to find investigations and narratives that reached deep into the news or beyond them. These weren't easy to identify or to shepherd through the paper's layered editing regime, though I felt privileged to do this sort of work.

It was late December 2017 with Christmas approaching, a Friday. My name hadn't appeared in the paper in a while, and editors were grumbling about my low yield. The sirens of Pence's motorcade were fading into the last half hour of the afternoon when my phone rang. Bob Foresman was calling.

I had met Foresman through contacts in Ukraine. I'd last seen him in Manhattan months earlier. We had shared a lunch at a ground-floor café across the road from the Rockefeller Center skating rink. Foresman had said then that he had something important to share but that the time wasn't right. Now with the phone to my ear, I heard Foresman take a deep breath. He launched into a story, what he knew of it. He said that a young man from Michigan who had worked with the FBI in counterterrorism had disappeared in Russia. Foresman was a charismatic and candid speaker, but his presentation faltered as he tried to explain the meaning of the Reilly events.

The family was desperate, Foresman said. He said he had done as much as he could to help the Reillys but could go no further. We commiserated over their ordeal. He passed me Terry's phone number. "Maybe you can do something for them," he said.

I agreed. Maybe I could. I had lived in Moscow. It had been five intense years. I had later lived in Kiev. I had been working as a reporter in the two countries for fifteen years, making numerous trips into and out of them. I had traveled for work and pleasure in the former Soviet Union and developed friendships and reporting sources in that part of the world. I told Foresman I doubted that I could find answers for the Reillys, but I conceded that I probably had more at hand than they did.

I also had the support of the newspaper. The *Journal*'s reputation could encourage people to share information about Billy Reilly. Then again, the paper's support came with conditions. I could tell from the little that Foresman had shared of the Reilly case that I would have to commit considerable time and effort if I were to make an article out of it. This was an open-ended project, the sort of thing that *Journal* editors did not favor. Their concern was news, its daily variety, and they expected reporters to produce regular bylines. I told Foresman I would look into Billy's story but could make no promises.

I laid down the cellphone with one hand and dialed on my desk phone with the other hand. Terry Reilly answered.

I identified myself, and she gasped. The panic in her voice was unmistakable. She must have thought I had called with dire news of Billy, just as she had once expected the worst from FBI agent Tim Reintjes. I told her that I had only just learned of her son's disappearance and wanted to know more. Relieved, she transferred the call to speakerphone. Bill said hello, his voice faint in the background.

Our call was brief, and by the end of it both Terry and Bill sounded optimistic. They appeared pleased that someone from the press was taking an interest in Billy. This could possibly inject energy into their flagging search. Their hope, after two and a half years without word from their son, sounded to me strong and real. I imagined their ceaseless emotional strain.

It was important to me to meet them in person. Early in 2018, I arrived in Detroit. I rented a car at the airport, and drove north. I had gone to college in Michigan and was now again charmed by its climate. The ground was packed with snow and ice, and it was also raining. Clouds locked in the sky as if there'd never been a sun. I nearly failed to notice Oxford appearing up ahead like a frontier town in the storm of the year. I diverted to the west, and the land opened to the lakeside.

Terry and Bill welcomed me into their home, and I could tell that this was difficult for them to do. They were anxious. The hope I'd heard on the phone must have been impossible to sustain, even when there was no one to impress. Faith probably came and went. Every day for them was a new day without Billy. They were unsure if he was alive but certain there was something important they were failing to do. Their search had exhausted and confused them, and their fire had all but gone out. Now here was one more person, come to comb through the embers.

The front door opened to a hallway that was about six feet across and boxed in by a low ceiling. A powder room was on the left side of the hall, followed by a compact kitchen and a rim of countertop. This gave way to the living room and its sofa and chairs and TV, and the rolltop where Billy had worked on the PC. Through the back window was the lake where he liked to fish. The rain had turned to sleet and was pockmarking the lake's slushy surface. It felt good to be indoors.

Scant winter light penetrated the home. As Tim Reintjes had once done, I sat on the couch. Bill and Terry took two chairs, and we looked at the floor a while, searching for a way to begin. Terry fondled the silver cross that hung on a chain around her neck. Their dog sat in her lap and eyed me. When Terry and Bill spoke, sorrow and fatigue frequently swallowed their words.

We talked about Billy's childhood, and their thoughts began to gather. They described his troubles in school, his solitude, and the communion he'd found on social media. Terry explained how Billy had learned languages through diligence and private study and how global affairs had grown to fascinate him. "He was kind of a nerd, really," she laughed, betraying her maternal pride. I noted her usage of the past tense. It was nearly three years since Billy had left for Russia.

Terry and Bill were gratified that their son was different and that he had achieved something in his idiosyncratic way. Their love for him was strong and uncomplicated. They couldn't understand what had happened in Russia. Billy had an inoffensive nature, they said, and no experience with weapons or war.

"He just disappeared off the face of the Earth," Terry said. "There's not one sign of anything." She said that their lives had "just stopped."

"Immediately slam on the brakes, and that's what we've been doing," Bill said. "This is our whole focus."

They had searched online for emotional support. There they'd met a couple whose son, like Billy, had been attending college in Chicago. "And he said, 'They're opening up this new rain-forest somewhere in the Caribbean somewhere,'" Bill said. "And he says, 'I'm dying to go.' And he just walked down the path. That was the end of it. It was like seven years ago." Terry and Bill understood they had joined a club whose members are miserable for belonging to it.

"The thing with this thing, Billy didn't just walk down a path," Bill added. He said his son had not been aimless and that the FBI must have played its part in his travels to a country that had made a mystery of his life. "I just always think about that crazy saying I think Churchill said, where Russia's a riddle wrapped up in an enigma. I just hate thinking that."

It was evident that Billy and Terry were made of three parts. They were devastated to be without their son. They were fearful for what had happened to him. And they had given over to the sleuth that lies within us all.

Their moods and recollections prompted the Reillys to jump forward and back along the timeline of their story. They seemed to want to share everything at once. They glossed over moments that sounded important. I encouraged them to share details in a linear fashion so that I could understand the timeline. Terry apologized. "Sometimes we move ahead because we've gone through so many different things," she said.

I asked why Billy had chosen to work with the FBI. "He really liked fighting the bad guys and kind of getting to know them and then, '*Kapow*, you're done,'" Terry said. "He was gung ho, you know. He was going to do something about the ISIS."

We discussed the Boston Marathon investigation, Aws Naser, and conversations Billy had pursued with international terror suspects on social media. It was clear that he had shared many details with his parents while keeping others in reserve. "He'd tell us what he wanted to tell us," Terry said.

"He'd almost whispered around here," Bill put in.

The Reillys shared many anecdotes of intrigue and doubt. Terry described the dinner that Billy said he had attended at an Embassy Suites hotel near the FBI office in Troy. Reintjes had been there, Terry said, along with the Russian man Billy later referred to as "the professor" and "the biologist." The Reillys described the fourth man who had been at the dinner. "Billy said the guy had been in Iraq or something, and his whole face was burned and his hands, and he said he was really kind of scared," Terry recalled. "He said he doesn't know whether he was a CIA guy or who he was with."

"Real tough guy," Bill added.

"I think Billy was thinking about working for the CIA," Terry said. "He was kind of talking about it."

Later, Terry caught herself. "I mean, I know you're not even going to believe some of the stuff I say."

They showed me a grainy picture Billy had sent from Rostov-on-Don. His head was shaven, and a man beside him had an arm across Billy's shoulder. They were grinning into the lens. Terry and Bill hadn't discovered the identity of the other man in the picture, and they remained puzzled by the cryptic nature of Billy's communications. "When I think about it now, what the hell was he telling us?" Terry asked. I saw that their inability to solve the riddle compounded their anguish.

"He said he was coming back," Bill said. "I thought he was going there, doing whatever, that humanitarian thing, and then come back and he was going to school in Chicago." Bill said he had bought a fishing cabin in Standish, 100 miles north of Oxford, off Saginaw Bay where Billy could fish for walleye. "We vinyl-sided it, the whole thing," Bill said.

As I listened to the Reillys and followed their digressions, I weighed the prospects of my own deeper involvement. Was this an article for the newspaper? The more Terry and Bill said, the more the story unspooled. I told them I could contact the FBI, the State Department, people on Capitol Hill, and others whom I knew or might access in Washington and Moscow and Kiev. I speculated about the persuasive effect the *Journal*'s interest could have on people who hadn't been forthcoming with the Reillys. "You seem just heaven-sent," Terry said. I told her that the only promise I could make was to work my hardest. "If you can't help us, I don't know where else we'll turn," she said.

It was time to confirm basic facts. Terry showed me emails she had exchanged with Reintjes so that I could see they had been in contact with one another. She handed me his business card. The number on it matched the number listed for "Tim" on the phone Billy had left behind. This confirmed for me that, on that phone, Billy had indeed been trading text messages about his Russia trip with his FBI handler. I saw nothing to suggest that the Reillys were feeding me a fabrication.

"I come up with so many different versions," Terry said. "It depends on my mood. I think something really horrible happened to him because I don't know what else it could possibly be. And other times I say, 'Hey, you know, maybe it's the CIA thing.' Things point to that, too. I just don't know."[2]

The Reillys suggested that their son had offered his counterterrorism services to the FSB and been accepted into its ranks. I conceded that anything was possible, but this theory revealed how desperate their belief had become. I didn't think that Billy possessed the level of expertise required to overcome his American origin, a decided obstacle to joining an organization as professional and cautious as the FSB. I knew that Billy's case could benefit from dispassionate observation. And I knew that Billy was an adult, responsible for his decisions. He might well have gone to Russia on his own. He might have crossed the border into Donbas and taken up arms for Russian aims.

It would be easy to fall into the profusion of information the Reillys shared. If I was going to pursue this story, I would have to learn why Billy had gone to Russia and what had happened to him there. These would be the two hardest questions to answer, yet they were the foundation of the case. Instinct told me that solving one mystery could unlock the other.

The following afternoon, I drove to Dearborn. I parked outside a stucco-and-glass fast-food restaurant, Panera Bread, a soulless convenience of the type Billy had plotted to escape. I entered the café and found a woman, thirty or so, wearing a headscarf and sitting at a table alone. It was Catie Cherri.

We talked about her brother. "Billy would meet the FBI men in this place," Catie said. She was expressionless, her voice flat. She seemed cautious. I tried to disarm her, but it wasn't easy. She said that a public revelation of Billy's FBI affiliation could cause her trouble, even now, nearly three years after her brother's disappearance.

I sought her insight into Billy's character through things he had done, people he'd known, but there wasn't much to grip. "After college, he drifted," Catie said. "He had no social connections."

She explained Billy's conversion to Islam and her parents' struggles to understand the choices their children had made. She hinted at conflict and a motive for Billy's efforts to reach out into the world. "He wanted to get out of here," she said.

Despite the family differences, Catie sounded similar to her parents when she discussed her brother. Respect and fascination surfaced in her voice. I saw that she shared many of the views that Billy had developed. She spoke against US policy in the Middle East and did not hide her revulsion at the twilight of the American compact. She said it was nearly impossible for people her age in Michigan to find jobs that were worth anything. Her long hours at a health clinic barely kept her family going, she said. To Catie, Billy had lived a life in protest of the status quo, and she regarded him in philosophical terms. "He was on a different plane than everybody else," she said.

Catie theorized about Billy's fate. She told me about the email printout she'd seen on the parlor coffee table at the house in Oxford. "Billy said it was from the Russian government and they wanted to work with him," she said. "He was pretty excited about it." I assumed the communication had been from Mikhail Polynkov or one of his associates but couldn't be sure. "Billy didn't want to waste time on things that weren't important. He really wanted to have a big adventure. He knew there'd be a risk, and he was okay with that."

Discussing Oxford, Catie said that no major interstate highways passed by it, emphasizing the town's remoteness and insularity. She sounded glad to be living elsewhere, and I detected envy of her brother's ability to make an interesting life, even though he had come to crisis. Catie appeared to be resigned to Billy's disappearance, speaking of it as though it had been preordained, even something he had sought. "Billy always wanted something bigger than our lives," she said.[3]

I left the meeting with a fuller view. Terry and Bill had blamed the FBI for Billy's disappearance, yet Catie hinted that her brother had gone his own way to Russia. I wondered if there was a middle road, if both versions could be true?

In Oxford two days later, I slipped back into conversation with Terry and Bill. They explained that Billy had wanted a salaried position with the FBI.

They said that "the men" had encouraged him, but that he had lost faith in their promises. "Several times he said, 'They're just really, you know, taking me for a chump,'" Terry said. "'I'm doing all this stuff for them and what am I getting out of it?'"

I theorized inwardly that Billy had felt an urge to prove himself, to impress his FBI handlers in order to gain their support for employment. Terry offered a similar assessment. "My opinion," she said, "which, I don't know, is that I think, you know, he volunteered to do something in Russia."

I told the Reillys that I would return to Washington and research the material to make my sense of it. They handed me a raft of documents. They shared screenshots of Terry's text conversation with Billy during his travels in Russia and the messages he had traded with Reintjes, his handler, in the ten months preceding the trip. The Reillys allowed me to copy the family PC's hard drive and the drive of a laptop Billy had used.

They provided all of this without caveat. They expressed no worry about how I might portray them or Billy in an article. They wanted their son back, and they needed help. I saw how the Reillys' trusting manner had made them vulnerable to the FBI.

Terry spoke about the first visit that agent Tim Reintjes had made to Oxford, when he had declared ignorance of Billy's presence in Russia. "How did they know he was missing?" Terry asked. "What made them think enough to come to the house?" I recognized this as the central question, uniting Billy's intent and fate. The FBI had discussed the Russia trip with him before he had gone there and had evidently later learned contemporaneously that something had befallen him. Given the matter at hand and its stakes, coincidence didn't provide an acceptable explanation for Reintjes's visit.

Daylight faded along with our theories. I had asked enough of Bill and Terry for now, and they had given me plenty to study. At the door, we said our goodbyes, and I stepped out into the cold and slanting rain. A hand gripped my arm. I turned to see Terry. She said, "We just know you're going to find Billy."[4]

CHAPTER TWENTY-SEVEN

Reticence

I acknowledged Terry's faith. From what I knew about Russia, the FBI, and the sphere of spies and intrigue, I couldn't share it.

Early in my Moscow years, I came to know a former KGB officer, Viktor Cherkashin, who had served as a senior spy in the Soviet Union's embassy in Washington. Cherkashin had handled Robert Hanssen, an FBI agent and computer specialist who secretly supplied the Soviet Union, and later Russia, with classified information over a staggering period of twenty-two years. Hanssen fed Cherkashin information about how the FBI conducted counter-intelligence, including details of a tunnel that the Bureau had dug beneath the Soviet embassy in order to listen to conversations there. The Soviet Union paid Hanssen in cash and diamonds. FBI counterintelligence agents unmasked him in 2001, and he received fifteen consecutive life sentences. He has been housed ever since at the supermax prison in Florence, Colorado, along with Boston Marathon bomber Dzhokhar Tsarnaev, underwear bomber Umar Abdulmu-tallab, and a host of terrorists, spies, turncoats, and crime-syndicate capos.[1]

Cherkashin also handled Aldrich Ames, a CIA officer who worked as a double agent for the Soviets and Russians in the 1980s and '90s. Both Ames and Hanssen provided the KGB with names of Soviet citizens who were working covertly for the United States. These disclosures allowed KGB counterintelligence to round up and execute many of these people, resulting in the near-wholesale elimination of American assets inside the Soviet Union. For years afterward, the CIA had no clear vision into the USSR.[2]

In the Soviet Union, Cherkashin was a star within a system of privilege and resolve. KGB officers occupied a high rank in Soviet life. There was pride in the organization, national purpose. There were perks: apartments, cars, vacations. But when the Soviet Union fell, that status evaporated. The nineties in Russia were the decade of the *biznesmen*, the oligarchs. The security services were no place for ambition. Some intelligence officers were happy enough to accept money from their Western counterparts, defect, and bring along their secrets. Others took their own lives rather than face demoralization or financial ruin.[3]

When Putin took office in 2000, he began to make changes. Putin himself had spent decades as an officer and administrator in the KGB and FSB. He had momentarily led the FSB months before Yeltsin stepped aside and placed Putin in his stead. Putin determined that the security services, known in Russian as the *siloviki*, would have a seat at the table.[4]

I first met Viktor Cherkashin not long after that, in 2002. Officially, he was out of the services, but he was still a man of the KGB. He hadn't defected to the West, though he'd had offers. But he still needed to earn a living. His past was his most marketable possession. Cherkashin decided to write a book. As it turned out, he and I had the same New York book agent.

The agent put us together as a writing team. I visited with Cherkashin in his Moscow home and met his family. I came to know him. He was a well-traveled, cultured man with graceful manners. His stories about Ames and Hanssen were riveting. But I found his easy charm unsettling, considering the deadly games he had played.

The publisher offered an unfavorable split, and I declined the Cherkashin project. He found another ghostwriter. Together they produced a worthy and entertaining book. It appeared with inopportune timing.

Putin had reworked a deal with the oligarchs, but it wasn't going smoothly. Businessman Mikhail Khodorkovsky had accumulated wealth through the rigged privatization acquisition of Siberian oil companies and by 2003 had become Russia's wealthiest person. He professed to have turned a page from Russia's excessive and exploitative nineties, structuring his company, Yukos, on the Fortune 500 model. This won him supporters in London, New York, and Washington who knew little of Russia or the tactics Khodorkovsky had used to gain and maintain his fortune. Khodorkovsky was no saint, but he was among the best in Russian business. He was financing Russian political parties that opposed Putin, believing that his wealth and Western business connections would protect him.

In October 2003, commandos stormed Khodorkovsky's jet when it touched down in the Siberian city of Novosibirsk. The oligarch would lose Yukos and his billions and be banished to distant penal colonies, emerging from prison a decade later a broken man.[5]

Khodorkovsky provided Putin with the object lesson he needed. Overnight, the oligarchs were tamed. This cleared the path for the *siloviki* to a portion of the country's riches. With Putin's patronage, they began to play a major role in Russia's largest industries. Hydrocarbon prices were soaring globally. Cash was flowing into Russia. The *siloviki*'s financial clout and political cover enabled them to regain the place of power in society that they had occupied in Soviet times.[6]

Despite their demoralizing nineties, the *siloviki* had never relinquished their jaundiced view of the United States. Now that they were back on their feet, they tightened their ranks and refastened their grip on state secrets. They revived a sense of national purpose within the security services and an unhealthy measure of Soviet-style paranoia in society at large. Viktor Cherkashin was caught in the midst of these changes, having misread them. By going public with his secret past, releasing his memoir in English and in the United States, Cherkashin placed himself aslant of the FSB. The FSB learned of the book too late to prevent its publication. But by pressuring Cherkashin's family, the agency prevented him from traveling to the US to promote it. It didn't matter what Cherkashin had previously achieved. His allegiance was now in question.[7]

The Cherkashin episode illustrated an important point. The 1990s had been a middle period only, a hiatus in a lasting conflict. There had effectively never been détente between the US and Russian security services. And access to sensitive material in Russia, once freely for sale, was constrained once again after Putin had solidified his power, especially if, as in the case of Billy Reilly, that information concerned the United States.

*   *   *

I had dipped into FBI cases over the years. In the course of reporting various articles, I'd met with agents in Las Vegas, Manila, Moscow, New York, Rome,

Washington, and other places. Most of them were professional, committed, and mindful of the responsibility they bore. On a few occasions, FBI agents encountered elements of my reporting and wanted to know how I had contacted certain figures in criminal worlds, similar to the Bureau's initial outreach to Billy. One agent was interested in a story I had written about a Russian tech figure whose head had been staved in, a murder in Moscow that has never been investigated.[8] These meetings were tricky, as I wouldn't divulge my sources but wanted to remain polite.

In 2010, FBI counterintelligence agents in New York made headlines when they rounded up a cluster of Russian spies they called "the Illegals." These were agents of Russia's Foreign Intelligence Service, or SVR, the inheritor of the KGB's overseas mission. Most of the Illegals had been working for years under assumed identities in the United States, harvesting intelligence from contacts in government and business. Several of these Russian spies had worked and lived undercover in the US for more than a decade. The FBI arrested the ten Illegals (their paymaster escaped via Cyprus) and exchanged them on an airport tarmac in Vienna for four people held in Russian prisons. The case later served as the inspiration for a popular US TV show, *The Americans.*[9]

The least experienced but most photogenic of the group, Anna Chapman became the face of the Illegals. In her twenties, she colored her hair red and kept fit. I met Chapman in Russia in 2010 and spent time with her over several months, gathering reporting for an article.[10] Capitalizing on her celebrity, she lent her name to various business ventures. I accompanied her on a trip to Voronezh, a city in the Russian south, where she was weighing an investment in a circus. In Moscow one evening, Chapman and I emerged from a movie premiere to a hail of paparazzi flashbulbs. The next day, a tabloid falsely identified me as her fiancé.[11]

As amusing as my acquaintance with Chapman might have been, she struck me as a clumsy operative, easy prey for FBI counterintelligence. The Bureau had observed her transmitting information from her laptop in a Manhattan coffee shop. An FBI asset working undercover had duped her in a meeting into implicitly confirming her role. It was hard to believe that the SVR had dispatched her into the FBI's ambit. Was this due to a breakdown in professionalism, the close of the Cold War weakening the Russian spy apparatus?

I later came to know Gennady Vasilenko, one of the four people Russia had exchanged in Vienna for Chapman and the other Illegals. Like Viktor Cherkashin, Vasilenko had been a KGB officer in the Soviet embassy in Washington in the 1980s. In those years, he had developed a puzzling friendship with a CIA officer, Jack Platt. In the 1980s, FBI turncoat Robert Hanssen included Vasilenko on a list of assets he shared with Cherkashin, and the KGB sidelined Vasilenko. In 2005, he wound up in Russian prison on a dubious weapons charge. He languished there for five years. When the United States was searching for people in Russian custody to trade for the Illegals, Vasilenko's old CIA friend, Jack Platt, succeeded in including his name on the list. Following the Vienna swap, Vasilenko settled in Virginia on a rural spread outside Washington. He built a Russian-style sauna at his home, and he and I later took long sweats there. He said he missed Russia but accepted that Virginia was better than prison.[12]

Speaking with Vasilenko, Chapman, Cherkashin, and other spies and former spies in Russia and the US, I learned about their powerlessness. At one time, they were endowed with special license. Later used and sidelined, joined in similar fates, they harbored resentments. It was not a surprise to me that agencies prevailed while individuals withered, though this was an education. The instinct to self-regard was a characteristic all agencies shared, including the FBI.

In 2010, I visited the FBI's New York field office on Lower Broadway in Manhattan. I met with the case agents who had identified, surveilled, and captured the Russian Illegals. The agents were eager to describe their success.

I returned to the FBI's main New York office five years later to discuss another agency coup. FIFA, global soccer's Zurich-based governing body, was a den of bribery, fraud, and kickbacks, yet police and governments in Europe and beyond showed little enthusiasm to investigate it. Two New York FBI agents assigned to combat Eurasian organized crime learned from sources that Russia might have bribed FIFA officials to gain the right to host the 2018 World Cup. This enlightened the agents to FIFA's problems, and they launched a sweeping investigation that toppled FIFA's leadership. As with the Illegals case, I found the FBI eager to publicize an investigation that resulted in high-profile convictions and burnished the Bureau's image.[13]

In 2015, with the FBI taking a bow over the FIFA case, another investigation, in Las Vegas, was wounding the Bureau's credibility. The previous summer, the

FBI had been investigating a Malaysian man, Paul Phua, whom it suspected of running an illegal sports-betting operation in the Caesars Palace hotel. Phua was a major gambling figure with suspected Chinese underworld ties and was known as the world's biggest bookmaker. The FBI appeared to have caught him red-handed, but a judge tossed the case on a technicality. Agents had lied on a search-warrant petition.[14]

I wrote about the Phua case, but this time without the FBI's participation. If FBI agents wanted something from you, they could be charming, but they usually stonewalled you when things didn't go their way. For the FBI, the Billy Reilly affair, like the Paul Phua case before it, could generate only negative publicity. My brief and intermittent engagement with the Bureau suggested that agents wouldn't be forthcoming about Billy.

That year, 2015, I was padding out my knowledge of the FBI. In the spring, I took a train from New York to Washington. At the intersection of Pennsylvania and H Streets stood the headquarters of the International Monetary Fund and also the World Bank. Along a third side of the square were the offices of Wilmer Hale, an influential law firm. I took an elevator to an upper floor and followed a secretary into an office. Rising from behind a desk and extending his hand was Robert Mueller, the former FBI director.

Mueller was an interesting study. He had attended privileged schools, St. Paul's School and Princeton, though his family had not been particularly wealthy. Unlike most of the people he knew from these schools, Mueller joined the Marines and fought in the Vietnam War. He returned to the United States a decorated combat officer and picked up a law degree. He didn't chase corporate wealth but instead pursued justice for the victims of violent crime. Mueller became a federal prosecutor. He was known to be no-nonsense.[15]

Mueller had retired from the FBI a year and a half earlier. It would be another two years before he would accept the job of special counsel and oversee the investigation into alleged ties between Trump and the Russian government.

Mueller and I preferred to discuss the past.[16] He told me about his experience on September 11, 2001. He had been attending a briefing that morning in an FBI conference room when agents informed him of the first World Trade Center strike. Later, in an underground situation room, he received word that a hijacked plane was heading toward Washington.

"What I remember is sitting there thinking, *What's the target?*" he said. "*Is*

189

it going to be the White House? Is it going to be Congress? FBI? What about my wife?" At the time, Mueller had been FBI director for only a week.

He described his first post-9/11 briefing in the Oval Office at the White House with President George W. Bush. "I prepared and started off by saying things like, 'Mr. President, we've got command posts at each of the incident sites and we're starting to identify the individuals.'"

Mueller said that Bush had replied, "That's all well and good, but my question to you today is what is the Bureau doing to prevent the next terrorist attack?"

"I'd always been used to investigating after the fact," Mueller continued. "Having that question put to me stood me up in my tracks. And that's a question that he asked just about every day I briefed him. With President Obama, it's been the same. The same question: 'What's the Bureau doing to stop the next terrorist attack?'"

Even after more than a dozen years since 9/11, the attacks were nearly all Mueller and I talked about. They had changed our world. They had changed the FBI. In the attacks' aftermath, it had been up to Mueller, not those who might later criticize him, to be decisive. His dilemma was clear to me. Mueller was a lawyer and a former prosecutor, bound by law. But the circumstances after 9/11 forced him to stake out extrajudicial territory.[17]

"It was understanding that you didn't focus on whether something was admissible in a courtroom in terms of grasping a particular fact, but putting together all pieces of information to put together a mosaic of what is happening and what might happen in the future," Mueller said. "The usual metrics of the arrests, indictments, and convictions are inadequate, and the question has to be: What is the threat? What do we know about the threat? What specifically do we not know about the threat? Then go out and fill in that gap."

Mueller would oversee the FBI's fundamental change, with the Bureau beginning to look beyond the courtroom. "As you're developing intelligence," Mueller told me, "you're out of the criminal justice superstructure."[18]

The date of my talk with Robert Mueller was March 24, 2015. As we sat in his Wilmer Hale office, I hadn't yet heard the name Billy Reilly. Billy was in Oxford and within two months would embark on the trip to Russia.

Mueller's comment about how the FBI had begun working beyond "the criminal justice superstructure" had implications for Billy and my chances of learning what had happened to him. The FBI was an institution of regulations, but Mueller suggested that those regulations, after 9/11, had blurred. Billy's FBI handlers could be beyond reproach or oversight. If they were, then my experiences with previous FBI cases suggested that I'd never learn much about how they had directed him.

And even though I knew Russia and had contacts there, I remembered the lesson of Viktor Cherkashin, Vladimir Putin, the spies, and the *siloviki*. If Russia had swallowed up an American, one connected with the FBI, the security services would make it nearly impossible to find him.

Despite these long odds, I believed I had to try. I had questions about the FBI's handling of the case, and I'd seen firsthand how desperate the Reillys were. Journalism, at its best, performs a public service. The idea of walking away from the Reillys felt like professional negligence. I decided to take on their story.

CHAPTER TWENTY-EIGHT

Quest

I sought to understand Billy. I thought that greater than the sum of the case's date-and-place parts were Billy's various shades. At different ages, we are different people. Our needs change, and we seek to fulfill them.

I considered the role that age plays in the choices we make. Billy was twenty-three years old when he started with the FBI, twenty-eight when he left for Russia. I remembered how desperate I had sometimes felt between twenty-three and twenty-eight, and how I had also gambled in those years.

When I was twenty-three, I was living in New York and working at a magazine as a fact-checker. I found the work stimulating. The editors at the magazine promoted me. I wrote my first article. I tore out that page from the magazine and slid it into a portfolio book I scrounged from the mailroom.

I ran errands for the established writers who wrote our difficult stories. I picked up their reporting techniques and a few of their vices. The editors let me write again and this time a little longer. Hunter S. Thompson visited the office one afternoon holding a glass of Chivas and smoking from a cigarette holder. At the Christmas party in the Flatiron, my boss slung his arm across my shoulder and said I'd have all kinds of opportunities. I was on my way. By thirty, I'd have a job as an editor and write on the side, pick up a book deal, make it to the publishing parties. Convenient visions, but I wouldn't realize them. I would derail my own progress.

And it was for no rational reason. As I turned twenty-four, a sensation stirred within me. A reckless idea, a call to action.

Quest

The professional path I had staked out began to seem overly conventional. I developed the impression that working in an office was the way to conformity of thought. Those were sincere days, and the notebook I carried proved it. I scrawled my thoughts across its pages, working out my ideas. The urge I felt intensified, becoming too powerful to control.

I consulted experienced colleagues. They gave sensible advice: stick with the job, advance within it. I didn't listen to them. My urge was pushing me to reach beyond what was sensible. I wanted to do something bold. I quit the job.

I decided to face down the world, and Africa came to mind. This felt like a quest. Its goals would emerge. I thought of Peter Beard's beetles, of *Green Hills of Africa*, my own poor versions of what other people had achieved. My original ideas would come. When I booked a flight to Cape Town, it felt like an artistic expression.

I leaped up the stairs from Houston Street three at a time, my notebook bulging from my back pocket, as though its script and stanzas had swollen its pages. I returned to my single room with its view on the rainy gray plaza, feeling wildly alive at the decision I'd made. I was making a break. I was answering the urge within me, not shrinking from it, not letting it idle and die. I was twenty-four, and life was electric with meaning.

My friends from the magazine regarded me as though I'd lost hold. I was no longer doing what they were doing. I had breached their structure. I shared drinks with them, ducking in and out of the rain and into the bars, and I could see it. I was a dreamer to them, damp and reckless. In time, they no longer invited me. I'd thought I would miss them.

*   *   *

In the Eastern Cape, I bunked with an Afrikaner family. The father said hateful things about black people while insisting he wasn't "a racialist," and at first light I was gone. I rented a car and drove the Garden Route through fields alight with flames. I picked up hitchhikers and set them down. At a right-hand wheel for the first time, I turned toward an oncoming truck, nearly paying the ultimate price for a simple mistake. I took a room in a flophouse in Durban and lay awake amid the night's groaning. I moved on, kept going, headed north, took trains.

In Harare, Zimbabwe, I was an ethnic minority, a new experience. A toddler shrieked at me, as though he'd seen a ghost, and ran into his mother's arms. I went to nightclubs and walked the streets and sat for hours in cafés. People stared, probing for my story. People seeking money trailed me, and down an alleyway at night one confronted me and I managed to smooth talk my way out of it.

I made a local friend, William. His intentions were unclear, and it was pointless to inquire. I had placed myself there, in Africa, seeking adventure. I let go so it would have no trouble finding me.

Late one night, William directed a cab out of the city, a half hour beyond the streetlights. He pointed the driver to the side of the road, stepped out of the car, and walked into the night. I waited in the back seat, and the driver panicked, saying this was no place to be. He swung the wheel toward town when William reappeared from the darkness. He had a woman on each arm, presumably one for me.

Another train, a new direction. One could still make out the faded etchings on the glass in the cabins, the interlinked Rs of the Rhodesia Railways. The train derailed at night. We humped our gear along the tracks through the tall grass in the dark.

At Victoria Falls, I miscalculated. It had seemed like tourist-brochure escapism until our raft capsized on the Zambezi River. Below the surface, someone's boot kicked me in the head. When I came up for air, the raft was fifty yards distant and trailing away from me. On the near bank, crocodiles slipped into the water.

I shared a fried chicken on the train with two men from Marseille, their beards raggedy from the road. Together, we camped for days in the Okavango Delta. We walked the lion's grass when the sun was high and edged up on rhino and Cape buffalo, the monkeys shrieked warnings from the trees. One night, with the Frenchmen and our guides asleep in the tents, I stared into the fire, its crackling the only sound on the savanna. I savored the choice I'd made and how far it had taken me. The guys at the magazine in New York were just leaving the office, trying to think of something to do. A lion roared no more than fifteen feet away from me, in the darkness beyond the fire.

I had close calls in Africa. I was an easy mark, a novice in the world. Like Billy, I took risks and was unable to calculate them, though I managed to make it through. We've all courted danger. We've all made choices that led us beyond our control. We've all been caught out in the rain.

CHAPTER TWENTY-NINE

Easy Mark

In 2018, having returned to Washington from Detroit, I unpacked the materials the Reillys had given me. My attention fell to the text-message correspondence between Terry and Billy, which I read in screenshots Terry had taken on her phone.

In May and June 2015, while Billy had been in Russia, mother and son had exchanged roughly 3,000 messages. Most of them were conventional, relaying family gossip, news from Michigan, details about meals and moods and sleep habits. The only pattern I could discern was Terry's insistence that Billy consider returning home. She began writing such messages as soon as he had arrived in Russia. Billy would routinely put her off, writing that his departure date remained unclear.

One message caught my attention. On June 14, 2015, ten days before Billy's last phone call, Terry had written to him: "I need to talk to you. Kind of something that scares me."[1]

This immediacy stood out from the rest of their correspondence. The resumed calm of the ensuing messages suggested that Billy had called his mother in the interim and resolved her concern. I phoned Terry and asked if she recalled what had frightened her. She said it had been the credit cards.

During my initial visit to the Reillys' home, Terry and Bill had explained that Billy had run out of cash while he was in Russia and that they had wired him money several times. A relatively inexperienced international traveler, Billy had made inadequate financial preparations for his trip. He hadn't brought enough cash with him. Nevertheless, Terry and Bill told me that Billy had brought credit cards. I didn't understand why he wasn't using them. Most businesses in Rostov-on-Don, linked to international payment systems, would have accepted them.

Terry told me she had become frightened when Billy's credit-card bills had arrived at the house in Oxford in mid-June 2015. After she emailed me the bills, I saw that on May 20, 2015, while Billy was on his Volga sojourn in Balakovo, a small city on the left bank of the river 350 miles north of Volgograd, he had made three charges to his Citibank card. Two purchases at a phone store totaled 33,918 rubles, or $676.83 at the existing exchange rate. The third charge, for 11,380 rubles, or $226.83, came at a shop selling video equipment. The purchases totaled nearly a thousand dollars in a single afternoon. Such free spending was uncharacteristic of Billy, and it signaled outside influence.[2]

*   *   *

I would much later discover clues to this influence in a database of private messages from the VKontakte social network. A group of hackers based in Odessa, in Ukraine, and calling themselves RUH8 had compromised the VKontakte accounts of scores of people active on the separatist side in Donbas. Within the database, I discovered a man named Andrey Demchuk.

Demchuk went by the call sign Pirate, which was fitting, since he had served in the Russian navy, expressly in the marines, two years as a radar man out of Sevastopol, on Crimea's western coast.[3]

Since the fall of the Soviet Union, Russia had annually paid $97 million in rent to Ukraine for the use of the Sevastopol naval base. It was an arrangement that Russia found degrading though indispensable, for Sevastopol had been the home of the Soviet Union's Black Sea Fleet, and before that of the Russian Empire's reaching back to the eighteenth century. Without Sevastopol, Russia would be locked out of the Black Sea and consequently the Mediterranean, which was incompatible with Russia's conception of its national security. For Ukraine, the agreement was lumped into the calculations of the larger, challenging relationship with its neighbor. It was unrealistic at the time that Kiev, with its unproven army and negligible navy, could dislodge the Russian fleet from Crimea, even if it considered doing so.[4]

For more than twenty years, Russian officials had decried the errors of fate that had left Crimea, a peninsula of strategic importance and high-cliff sea views, in Ukrainian hands. Nikita Khrushchev, a southern Russian whose path to the Soviet premiership began in Donetsk communist circles, assigned Crimea to the Ukrainian Soviet Socialist Republic, a constituent part of the Soviet Union, in 1954. At the time an administrative formality, this decision turned profound thirty-seven years later, when the union dissolved and the peninsula became inaccessible to Russia but for the naval-base lease.[5]

In the Russian consciousness, history had granted Moscow the Crimean title. A more complete view showed that Russians had controlled Crimea for only a recent portion of its human settlement. Greeks had predominated on the peninsula, and Ruthenians had controlled it, and Armenians and Genoese had lived there, and they had given way to Ottomans. Russia had captured Crimea in the eighteenth-century Russo–Turkish War. This event, viewed through a Russian chauvinistic lens, was distant enough to appear as the beginning of time. The Ottomans had effectively signed over the peninsula a year before the Battle of Bunker Hill.[6] Yet history provides no indelible deed.

Sevastopol was the site of one of Russia's most glorified battles. It was the signature clash in a later conflict, a vain defense of the seaward fort from joint English, French, and Ottoman siege in the Crimean War. This was a signal event of the mid-modern period, galvanizing Russian identity in the 1850s. Russia would lose Sevastopol yet retain Crimea. Generations of Russian, then Soviet, schoolchildren would be weaned on *The Sevastopol Sketches*, Leo Tolstoy's 1855, near-contemporaneous fictional account of his experiences in uniform at the siege, published when he was twenty-seven years old.[7]

Andrey Demchuk, the man I located on the hacked VKontakte database, served in Sevastopol as a young marine, mustering out of the service in 2007 and withdrawing to his Volga River hometown of Ulyanovsk. He married and had a daughter and hired himself out as a clown and singer for parties, but civilian life lacked grandeur. In 2014, Demchuk looked on as the Russo–Ukrainian divergence exploded into conflict in a place he knew well. Demchuk missed Crimea, and the uniform.[8]

As Billy would later do, Demchuk contacted Mikhail Polynkov, the volunteer-fighter recruiter, via VKontakte and found his way to the Rostov-on-Don base. From there, Demchuk crossed into Donbas and joined the war.[9]

Demchuk's service ran from 2014 and into the spring of the following year, when he recrossed the border to the Rostov camp as Billy Reilly was making his curious arrival there. A year younger and a head taller than Billy, Demchuk resembled the countless insurgents Billy had known in digital form on his screens in Oxford. Close to Billy's age and already a veteran of conflict, Demchuk possessed what Billy coveted, a secret knowledge, a daring aura, a war of his own. Two days after Billy arrived in Rostov, he and Demchuk boarded a train heading north.

This was the start of Billy's Volga sojourn, which had mystified his parents. I was beginning to fill in the gaps of his 2015 text messages home to his mother.

Another man joined Billy and Demchuk. Andrey Kisilev had also been a Russian marine. He and Demchuk had grown up together in Ulyanovsk.[10] They could have been brothers, each with Slavic features and hair styled short. They looked like any pair of unassuming young men from any Midwestern American town, except for the knowledge of war they held within them.

Billy's chaperones confessed poverty, prevailing upon him to finance their trip. They pledged that Polynkov would make Billy financially whole once they had concluded their travels and returned to Rostov. Far from home and making new pals, Billy put up no fuss. Adventure had its costs. Billy bunked with Demchuk. They visited neighboring cities. It was Demchuk and Kisilev who snapped the photos of Billy at the Stalingrad memorial that he had sent home to his mother.[11]

Billy talked increasingly with his travel companions about Donbas. He might have understood the dynamics between the political and paramilitary factions there, having soaked up open-source information, but Demchuk had a visceral sense of the situation. He knew people in Donbas, had fought on its terrain. US intelligence agencies were playing catch-up, struggling to penetrate Russian networks on either side of the border. Any sort of human intelligence at this stage held possible value, hinting at Billy's possible purpose.

As Billy concluded his Volga travels, Mikhail Polynkov, the volunteer-fighter recruiter, learned of the purchases made on the American's credit cards. On May 31, 2015, Polynkov wrote to Demchuk over VKontakte. "What's this shit with Vasya?" Polynkov asked, using Billy's Russian pseudonym. "Why the fuck did you clean him out?"

Polynkov wrote again a few minutes later: "Do you realize what benefit his money would bring to the unit?"

As I read these messages sent years ago, they remained visceral and alive. They provided a possible subtext that underpinned Billy's fate.

Billy and Demchuk had returned to the Rostov base when Demchuk replied to Polynkov. "As to cleaning him out," Demchuk wrote, "he and I have an agreement." Demchuk explained that he would be leaving soon for Donetsk. "When I get there, I'll give it back."

Polynkov inventoried his expectations: "700 dollars. 11 thousand rubles, a credit card. Money for two iPhones." These figures closely corresponded to the amounts on Billy's credit-card bills that had alarmed Terry Reilly. "He's got nothing left," Polynkov wrote. "Don't you think it's overkill?"[12]

The VKontakte messages and the credit-card charges made it plain: Polynkov and his associates had taken Billy for an easy mark. I had to consider that a simple, typical motive, money, explained Billy's disappearance.

The Rostov volunteer-fighter base was expensive to run. Moscow had funded its establishment and early operations.[13] But once the dream of Novorossiya faded and Igor Strelkov fell from favor, removed from his post as DNR Defense Minister and recalled to Moscow, fiscal conditions at the Rostov camp worsened. The camp's finances were stressed, managed by men who handled a rifle more cleverly than they did a ledger.[14]

The morning after Polynkov's exchange with Demchuk, on the first day of June 2015, Polynkov received a VKontakte message from Bronya Kalmyk, the man who managed the day-to-day operations of the camp.

The message contained an inventory of food and household items for the camp: chicken legs, soap, coffee, and forty additional sundries that fortified the volunteer fighters along their transit to Donbas. The largest line item, nearly double the second-costliest entry, was cigarettes, with a monthly allocation of 31,200 rubles, or roughly $400 at the existing rate. The monthly sum, as Bronya calculated it, came to 110,000 rubles, or about $1,500, a considerable amount for these people in Russia who had no jobs or steady, honest income.

"This is for a month???" Polynkov responded. "What the fuck. Gotta figure this out."

Later in 2015, Bronya wrote Polynkov to say that "there's no money even for bread."

"I would mothball the base," Polynkov responded. "No fucking money. I'm already overdue on my rent by almost two weeks."[15]

Like others at the Rostov camp, Billy was ignorant of these financial difficulties. On June 3, 2015, he contacted Polynkov. "I don't know what's happening," Billy wrote. "I paid for the trip to Balakovo and Ulyanovsk and two iPhones for Pirate and a video camera. Pirate said that you said that I had to pay and that he would repay me the money."

"I gave Pirate no such orders," Polynkov replied. "To put it bluntly, he's deceived you."[16]

Theft had become a way of life at the base. Bronya Kalmyk often persuaded arrivals to stow cash and gear for safekeeping in a base locker. When these volunteers returned from a tour fighting in Donbas, they would often find their money and possessions diminished or gone, with Bronya offering only a shrug. "Walkie-talkies, GoPro camera, bulletproof vest, bulletproof helmet, first aid kits, folding saw, tactical neckerchief, a hair clipper, a calimator sight and a rail for its attachment, binoculars," one fighter wrote on VKontakte about the base. "In general, they stole everything of value."

Billy had brought no such items to the camp, but he unwittingly contributed his share of resources. Three days after he contacted Polynkov about his purchases, Billy fell victim to ATM fraud. On June 6, four ATM cash-advance withdrawals were made using his Chase credit card, for 4,769 rubles each. The total was 19,076 rubles, or $356.12. On the next morning and over the following four days, a total of ten ATM cash-advance withdrawals appeared on Billy's Citibank account, for a sum of $869.27.[17]

This was not the end of the schemes. In calls with Terry, Billy mentioned his receipt of a press pass. Bronya had suggested that Billy join a humanitarian convoy as a videographer and explained that he would need to pay for media accreditation, though no relevant accrediting body required such a fee.

On June 8, Billy wrote to Polynkov: "Bronya said that I need to pay 14,500 rubles [roughly $250] for a press pass. Yes?"

"You probably need to pay," Polynkov replied.

It was clear that Billy was being maneuvered. Over the years, he had amassed great knowledge of Russia and other countries, but he had little hands-on feel for the world and its gray shades. He was still, in part, the young man at home in his bedroom, his face lit by the glow of his cellphone screen, thrilling to faraway adventures. Now that adventure was his, he was paying its price.

Few lessons are free, and it's through such episodes that we learn. Although it took them several weeks, Billy and his mother finally accepted the fact that the men who ran the Rostov base were taking him for a ride. On several phone calls in mid-June 2015, Billy and Terry jointly inspected the Chase and Citibank bills, inventorying purchases and withdrawals that Billy realized he hadn't made. The total came to $2,129.05. This was a healthy sum to Billy, on the road in a foreign country, and also to those who were pulling his cash out of ATMs in Rostov.[18]

Terry and Billy were combing through bills and flagging charges and withdrawals even on June 24, the day of their final phone call. By this time, Terry, with Billy's acquiescence, had canceled his cards and begun wiring him cash. The cards were useless. In a way so was Billy, no longer a source of easy funding for the intrigues Polynkov and his group continued to formulate.

CHAPTER THIRTY

Conspiracy

I n addition to the messages she had traded with Billy, Terry had supplied me her son's text-message correspondence with agent Tim Reintjes. This was the exchange that revealed the FBI's foreknowledge of Billy's Russia trip. At my desk at the *Journal*, I began reading.

The collection of messages between Billy and Reintjes was voluminous. Over more than 300 days between the start and end of this conversation, the two traded nearly 1,300 texts. This was in addition to their phone calls and meetings, which appeared to have been frequent. This confirmed for me that their relationship had not been fly-by-night. They had maintained close and consistent contact. In the texts, Billy was responsive, resourceful, and accountable, for Reintjes a trusted counterterrorism partner. This proved for me that Billy was indeed a bona fide CHS.

I searched for signs of the alienation that Terry and Bill said their son had begun to feel in the latter stages of his relationship with the FBI. Reintjes and Billy traded operational chatter about cell phones, computer systems, communications applications, and the ways Billy applied them in his Bureau work. They frequently discussed Billy's file uploads via Dropbox and meetings at establishments such as Wendy's and Home Depot. Reintjes sometimes directed Billy to bring his iPod to the appointments, since Billy used the device to record calls with counterterrorism targets. In all of this back-and-forth, I found no evidence of a souring relationship.[1]

I looked instead for proof that the FBI had sent Billy to Russia. Reintjes had been careless in leaving behind text messages revealing his knowledge of Billy's trip. Maybe additional corroboration was threaded through the correspondence.

I couldn't find it. It wasn't there. The substance of their communications concerned Islamic fundamentalist terror almost exclusively. There was very little in the texts about Eastern Europe.

Terry had also given me hard drives from two computers Billy had used, a laptop and the family PC. Only one file out of the thousand or so documents on these drives discussed Russia or Donbas in any depth. It was labeled "DPR," and it provided an analysis of the so-called Donetsk People's Republic.

"Their ideology is a mix of Soviet nostalgia, anti-Western social conservatism and Russian Orthodoxy and Russian nationalism," Billy wrote. He discussed the separatists' usage of Grad rockets and Kornet anti-tank weapons. "They seem like quite a functional military unit. It seems they attract a lot of ex-military men, in many of their videos their soldiers seem like they are professionals—rather than just guys who picked up guns (contrary to what was seen at the start of the Syrian conflict)."

Billy's analysis of the Donbas brigades was sound, as his CHS reports customarily were. Besides this single file, there was little related to Russia on the hard drives, no FBI clues hinting at why Billy had ended up there.

*   *   *

In my search for indications that the FBI had sent Billy abroad, I returned to Michigan in April 2018. I understood Billy's digital skills but wanted to know if his performance in the real world had influenced his handler's notion of what this "keyboard commando" could manage.

I flew to Muskegon, on Michigan's western border, along the shore of Lake Michigan. A guard at a federal lock-up there, the Earnest C. Brooks Correctional Facility, escorted me through several metal gates and into the prison yard. It was a temperate mid-spring morning. Dozens of inmates were pumping weights or sitting around picnic tables in the sun. They eyed me as I followed the guard into a dormitory.

Two hallways of bedrooms extended from a whitewashed common area. The guard led me to a glassed-in room that contained a bookcase with dozens of worn volumes and magazines. Sitting at a table was Aws Naser, the Iraqi-American whom Billy had approached for the FBI in 2012.[2]

Naser, thirty, was a small man with fine features. We had been speaking about his case by phone and email, but I hadn't yet mentioned Billy, unsure who else might have been listening to our conversations. I had brought a folder with me to the prison, and I pulled a photo of Billy from it. Naser's eyes lit up. "That's Mikhail," he said, recalling the alias Billy had used.

Naser described their initial contact over YouTube, their first meeting, and Billy's attempts to draw out Naser through discussions of Islam. "From the first impression, he doesn't know anything," Naser said. "I could already see he had ill intentions. I know I'm being catfished." Naser explained how he had taken the wheel of Billy's car in their second meeting and led the FBI tail on a chase down Warren Road in Westland. Naser said that during this ride Billy "was trying to crawl out of his own skin."

Naser and I spoke for several hours, but a few words were all it took to rid me of illusions. Billy, an advanced operator on social media, fooled no one in the field. In person, he was unable to relax in a lie, to fake his identity.[3] This was something in his favor. But since Billy couldn't operate convincingly in his own language and surroundings, it was difficult to imagine his FBI handlers sending him to Russia, which was perhaps the most challenging theater for US intelligence operators. The FSB had inherited the KGB's accomplished counterintelligence division, and Russia's security services were on alert following the seizure of Crimea and fomentation of war in Donbas.[4] What could the FBI or another US agency have hoped to gain by dispatching Billy into such hazards, given that he had wilted in the field with Naser?

I returned to the text messages between Billy and Reintjes. Perhaps there was evidence not that the FBI had sent Billy to Russia, but the opposite, that a break in the relationship had led Billy astray. I discovered talk of the bombing plots that Terry and Bill said had finally fractured their son's link with the Bureau. On December 9, 2014, six months before Billy would leave for Russia, he messaged Reintjes about a conversation he was having with a counterterrorism target: "She saying I should do suicide bomb here."

"Ask how she would plan it and fund," Reintjes replied.

"I think she means like the one in Canada. Just like running people over or shooting by my self."

In October that year, an ISIS supporter in Quebec had driven his car over two Canadian soldiers, killing one of them.[5] Two days later, a man from Montreal had fatally shot a sentry at the Canadian National War Memorial in Ottawa, then died in a shootout with guards inside the nearby Parliament building.[6]

"She needs to direct you," Reintjes cautioned. "Don't infer."

Two days later, Billy texted: "Msg just said 'I know u can do it' about the op...Let me know what I should do if she goes on to say I should do op on my own here like something small like Ottawa."

"Say I still need direction, guidance and money," Reintjes advised.

Billy told Reintjes that his contact had received permission for Billy to conduct a major operation, suggesting that a foreign terror group was attempting to operate him.

These messages didn't prove that Billy and the FBI were growing apart. In fact, they seemed standard, the handler guiding the CHS through conversations with terror nodes in an effort to collect intelligence. But Bill and Terry said that their son had taken these exchanges with Reintjes as a threat to his safety. I didn't see it.

What I did see was that after these late-2014 bombing-plot discussions, the frequency of Billy's correspondence with Reintjes decreased markedly. Into the spring of 2015, the two continued to meet in person, but their messages drained of substance, with Billy providing token replies to his handler's queries.

I found a file on Billy's hard drives that suggested he'd made a break. In January 2015, he had downloaded a Russian-language volunteer-fighter questionnaire. This was a boilerplate form that Mikhail Polynkov's group required recruits to complete. The document asked about a person's combat experience, religion, debts, criminal record, motivation, and facility with weapons. Neither Billy nor Reintjes mentioned the questionnaire in their text conversation. They didn't discuss Polynkov or mercenaries in Donbas. It appeared that Billy had taken this step alone.[7]

On March 10, 2015, Billy sent his first VKontakte message to Polynkov. Billy failed to reference this contact in the texts with his FBI handler. I sensed that Billy was edging away from the FBI, drawn into the orbit of Russia's volunteer fighters.[8]

*　　*　　*

Billy's texts with agent Reintjes were leavened with contradictions. Once I thought I understood their relationship, I'd read an exchange that turned everything on its head.

In a November 2014 text, Billy mentioned traveling to Syria, a trip he had discussed with a terror target. The next day, Billy received a Turkish visa.[9, 10]

This suggested a path common for ISIS recruits, a trip to Turkey and an illegal crossing into Syria. It was the very route that Daniela Greene, the German-speaking FBI translator, had taken when she had defected from the Bureau's Detroit office to marry the German rapper Deso Dogg. To me, Billy's visa proved that he intended to travel to Turkey.

There was more. On one of Billy's drives, a 2013 document summarized a Skype conversation with a terror target. "He asked me what is going on about going to Syria," Billy wrote. He mentioned flying to Istanbul, making his way to Antalya, and meeting a chaperone for the Syrian border crossing into ISIS territory. "I told him I had problems getting a visa, and maybe I can try with a Russian passport or try to go via aid convoy."[11]

An aid convoy. This caught my attention. It was the very reasoning for going to Russia that Billy would give his parents in 2015: joining a humanitarian aid convoy crossing into Donbas. Volunteering to assist an aid convoy was a tactic that a US asset like Billy might use to enter restricted areas.

These discoveries altered my views about Billy, his late-stage FBI relationship, and his trip to Russia. His inadequacies in the Naser case should have sidelined him from hazardous fieldwork. But the material on Billy's hard drives and in the Reintjes messages showed that the FBI or another agency had indeed considered international operations for Billy. A US agency might well have sent Billy to Russia, since there was evidence of previous thought of sending him to Turkey. Dealing with volunteer fighters on the way to the front lines in Donbas was no simpler than getting mixed up with migrations to ISIS.

I still believed that this was improbable, but I myself was continuing to learn what the FBI, or other agencies, would and wouldn't do. It was possible that Billy hadn't been withdrawing from the FBI after all.

I resisted the urge to assume. However, the notion that Billy had taken a private trip to Russia didn't appear to align with the text messages he had traded with Reintjes in the days before his departure, nor with the handler's later visits to Oxford. Reintjes's deceptions and the timing of his initial visit to the Reillys' home cast the FBI's behavior in doubt. If Billy had traveled to Russia on his own and been beyond the FBI's sight there, how did Reintjes know that something had happened to him, thereby causing the home visit? And if Reintjes didn't know that Billy was living among Russian mercenaries, why had he asked the Reillys which side Billy was on?

Taken together, the Turkish visa, discussions about travel, the talk of aid convoys, and Reintjes's actions in 2015 hinted at a resolution of the central question: Did the FBI send Billy to Russia, or did Billy go there on a quest of self-realization?

I knew who had the answer.

*   *   *

Tim Reintjes wasn't my adversary. He had wanted to be an FBI agent since he'd been in high school. He had openly talked about it with friends and teachers for years. I imagined he had been inclined to altruism, motivated to protect the weak. He performed a vital role, and I valued it.

I phoned the FBI's Detroit office. The receptionist patched the call through. Tim Reintjes picked up the phone and identified himself. I said hello, and he returned my greeting. He was direct and professional. I explained that I was looking into a matter related to William Reilly, who had worked for Reintjes as a CHS.

I paused, listening for an indication that the topic of this unsolicited outreach affected Reintjes. He said nothing.

I said that I understood that Billy had disappeared and that his parents were searching for him. Reintjes's voice was calm. "I'm not familiar with any inquiries," he said.[12]

CHAPTER THIRTY-ONE

A Dangerous Challenge

From the moment I learned of Billy's interest in Amera Lomangcolob, their relationship had suggested an alternate narrative. Had she been exciting his mind with explicit promises and photos, or had he been luring her under directive from the FBI? Had the two ultimately met one another?

As I read through the texts that Billy and his mother shared in debating and arranging his Bangkok side trip to see Lomangcolob, I saw that they were written in many shades. As Billy's frustrations mounted over delays at the Rostov base, threatening his trip to Thailand, he wavered in his commitment to it. Terry employed what tricks remained to her.

"Don't forget you can always change your mind," she texted Billy in mid-June 2015. "You've already done one off the wall nutty trip already."

"Ill keep that in mind," Billy replied.

"Just let me know and I'll have that home ticket booked."

Terry asked Billy days later if he was "still doing the creep side trip?"

"I dont now about side trip, she's really bad," Billy wrote, "shes having a schizophrenic day again."

"It really does sound dangerous. Not kidding. You really could be killed. What is she saying?"

"Crazy talking," Billy replied, "she said id leave her there and hate and things like that. Worse than yesterday. Yeah. Like when sending her back, she might go crazy." It appeared that Lomangcolob feared Billy would leave her behind in Bangkok after returning to Detroit.

"I'm glad you changed your mind," Terry wrote. "I think something bad would have happened." As much as Terry tried to guide Billy home, his desires remained fluid.

"Maybe delay that," Billy wrote, "while i see what to do with her."

"Oh no what now. Not a good idea. Just tell her your sick. She seems to be a manipulator."

"Ill think about it. Sort of a dangerous challenge."

What was Billy planning to do with Lomangcolob? On his hard drive, I had discovered the pictures Lomangcolob had taken of unwitting Westerners in the Filipino shopping mall. And I remembered the talk of Billy staging a Detroit terror attack. I hadn't met Billy and couldn't gauge what he was capable of doing. Neither, it seemed, could Terry.

"I think you have gone completely out of your mind," she texted him in June 2015.

"Maybe," he replied.

In the second half of June, Billy reached a crossroads. With the date of his flight to Bangkok approaching, he faced a choice between waiting for his adventure to materialize over the Ukrainian border and chasing desire in the Far East. The options were equally unappealing to Terry, but the side trip seemed to her more perilous as Billy continued to surface it. "I think you have gone completely wacky," Terry wrote.

"Adventure," he wrote.

"No adventure of your throats slashed. Please reconsider. This really scares me."

"That's the best part of adventure."

"You need to think it through more," Terry reasoned with him.

"I will think about it," he replied.

"She's crazy," Terry wrote. "You can't rationalize with her."

Billy had already aborted one trip to Asia to see Lomangcolob. Would he have the courage to follow through now? "Adventure is one thing," Terry texted, "but this sounds like suicide."[1]

*　　*　　*

By the summer of 2018, I had been working the Reilly case for six months. That's how long it had taken me to piece together an understanding of events from the research materials. I felt my knowledge solidifying but needed to know more. There were fundamental questions I couldn't answer in Washington. The case's many threads led to Russia, and I knew I would have to go there.

First, I took a train to New York. I met a contact of Bob Foresman's at the InterContintenal Hotel on East 48th Street in Manhattan. The man appeared irritated by our meeting, as though he were taking a risk by seeing me. In the hotel lobby, he made sure that my phones were switched off and stashed.

He said he had family relations in Rostov-on-Don and that these people were involved in local government. I knew what that meant. One didn't achieve such positions without influence in Moscow, and muscle, and a hand in the Ministry of Internal Affairs.

"I called them and asked them about this case, and they looked into it," the man said. "They came back and told me, 'Don't ever ask about this ever again.'"[2]

This indicated that in Russia, Billy's case was both known and so volatile that even people in power feared it. I was surprised. Billy was important to his family, but I couldn't imagine that he was a national-security operative of great value. Drawn to simple premises, rather than those requiring leaps of imagination, I theorized that Billy had been the victim of a crime in Russia, not a centerpiece of espionage.

But I couldn't discount anything. All options were in play. In June 2018, I booked a ticket to Moscow. On the drive to Dulles International Airport, in Washington's Virginia suburbs, I phoned Bob Foresman. He offered to make introductions for me in Russia, and he offered something else. "Be careful while you're over there," he said. "This may be a case where the two countries are aligned."

CHAPTER THIRTY-TWO

Moscow

Afternoon sunlight filtered through the drapes of the teahouse. The place was called Chaihona No. 1, and it was situated near the main entrance to the Moscow Zoo, close to one of the city's seven Stalin skyscrapers. The neighborhood was named Barikadnaya, for this was a location where anti-tsarist militias had erected barricades in a 1905 rebellion that served as a precursor to the revolution of 1917.[1]

I was sitting at a corner table amid the room's low chatter when Dmitri Tyurin, the Russian private investigator who had worked for the Reillys, appeared in the doorway. Tyurin was casually dressed in a short-sleeved shirt. He was forty-five but appeared to be younger, with the lean build and erect carriage of someone who exercises regularly and watches his diet. He wore his brown hair over the ears, and his smile was toothy, pitched at a mischievous angle. His eyes, bright and animated, foretold adventures.

Terry and Bill had provided me with Tyurin's investigative files. I had pored over them and seen that he'd put his shoulder into Billy's case in 2015 and 2016. Laced through his notes were provocative threads and contacts, officials in Moscow and Rostov-on-Don who might hold evidence and information that Tyurin's personal relationships could loosen.

When I'd told the Reillys about my plans for Moscow, Bill contacted Tyurin for the first time in two years. Recognizing a potential benefit to having Tyurin rejoin the case while I also pursued it in Russia, the Reillys set aside their doubts about him, desperate for results. They rehired him.[2] Over lunch,

211

I sensed a motivation in Tyurin beyond the money Terry and Bill had recently wired him to reanimate his search. Two years on, Tyurin was still sore at his inability to crack the case.

Tyurin had an open manner, and he was easily enthused. I detected a slight stutter. At the crux of each anecdote he shared, Tyurin's voice hesitated, giving the impression of an investigator, pursuing discovery, overcome by the thrill of solving a puzzling question.

Tyurin said he had recently spoken with an Interior Ministry contact and learned that Billy's case had been suspended since at least 2016. Despite the assurances of officials at the Rostov-on-Don Investigative Committee, who'd told the Reillys they would open a missing persons case, this meant that neither the Americans nor the Russians had been doing anything about it for more than two years. That left the field open to us. Yet I feared that Tyurin's leads would be worthless after so much time. An Interior Ministry department chief had pledged to facilitate Tyurin's contact with additional officials in Rostov. That's where he and I resolved to go.

Tyurin mused about life at the Rostov base. "These people were all able to leave behind their frustrations. There was a party every night in the camp. Every guy has a great singing voice. They all play the guitar. Many young women come to the camp. They cook. They are attracted to men in uniform. There is sex. Arms, adventure, freedom. And a girl going to sleep happily with no money paid." Despite Tyurin's colorful portrait, I knew that the movement of fighters through Rostov had been no glorified camping trip. I continued to have difficulty imagining Billy there.

So did Tyurin. "In this case, I have not been able to understand Billy's motivations," he said. "He didn't fit in at the camp. These volunteer fighters are disenchanted with the modern world. They have debt. Family stress. There is alcoholism. So they go to fight in Ukraine. Billy was also disenchanted. But in a different way." Tyurin said that he knew plenty about Russian prison life, having read about this underbelly, opaque to outsiders, which was governed by criminal hierarchies. He likened the environment at the Rostov camp to that of a Russian penitentiary. "Psychological pressure and humiliation. Billy may have been exposed to this in the Russia character." People at the camp might have preyed on Billy, Tyurin said.

I suggested that credit-card and ATM fraud provided a clue to Billy's story in Russia, but Tyurin offered a baser version. "At the time of Billy's arrival, there was a lot of TV propaganda blaming the US for the war in Donbas. What if there was a young guy whose family had been killed there? And he went to Billy and challenged him? 'You're to blame.'"[3]

We sketched a plan. Tyurin said he would broker a meeting in Moscow with Mikhail Polynkov, the recruiter. After that, we would make for Rostov, picking up the investigative trail that Tyurin had abandoned two years earlier.

After so much time spent in solitary theorizing, I welcomed the exchange with Tyurin. And I could imagine no better investigative partner. Tyurin knew the case and was motivated to solve it. He had built trust with security-services officials over the years of his work as a private eye. I had no such pool of contacts. Tyurin would also bring peace of mind to the enterprise, with his native understanding of our outstretching landscape and its many brambles and sinkholes.

I didn't care to romanticize the hazard of our task. We weren't digging into the source of an oligarch's fortune or, say, investigating Russia's defense sector. We were looking for a junior person whose narrow experience and knowledge held limited value. Even so, the queries we were pursuing were provocative. There were people in Russia who were concealing the answers, and I didn't know how determined they would be to make sure they remained hidden.

In Russia, it was important to be honest with yourself about risk. Many journalists in Russia over the years had risked everything in the process of their work, targeted because of the facts they uncovered. In 2000, an assailant attacked Igor Domnikov, a newspaper reporter for *Novaya Gazeta*, striking him repeatedly in the head with a hammer. Domnikov fell into a coma and died thereafter. In 2004, gunmen slew Paul Klebnikov, an American magazine writer and editor who was investigating several oligarchs, as he left his office in central Moscow. Two years later, Anna Politkovskaya, who wrote about Kremlin policies in the north Caucasus, was returning home from a market, her arms laden with groceries, when she encountered a man in the vestibule of her Moscow apartment. Two bullets to her chest, another to her head, martyred for her cause.[4] In 2009, journalist and human rights activist Natalya Estemirova was kidnapped near her home in Chechnya. Her body turned up later that day in the woods.[5]

These reporters had been fighting to change Russian society, their crusades ennobling their lives. I wasn't in their class, but Billy's case edged me closer to the dangers they had faced. Given the international gravity of events in Donbas, revealing the truth of Billy's fate could expose secrets within the American and Russian security services.

I believed, perhaps naively, that no one started out wanting to kill a reporter. Murder brought scrutiny. First would come a warning, a message that you'd done your job too well, had pressed too close to information that someone was willing to prevent you from revealing. For most reporters, a warning was enough. It was a chance to exit the scene under your own power.

After lunch, in the teahouse driveway, I watched Dmitri Tyurin walk out to the road. I was careful not to be credulous of his motives. A contact of mine who had experience in these areas had explained that Russian private eyes were not entirely private, that they took direction from state investigators or the security services and disseminated approved information. It was easy to sell a cover story, especially with a manner as disarming as Tyurin's, and to a foreigner in particular. Maybe Tyurin's principal task wasn't finding Billy but instead recording my moves and intentions. I puzzled over Tyurin, as he probably puzzled over me, but there are questions one can never answer.

CHAPTER THIRTY-THREE

Red Square

I first thought seriously about Russia in 2002. I fell into conversation with a friend, Angus, who had moved to Moscow for a job. His Moscow stories of nightclubs and ballet dancers and connected guys appealed to me.

I made it to Moscow that summer within what I would later understand was a special window of time. It was four years since the ruble had crashed, and rising oil and gas prices had since revived the Russian economy.[1] Moscow was the largest city in Europe. I found it to be a raucous yet sophisticated place kind of like New York.

Vladimir Putin had been Russian president for only eighteen months. His style was still taking shape. It was more than a year before he authorized the arrest of the oligarch Mikhail Khodorkovsky. Many people in the West regarded Putin favorably. He had even forged something of a friendship with George W. Bush. The two had spent time together on Bush's Texas ranch.[2]

The Moscow people whom Angus and his friends Stefan and Arthur introduced me to on my first trip were old enough to have come of age in the Soviet system, though young enough to adapt to the new ways. They had profited in the capitalist system, yet were heirs to the former collective. They shared what they had. They were vibrant, energetic, curious about the world. They didn't seem to plan for the future, yet they were optimistic about whatever would come. They didn't save life for later. They spent it. Friendships with them came easily and seemed to hold.

When you wanted to go someplace in Moscow, you stepped to the curb and extended your hand, and a car would break from traffic. You would tell the driver your destination and talk price. He would grin and say, "However much is enough." You'd sit up front, rubbing shoulders with the driver as he worked the gear shifter. The Soviet-made car would groan, never breaking thirty-five as it looped through town. This would give you and the driver a chance to talk. That's what he'd want to do, the money for the ride feeling incidental. He would pick up on your accent, surprised that you were American, and he'd have many questions. Liberated in your company, he'd swear and say wild things, tell off-color jokes. When he'd learn that you lived in New York, he would turn solemn, expressing his sympathy for the 9/11 attacks that still burned in recent memory. When you'd arrive at your destination, you'd place a ruble bill on the dash and shake the driver's hand, sharing a look of gravity. Standing on the curb, you'd watch the car slip back into traffic, dissolving into the cityscape. You'd feel like you'd made a friend you'd never see again.

During that first visit to Moscow, I felt a familiar rumble. I had once paid my dues for a magazine job I'd then left behind. I had scrapped that to make a new life as a freelance writer. I was now at a new age, with new needs, and I felt drawn to new challenges, believing that Russia would present them.

My plan was unspecific and chancy: learn the language and the city, sell a few articles, sketch out a book, take the ride, follow wherever it led. I moved to Moscow, and Angus took me in. He lived in a large private home from the late-tsarist period on Gagarinsky Lane in the center of the city. The house was a building of many small rooms and Gothic darkness, with an elderly woman, bedridden and tended by nurses, dying on an upper floor.

We lived in a detached portion of the property, a two-floor carriage house with a windowless basement and a bright, high-ceilinged gallery we referred to as the loge. Its showcase windows overlooked a private garden of birch trees and flowering plants bound by twelve-foot whitewashed stone walls. Looming above the scene were the white-marble tower and gold-leafed dome of Christ the Savior Cathedral, the city's largest church. Floodlights lit the dome through the night. It looked like an immense candle.

A pleasing setting, this provided me no conventional introduction to Russia. At night, our house on Gagarinsky transfigured. When the city's nightclubs closed, people would arrive at our place to continue the party. The door was always open. These people turned the basement into a dance floor, the loge into a lounge, and hung around sometimes for days. I watched these people lead their wild lives and began to pick up their language and manner.

Americans in Moscow were few, though I met several who had made fortunes there applying financial acumen. Women clinging to them, they swaggered around the city with cars and drivers. They talked about yachts and quail-egg breakfasts and how they could never go home again, having thrown off its conventions. They referred to government ministers by their nicknames.

There weren't many Western tourists either. Prague was about as far east as they ever made it. Russia presented a high barrier. Moscow was too big-shouldered.

I wrote articles for glossies in New York. *Vanity Fair, National Geographic, The New York Times Magazine, Playboy.* I filed dispatches from Moscow and the Caucasus. I flew on helicopters in the Siberian Arctic, writing about gas pipelines and reindeer. Outside Vladivostok, I spent time with a member of a criminal gang who'd served two terms for murder. Later, he would visit Moscow and look me up, and over beers he would tell dark stories.

In Russia, I did things I'd never imagined one could do. Life and work fused. I valued friendships with people who were different than I was, drawn to human variety instead of seeking comfort in people like me. I felt a sense of great reward, though these years sometimes gave me the blues. I knew that this was my life's great adventure. It would end one day, and I would never equal it. I stayed in Moscow for five years, chasing the feeling.

Before Russia, I had been like Billy, young and formless. I'd sought to address my shortcomings, just as he would later feel the need. Billy's urge to expand himself had driven him toward danger. Going to places that others feared would be his right of passage. His impulse was familiar to me.

Russia was Billy's venue, as it had been mine, yet the place had changed in the decade-plus between my arrival and his. Like many people who knew the country, I hadn't foreseen what was coming, though perhaps we all should have. Putin asserted his control in pursuit of "managed democracy." Cynicism and paranoia, the traits of a leader who stays in power too long, overspread society. Russia became less freewheeling. Moscow's Weimar period faded. Without notice, it was over.

The Kremlin grew emboldened, and our countries' political classes clashed. Russia went to war with Georgia for a dozen days in 2008.[3] Then came Crimea and Donbas in 2014, further hardening our feelings toward one another. It was no longer such an easy thrill being an American in Russia when Billy arrived there in 2015.

I had left Russia in 2008 but continued to visit on assignment. The visits were meaningful yet sometimes gloomy and wistful. Russia was saddled with the endless prospect of a single political leader. Freedom of thought, a variety of ideas, an appreciation of difference, these concepts declined, Putin's dogma consuming them. My own country suffered from limitations on free expression, but the swing of Russia's pendulum was far more drastic.

The old Soviet cars had all but disappeared from Moscow's roads, a sign of prosperity and the passage of time. Drivers no longer stopped at the curb when you extended your hand. When you wanted to go somewhere, you would order a car through an app on your phone. When the driver would learn that you were American, an instinct for conflict would arise within him. He'd challenge you to defend US policies. He'd tell you about Russian infallibility. You would remember the rides you'd taken in Moscow years ago and their amiable interactions. They'd evaporated through the years and changes. The only reliable thing to say about change is that it will come. You will be glad enough if you have enjoyed the good times.

* * *

A taxicab took me from the teahouse where I had met with Dmitri Tyurin and sped along the high walls of the Moscow Zoo. A friend of mine lived nearby. I had met him on that first trip to Moscow in 2002, and we had remained close. People in Moscow called him the General, the rank he had once attained in a state agency. Late many nights, with the zoo's lions roaring, he and I would leave his apartment tower on prowls of our own.

The cab gained the road that described inner Moscow, the Garden Ring. I absorbed many changes. Billions of dollars had poured into municipal improvements in preceding years. Moscow friends of mine had groused over Mayor Sobyanin's reconstructions: torn-up roads and sidewalks, bike lanes, snarled traffic, delays and dirt. The improvements had now been completed in time for Russia's hosting of the World Cup.[4]

The 2018 World Cup was underway. Moscow was in a state of mass celebration. People loaded into bars to watch the tournament's opening-round games and gathered on streets closed to cars, shaping the World Cup carnival. A debate was underway: Were Italian fans the most festive, or was it the Spanish? Or the Mexicans? The days were bright and warm and lengthy. The early successes of the Russian team enriched the local mood.

The cab turned down the Boulevard Ring, the leafy inner circuit that slashed through the city's old quarters, making its way south toward the Kropotkinskaya metro station and my first Moscow home. We slipped onto Gagarinsky Lane, past the corner café where I used to meet sources. Pairs of people were walking along the narrow stone sidewalk. Our car approached the old house where Angus and I had lived.

We drove alongside the property, and I turned my head to take in our old carriage house, anticipating the sight of it, the return of dormant memories and emotions. But our carriage house was no longer there. It had been razed. The basement after-hours nightclub, the loge and lounge, the people, the time, all gone, imagined.

CHAPTER THIRTY-FOUR

Walden

D mitri Tyurin was waiting in the afternoon beside a canal along the Moscow River, Krymskaya Embankment. He struggled to contain his excitement over the news he had learned. "Billy's case has been elevated from Rostov to the national Interior Ministry database," he said. The search for Billy had gone federal.

In a small café, we were the only customers, yet Tyurin leaned in close to relay information. He said that his Rostov police contacts had told him that they no longer had jurisdiction of the investigation into Billy's disappearance. "The whole case is in Moscow," he said, "and it has been for a while."

Still, Tyurin puzzled over the behavior of his contacts within the state security structures. Over the years, they had accepted payment in exchange for information, but now they were asking questions. One encounter troubled Tyurin, a conversation with a contact who had access to what was called the Zonal Information Center of the Main Department of Internal Affairs of Moscow, an information database known as ZAITS.

The man had asked if Tyurin was sure he was doing the right thing, "because Billy is flagged, and we don't know why." Tyurin said someone with administrative control had placed a red checkmark next to the case in the computer system. This prohibited the dissemination of information. This status was serious enough to discourage government officials from seeking side income by sharing case details with Tyurin.

Tyurin couldn't imagine why his contacts and their superiors would find

Billy's case important. "The police are not political," he said. "The office is about making money." He drew a distinction between the police (Russian federal investigators) and intelligence and counterintelligence operatives and officials who carried out Kremlin directives. Tyurin concluded that there was no monetary motivation behind the prohibition on information about Billy. He feared that the flagging of Billy's case led to a political authority.

Tyurin said he had obtained Russian immigration records, which showed Billy's arrival in the country on May 15, 2015, but no departure. Even this was up for grabs, Tyurin explained. Years before, immigration authorities had been unable to locate a departure record for a British client of Tyurin's. But Tyurin and his client were already out of the country. They had driven into Ukraine, and border guards had failed to record the departure. Tyurin suggested that Billy had, in fact, already left Russia.

Tyurin indulged in musings. With a pen, he doodled on the receipt for our lunch. "I once went on a kayaking trip down the Snezhnaya River in Buryatia, near Lake Baikal," he said. "This was 2015. I met a local. He said, 'Hey, do you want to meet these American guys who live nearby?' There were two Americans who had built a cabin there."

Tyurin described Russia's middle expanse, millions of square miles of forests and rivers and wildlife and few people. He said he had once worked for a man who helped American couples adopt Russian children. Traveling on this job to Chita, north of the Mongolian border, Tyurin had encountered an American whose Russian visa had expired years earlier. "He had become the leader of a religious sect," Tyurin said. "He had about ninety followers in his church. For some Americans, coming to Russia would be a way to get away from American life, which is not for them. Maybe Billy chose this path."

Tyurin laid down his pen. Uncoiled across the café receipt was a single word: "Walden."

We walked along the canal, approaching Christ the Savior Cathedral. Sunbeams were bearing down. Tyurin pieced together his ideas into a coherent theory. "I think there has been an order from the top to present one cover story," he said.

Tyurin gestured toward the water that flowed between the canal's granite embankments. "If you throw a stone into the water over there, it will create circles," he said. "But if you throw a stone into a swamp, there will be no circles. Among these officials, it's impossible to generate any reaction."

Yet Tyurin suggested that he knew how to penetrate the cover story, circumventing the limitation placed on Billy's case materials within the ZAITS database. Tyurin said he had contacted a government official who had the necessary power. "I will see him in the next day or so," Tyurin said. "And then we'll go to Rostov."

A cab dropped me at a hotel off Prichistenka Street, down a hidden lane. It was a careworn place, but I was lucky to have found a room there, given the rush on hotels citywide during the World Cup. The middle-aged women at the front desk eyed me as I came and went. I packed for Rostov and thought of what Tyurin and I might achieve there. After months of combing through inert files at my desk in the *Journal* office in Washington, I was taking the steps toward the people and places that held the secrets of Billy's fate.

Preparing for the trip, I scanned my notes in the hotel café. A Soviet drama played on TV. People were hunched in whispers and smoking. The butter was melting in the kasha when the girl placed it on the table.

My room, done in green taffeta, had a grandiose armoire. Through a window, I saw a watchman and maid sitting on a bench, their cigarettes going, their stares leveled at the courtyard gravel. For a couple of days, I was absorbed in thought before I realized that I hadn't heard from Tyurin. He had stopped returning my calls and text messages. Like Billy, he had disappeared.

CHAPTER THIRTY-FIVE

A Reaction

I was locked in a reporter's dilemma, on the road and immobilized, inhaling the air conditioning and running up the hotel bill. Packed and ready to leave for Rostov, I now put the trip on hold. I extended my Moscow stay a day at a time, believing that Tyurin would reappear. When he didn't, my thoughts turned dark.

It was hard to be patient, easier to get moving. On a cool morning, I jogged across the Krimsky Bridge, a steel-suspension structure from the Stalinist prewar period. Down below, the sun sparkled on the Moscow River. Traffic whipped along the bridge's middle lanes, the cars' tires thrumming along grooved pavement. On the pedestrian walkway, I passed a young couple holding hands. An elderly woman lugged a sack on one shoulder. I reached the far side of the bridge and darted down a flight of stone stairs that led into Gorky Park.

I ran south through the park along the river's embankment toward the trees, replaying the points of Billy's story in my mind. The letter Catie had seen, which Billy suggested was an invitation to Russia. The side trip to Thailand to see Lomangcolob. Agent Reintjes's first visit to the house in Oxford. The correspondence between Mikhail Polynkov and Bill Reilly. Mohammed Cherri's inspection of Billy's social media accounts. These elements continued to frustrate the formulation of a conclusion. I remembered what Bob Foresman had said about two adversarial countries finding common cause.

A few miles into the park, I approached Luzhnetskiy Bridge, which carried over the river into a park around Luzhniki Stadium, a site for the 1980 summer Olympic Games. As I passed under the bridge, a train rattled along tracks overhead, its clatter resounding through the stone underpinning. A man appeared from the shadows. I heard a bicycle approach from behind me. I spun around. On the bike was a young girl. She and the man went separate ways.

I realized that I was manufacturing intrigue. There must have been a simple reason for Tyurin's withdrawal. While it was true that Russia was a place of long shadows, life there was also full of ordinary troubles. A friend once told me: If you have a problem with problems, don't come to Russia. Tyurin was likely dealing with a problem of his own. Maybe he was on a bender, a *zapoy*. That happened. And when it did, nobody asked questions. In Russia, unexplained absences were routine. I allowed Tyurin his absence. And I got to work.

Absolute power in Russia, Putin, was inaccessible. But remaining levels of influence were permeable. Having friends who could stamp a document or waive a fine was an essential part of life. Early on in Russia, beginning with my time at the Gagarinsky house, I had met people who worked in the ministries, city government, the military, the border service. Without Tyurin, I would have to find my own way.

I started seeing old friends, meeting them at offices, apartments, and cafés. I mentioned my search, waiting to see who'd engage. I called the General. He had always fulfilled his word and had broad contacts. I had witnessed him on many occasions solve a problem with a single phone call, no matter its type or difficulty. Years ago, enjoying himself at a party and late for a trip to Italy, he had once delayed the departure of an Al Italia flight from a Moscow airport. He phoned a contact at the airport, and the flight boarded but idled. The General strolled onto the plane sometime later, and only then did it move toward the runway, its passengers ignorant of the reason for the holdup.

He and I met at a restaurant. He had never looked like a general. He was slightly built, in his forties, and his chestnut hair swept across his forehead. I'd met him in the Gagarinsky years, and his smile had the mischief of the old times. Over dinner, I told him Billy's story. The General asked for dates, passport details, photos. He said he'd see what he could do.

On another day, I was in a boat heading north of Moscow toward the city of Tver. I had gone at the invitation of a friend who had contacts in the Duma, the lower house of the Russian parliament, and in businesses governed by muscle and state contracts. He and his wife were old friends of mine, and they spent weekends on this extensive berm of land that lay in a crook in the Volga River. They had a helipad and an enormous garden. Hanging on a wall in the living room of their main house was a large framed portrait of Putin. His lips pursed, he was squinting.

My friend and I swam in the Volga and took a sauna at the waterline. Red-faced from the heat of the *banya*, we sat on the deck and watched freighters navigate the river's elbow. This slow drama played out in silence a half mile away, and in robes and felt *banya* hats we discussed Billy's story. "How could no one have a record of him?" my friend asked. He promised to ask around.

I returned to Moscow and knocked on many doors, hoping that the right one would open. A German expat with valuable connections said she'd tap her underworld ties. Over vodka and *zakuski*, Sasha, an old friend with Donetsk contacts and a fleet of sedans and bodyguards, offered to take me there in search of Billy. We sketched out a plan, but it and the vodka had worn off by morning.

In late June, I contacted Mikhail Polynkov, the recruiter.

I was encouraged by an evolution of his political philosophy. Polynkov had written on his LiveJournal blog, *A Soldier's Truth*, that his regard for Putin and the Russian power structure had soured. The Kremlin had removed Igor Strelkov, Polynkov's associate, from his position in the DNR and nixed talk of reviving Novorossiya. Moscow made it clear that it had no current intention to incorporate Donbas, as it had done with Crimea. Donbas would remain a buffer zone with unofficial status, at least for the time being. Polynkov wrote on his page that the Kremlin had betrayed the movement.

"The perpetrators of what happened to our country in the nineties are alive and well, are at the head of the government and continue to rob and rape our country and all of us for their own enrichment and perverse pleasure," Polynkov wrote. "There is no money for anything other than yachts for oligarchs and imperialist feuds."[1]

Polynkov published prolifically, and I hoped to encourage him to communicate further. He asked that I send him an email explaining my goal. I received his reply the following morning. "Please forgive me," he wrote, "but I decline to meet." I wrote him again and called. Polynkov didn't answer.

I took a cab to an address where I'd learned Polynkov had an office for the Novorossiya movement, on Nikoloyamskaya Street in Moscow's west-central

Taganka district, just beyond the Garden Ring south of a bend in the Yauza River. From the street, I walked into a courtyard. It was ringed by squat buildings on three sides. The building numbers were poorly labeled and their doors were all locked. The place felt deserted.

Trash was piled in the courtyard. I nudged it with a shoe. A shattered printer-ink cartridge, a dented wastebasket, a desk chair, the objects of an abandoned office. Several flyers were scattered across the crabgrass. "Help Our Heroes," read one. Another said: "Be a Part of History." The flyers' small print described a funding drive for the Russian military effort in Crimea, four years earlier, evidence that I was in the right place but at the wrong time.

A door opened in one of the buildings, and a man emerged on a landing. He lit a cigarette. I told him I was looking for the office for the volunteer fighters. "They were here," he said. "But they moved out a long time ago." My further attempts to locate Polynkov bottomed out.

I turned my attention to Bronya Kalmyk. I knew he had secrets. Here I hit another snag. An open-source digital compendium of Donbas participants, administered by the Ukrainian security services, stated that Bronya had been "liquidated" the year before.[2]

There was someone else in Moscow besides Polynkov and Bronya who I knew had met Billy, Elena Gorbacheva, the photojournalist. She agreed to meet at a café close to my hotel, along Prichistenka Street. Gorbacheva took me back to the day in May 2015 when Billy had arrived in Russia. She said she'd gone to Polynkov's office to interview Serbian fighters. Polynkov had pulled her aside. "He said, 'You speak English, right? Can you help me with something? There is a strange guy who came from the US, and I don't know what to do with him.'"

She described how she and Polynkov had gone to the train station and met "Vasily." She said Polynkov had tried to dissuade Billy from traveling to Rostov. "There was nothing we could do," she said. "He already had his train ticket." On her phone, Gorbacheva showed me the photos she had taken of Billy on the train platform.

"I wanted to write an article about Vasily," she said. "My editor said wait and see what happens. I called Polynkov later. He said Vasily had disappeared."

It was impossible to tell if Gorbacheva was holding back or if she was truly ignorant of Billy's fate. "If you find out what happened to him, please let me know," she said. "I still want to write about him."[3]

Days passed. I had hoped that my experience as a reporter and my contacts in Russia would combine to produce results. But the case was resisting my efforts.

One evening, the weather warm and inviting, I met the General on a street corner at the edge of Patriarchs Pond, a freshwater brook in the center of town. "I've been asking around about your lost American," he said.

This neighborhood was pricey and usually subdued. But with the World Cup in Russia, cafés and restaurants had opened to entertain the many foreigners who had flooded into town. A Ferrari zipped down the street in front of a row of bars, their action giving out onto the sidewalks. A crowd of mixed nationalities, ethnicities, and languages had come together. People were talking loudly with cocktail glasses in hand.

The General had grown up in a different kind of Moscow, a closed society. After the Soviet Union had fallen, he had watched the city change. He had seen how people had become freer, more adventurous, connected to the larger world. The General gestured toward this World Cup crowd. "This could be Paris," he said. "Or maybe even New York." He laughed. Because he knew that the World Cup crowd was a mirage. Under Putin, Russia was retreating, suspicious of the Western world.

"How does the FSB feel about your project?" the General asked. I told him that I would be surprised if the FSB cared about it, since Billy was so junior.

The General pushed back. "Some strange things started happening. They started listening to me." I asked how he could be sure. "I have a little experience with this," he said.

His troubles had happened so long ago that I'd nearly forgotten them. An arrest and incarceration meant to wear him down. To win his freedom, he had signed over his *dacha*, or country house. Someone even with his influence couldn't escape the system of the *siloviki*.

He grew serious. "Look, I'm a Soviet patriot," he said. "I don't want to get caught up in anything."

*   *   *

The following morning, I went for another run in Gorky Park. I navigated an interior lane. Twenty minutes into the run, I noticed movement up ahead along the path. A van was driving toward me, a black Mercedes. Its windshield was opaque. A thin strip of red and blue lights was fixed to the van's roof.

With the World Cup in town, all branches of Russia's military and police were on alert to crime and terrorism. I'd seen as much at the Winter Olympic Games in the southern Russian city of Sochi in 2014. Cops and investigators were stationed all over Moscow in the summer of 2018, poised to handle everything from drunken fans to bombing plots. It would have been strange if special-operations units weren't combing Gorky Park.

I maintained my pace and jogged by the van. It drove on in the opposite direction.

Then I heard the van's engine downshift. Looking over my shoulder, I saw that the van was turning around and now driving in my direction.

It drew level then drove ahead of me. It executed a quick turn and parked perpendicular to the path, blocking it. The van's tandem side doors faced me, poised to open. I was powerless to prevent whatever would happen.

But nothing did happen. No hooded phantoms emerged from the van. I veered around it into the grass along the edge of the pathway and kept running.

Back at the hotel, I realized the absurdity of what I was trying to achieve in Russia. I was a twig on the edge of a bonfire, about to be sucked in. I thought of Terry Reilly and how she had gripped my arm on the threshold of the house in Oxford, certain I'd find her son. I'd never find Billy. It was silly to think I could.

I was in my hotel room later that day when my phone rang. It was Dmitri Tyurin calling. He had reappeared. Tyurin's jaunty mood was gone. He sounded afraid.

Tyurin said that a security-services official had summoned him. The man had upbraided him, demanding to know why he was looking into the Reilly case despite warnings from underlings. Tyurin said that the official had threatened to revoke Tyurin's private investigator's license, and potentially do more, if he continued probing Billy's disappearance.

Tyurin's voice quivered. "I need some time to realize if I am under their scrutiny," he said. "They can go all the way."

I asked how we could proceed with the investigation. "In my opinion, it's not possible," he said. "We have reached a point where no further action is needed. We are not to go further. If we keep going in this direction, I can't imagine what may happen to me or others."

Tyurin talked quickly, straining to express a message. "I want you to be extremely careful. Take it as a basic fact that there is something very special about this case. Do not press in places where you are not sure, because there could be a bad reaction."

The line fell quiet. I didn't know what to say.

A bad reaction: that's what he had said, and there was no way to mistake the message. It was the message many reporters before me in Russia had received in advance of grave measures. Tyurin had given me the warning.

He said that we could no longer meet, and he suggested that we limit our communications. "All these things happening now, the police wouldn't do all this to cover up a crime." I asked what he meant.

He said, "There is a very high probability that Billy is alive."[4]

CHAPTER THIRTY-SIX

With Those Guys Now

A cab dropped me near the Moscow Zoo. I was confused. Billy was alive? He had been silent for three years. Tyurin presented no evidence for his assumption, and maybe he'd been directed to throw me off the scent. Still, I had to consider the possibility.

I rode the elevator to the General's apartment. I needed to blow off steam, reset my thoughts. We had a drink. As the night drew on, the General asked how my search was going.

He could tell I was troubled, and he offered a suggestion. "Do you remember Nastya?" he asked.

I drew a blank. Nastya was short for Anastasiya, and in Russia who didn't know many of them? "From the Gagarinsky house," the General said. "She was often there."

The General described her appearance, and I tried to extract her from among the kaleidoscope of faces from those years. He explained that Nastya had been a designer. She had created the interiors of Shambala, a Moscow nightclub with an Indian theme, long since shuttered.[1] "Nastya," said the General, "you remember."

A face came to mind, elegant and lean, framed by dark hair.

The General worked his phone. He showed me a picture on its screen. It was a small, blurry image from social media. There was a person I had once known, Nastya Mikhailovskaya.

In the picture, she wore green fatigues and a severe expression. In her lap, she nuzzled a bobcat cub. I quickly gathered why the General had mentioned her. I had seen many similar photos on Billy's hard drives, men dressed in this way, with rifles strapped across their chests and exotic cats in their laps. Mikhailovskaya's social media avatar presented the unmistakable pose of the militant, the radical, the freedom fighter. "Yeah," said the General, "she's with those guys now."

*   *   *

It was an Italian place, Il Pomodoro. A World Cup match played on a TV screen. I was reading the menu when Mikhailovskaya breezed in. She scrutinized me with large green eyes.

We took a table outside on the sidewalk, where a tablecloth, buffeted by the breeze, suspended above us and filtered the sun. Mikhailovskaya had brought her dog, one of medium build and a thick white coat. It sat at her feet with a hunter's coolness. She said that the dog's name was Sever, the Russian word for north. He was half Husky.

"The other half?" I asked.

"Wolf."

Mikhailovskaya and I had known each other once. We had been members of the *tusovka*, the party. That was years ago, before relations between our countries had soured. Now it felt like there was something at stake between us. The General had said she was "with those guys," and to me that meant only one thing.

Mikhailovskaya said that she had been involved in the war in Donbas nearly since it had begun. She traveled there regularly, bringing food and clothes to civilians who needed them, she said. She organized field trips for children. I knew there was more, but I wouldn't get at it by pressing her. We ordered a pizza.

I knew that my motive was pure, but Mikhailovskaya had no cause to believe that. Her eyes scanned for clues to my intentions and fell upon the book I had brought to pass the time. It lay between us on the table, *Life and Fate*, a World War II saga suppressed in its day. Mikhailovskaya scrutinized the cover and asked me what I knew about Dostoevsky. I wasn't there to talk about books, but I'd take any entry point to a discussion. I sensed her softening enough to accept a change in topic.

"I'm looking for an American who disappeared in Rostov," I said. "Or maybe in Donbas."

Mikhailovskaya appeared interested. "What was he doing there?" she asked.

I rattled off a lean version of Billy's story. I wasn't far along when Mikhailovskaya shot her arm across the table and touched my wrist. "He was at the camp in Rostov?" she asked. "No. Impossible."

"He sent pictures to his parents," I said. "He was there. I'm sure of it."

"But how did he get there?"

"He met a guy online named Polynkov."

Mikhailovskaya leaned back and took me in. "Mikhail?" she asked.

She knew Polynkov. In fact, she knew them all.

Mikhailovskaya had served as press attaché for Igor Strelkov, the alleged GRU (military intelligence) officer who had kicked off the war in Donbas. She said Strelkov was Polynkov's boss, confirming a fact I knew to be true.

It was my turn to sit back and marvel at the connections. Mikhailovskaya was the sort of person I'd been hoping to find, a chaperone into a restricted world. I made sure to maintain an even manner, fearing that my exhilaration would tip my hand. Now wasn't the time to play it.

Mikhailovskaya spoke English well, and I asked her where she had refined the skill. She said her father had been in the KGB and was involved in the Moscow theater scene, where playwrights and actors often seemed to have dangerous ideas. As an adult, Mikhailovskaya said, she had visited the US and distributed Russian films on behalf of the Ministry of Culture. She had hosted screenings, interviewed American personalities for Moscow newspapers and magazines, traveled west and south, saw the country. The consular cultural department (a frequent cover for espionage), a father in the KGB. I knew what this generally meant but reserved comment. These were the roads that could lead to Billy.

At the time of the Second Chechen War, in the early 2000s, Mikhailovskaya went to the Caucasus, she said. Later, in Donbas in 2014, she started working with Strelkov at the behest of Aleksandr Dugin, a Russian nationalist ideologue who influenced Kremlin thinking. She said that Strelkov had secured initial financing for the volunteer-fighter base in Rostov-on-Don. "It was really a distribution point," she said. "It was not a training camp. The training is done in DNR, not in Rostov. The volunteers usually stayed only a couple of days at the dorm, then went into DNR." Mikhailovskaya's sketch harmonized with others I'd heard.

"But why did he go there?" she asked about Billy. I said I had few answers. "And what about his family? Have they looked for him?"

I described the efforts the Reillys had made, and how they bore the burden of their son's choices. Mikhailovskaya mentioned a child of her own, a daughter married and living far away in Australia. They rarely saw one another. Another child was readying for college and would soon leave her on her own. I sensed a mother's longing, though I couldn't be certain.

Mikhailovskaya said she would join my search, make introductions, and help me find answers.

Her offer seemed too promising. Given her background and circle, I doubted that our motives aligned. I figured that she might have been assigned to me. In Russia, on a task such as mine, one generally picked up a minder, a local person of friendly disposition whose cards never played face-up. A deflector. An informant. I couldn't be sure if this had factored into the General's suggesting Mikhailovskaya.

And I didn't care. I would get a minder anyway. There was no way around it. At least it was someone I knew. And I reasoned that operating under Mikhailovskaya's gaze gave me license to continue the search for Billy, despite Tyurin's warning.

The sun of the afternoon was gone. The back roads Mikhailovskaya and I walked were still, a lone car zipping now and again through the street lamps' yellow shafts. We reached Mikhailovskaya's apartment building and walked past it toward the embankment of a canal. Sever, her dog, stayed close off the leash.

"What was Billy doing here?" Mikhailovskaya asked. Speaking English, she pronounced his name with a Russian accent: "Beely."

I told her I'd like to know.

She eyed me. "I wonder what your real goal is," she said. "You Americans are sly."

Our eyes locked. I had to give something. I had no interest in giving any impression that I was a spy, withholding information she might already know. "There's an FBI connection to this case," I said.

She looked away. "I don't care." Neither of us could know the other's aims. All we had was what we shared. "I remember you from the house on Gagarinsky," she said.[2]

CHAPTER THIRTY-SEVEN

Black Hole

Mikhalovskaya and I made plans for Rostov, but first I pursued a side trip: Kiev. I endeavored to follow my contacts there down a path to information relevant to Billy. There was a Ukrainian half to my life in this part of the world.

I'd first visited Ukraine in the same year as my initial trip to Russia, 2002. An American friend, Arthur, was marrying a woman from Kiev, Lesya, and they invited me to their wedding there. I made fast friends in Ukraine, local and foreign. People there were warm, friendly, and eager to make and sustain contact, always available for a dinner, a weekend at the *dacha*, a night out.

Once I moved to Russia, I often went to Ukraine, taking the quick flight from Moscow or the sleeper train that always left you with colorful stories. I traveled beyond Kiev, to Donetsk, Kharkiv, Simferopol, Odessa, Mariupol, Lviv, and places in between. The connection I developed to Ukraine was as strong as the bond I came to feel for Russia. Later, I lived in Kiev, and when I left it, returning to live in the US, I nearly did so with a wife.

In those years, I told people who asked me that Kiev was "Moscow light," a moderated version of the same drink. From my foreigner's perspective, the cities operated by the same general rules and customs, with the differences difficult for me to distinguish without more time and feel. What I could immediately discern was that Moscow was a hard city, overwhelming in scope, where force and clan affiliation prevailed. Kiev was smaller, greener, gentler, even a little provincial. Stakes were lower there. People had less to prove.

I found that many Russians wanted you to know how special it was to be Russian, whereas the Ukrainians I knew didn't appear to carry much of an historical burden. A friend once said that if Moscow was equivalent to New York, Kiev was something like Detroit.

The differences ran more deeply than this, and I would come to feel them. One country, Ukraine, sickened with political and financial corruption, was a democracy of surprising electoral outcomes and politically engaged people who were often disappointed in their leaders but fought for a say in things. The other country was solidifying into a dictatorship and personality cult, corrupt not just in specific ways but at its core. The preponderance of its people, while extolling their hardiness and individuality, were frightened into political inactivity. In the years that I lived in that part of the world, it was difficult to foresee that these differences would result in war. Maybe I just didn't want to accept what was possible. Independence had deceived Ukraine into believing that Russia would let it be.

In April 2014, after the shock of the initial uprising in Donbas, Kiev, under an acting president, Oleksandr Turchynov, had launched what it called an anti-terrorist operation. This counteroffensive was so successful in regaining territory from the separatists that, by the end of August that year, Russia began sending artillery and personnel over the border in what some observers called an open invasion. The offensive recouped lost territory for the rebels but couldn't overcome Kiev's resolve. A 260-mile front line solidified.[1]

When I arrived in Kiev, flying from Moscow via Minsk, in the summer of 2018, Ukraine's war in Donbas against Russia and its proxies was more than four years old. I had traveled to Kiev reasoning that the Ukrainians had cause to reveal information about Billy that the Russians might endeavor to hide. I started asking around about Polynkov, Bronya, and the other characters in the story. I met with local reporters in Kiev and spoke with government officials who handled prisoner lists and intelligence. I explained that Billy might be captive on the other side of the line of engagement. My contacts searched POW files but failed to locate mention of him.

I thought I might find more success in Ukraine by contacting people there who had links to Russia. A black van waited in the driveway of the Hyatt hotel one afternoon. The man at the wheel wore an earpiece. He drove me to an office complex on the edge of a park and handed me off to another man who wore his own earpiece. We exchanged no words, and I followed him through a doorway. We rode an elevator up several floors, and he passed me to a third man, also wearing an earpiece. I took a seat in an office filled with Russian Orthodox icons and imagery. Andriy Derkach walked in.

Derkach's father, Leonid, was a polarizing figure in Ukraine. He had served twenty years in the Dnepropetrovsk office of the KGB, in the eastern part of the Ukrainian Soviet republic. He was close to Leonid Kuchma, the second president in an independent Ukraine, who presided over the establishment of the system of political corruption that has since plagued the country. Rumors of ties to organized crime dogged Leonid Derkach for years. He once led the Security Service of Ukraine, the country's approximate analog to the FBI.[2]

Andriy Derkach, the son, was a deputy in Ukraine's parliament, the Verkhovna Rada, but was better known for having inherited his father's legacy. Andriy had earned a law degree in Moscow at the Dzerzhinsky Higher School of the KGB, an institution that later changed its name to the FBS Academy. Derkach couldn't shake accusations that he was an FSB officer, or at least a Russian agent, one of many in Ukraine who frustrated war designs and national unity in government and the legislature. He denied the accusations.

Derkach symbolized a central dilemma for Ukraine. In the country's lasting struggle with its stronger neighbor, it was often difficult to know which side lawmakers, military officers, and government officials were supporting. Even when people clearly pursued Russian interests in Ukraine, financial and political clout routinely allowed them to operate.

Derkach ran a TV network and produced an investigative-reporting show. Later, when Donald Trump was the US president, Derkach would partner with Rudolph Giuliani, the former New York City mayor who provided legal counsel to Trump. Derkach and Giuliani publicized information that they said confirmed that Joe Biden, Obama's vice president who would win the presidency in 2020, and a son, Hunter, had engaged in fraud in Ukraine. While his father had been vice president, Hunter Biden had earned considerable payments while sitting on the board of a Ukrainian energy company that was battling corruption allegations. Despite Hunter Biden's indiscretions, Derkach, given his reputation, undercut the material he and Giuliani put forth, especially since it lacked coherence.[3]

For me, Derkach represented a journalistic tenet: a reporter's right to interview anyone. More than a right, it was a duty. You had to talk to everybody, even to alleged spies. Sometimes they know things. It's up to you to figure out the truth. You had to be careful they weren't using you. Working for the *Journal*, I regularly encountered people who shared material that was simply false. But I remained open to talking. You never knew what you might hear.

Andriy Derkach was an extroverted man. But he was tied up in the trappings of being Leonid Derkach's son. There had been the phalanx of bodyguards wearing earpieces. Stranger still was the odd noise in Derkach's office. A speaker mounted on his desk was emitting white noise, the sound of dozens of overlapping conversations, meant to frustrate audio surveillance.

Derkach handed me a file on Billy Reilly. In the folder, I was surprised to see a photocopy of Billy's main passport page. There were records of his train travels in Russia. There was even a copy of Billy's final phone bill. None of the Ukrainian ministries had given me anything like this. I assumed that the materials had come to Derkach from contacts in Russia. When I asked about the origin of these materials, Derkach shrugged. "It looks like this guy got in over his head," he said.[4]

I called on Oleg Babanin, who handled press inquiries for Viktor Medvedchuk, who years before had been the head of the presidential administration under former Ukrainian president Kuchma. At the time a Rada deputy, like Derkach, Medvedchuk was known for his relations with Putin, who, it was said, was the godfather to one of Medvedchuk's daughters. Since 2014, Medvedchuk had managed several prisoner exchanges between Kiev and the separatists and was someone who, I thought, might petition the Russian side on behalf of the Reillys.[5]

I met Babanin in a café. He was downbeat about our chances. "It's very difficult, if not impossible," he said. "If they don't want to tell you something, they won't."

If Billy had disappeared in Donbas, some people there would know about it. Soliciting assistance in Donbas from afar appeared to be impractical, and I considered traveling there. But this was a tricky proposition. Reporting in Russia presented colorful challenges. But going to Donbas and asking questions about a missing American in the midst of war could court its own peril.

Press offices in the pseudo-governments of DNR and LNR had issued accreditation for many reporters in the first years of war. A press credential provided a measure of protection. It indicated that the local power welcomed the visit. By 2018, when I applied, policy had shifted. The so-called republics were slow-rolling the issuance of credentials. Even reporters from Russia weren't getting in. My applications were denied.

Still, there had to be a way to get there. Entering Donbas from the Russian side was possible. Ukraine no longer controlled its border with Russia. But Kiev proscribed this illegal method of entry to its sovereign territory, banning those who took it from entering Ukraine for years to come. Maintaining access to Ukraine was important to me professionally. Also, if I took the route into Ukraine from the Russian side, I would expose my *Journal* colleagues to similar penalties.

There was one tolerable way to enter Donbas. One could take a train from Kiev to Kramatorsk, a city in the east, then flag down a car to Donetsk, sixty miles south. Taking this route required a press card, which I received from the Joint Forces Operation, the Kiev military and political body that administered Ukraine's war effort.

I had visited Donbas in the years before the war. I'd gone to Donetsk and to vacation towns along the Azov Sea. I hadn't been there since the war had begun and lawlessness had consumed the territory. People I knew in Kiev warned me against going there, but they didn't have firsthand knowledge of what was happening there now either. I wanted to get an informed opinion before booking a place on the train to Kramatorsk, or abandoning the plan.

For years, I had known the Konstantinovsky brothers, Slava and Alex. Fraternal twins, fifty-seven years old and a shade under six feet tall, they were intense. Their heads were shaven, and their features called to mind Yul Brenner. They spoke without filigree. The Konstantinovskys couldn't outrun whispers of criminal exploits and connections, though they denied them. For years they had owned two of Kiev's most exclusive restaurants, Concord and Decadence. Many people in town referred to them as the Karamazov brothers, a reference to the Dostoevsky novel. In the 1958 film adaptation of the book, Yul Brenner had played the lead.[6]

The Konstantinovskys told many stories. There was one from Brooklyn decades ago, when they had worked as bouncers at a nightclub there and Slava had extinguished a cigarette on the eyeball of a troublesome patron. Slava once told me that he no longer engaged in such behavior. He said he had quit smoking.

In 2006, the brothers had learned that a rival had placed a contract on them. They went into hiding at a Kiev apartment, reappearing only when the Kiev police and the FBI arrested the man who allegedly wanted them dead.[7]

When events erupted in Maidan in 2014, the Konstantinovskys leapt into the fray. Slava, a Rada deputy at the time, joined the parliamentary national-security committee. He formed and funded an ex-officio armed battalion that fought separatist and Russian forces in Donbas. The Konstantinovskys understood how to navigate systems of violence and the terrain of the Donbas war better than anyone I knew.

I met Slava Konstantinovsky one evening at Concord during my summer 2018 visit. The dining room had its share of men of apparent no-nonsense in well-fitting blazers and women whose looks commanded a second glance. The lights were turned low. Candlelight flickered across Slava's snub features. I shared the story of Billy Reilly and my hopes to locate him. I probed Slava for the mechanisms by which I could work in Donbas.

He predicted I would be kidnapped. "It's like the Wild West there," he said. "But worse."

I was surprised. Slava was no shrinking violet. In my years in this part of the world, I'd learned that regulations were usually just suggestions, that money and personal connections were the only law. With them, and with determination, one could achieve almost anything. I told Slava that it was important to find answers for Terry and Bill, that I accepted taking a few chances.

Slava didn't budge. He described basement torture chambers in Donbas. He said people in Donbas had lost their sense of proportion.

I sought gaps in Slava's reasoning, pressed him for alternatives. I suggested that some formation of his muscle could clear a path for me.

"If you go in there and find nothing and make it out alive, it's the best thing that can happen to you," he said. "And that won't happen. You won't make it out of there."[8] I understood I could go no further. Donbas was a black hole.

The following afternoon, I received a call from Paul Beckett, my boss, the chief of the *Journal*'s Washington office. I briefed him on my work and what remained of it. He was encouraging yet firm. "Start thinking about wrapping it up and heading back," he said.

I had time for another move or two. I booked a return trip to Russia. Nastya Mikhailovskaya was waiting.

CHAPTER THIRTY-EIGHT

Cossacks

The Aeroflot plane pulled into a gate at Platov International Airport on the outskirts of Rostov-on-Don. I was seated in row one, first in line to disembark. The stewardess muscled open the cabin door. On the other side of it, several uniformed policemen were marshaled along the ramp. The lead cop stepped onto the plane.

He saluted the stewardess and addressed her sharply. "We need every male passenger to show their passports on the way off the plane," he said. "Make the announcement."

The attendant informed the cabin over the intercom. Murmurs circulated.

The cop turned toward me, and I handed him my passport. I was fairly certain that I wasn't his target. But this display underscored the fact that I was now powerless to local authorities, having returned to Russia in pursuit of Billy in his last known location. The cop's eyebrows raised as he leafed through the passport. A woman behind me whispered, "What's this all about?" and a man replied dryly, "Welcome to Rostov."

The cop's eyes dashed across the booklet's pages, and he shook his head. I saw that he hadn't been expecting a US passport. He handed it back as though I'd wasted his time. Soon I was in a cab headed toward Rostov-on-Don.

*   *   *

In the 1740s, Russian empress Elizabeth, a daughter of Peter I, learned of a settlement that had arisen along the Don River on the rim of the realm, where freedmen and Turks conducted trade yet paid no tax on it. Elizabeth's authorities established a customs house and fort where the Don delta emptied into the Azov Sea. A settlement emerged at the fort, which was named for a bishop of Rostov, a ninth-century Kievan Rus town on Russia's Golden Ring, a grouping of historic cities north of Moscow. By the dawn of the 19th century, the second Rostov, on the Don, had gained prominence in trade, necessitating an appellation to distinguish it from the first.[1]

A predominant group then in Rostov-on-Don were Cossacks. These were people who had escaped serfdom in the Russian empire or, Slavic and Turkic, had long existed in semi-itinerant clusters. There were convicts and outlaws among them, too, people who had fled to the borderlands.[2]

Cossack hosts spread across the lower basins of great rivers, including the Dnieper, Don, and Volga. In 1648, Bohdan Khmelnytsky, a minor noble from eastern Ukraine, led a Cossack uprising that dislodged Polish landowners and massacred their Jewish estate managers. Six years later, Khmelnytsky concluded the Pereiaslav Agreement, swearing allegiance to the tsar and granting Russian control over a large portion of Ukrainian lands.

With skill in saddle and saber, the Cossacks defended the empire's blurry borders in exchange for a measure of self-rule. They were parts knight, cowboy, and brigand, the riders of the Slavic range.[3]

The Cossacks clashed with the Soviet system that emerged after the Russian Civil War. The Soviets terminated the agreement that had granted the Cossacks special status, subduing the group to the collective. *And Quiet Flows the Don*, the Cossack elegy, appeared in these times, published in serial form between 1928 and 1940. The tale of Cossack life through war and revolution won Joseph Stalin's favor even while he repressed the group. The book's author, Mikhail Sholokhov, grew so close to power that he became known as "Stalin's writer."[4]

In World War II, some Cossack units fought on the Soviet side, while others, intent on regaining their lost autonomy, threw in with the Germans. The Nazis took Rostov-on-Don when they invaded Russia in 1941, lost it a week later, and regained it in the summer of '42. The Germans murdered all of the Jews who lived in Rostov, 27,000 or so people, marking the greatest Holocaust crime on Russian soil. For six months the Nazis occupied the city, leading many Don Cossacks to entertain thoughts of regained independence.[5]

The Nazis pressed their offensive toward the Baku oilfields, and here they struggled. The Soviets flooded the plains around Rostov-on-Don with a new sort of cavalry. The T-34 tank had advanced armor and a powerful cannon, and factories beyond the Urals produced two dozen of them per day. When the Germans retreated, the Cossack bill came due.[6]

Stalin had drawn a border through Cossack lands, splitting those in the Ukrainian Soviet Socialist Republic from those on the Russian side, but Cossack worries were greater. Stalin avenged their Nazi collaboration, eliminating the Cossack hosts via deportation to internal exile, or by bullet.[7]

Only in perestroika would the Don Cossacks return to Rostov-on-Don, but by then their way of life had ceased to exist. Putin later championed the group's reconstitution. The subject of the Cossacks' Nazi collaboration is too sensitive, even now, nearly eighty years later, to mention. Instead, mythology has taken hold. It describes the pre-Soviet Don Cossacks, the horsemen of the plains, independent but loyal, self-sacrificing and disciplined, patrolling the frontier. At Rostov's airport, a video set to a cinematic score plays on a cylindrical display, horsemen gliding through wheat fields.

When war broke out in Donbas in 2014, it promised those who identified as Cossacks a renewal of purpose, the rejoining of lands that Stalin's decree had separated on either side of the Russian-Ukrainian border. In the Donbas war, those who claimed Cossack heritage could reach back into the past to those who had fought the tsar's wars before them, reviving the order of the cavalry.[8]

*   *   *

A hotel in Rostov on the left bank of the Don gave form to the Cossack ideal. The staff at Petrovsky Prichal ("Peter's Pier") wore period dress of military caps and belted tunics and were proficient if stern. The cast-iron cannons at the end of a pier reaching into the Don were in working order, fired each evening.[9]

The Cossack character, forceful and decisive, was central to Russian identity and typified the character of the current Kremlin class. In Petrovsky Prichal's billiards room, framed pictures memorialized the visits to the hotel of Russian foreign minister Sergei Lavrov and Dmitri Medvedev, once a president. There was also a photo of Putin, who had visited Petrovsky Prichal in the early years of his reign, as he was formulating his style of control.

Putin was the topic on-screen in the hotel lobby when I arrived. A state-TV newscaster discussing a Helsinki meeting that the Russian president would soon take with Donald Trump. The TV anchor predicted that the two would discuss the case of Maria Butina, a Russian national living in the United States. Through relationships in the National Rifle Association, she had attended Republican Party events and met party officials and candidates for national office. US federal prosecutors suspected that Butina was working on behalf of a Kremlin-connected banker to influence American politics.

As talk of Butina had circulated in Washington, she and I had traded messages and made plans to meet. I wanted to understand, if I could, if she was effectively advancing Kremlin goals, or if she was just another Anna Chapman, or a Billy Reilly, an amateur. The FBI got to Butina first, arresting her in Washington in July 2018, days before the Putin–Trump Helsinki talks.

Butina pleaded guilty to conspiring to work as an agent of a foreign government, and the United States deported her. Russia's leaders made Butina a *cause célèbre*, pearl-clutching over how inhumanely the US had treated her. Butina went on to become a Duma delegate with Putin's political party. When Russia launched a full-scale invasion of Ukraine in 2022, initiating a campaign of targeted civilian killings, Butina recorded supportive videos on social media.[10]

Butina struck me as too public, clumsy. Her efforts were bound to capture the attention of FBI counterintelligence, which, in the end, they did. But perhaps she was in keeping with the times, in which even an outsider like Billy could become deeply involved in national-security matters.

On the dock at the back of the hotel property, sitting at a table beneath a white cloth canopy, was Nastya Mikhailovskaya. Sever, her dog, sat on the deck beside her.

She was on a phone call and talking about Billy. "An American, yes," Mikhailovskaya said. "He came here through Polynkov."

Her call ended, and she told me she had been speaking with a regional security officer. "He said that there is nothing we can do. The FSB wouldn't hold someone for three years."

I asked if her contact had speculated about what had become of Billy. "He said someone would have tortured Billy for information and dumped his body in LNR or DNR."

Cossacks

*   *   *

In the morning, Mikhailovskaya and I left the hotel by foot along the riverfront heading west. The sky was bright and clear. She wore a blue sarong and walked the shoreline, her feet dipping in and out of the water. Sever, the dog, ran ahead kicking up sand.

I asked Mikhailovskaya about her phone call from the previous day, how serious her contact had been about the suggestion that Billy had been tortured. "This is what they do, how they get information," she said. "They take people down into the basement."

Kidnapping victims and POWs in the Donbas war often found themselves held in the basements of buildings on either side of the front line, where their captors starved, crowded, assaulted, and sometimes disappeared them. In Washington, in pursuit of a different story, I had met a Ukrainian militiaman who had lost his sight and hands and had spent months in one of these places on the Russian side, somehow surviving the experience and gaining his liberty in a POW swap. The Russian word for basement, *podval*, carried meaningful subtext.

Intelligence reports later revealed, in one incident of many, that in April 2014, special-operations groups led by Igor Strelkov had abducted Volodomyr Rybak, a city councilman from the town of Horlivka, thirty miles north of Donetsk, and Yuriy Popravka, a student at the Kiev Polytechnic Institute. Their bodies were later discovered in a tributary to the Seversky Donets River. They had been stabbed, burned, and disemboweled.[11]

I followed Mikhailovskaya along the river and wanted to trust her. She and I walked for less than a mile when she turned off the beach and up a pathway leading south. We cleared a stand of trees. Looming before us was the Rostov Arena, the World Cup venue, a modern stadium built at a cost of $300 million. The Brazilian national soccer team had played there just days before.

"I think we're getting close," Mikhailovskaya said.[12]

I followed her down an alleyway. Up ahead of us, several cars were parked in front of a cluster of buildings, the largest a warehouse of corrugated metal. A few patrol boats sat beside it, affixed with military insignia. Tall fences ran along either side of the pathway we were walking, and dense vegetation closed in overhead. I felt boxed in. I was about to turn around when several German shepherds flashed out of the warehouse and bolted toward us, barking loudly. It occurred to me that Mikhailovskaya had led me into a trap.

A voice called out, and the dogs came to heel. A man emerged from the warehouse. He was barrel-chested and wore a light-blue military uniform shirt. He waved his arms back and forth in front of his torso several times. "This is a closed zone," he yelled. We had taken a wrong turn.

I followed Mikhailovskaya back to the beach, and we continued west. Along the riverbank, we encountered groups of people sunning themselves on folding chairs. Several windsurfers with sails of many colors rode the breeze along the river.

That's when I saw it.

The clock tower, the Voroshilovskiy Bridge: the landmarks from the photo Billy had sent home in May 2015. We picked up our pace and in twenty yards, Mikhailovskaya and I were upon it, Mikhail Polynkov's volunteer-fighter camp.

It was a low building forty yards or so in length, fifteen yards deep, one and a half stories tall. It had a new coat of blue paint. I had seen photos of the building taken during the height of the Donbas war. There were plenty of images on social media. Bronya had been present in some of them. Volunteers had gathered on the railing of the building and taken group snapshots along the central stairs. But now there was no one around.

Mikhailovskaya called out, and two men emerged from a doorway of the building. They were middle-aged, fleshy in washed-out T-shirts, and had short haircuts. Mikhailovskaya told them she knew Bronya and Polynkov. One of the men placed a hand against his forehead as Mikhailovskaya talked, shading his eyes. The other man fastened his gaze on me.

"We had to move the camp," the first man said. He pointed to the Rostov Arena, its roof visible above the trees.

Governments that hosted the World Cup, the Olympic Games, and other major sporting events often cleared slums and vice districts before fans arrived, painting a false picture of the local environment. In Rostov, Russia addressed a different concern. The Kremlin had repeatedly maintained that it wasn't directly involved in the Donbas war, that citizens of the DNR and LNR were waging their own local rebellion. The Rostov fighter base muddied that narrative, and foreign soccer fans didn't need to see it.[13]

Mikhailovskaya tried to strike up a conversation with the men, but they appeared disinterested. Finally, she asked if they'd heard about an American named Vasya, or Billy, or William who had been at the camp years before. The men shrugged.

I walked down to the waterline and looked across the river to the clock tower. Crossing the faraway bridge overhead, cars slipped into the city, the sounds of their engines faintly audible. Billy had stood in this spot. He had been frustrated over his inability to cross the border into Donbas.

Billy's life had hung in the balance on this sand, and had he known it? He could have slipped out of the camp at night, taken a train to Moscow, and boarded a flight back home to Detroit. He could have found a spot on a boat, which he liked to do, and sailed from the Rostov port and into the Azov Sea, the Black Sea, and then the Mediterranean. He didn't. Traveling to Russia, just being here, wasn't enough. He wanted more, whether for himself or a US agency. Billy's ambitions left him exposed on this wide-open beach.

In that year, 2015, Russia's approach to Donbas was changing. When Ukrainian forces made gains or a big push, Russia would take a stronger hand, injecting troops and supplies to aid and direct the Donbas separatists and the volunteer brigades. Would-be Donbas military and political leaders fell out of Moscow's favor as abruptly as they gained it. Many met with violent deaths. A new group formed, Wagner, a Russian private military contracting company that enhanced the Kremlin's deniability.[14]

The wider world first learned of the existence of Wagner in February 2014, during the disarmament of Ukrainian soldiers in Crimea. Wagner had supplied some of the unmarked soldiers who came to represent Russian involvement there, the "little green men" who wore military fatigues but no identifying insignia.

After Russia secured Crimea, several hundred Wagner mercenaries decamped east, as fighting opened in Donbas. Although private military contracting companies were rife throughout the world, and many were owned or staffed by former US servicemen, this was a new phenomenon for Russia. It took the West by surprise. Fighting freelance was illegal under Russian federal statute, punishable by as many as fifteen years in prison. But Russian laws, like some US laws, could be ignored in pursuit of the national-security interest.[15]

Since Wagner was not an official element of the Russian armed forces, the

Kremlin could say it had no control over the group. This dovetailed with Putin's continued assertion that the Donbas war was an internal Ukrainian issue. Although the United States and European Union applied sanctions against Russian agencies and officials over Donbas, Russia's shading of its activity there complicated the international response to the conflict.

Wagner was effective, yet it didn't have a large staff or surfeit of specialists. The group needed more men as its mission expanded into Syria, supporting President Bashar al-Assad.[16]

Wagner was after fresh bodies. One location where its agents could find people to fill their ranks, good with weapons and foolhardy enough, was the volunteer-fighter base on Rostov's Don River bank. Syria, a country that fascinated Billy, presented another version of his fate.

*　　*　　*

My doubts about Mikhailovskaya grew. Had she known that the fighter camp would be empty? Was she leading an exercise in wasting my time and wearing me out, presenting a prepared picture?

Finding the camp devoid of activity did appear to motivate her. Over the ensuing days and evenings, she worked her phone, pressing old contacts and making new ones. She often called the security man who had mentioned the *podval*. She told me that his name was Valery, and I did my best to eavesdrop when she phoned him.

The tone of their calls revealed that Valery was against helping us. But Mikhailovskaya pushed him. "You have children," she said on one call. "What does it matter if he's American or Russian? What if he was your son?"

I continued to puzzle over her motivation, since she sometimes expressed her antipathy for the US. One evening, we were sitting on the dock at Petrovsky Prichal, with the sun sinking over the Don. "We consider America our enemy," she said. "Everywhere the United States goes, it brings death and destruction. Iraq, Afghanistan, Libya, where they killed Muammar Qaddafi. We are against this policy where America rules the world."

I held my own opinions close. I had lost interest in having political discussions in Russia. I knew that my country sometimes pursued foreign military actions that undercut moral authority. Countries were not moral enterprises.

Mikhailovskaya spoke in absolutes, failing to acknowledge the suffering that her own country was inflicting on Ukraine. She appeared to view the Russian president, like so many Russians did, as without flaw.

"Watch this," she said, calling her dog, Sever, to attention.

"Putin," she said. The dog leapt to its feet. "Putin," Mikhailovskaya repeated. "Putin." Sever craned back his head and howled.

*   *   *

I had been corresponding with Terry Reilly throughout my stay in Russia. She and Bill were useful resources. They had been down many of these same roads before me. A few days into my Rostov visit, Terry told me that she and Bill had developed a new plan. Fixed between two milestones, the third anniversary of Billy's June 2015 disappearance and his approaching thirty-second birthday in September, they decided to confront the FBI.

The Reillys drove to Detroit. At the FBI reception desk, they talked to a receptionist who sat behind bulletproof glass. They asked to speak with Tim Reintjes.

The woman left her chair and soon returned. "He has no new information," she said.

"*We* have some new information *for him*," Bill countered.

The woman waved them off. "He'll call you if he wants to talk to you." The Reillys left the FBI office feeling defeated again.

On the drive home, Terry phoned me. "He's a coward," she shrieked. "Sitting behind his little desk. He didn't even have the decency to come out and talk to us. We've gotten no help from the government. Not one iota."

She began to cry but quickly gathered herself. This was the Reillys' odd mix of emotions. They often felt dispirited as they wandered the FBI's hall of mirrors, but the love they had for their son wouldn't let them lie down. "We'll never give up," Terry said.[17]

The Reillys' resolve inspired me. After my call with Terry, I pressed Nastya Mikhailovskaya to develop new options through her network of contacts. She said she was leaving for Donbas soon, but she promised to continue to help. She told me was working on brokering a meeting that might break open the search.

We were sitting on the dock at the hotel one evening when her phone rang. Valery, her security services contact, was calling. Mikhailovskaya glanced at me several times during their conversation, as though they were discussing me. "Valery, come on," she said coyly, laughing. When their call ended, I asked what she had found so amusing.

"He asked, 'Are you still with that American guy? Why isn't he in the *podval* already?'" I stared at her. "Oh, he was just joking," she said.[18]

CHAPTER THIRTY-NINE

A Different Country

I rode a small elevator five floors to the Rostov branch of the Investigative Committee. When the doors opened, there was no bulletproof glass, no receptionist, just an unadorned, low-ceiling hallway lined with many offices, their doors closed.

I tried one of the doors. Two men were arguing from either ends of a tandem desk. Halting their debate, they directed me to another office further down the hallway. There I found a doughy middle-aged man tucked behind a desk. He had a dark, bushy mustache. I told him I wanted to speak with the investigator working the Billy Reilly case.

The man shot to his feet. His face flushed red. He pointed at me. "You are William?" he shouted. I was sorry to disappoint him. But at least I knew I was in the right place.

The man directed me to a third office down the hall. There a man in his thirties with sandy-colored hair sat at a desk. He wore a lavender officer's blouse with gold-starred shoulder boards. Framed pictures of Putin and Dzerzhinsky hung on the wall behind him.

Two men and two women in their twenties were clustered around him, gazing at a photo album over his shoulder. I felt like I had interrupted a meeting of the high school yearbook committee. They all appeared overly young for the serious work of investigating crimes in Russia.

The officer introduced himself: Sergey Shvetsov. He saluted, and we shook hands.

251

I asked him about the Reilly case. He said he was overseeing it but that he knew little about it. Shvetsov explained that he had been on the case for only a month or so. He had replaced a colleague of his, Alexander Ganus, who no longer worked with the department. I asked where I could find Ganus, but Shvetsov said he didn't know.

I expected few straight answers from the Investigative Committee but waded into my inquiries. I asked Shevtsov what he thought had happened to Billy. He said that Billy had likely crossed the border into Ukraine. "In that case, there's nothing we can do," he said. "That's a different country." Billy's case presented endless opportunities to pass the buck.

Demonstrating that he had nothing to hide, Shvetsov directed one of his assistants to retrieve a folder from a shelf by the door. The folder was choked with papers, hundreds of them. String threaded through the punch holes of the documents and held the stack together like a diner menu. This was the Investigative Committee's Billy Reilly case file.

Imagining its great value, I sensed opportunity. If no one in uniform had made a real effort to find Billy, I might be the first one with an unvarnished aim to mine the file for leads.

When I reached for it, Shvetsov said I would need to complete a request form. He suggested I call later in the week.[1]

I filled the following days combing Rostov for the places listed on Billy's credit-card statements. There was a grocery, Auchan, and M.Video, an electronics store. I visited the bank where he had picked up the Western Union wires that his mother had sent him. The main train station in town where Billy had departed on his Volga sojourn looked like any other. The small commuter depot, where Andrei Chikatilo, a serial killer known as "the Butcher of Rostov," or "the Rostov Ripper," had searched for victims in the late Soviet period, felt transient, desolate.

At Smirnov, the café behind Polynkov's base where the volunteer fighters had stuck Billy with the tab, I had a beer with the owner, who said he didn't remember any American. In this city-dust and gloom and low sunlight, people still pointed out the store on Bolshaya Sadovaya Street that in the USSR sold milk. Rostov was full of curiosities that marked a lost time.

I saw Billy taking these same steps, consuming these sights, and I imagined the effect they'd had on him. He had never been away from home for such an extended period of time. In Rostov, Billy would have seen how life is when viewed from new angles, how foreign, but also how similar to what we think is unique about ourselves. In Rostov, his conception of adventure had fallen away, replaced by the reality of its surprises and tedium.

I needed to know more about Billy's life there and thought of someone who could help me fill in the blank places. I met a local private investigator in a shopping-mall parking lot. He handed me a sheet of paper with an address on it.

The address was in the center of town. I walked down an alleyway and into a courtyard. Arriving at a residential tower, I spoke with the doorman guarding its entry. I asked for Alexander Ganus, and the doorman pointed through the lobby window. Ganus was pacing the courtyard, talking animatedly into a phone.

Ganus was the former Rostov Investigative Committee official who had led Billy's case. He was the one who had taken sworn statements from Terry and Bill when they had visited the office with Russell Bentley and his wife, Lyudmila, in 2017. Officially at least, Ganus had conducted more work on Billy's case than any other Rostov investigator.

Ganus was tall and thin and wore his hair short. He looked to be in his thirties. When he finished his call, I introduced myself and said I knew Billy's parents. Ganus looked surprised, but he quickly regained his composure. As an investigator, he was used to curious encounters.

Even if Ganus didn't know where Billy was, he knew what the Investigative Committee and maybe even the Interior Ministry or the FSB thought of the case. He could help me see through the smoke screen if he was so inclined.

He wasn't. His back going rigid, Ganus said that Russian law allowed the dissemination of case details only to a victim's family. He was retreating to protocol, yet he left an opening. "I could definitely help," he said in a low voice. "I can get answers for the parents."

I asked what he could do. "I have a lot of people in Donbas," he said.

"That's where Reilly ended up?" I asked.[2]

Ganus looked across the courtyard. His eyes fixed on a distant point as he deliberated. He said that his work had a price. I could have expected this though I was still disappointed. I understood his need to earn a living, but was there no one who had pity for the Reillys? Surrounding them were people with uncertain intentions. Dmitri Tyurin had taken pay from the Reillys yet produced no hard results. I didn't know what Nastya Mikhailovskaya's motive was, but she had one. Even I had a motive, as I was gathering material for an article. Meanwhile, Terry and Bill suffered.

I told Ganus that I didn't pay for information.

I later passed his number to the Reillys, and they told me that they called him with the help of an interpreter. They said Ganus asked them to wire him $10,000, although he failed to summarize what that money would buy. They declined his offer.[3]

Parting ways with Ganus, I returned my attention to obtaining Billy's investigative file. Several times, I called the number Shvetsov had given me, but the voice on the end of the line told me to try again later.

I was running out of time. Paul Beckett, my boss at the *Journal*, phoned again, and I could tell that his patience was wavering. I had been away from Washington for more than a month. That provided hardly enough of a chance to solve the Reilly mystery. This work required patience, diligence. But if I wanted to continue doing it for the *Journal*, I'd have to return soon from the field.

Pressing now, I took a cab to the Investigative Committee offices. Sergey Shvetsov was standing on the curb flanked by his female aides, returning from lunch, working a toothpick between his teeth. He smirked at me, apparently surprised I was still in town. Up in his office, he gave me the Reilly file as though conceding defeat.

I cracked open the file on a desk and began photographing its contents with my phone, working quickly before Shvetsov could have a change of heart. I glimpsed each sheet as I shot it and recognized documents I already possessed. Photocopies of Billy's passport. Pictures he had texted home. Most of the documents were new to me, however, forms typed on the letterhead of Russian state agencies, stamped and flourished in signatures.

* * *

On the dock at Petrovsky Prichal, I scrolled through the pictures of the investigative file. I quickly realized that Billy's case folder, all 300-plus pages, could have been a quarter of its size. The documents consisted mostly of request letters sent to government agencies, notices of the forwarding of such appeals to other offices, and denials from these third agencies, the correspondence a closed loop producing the appearance of activity. Yet in this sea of bureaucracy, I did discover sunken treasures.

In the materials I had found on Billy's hard drives earlier in the year, and in the text messages he had exchanged with his mother, Billy had appeared tightly bound to Amera Lomangcolob, the alleged terror node. The nature of their relationship had never been clear to me. The side trip to the Far East, and whatever he and Lomangcolob were engineering there, had been a provocative possible explanation for Billy's disappearance. It could have explained why he had never turned up in Russia, having left it for Thailand. The flight to Bangkok that Terry had booked for him had transited from Moscow via Doha, Qatar. As I flipped through the Investigative Committee file, I stopped short when I came upon a document from the US embassy in Qatar.

The letter stated that Qatar had no record of Billy's arrival there. It was unmistakable: he had missed the first leg of his Bangkok side trip. Billy had never gone to see Lomangcolob in Thailand. Terry's motherly appeals via texts and phone calls had guided him away from a potential crisis in the Far East.

Another document in the investigative file contained information I had been seeking for months, GPS data for the cell phone Billy had used while in Russia. I couldn't independently verify the document, but it stated that Billy's phone had continued to transmit until July 3, 2015. By local Russian time, this date was eight days after Terry and Bill had last heard from their son.

The document said that during the week-plus period between the suspension of communications with his parents and the final disabling of his phone, the device had been transmitting its signal from Rostov-on-Don, not from across the Ukrainian border in Donbas. This was some evidence, perhaps, that he hadn't crossed into Ukraine. But the fact that Billy had apparently lost control of his phone, to which he was so attached, was troubling. I thought about those lost eight days, a critical period of time.[4]

I puzzled over the meaning of the information contained in the Investigative Committee file. It was possible that the file was a sham, a paper trail crafted to support an artificial conclusion. But if these documents were genuine, then Billy might never have left Rostov. He might have chosen to sever contact with his parents, or maybe he had been separated from his phone. This new information narrowed my hopes but not the search. I thought of what Dmitri Tyurin had said, that Billy was likely alive. I wanted to believe that.

Several men in Cossack tunics passed by my table on the way to the end of the dock. Watching them go, I realized that the case file lacked an obvious element. Tyurin had told the Reillys and me that the Rostov Investigative Committee at one point had interrogated men at the volunteer-fighter base. In the file, I discovered the summary of an interview.

The subject of the interview was a man named Vyacheslav Korshunov. The document stated that he lived in a village called Krasny Sulin, in the Rostov region. Ganus had taken the interview in October 2017, more than two years after Billy's disappearance.

Korshunov shared a personal history in the interview. He said that when fighting started in Ukraine in 2014, he had decided to take up arms, joining a volunteer brigade named Rome. He assumed the call sign *Funt*, or Pound. Korshunov said he had been based in Donbas, in the town of Sverdlovsk, in the Luhansk region. Sometime in 2015, the exact date eluding him, he said, he had found himself in the town of Darevka in the so-called LNR. A group of volunteer fighters had gathered there in a field.

The interview summary quoted Korshunov: "I met a guy who was from America who they called William Paul Reilly. I hung out with him through guys who had been with him and who knew English. I can also speak English, but not totally."

The testimony stopped me cold. Here was an alleged eyewitness account, possible evidence that Billy had indeed crossed the border into Ukraine. I wanted to maintain my skepticism, but the words on the page pulled me in. Had Billy taken that final leap from Oxford and into the war? This was the place he had always wanted to be, in the midst of armed struggle, history as it is made. Everything I knew about the people who waged this war, and about Billy, indicated that he and they were ill matched. Yet in his interview with Ganus, Korshunov said Billy had been there.

"William said he had followed the war in Ukraine through news channels and couldn't not come and join a volunteer brigade," the testimony read. "I was really interested to listen to a foreign citizen's impressions of Russia and Ukraine and hung out with William a long time."

Korshunov testified that the volunteer groups stayed in Darevka for the day. "After this, they formed us into brigades and we headed toward Raevka, LNR. I don't know where they sent William's brigade. And I didn't see. Later, I heard from someone that William was in the neighborhood of the Donetsk airport. I didn't hear anything else about William."

I read this document several times, feeling for its meaning. The mention of the airport was curious. The Donetsk airport had been completed two years before the fighting began and was a leap forward for the city, an $860 million symbol of the region's growing economy. Once the fighting started, the airport became a focus, as each side struggled for control of it. They destroyed the airport in the process, with heavy human losses.[5]

I remembered what Bronya Kalmyk had told the Reillys' interpreter by phone in 2015, that Billy had been 300, the code for someone wounded in battle. But I knew that the fighting for control of the airport had concluded in January 2015, four months before Billy's arrival in Russia. Korshunov's reference to the airport felt like a red herring. The battle for the airport was the sort of kinetic event that could serve as cover for all manner of happenstance, including disappearance and unexplained death.

The interview summary was larded with strange elements. Korshunov mentioned Oxford, Michigan, along with Terry and Bill by name. I didn't imagine that Billy had shared such information with a stranger. And if he had met Billy once and only briefly, Korshunov was unlikely to have recalled such details, especially since Ganus had taken this interview more than two years after the supposed encounter in the field outside Darevka. Plus, Korshunov said himself that he didn't speak English well, and Billy's conversational Russian was substandard. How could they have communicated adequately? The inclusion of Billy's complete name seemed odd also, but maybe in Russia, a culture of patronymics, it was not. I took into account the likelihood that Ganus himself had inserted these details, and that he'd done so not to deceive but as an official including identifying details, inadvertently subverting Korshunov's testimony.

My head spun with the possibilities and contradictions in Korshunov's interview. The summary's final line appeared particularly calculated. "I have a very good memory for faces," Korshunov said.[6]

The testimony proved one of two things: either Billy had indeed made it to war in Donbas, or Ganus, the investigator, was complicit in the construction of a cover story. Either way, Korshunov presented a tantalizing new thread.

And this compounded my practical dilemma. I had to find Korshunov and ask him my own questions. However, Mikhailovskaya had called to say that she'd succeeded in brokering the critical meeting she had previously mentioned. I couldn't remain in the field for much longer if I wanted to hold onto my job. Paul Beckett was recalling me to Washington.

I calculated that I had time for only one final errand.

CHAPTER FORTY

A Drive

The M4 highway carried evenly through far-reaching steppe from Rostov-on-Don toward Moscow, four lanes in either direction. Andrei, the driver, preferred smoking to talking. The scenery provided its own manner of interaction. There were no billboards along its margins spoiling it. We steered through it and were a part of it. We approached towns. Wooden stands dotted the highway margins with fruits and vegetables. Dried fish hung head-down on laundry lines. Signs beckoned: honey for sale. We left towns behind.

Fields of sunflowers, cultivated for their oil, surged into view. Beyond lay the plains, yellow and bare after the wheat harvest. The landscape extended for versts along the steppe, offering great vistas. Far to the northeast, a dark cloud hovered, emptying rain on the earth below it. We drove for hours into the sun.

The phone in my pocket vibrated. It was a text message from the *Journal's* security department. My colleagues and I sometimes covered war and protests, and the paper kept an eye on us. The murder of Daniel Pearl, the *Journal* reporter abducted in Pakistan in 2002, remained an example of the potential dangers of this work. In recent years, the paper no longer allowed reporters a free hand in the field. Before my trip to Russia, I had agreed to alert our security chief to risky contacts and meetings. The day before the drive out of Rostov, he and I had vetted my driver and route. I had granted the security unit access to my location through an app on my phone. As Andrei drove onward, the security team back in the United States monitored my progress and checked in with me periodically, asking me to confirm that all was well.

I didn't mind the coverage. But as Andrei and I burrowed into the steppe, I knew that there was little our security unit could do if trouble came. The group would know my final location and not much more. No one would come to save me. Billy's predicament had shown how feckless or helpless the State Department could be when bad things happened in Russia. But moving out beyond safe harbors was the way to solve Billy's mystery.

Andrei had driven four hours north of Rostov when he turned off the highway, steering the local road toward Veshenskaya, the home of Mikhail Sholokhov, the author of *And Quiet Flows the Don*.[1]

The potholes were so deep and numerous that our progress reduced to a crawl. The car's radio lost its signal and pumped out static. The road bent distantly into uncultivated lands.

We had driven seventy miles off the M4. Seeking our bearings, we found a squat building set back from the road and parked there. Inside, a slow-moving man with white hair stood lonely behind a cashbox, sundries scattered on the shelves behind him. Sitting on a counter in plastic bags were *bubliki*, a sort of small, hardened bagel. The clerk poured out coffee, ten rubles a paper cup, or about a cent. Wind kicked up outside and whistled through the cracks in the walls.

My thoughts turned to Aleksandr Solzhenitsyn. He had grown up in Rostov-on-Don, poor and fatherless. In 1971, the year after he had won the Nobel Prize, Solzhenitsyn took a road trip with a friend in the local region. They stopped at a store that might well have been something like this one.

They returned to their car from the shop and resumed their trip, and Solzhenitsyn took ill. At a hospital, doctors discovered burns on his body but could neither explain them nor relieve his pain. They made a dire prognosis. Solzhenitsyn, however, recovered. The episode added to his lore. Only after the Soviet Union's fall, a retired lieutenant colonel of the KGB, writing in his memoirs, revealed the details of an encounter in the roadside store. An umbrella tipped with poison, a bungled assassination.[2]

Standing on the steppe, I couldn't be sure of the risk I was undertaking. All I knew was where we were headed. The instructions had been simple. Drive until you see the tank, where the roads to Veshenskaya and Bokovskaya diverge. The café will be across the road.

A Drive

Andrei stubbed out a cigarette. He said we were getting close.

We drove an hour more along the road that was perforated with potholes. The landscape rolled by in its evenness and beauty. Up ahead rose a man-made object.

It was a tank, the one foretold, a T-34. This T-34 was raised on a plinth, a monument to Soviet glory. The T-34 had halted the advance of the Heer, Germany's land forces, and now it halted ours.

Nearby was the café. It was shrouded by a stand of trees, and wisps of gray smoke were curling from its chimney. A worn sign dangled in the breeze beneath an awning: Fireplace Snackhouse. Parked out front of the café was a white Volga sedan. The setting, remote and windblown, had the feel of America's Western frontier, before the railroads, before the law.

I stepped from the car and approached the café. I saw that there was a courtyard in front of the building and that a stone wall bordered it. Within the courtyard, several picnic tables burned in the afternoon sun.

At one of the tables sat a man, in his thirties or so, and across from him a boy of maybe ten. They were dressed like country people who dirtied themselves working the land. They ate quietly.

There was one other person in the courtyard, a man at a nearby table. He had a large head and Asian features. He wore camouflage pants and jacket, with metal stars pinned to its shoulder boards. He nodded when he saw me.

In front of him, resting on the table, were three white ceramic plates. They were empty but for a shimmer of grease. He was chewing a final bit of food. Wiping his mouth with a sleeve, he invited me to sit on the bench across the table from him.

I shook the man's fleshy right hand. This caused the medals pinned to his jacket front to tinkle against one another like pieces from a board game. This drew my eye to them, and from there to the name tag that was stitched over the left breast of his jacket: "Bronya."

I had declined to search for Vyacheslav Korshunov and instead took Nastya Mikhailovskaya's brokered meeting, because Bronya Kalmyk had not been liquidated, as the Ukrainians had alleged. The manager of the Rostov volunteer-fighter camp was sitting before me.

Agents from Ukraine's security services often spread false reports to demoralize their foe, even phoning people in Russia to report the deaths of loved ones who were still active in battle. These were the psychological tactics of war.

Bronya was a burly man, very much alive. A belt strained across the arc of his belly. Acne scars sprinkled his cheeks. His hair was shaved close to the scalp. He had few teeth, only one I could see, and it hung crookedly in his mouth as though it were about to drop.

Bronya was uneasy. His eyes darted in many directions. He said he was leaving, that he had to return to the volunteer-fighter camp, which he said he had relocated to a nearby farm. He reached for a wooden cane.

"Hold on," I said, having come so far. "Let me show you something."

I held up my phone. On it was one of Elena Gorbacheva's photos from the Kazan train station in Moscow, the day that Billy had arrived in Russia in May 2015. At the sight of the picture, Bronya's features brightened. He jabbed an index finger at the phone. "That's Vasily," he bellowed. He set aside leaving for now.

I asked Bronya how he had met the American. "In Rostov at that time, there were a lot of people in fatigues," he said. "He probably asked one of those guys where to go. I had a lot of foreigners at that time. French, Italian, Australian, American. Vasily just showed up. I never heard anything about him from Polynkov. He came. And he left in a couple days. Then he came back."

A pack of cigarettes lay on the table, Donskoy Tabak, a brown wrapper, gold trim. The cigarette looked like a toothpick between Bronya's large fingers as he lit it and took a pull. He described Billy at the Rostov camp, saying that he had fallen in with a rough crowd. "'Russian vodka,' he would say. If he drank fifty grams, he couldn't stop. He was drunk all the time."

Billy hadn't been much of a drinker. That's what his family had said. Adventure encouraged one to try new things.

"All different kinds of people came to the base," Bronya said. "Some were drunks, some were drug addicts, some were crazy, some were aggressive." Bronya said that several men at the camp found Billy an easy mark, stealing his money.

I knew that some of what Bronya said was true. But would he be truthful about the portions of the story that mattered? I asked what had become of Billy.

"Vasya wanted to go to Donbas," Bronya said. "But he didn't want to get a stamp in his passport at the border. When he got home, your CIA would arrest him." Bronya laughed, and his medals tapped out a tune. "I told him there was another way he could go." Bronya's voice dropped to a confidential tone. "He told me he didn't want to fight."

I had expected Bronya to boast and prevaricate, but here he spoke what felt like the truth. I pressed for more of it. I asked what Billy had intended to do, if not to join the battle.

But Bronya suddenly wasn't paying attention. He was looking beyond me.

The father and son at the next table were gone, and three men were entering the courtyard. They were tall and athletic. Their short haircuts were fresh. Their clothes were new and had a casual style, like the sort one might purchase in a city. The men took seats at a nearby table and fell into quiet discussion, close enough to pick up what Bronya and I were saying.

The arrival of these men appeared to unnerve Bronya. He spoke loudly, with a swaggering quality. "I gave Vasily a helmet," he said. "And a flak jacket, a shoulder holster, and an outfit of camouflage fatigues."

I reminded Bronya that he'd just said that Billy had no interest in fighting. Bronya waved me off.

Changing the subject, he said that the separatists periodically gained control of portions of the Russia-Ukraine border and secreted people and matériel through them into Donbas. He said these passageways were called black corridors.

"There were a few other foreigners with Vasily," Bronya said. "I told them to leave their SIM cards behind, because the Ukrainians locate the pulse and send in rockets. The black corridor opened. I put them in the red van, the one Strelkov gave us. And they went across the border."

I asked him where the van had gone once it had driven into Donbas. Bronya said that commanders had assigned the foreigners to fighting brigades.

If Bronya was telling the truth about Billy being deposited into the care of Donbas commanders, this appeared to match Vyacheslav Korshunov's Investigative Committee account of the volunteer-fighter roundup outside the village of Darevka.

I told Bronya about Korshunov's account, but Bronya tilted his head, doubting that it was true. His voice dropped to a whisper. "Vasily was naïve," he said. "I told him to stay away from those guys." Bronya's eyes flashed to the men sitting at the nearby table. I knew that amid Russia's war in Donbas, there were competing factions: local Donbas fighters, intelligence operatives from Moscow, and many more in between struggling over power, money, and ideology.

Bronya appeared to catch himself, and again his tone and direction shifted. "He probably got involved in an attack, and they buried him somewhere in DNR. Do you know what's left of a body after a tank rolls over it?" I was trying to separate Bronya's fact from his fiction, when he abruptly swiped his pack of cigarettes off the table. "I've told all I know," he said.

With difficulty, he rose from the table and grabbed for the wooden cane. He relied on it as we proceeded to the exit of the courtyard, passing by the three men, who didn't watch us go.

Out by the road, Bronya rested a hand on the hood of the white Volga sedan. This car had been the preferred model of the Soviet apparatchik, a marker of status and influence. It still held meaning these decades later, like the T-34, each a symbol of former Soviet glory that many Russian people resisted relinquishing.

Bronya wheezed from the effort it had taken him to make it to the car. He looked out over its roof, across the plains. The sun had passed its meridian and its shafts were slanting, causing him to squint.

"Why did Vasily come here?" he asked. "For adventure? He could have gone to the next town for adventure. Why did he need to come all the way to Russia?" It sounded like Bronya was mourning someone he'd known who'd been lost.

He caught himself. A thought occurred to him, and he laughed. "It would be better if we had a war against America," Bronya said. "I want to go to Fifth Avenue. That's where Angelina Jolie lives?" He looked at me searchingly. "I'll go there and fuck her," he said.

Bronya climbed into the white Volga. I watched the car go.[3]

Andrei and I drove some distance from the café. I pointed him to the side of the road. I needed to get everything down in a notebook before I lost the details of my talk with Bronya.

There were facts and story points. There were the places in between them where I believed the truth about Billy lived and was hidden. I took down Bronya's version of Billy's crossing into Donbas and thought of Korshunov but was unprepared to credit either of them fully. I thought of the three men in the café courtyard and if they had come to put eyes and ears on us. I thought of Russia's unknowable layers of secrecy. I wrote in the notebook, my thoughts compounding.

My phone vibrated. The *Journal*'s security unit was requesting a status report. "When will you move from the tank?" the message read. Through the car's windshield, I saw Andrei, a cigarette in his teeth, leaning against the T-34.

CHAPTER FORTY-ONE

Washington

I returned to Washington in July 2018 armed with information and credibility. Now was the time to approach the Reillys' elected representatives on Capitol Hill. Billy had been missing in a cloud of FBI suspicion for more than three years. He deserved an advocate in Washington.

My goals were modest. I didn't expect to persuade Michigan senators Gary Peters and Debbie Stabenow to phone FBI director Christopher Wray. And I knew that their offices couldn't solve every problem that came their way. They were busy with the senators' committee assignments, drawing up legislation and politicking for votes in the Senate, managing campaigns, and fielding constituent petitions. Like the Hostage Recovery Fusion Cell, the senators' offices had to pick and choose. They had helped the Reillys years before and come up empty. But had they done enough? If I could scare up a lead or two from them that I could pursue on my own, I'd count it a victory.

I hadn't spent my career in Washington, and I might have been a little naïve.

Press staffers for Peters and Stabenow offered little. They declined to arrange off-the-record talks with senior colleagues of theirs who might have known details about the case and the FBI's involvement in it. It was demoralizing that so little information about Billy's disappearance, never mind any accountability, could be summoned in my own country.

I found another way to try for it.

Beneath the Capitol dome, behind the wall closest to the rostrum of the Speaker of the US House of Representatives, there is an anteroom. The room is known as the Speaker's Lobby. It is rectangular and lit by chandeliers. Portraits of House Speakers of the past line the walls. Several doors lead from the room directly onto the House floor.

The House chamber came into use in the 1850s, with only House representatives allowed to enter it. Ordinary citizens could loiter in the Speaker's Lobby and pass notes to representatives with the help of people known as doorkeepers. A petitioner would write a note and hand it to a doorkeeper, who would then deliver it to congressmen on the House floor. This would alert the representative that someone was waiting to talk in the Speaker's Lobby. By some accounts, it was in this room where the practice of political lobbying began.

Today, the Speaker's Lobby retains its clubby charm. Doorkeepers continue to deliver notes into the House chamber, although now access to the Speaker's Lobby is restricted.

The general public is barred from the Speaker's Lobby, and so are, interestingly, the press secretaries of House representatives. Reporters holding a Hill credential are one of the few groups that may enter. The Speaker's Lobby is one of the only places on Capitol Hill where a reporter can be sure to speak directly with a member of Congress without the presence of a press manager, as long as the representative responds favorably to a note delivered by a doorkeeper.[1]

In the summer of 2018, a doorkeeper carried my note into the House chamber, and in a few minutes Mike Bishop entered the Speaker's Lobby looking for me. Bishop, a Republican, had represented Michigan's eighth district since 2015. A lawyer and real estate broker, he served on the House Judiciary Committee, which performed oversight of the Department of Justice, including the FBI. His office had made calls on the Reillys' behalf after Billy had disappeared. Bishop's committee assignment had given him relevant insight and context.[2]

I waved down Bishop and shared my shopworn summary of Billy's story. Bishop took in the information, his brow creasing. "This is the first I've heard of it," he said.

He explained that he'd had his share of encounters with the FBI and groused over the partial responses that Bureau officials routinely gave to Judiciary Committee inquiries. "It's very hard dealing with the FBI," he said. He explained that the Bureau always seemed to avoid oversight.

Bishop had experienced similar obstinacy with the State Department. He told me that in Tanzania the year before, he had visited the US embassy in support of a constituent who had died while on a safari. "The woman at the embassy turned me away. She said they didn't want to upset US–Tanzanian relations. And I'm a congressman." Exasperated by bureaucracy and appearing to sympathize with the Reillys, Bishop connected me with one of his staffers.[3]

On a call, the staffer said he had tried to assist the Reillys years earlier. The State Department, he said, had provided nothing of significance. He had pressed the US embassy in Moscow to coordinate with the local Interior Ministry, but the Russian side was unresponsive.

There had to be more. I phoned Bishop, and we spoke several times. He sounded frustrated, as perplexed as I was at how the Bureau managed to elude obvious questions. "The FBI had control of the narrative," Bishop told me. "They had control of the evidence and could tell us what they wanted us to hear. And we had no way of refuting it."[4]

*   *   *

Mike Bishop was a US congressman sitting on the House Judiciary Committee and performing oversight of the FBI, and he couldn't get answers for Billy in Washington. How was I going to manage it?

I didn't know, but I had to keep trying. I believed that Andy Arena could provide worthwhile context. Arena had been the special agent in charge of the FBI's Detroit office when Billy had signed on to work there. Arena had also been instrumental in the adjustment of the FBI's usage of sources and informants after the revelation of the Whitey Bulger scandal.

Arena had left the FBI in 2012 so could now speak freely. He lived in Metro Detroit still, and there led the Detroit Crime Commission, a law-enforcement consultative board. Unlike many FBI agents and officials I'd encountered, who appeared threatened by the possible revelation of information, Arena was candid.

We discussed the lessons of Whitey Bulger. "You get in trouble real quick if you mishandle a source," Arena said. "You never ever trust a source. Agents get too comfortable. Then they find out the source is running a rogue operation." Arena raised the possibility that Billy had done just this in Russia.

When I described the case's curious points Arena appeared to change his mind. He focused on the initial visit that agent Tim Reintjes had made to the Reillys' home. "You don't just go out there. Something caused it." I encouraged Arena to talk through this theory.

"It sounds like they may have been having contact, and contact went cold, or he called and told him there was a problem," he said. "Either they knew that something happened, or they got suspicious he was involved in something. It could have been when they found out, they panicked. It may have been a misfire."[5]

Considering Arena's inside understanding of the FBI and the Detroit office, his candor was absorbing.

I contacted several other former FBI agents. I met with one who said that Billy's case resembled other instances, he said, of the CIA co-opting FBI CHSs and dispatching them abroad. "This is all CIA-directed," the former agent said of Billy's case. "The FBI doesn't give a shit about Ukraine and Russia."[6] It was true that CHS, via contacts made between CIA officers and FBI agents in a JTTF and elsewhere, could end up working for the CIA.

A former CIA officer met me for lunch one afternoon at The Prime Rib, a steakhouse on K Street in Washington. The walls were coated in glossy dark paint, and an elderly man felt out jazz standards on a black grand piano. The former officer explained the concept of nonofficial cover.

The spy game had rules that adversarial countries observed as a way to maintain respect and restraint. The CIA placed spies in public jobs in overseas US embassies, often in the cultural or political departments. The official job was a uniform of sorts, which clearly declared one's allegiance. It was a way of letting the local counterintelligence agencies know who was who. That's how the game was played. A CIA officer in an official job in an embassy received what's known as official cover. The host country might harass or thwart the officer, but since the CIA was showing local respect, the rules of restraint usually protected the officer from arrest, or worse.

However, nonofficial cover, sending a CIA officer or asset to another country beyond the bounds of a diplomatic mission, was something different. It was among the most dangerous undertakings in espionage. It amounted to operating in civilian clothes behind enemy lines. For centuries, countries had executed adversaries who had operated in this way, out of uniform. This was what the Russian Illegals had done in the United States, and it was one reason why the FBI had made such a public spectacle of them. The CIA referred to people who worked under nonofficial cover as NOCs.

"A NOC can't have overt US government affiliation," the former CIA officer told me over lunch. "The NOCs have no way out." The likelihood that Billy had been a NOC was hard for me to credit. This seemed too deep for someone of his partial abilities. But I also didn't dismiss the possibility out of hand. "If he's a NOC and the Russians knew it, their response is serious. They will never give him up."[7]

The calls, coffees, and lunches I cycled through in Washington made for interesting conversation, but they provided only context. None of the people I met had direct knowledge of Billy's case. What they told me was speculative. Armed with a deeper understanding of these issues, I returned to my research files, searching for material that might yield evidence of the FBI's involvement in Billy's Russia trip.

The FBI's Confidential Human Source Policy Guide outlined how an agent could dispatch a CHS to another country. This was not done cavalierly, but through an elaborate process that required consent from several offices and divisions. Once the CHS was on the trip, the policy guide stated, "as a general rule, an employee based domestically is prohibited from contacting a CHS while the CHS is in a foreign country."[8]

This line in the policy guide reminded me of the text messages between Billy and Reintjes, the correspondence that the parents had discovered after their son's disappearance. In the final lines of the text-message exchange, on May 14, 2015, the evening before Billy had left for Russia, Tim Reintjes had asked, "Whatsapp, skype, viber?"

"Once I load the apps," Billy had replied, "I'll msg u the info." Later that night, Billy had texted Reintjes again: "The number I got for those is the new phone number."[9]

This last message aroused my curiosity. I called Catie Cherri, Billy's sister. Catie said that before his trip, Billy had been unsure if the phone he had mainly been using in Michigan would connect properly while he was in Russia. I knew from my own travels there that not every US phone did so, at least in earlier years. Catie said Billy had bought a new phone before he'd departed for Moscow. He had made certain to choose a model that would operate on Russian cellular systems.[10]

The final exchange between Billy and his handler suggested that they had devised a method of communication they would employ while Billy was in Russia. This plan appeared to overreach the limits outlined in the CHS policy guide.

In the FBI, there were always more rules to read. The Bureau is an organization of handbooks, guidelines, and policies. The CHS policy guide alone is 195 pages long, and it's no breezy read. If agents made their way through this and other required study, they also had to contend with the fact that some FBI regulations contradicted one another or were otherwise unclear, providing allowances for interpretation.

"Despite all the written guidance in the FBI CHS manual, this is a murky business at best," Don Robinson, the former FBI Moscow legat, told me.

The CHS policy manual, while stating a prohibition against communicating with a traveling CHS, also provided a condition under which an agent could do just that, as long as it was "a requirement for the success or safety of the operation." As I made my way through FBI rules, I encountered one loophole after another.

The policy guide stated that FBI technology and operations divisions would devise "suitable methodology and available tools for the communication," allowing an agent to "communicate an emergency communications plan . . . to a CHS traveling for operational reasons."[11]

It was clear: Buried amid the FBI's rules were the permissions to break them. Here was the possible reasoning behind the timing of Tim Reintjes's initial visit to the Reillys' house in Oxford in 2015. The guidelines in the policy manual, when paired with the text messages Billy had exchanged with his handler before leaving for Russia, suggested that Reintjes had been speaking with Billy during the trip, and that this was how the FBI had learned something had gone wrong.

*   *   *

While I dug through documents and chased government leads, I was also speaking with Nastya Mikhailovskaya, the Igor Strelkov affiliate who had brokered my meeting with Bronya Kalmyk north of Rostov. She and I tried to develop new avenues of inquiry.

I was guarded, trying not to be credulous, given Mikhailovskaya's *siloviki* background. But I wasn't making great gains in the US, and Russia was where Billy had disappeared. She knew people there who had access to information.

On one of our calls, she suggested that I speak with Valery, her Russian security-service contact who had joked about sending me to the *podval*. I wrote him a text message, and we struck up a conversation. I didn't know who Valery really was, or why he seemed so friendly. I simply followed the lead.

The name he gave was Valery Prikhodko. He told me he ran a non-governmental organization headquartered in the Rostov region and that his group combated religious extremism. The organization was called the Center for Assistance to the State in Counteracting Extremist Activities.[12]

Prikhodko said that the group had a staff of sixty-seven people in several Russian cities. He explained that he helped law enforcement locate Russians who had disappeared in the Donbas war, whether on their own or otherwise. He said that roughly 1,500 people had gone missing there in the last five years.

Prikhodko explained further, saying that his group tracked undesirables who hid or committed crimes in the lawlessness of war in Donbas: Escaped cons, bail jumpers, wanted men, the mentally unsound. His agents were seeded in the disputed territories and along the border and had brought such people to heel, returning them to jail in Russia. His group's mission and mission statement appeared to differ, and I puzzled over why Prikhodko was talking to me.

At first formal, our relationship turned familiar, with Prikhodko telling jokes and swearing roguishly. If he was another obstacle placed in my path, I couldn't tell. I kept talking to him, simply since he kept talking to me.[13]

Mikhailovskaya called one morning and asked me to send her a copy of Billy's fingerprints. She said that Prikhodko had asked her for this. Bill and Terry said they had searched for prints already and that there were none. But I remembered something. The Reillys had once mentioned to me that Billy, years before, during his time with the FBI, had applied for a firearm license.

A clerk with the Michigan State Police confirmed my assumption. Every petition for a gun permit in Michigan required the applicant to provide a set of his or her fingerprints.[14]

I couldn't imagine that any state police department would delete a set of fingerprints once it possessed it. Police and the FBI compiled databases of prints they used to identify John and Jane Does and the perpetrators of crimes. The clerk told me that Michigan retained all of these prints in a database. Billy's fingerprints had to be there.

I couldn't request them. Only a family member could. Terry and Bill submitted the paperwork. The Michigan State Police sent the Reillys Billy's fingerprints in a digital file, and I forwarded this to Valery Prikhodko.[15]

The prints might have gone some way to addressing the question of where Billy was, but the underlying reason for his trip remained elusive.

I spoke later with Don Robinson, the former Moscow legat. Robinson had left the position in mid-2015. He said he couldn't recall an exact date for his departure, but he and I determined that he had occupied the post when Billy had arrived in Russia in May that year. If he chose, Robinson could confirm if the FBI had officially dispatched Billy to Russia. He would have known.

Robinson said that he had at times approved CHS travel to Russia while he had been the legat there. Yet he said that by 2015, after the events in Crimea and Donbas the year before, and with US–Russia relations so soured, the FBI nearly suspended its practice of sending CHSs to the country. He said that such operations "were highly restricted and extremely rare in the best of times. Even if they were approved it would have been restricted to passive incidental collection. For example, a domestically operated CHS with family in Russia traveling home on family business. The CHS would not be tasked but would be debriefed upon return."

Robinson said that after Russia annexed Crimea in 2014, the US embassy in Moscow "became very risk averse, and even our open bilateral liaison contacts were scrutinized and restricted, so I can't imagine a scenario where we would even try for approval."

When I sketched a profile of Billy, Robinson said that a request to send such a person to Russia, especially in 2015, would have been squashed in FBI head-quarters. If he had received such an application, Robinson said, he would have denied it. "I probably would call the case agent direct and say, 'Are you reading the newspaper? Are you really sure you want to do this? This is a bad idea.'"

Robinson said he would have shared the request with someone known as the chief of station. This was the top CIA official at a US embassy, whose identity is classified. "The chief of station who was there at that time would not have approved that," Robinson said. "I guarantee that."

Robinson walked me through the steps that embassy officials would ordinarily take to evaluate an application to send a CHS to Russia.

A small committee would convene in the Moscow embassy. The legat would attend. The embassy's RSO, or regional security officer, would be there as well. RSOs work for the State Department's US Diplomatic Security Service and are responsible for the security of the people who work at embassies. Robinson said that in 2015, a member of the Secret Service was stationed at the embassy, along with someone from Homeland Security Investigations, the investigative arm of the Department of Homeland Security. He said that these two officials might join such a meeting. The Deputy Chief of Mission, the embassy's second-in-command, would likely be there as well, along with the ambassador. An FBI request to send a CHS to Russia traveled that high up the chain of command.

Robinson said that once the committee convened, the legat would make the FBI's case for the CHS travel, presenting the mission's objectives and operational requirements, along with known risks and a contingency plan.

This was a fascinating insight. It showed how law enforcement, intelligence, and diplomacy merged within a US embassy to weigh hazards and values. And it confirmed how seriously the US government took the prospect of sending a CHS to Russia. "It would have to go that far for it to actually be approved," Robinson said. "Ultimately, this decision would be the ambassador's."[16]

I had contacted several former senior diplomats, including John Beyrle, who was the US ambassador to Russia from 2008 to 2012. Beyrle was from Michigan, which I thought might induce him to assist the Reillys. Beyrle was a gracious man, and he was concerned for the family. But like others, he simply didn't know about the case and said he was in no position to gather information I was seeking. On a later trip to Moscow, I raised Billy in a meeting at the US embassy with ambassador Jon Huntsman and a senior aide. They said they knew of the Reilly case, but they had nothing to add.[17]

I hoped John Tefft would be different. Tefft had served in three ambassadorial postings before arriving in Moscow in November 2014. Tefft was the US ambassador to Russia in 2015, when Billy had arrived in the country and subsequently disappeared there.

Tefft and I traded emails in 2018. I provided a sketch of the article I was reporting and asked if we could talk. "I remember the case in general,"

Tefft wrote, "but don't have details." He advised me to contact the State Department's consular affairs office. "Sorry," he wrote.[18]

Tefft said he remembered the case, but Don Robinson said he said he'd never heard of Billy Reilly. Robinson couldn't tell me for certain what had happened. But he made a clear assessment. "I can tell you with a very high degree of confidence that this was not an officially sanctioned trip," Robinson said. "Even if it did come through as an official request, which it didn't while I was there, I guarantee it would not have been approved at the embassy level."

Robinson's comprehensive argument was hard to resist. Yet even Robinson said he didn't really know. He provided context only, with nothing specific to Billy. After many months, I was still seeking people who possessed details of the case that remained beyond my grasp.

Finally, after some effort, I managed to make contact with the Hostage Recovery Fusion Cell. This was the multiagency task force that was headquartered at the FBI building on Pennsylvania Avenue in Washington. It was in charge of the US effort to gain the release of Americans in captivity abroad.

My source worked within the cell and said that Billy's case was known there. The message that came back to me was that "eyebrows were raising" in response to my queries. Another person who worked at the Fusion Cell had said, "There's a lot more to this than there appears."[19]

*   *   *

The further I proceeded through this hall of mirrors, the more it distorted my understanding of Billy's case. Ten months into my search for him, the fall of 2018 brought the meeting I had always known would come.

One afternoon, I exited the *Journal*'s office with Paul Beckett, the head of our Washington bureau. We walked past the White House and down a slope where Pennsylvania Avenue banks east near the mayor's office. FBI headquarters came into view.

The J. Edgar Hoover Building had all the charm of a highway divider. Departing from the gravitas of Washington's monuments, the FBI building was blunt, unadorned. Its block-long facade on Pennsylvania Avenue was eight stories of manila concrete. Square windows punched into it in uniform intervals, which made the building resemble an enormous cheese grater that had been knocked on its side. Standing halfway between the White House and Capitol Hill, FBI headquarters was three million square feet of office space configured as a fortress.[20]

I had informed officials at the FBI of an impending article about Billy. I also wanted their help. FBI staff communicated regularly with reporters, though I understood that this story was unlikely to elicit a productive response. As I knew from previous work, the Bureau was seldom free with information. It was occasionally in the FBI's interest to correct or confirm material that reporters had gathered. I still hoped that the FBI would bring the *Journal* into Billy's case.

The Bureau could also disabuse me of misleading notions. I was ready to accept an alternative reasoning for agent Tim Reintjes's initial visit to the Reillys' house in Oxford. My reporting didn't suggest one, but I visited headquarters to offer the FBI the opportunity to set me straight.

Beckett and I had agreed that our discussion would be off the record, but this was a pointless concession. The FBI shared no information with the Bureau's press office. Officials denied my request to speak with Reintjes. Later, Brian Hale, who was then the assistant director of FBI public affairs, would offer the only comment the Bureau would utter on the record about the Reilly case.

Hale wrote to me in an email: "The FBI never directed William Reilly to travel overseas to perform any work for the FBI."

CHAPTER FORTY-TWO

Outreach

Terry and Bill had long since written off the FBI when the FBI took renewed interest in them. It had been three years since the Reillys' last functional conversation with anyone from the Bureau. Shortly after my own contact with officials at FBI headquarters, FBI supervisor Timothy Waters phoned the Reillys.[1]

It was Waters who had begun the interrogation of Umar Abdulmutallab, the Nigerian who had ignited an explosive in his underwear on a Northwest Airlines flight from Amsterdam to Detroit on Christmas Day 2009. That questioning included Andy Arena and was the first application of the FBI's High-Value Detainee Interrogation Program.[2]

In 2015, when Billy disappeared, Waters had worked in the FBI's operations division. He was now a supervisory agent overseeing Detroit's counterterrorism desk. A West Pointer, Waters had a reputation for being disciplined and rule-bound, and he had decades of experience dealing with sources and interrogations. He brought this savvy and grit to the FBI's reengagement of the Reillys.[3]

Terry and Bill were wary of Waters's sudden attention, since the Bureau had ignored them for so long, but they agreed to speak him, still aching to understand what the FBI knew. On September 17, 2018, Waters phoned. He said that Billy had been "off the radar." He said little of substance, and the Reillys phoned him days later to press for details.[4]

"We have absolutely no information as to where your son is at this point,"

Waters said. "We know there was some communication between you and him. The last we knew he was heading south from Moscow. But that's it. We got nothing else."

"Do you know that Tim Reintjes, he asked for Billy's itinerary just before he left," Bill said. "Do you know anything about that at all? Did he mention anything about Billy's itinerary?"

"I talked to him about it," Waters replied. "But it's not . . . I can't go into a lot of detail. What we thought was going on was very different from what he told you guys."

This was precisely what the Reillys wanted to know, what the FBI thought was going on. "'Cause all we want to do, all our whole deal is just to find out, like we've been working on for three years about where he is," Bill said. "We have no other—"

"I know," Waters cut in. "Honestly, sir, I'm telling you straight up. We have, we have no further information on this at all. Like none. And we did do, you know, some checks and things of that nature, and we have no information, is what it boils down to."

"Then what kind of information did you have?" Bill asked.

"There's just nothing I can talk to you about, sir," Waters said. "There's certain things that are confidential to the FBI. I'm not in a position to disclose those to you."

The Reillys boiled. Why was the FBI talking to them if confidentiality policies prevented the disclosure of any information? The Bureau often said that it couldn't reveal "sources and methods," erecting a wall between it and the public, while being the sole judge of what to reveal or conceal. Agents appeared able to withhold anything they wanted, employing any explanation. If the FBI or a sister agency was culpable in Billy's disappearance, the FBI could simply conceal proof of its involvement. Bill and Terry questioned why Waters had reinitiated contact, if only to continue suppressing facts they were desperate to have.

"Listen," Waters said. "I'm not trying to hide the ball from you, because I know—I *don't* know—but I guess I can remotely understand the pain and everything else that you guys are going through. I get it, and I understand it. I just, from our perspective, what your son was doing over there was completely personal travel and had absolutely nothing, nothing to do with the FBI. He was going over there, I guess, on a vacation, or maybe to see Moscow or tour the countryside or whatever it was. That was our understanding also. So when he came up missing, when you started talking, when you couldn't find him, it was a shock to us also. Honestly, we've looked at certain things, and we have no idea where your son is, is just the bottom line."

Waters sounded sincere, but he was contradicting himself. If the FBI were ignorant of the reason for Billy's travels or how he had disappeared, then the Bureau couldn't possibly possess confidential information about the trip. The FBI couldn't be blind and yet all-seeing.

The parents focused on what they knew. "The day after he left," Bill told Waters, referring to the drop in his son's communications, "that Tim Reintjes, he's never come to the house before, but here he was at the house."

"I have a different version of events of that," Waters replied. "I have paperwork that shows something different."

Bill brushed past what Waters said, squandering an opportunity to hold him to account. What was this paperwork, and what did it say? Reintjes had indeed visited the house in Oxford. He had given the Reillys his business card. He and Terry had exchanged emails with each other.

It was easy by phone for Waters to deny and deflect. Bill and Terry believed they could get better results by looking him in the eye. Bill cleverly redirected the conversation. "Even if we just somehow had a meeting somewhere," he said. "We just live in Oxford out here, you know."

"You're looking for further information from us," Waters cut in. "There's no information that we have that would be, that could help you in terms of . . . We have no information about what your son was doing in Russia. Like, none, zero."

"But I just don't understand it," Bill countered. "Billy gave him the itinerary. I don't see what's so top secret about that. Like, what would it be, you know?"

"The itinerary, I'll tell you this," Waters said. "The itinerary we were aware of was Moscow, through Kiev to someplace in Poland. We had no information about him heading south. At all. So, he obviously went over there with his own agenda to do something that, you know, that obviously we had nothing to do with whatsoever. It was a personal trip. We have no information on it at all."

Billy had never told his parents that he had planned to visit Kiev or

Poland. Such trips had never come up in the many text messages that Billy had exchanged with his mother while he was in Russia. Yet this proved nothing. Billy had adjusted the truth in the past. This habit threw many things in doubt.

Bill and Terry directed the discussion back to Tim Reintjes. "For three years," Bill said, "we've just always wondered how come Tim knew he was missing the day he was missing?" This was the central question for the Reillys, and if they needed confirmation of its importance, Waters provided it.

He hesitated. "Did you? Did you all . . . ? Well . . . It was . . . It was . . . It was not, um . . ."

Waters had interrogated the Underwear Bomber, and he would later lead the Detroit office as special agent in charge, but the pressure of this call with the Reillys had unsettled him.

"Let me get back with Tim and get some further details," Waters said. "And then maybe we can set up a meeting where you guys can come in and we can sit down and talk to you guys."

Bill's question had so flummoxed Waters that he invited the Reillys for an encounter that would surely be uncomfortable for the FBI.[5]

*   *   *

On September 26, 2018, five days after the phone call with Tim Waters, Terry and Bill drove down to Detroit. They steered along Michigan Avenue, a broad thoroughfare that sliced through the center of the city. Migrating bison had first carved this path a thousand years ago, and Chippewa, Fox, Potawatomi, and Sauk took to the route in search of game. The Great Sauk Trail, which is the name that English speakers later gave it, evolved into a horse path for traders, hunters, and settlers. It ran from the Detroit River all the way to Chicago, an artery through a rugged Midwest that was lost long ago.[6]

In place of that landscape was a paved inner city of towers and traffic. Along Michigan Avenue, five blocks from its intersection with Woodward Avenue and Campus Martius Park, a city hub, stood a gray monolith. The Patrick V. McNamara Federal Building was a million-square-foot reinforced-concrete fortification of twenty-seven floors in the 1970s Brutalist fashion. The building housed branch offices for numerous federal agencies, including the FBI. A US flag was posted in front of the building.[7]

To Terry and Bill, the building was the physical incarnation of the Bureau, foreboding and impersonal. This was the entity that had drawn in Billy and altered the course of his life. His parents had been here before, in the summer that year, when Tim Reintjes had declined to see them. Passing through a spinning door and into the tower's lobby, the Reillys now recognized a familiar chill. They felt like two small people without a chance.

They urged themselves forward with Billy in mind, through a lobby entrance that was reserved for the Bureau. Tim Waters was waiting in an FBI greeting room. Beside him was agent Reintjes.

Terry fought to control her emotions. Years had passed since the Reillys had laid eyes on Reintjes. He was the FBI agent who had known Billy best. Reintjes had directed Billy, utilized the information that Billy gathered. The two had talked to one another nearly every week for years. You couldn't avoid getting to know someone when you shared that much contact, which made Reintjes's behavior all the more painful for the Reillys. Terry focused her gaze on Reintjes, intent on making eye contact, but he looked away.

Tim Waters directed the group to his office. The Reillys were prepared to make the most of this encounter, three years in the making, an opportunity to hold the FBI to account.

After everyone had taken seats, Waters spoke. "I'm going to give you some confidential information." Waters said that in the last year, the FBI had adjusted its policy about sharing information with the families of CHSs who had encountered troubles. Previously, Waters said, some such families had taken their plights to the press. And this had generated unwelcome publicity for the FBI. Terry and Bill listened patiently for the confidential information that Waters promised to share.

"Be aware," Waters said, "that a reporter from the *Wall Street Journal* has been snooping around. If he gets it to the press that Billy has done work for us, it could be very dangerous. Billy could be killed."

For more than three years, the FBI had denied knowledge of what had happened to Billy in Russia. Waters himself had said so in phone calls in just the last week. Now he was suggesting that the FBI indeed possessed relevant information, that Billy was alive in Russia.

The Reillys didn't believe it. Instead, they now understood the reason for the Bureau's withdrawal in 2015, for the lies and confusion, for the hall of mirrors down which the FBI agents had led them. The Bureau didn't care about Billy. He was a CHS, a tool to be used and even discarded. The FBI was concerned about its image.

Waters asked pointedly: "Have you spoken to this reporter?"

The Reillys weren't prepared for this question. They didn't know how to answer it in their best interest. Bill fudged an answer. "A couple of times."

"Did you tell him about us?" Waters asked.

"A little," Bill said.

Waters shifted gears. He told the Reillys how positively the FBI regarded their son. "Billy was doing work for us, Internet work. He was what we call a source. He spoke Russian very well. He was extremely helpful to our country. He did a phenomenal job."

The Reillys asked if the FBI had paid Billy. Waters turned to Reintjes. "Every now and then," Reintjes said. "For gas and stuff. His time."

Bill sensed an opportunity, and he turned to Reintjes. "What was the itinerary Billy had given you?"

Reintjes had never admitted to his foreknowledge of Billy's Russia trip. Now Bill had asked him a direct question about it. Reintjes hesitated. "He said he was going to Moscow, then to Kiev and Poland," Reintjes said. This was his first acknowledgment of the discussions he'd had with Billy before the Moscow flight.

"He was visiting his Aunt Kathie in Poland," Reintjes went on. "He said his parents were going to meet him there. He was visiting his great-grandfather, Joe, in Kiev. He was staying at the Hotel Kosmos in Moscow for a couple of days. Then the Cosmopolitan in Kiev."

Billy did have an Aunt Kathie, Terry's sister. She lived in Michigan, but a physical disability limited her mobility. Her condition was severe enough to occasion frequent falls. Billy had often rushed to her side and helped her onto her feet. The Reillys had trouble imagining Kathie traveling to Poland. Terry and Kathie spoke often. She'd made no plans to travel to Europe.

And the Reillys knew of no relative in Kiev named Joe. Bill and Terry themselves had made no arrangements to join Billy in Europe, nor had they discussed any such plan in text messages with him.

Again, however, the possibility remained that Billy had given the FBI a false itinerary, concealing his intentions. Either Billy had lied then, or the FBI was lying now. Both parties had at times been unreliable narrators.

"When did you last speak to Billy in Russia?" Bill asked Reintjes.

"Never," Reintjes replied. "It's protocol, for surveillance reasons."

"Then how did you know Billy was missing?"

Reintjes said that when he hadn't heard from Billy in weeks, he had checked border-entry records and learned that Billy hadn't returned to the US. Reintjes said he hadn't known that Billy's communications with the family had ceased. "The day I stopped by was just a coincidence," he said.

Paired with Reintjes's earlier concealment of his knowledge of the Russia trip, his answer to this central question sounded to the Reillys like more double-dealing. "When did you last talk to Billy?" Bill asked.

Reintjes said that his final conversation with Billy had occurred a few days before the Russia trip, but the Reillys knew this to be false. They remembered how Billy had left home the evening before his Moscow departure, going to meet Reintjes one last time.

"Didn't you talk to him the night before he left?" Bill asked Reintjes.

"Maybe I did," Reintjes said.

The Reillys threw up their hands, convinced that Reintjes just couldn't be straight with them. He would admit only to partial truths.

They thought of one more card to play. "Who is Amera Lomangcolob?" Bill asked. Reintjes and Waters looked at each other. "That's an ongoing case, isn't it?" Waters asked Reintjes.

"It's confidential," Reintjes said.[8]

When the meeting ended, the Reillys walked out of the FBI office and onto the street, disoriented by the discussion. The FBI wasn't finished with them. In coming weeks, there were more calls. And Waters and Reintjes stopped by the house in Oxford. More and more, the FBI wanted to talk about the *Wall Street Journal*.

"If you tell that reporter anything, we won't be able to give you confidential information," Waters said in one conversation. This sounded to the Reillys like a quid pro quo, as though the FBI was bargaining with them. Waters said that a *Journal* article would create friction between the FBI and its Russian counterparts. "They'll think we sent a spy," he said. He asked the Reillys if they could persuade the *Journal* not to mention the FBI in any article about Billy.

"Can you just get the reporter not to write the article just yet?" Waters pleaded on a call with Terry and Bill in mid-October 2018. "We're going to try to talk to the Russians about Billy. But once the article's out, the Russians will think of him as an FBI agent."[9]

The Reillys didn't believe that Waters would even follow through. The more he talked, the clearer the Bureau's motivation became to them. "We've had enough problems with our image lately," Waters told them on a call. "We don't want anything else negative coming out."[10]

The hope that had arisen within the Reillys when the FBI had renewed contact was now gone. Terry and Bill believed that the Bureau had never intended to share information about their son's case. They concluded that Waters had reestablished contact solely to enlist the Reillys' help in damage control, to prevent the article from being written.

But it was already written.

*   *   *

Even though I didn't know what had happened to Billy after the suspension of his communications in June 2015, I realized that it was time to get down a draft of the article. It had been nearly a year since Bob Foresman had called to tell me about Billy. I'd expended considerable professional capital by pursuing the case all this time. I had to write an article from the facts I'd gathered, even if I was unsure how to conclude it. Paul Beckett edited the story through various versions. We submitted it to the editors in New York who oversaw the *Journal*'s front page.

Sometimes you must complete a project knowing that it is deficient. The page-one editors said that the article needed an ending. But I could scarcely conjure up Billy. The article sat.

I resisted the urge to feel I'd made a foolish gamble by looking for Billy at the expense of other projects. I wasn't finished.

One evening in December 2018, I was having a drink at a bar in Washington with a friend who had once worked as a federal prosecutor. We were discussing the Reilly case when my friend remembered he had an invitation to a party.

The Department of Justice was one of the last places I expected us to go. A cab dropped us at the DOJ building on Pennsylvania Avenue, its neoclassical style contrasting with the Brutalist FBI building across the road.

The chief of the DOJ's counterterrorism section, Mike Mullaney, was retiring after decades in government service. He had overseen all federal terrorist prosecutions for the last dozen years. In a high-ceilinged hall, a hundred or so people were milling about drinking cocktails and beer. My friend introduced me around. These were prosecutors and investigators, the people charged with applying federal law. Many of them had participated in the major terrorism cases of our time.[11]

I met a government lawyer who was prosecuting al Qaeda terrorist Khalid Sheikh Mohammed in the prison complex at Guantánamo Bay, Cuba. It was Mohammed who had murdered *Journal* reporter Daniel Pearl in Pakistan in 2002, or so he had said.[12]

The party chatter periodically subsided as people toasted Mullaney. I tried to follow along but felt like an interloper. I didn't understand the inside jokes. My attention was waning when a man I recognized stepped from the crowd and raised a glass. It was Paul Abbate.

Abbate had been the special agent in charge of the Bureau's Detroit office in 2015, the year Billy traveled to Russia. Now Abbate was the FBI's third-highest-ranking official, its associate deputy director.

I could scarcely believe my good fortune. Weeks before, I had gone through the front door at the FBI and achieved little. Now before me was a sudden opportunity, the sort every reporter covets, a social encounter with an elusive source. Like my visit to the Speaker's Lobby in the Capitol, there would be no handlers or press managers to impede my approach. I would have a special chance to try for answers for Terry and Bill.

From across the room, I studied Abbate as he spoke. He had a high forehead, and his hair was cut uniformly short, graying at the margins. Abbate wore a dark suit. He delivered his remarks in the style of the functionary, his dryness suited to the nature of the work he and Mullaney shared. FBI agents worked in concert with DOJ prosecutors. One group couldn't succeed without the other.

Abbate praised Mullaney, and as he spoke of national security and its ideals, my thoughts turned to Billy. In this room was the human core of the Department of Justice and the FBI. Government often appeared to be a monolith, but it was made of many people. This room was filled with people who could help Terry and Bill, if only they wanted to do it.

When Abbate's speech ended, party chatter refilled the room. I wove through the crowd and called out his name. Abbate turned to face me, flashing a disarming smile.

Tim Reintjes was Billy's FBI handler, and above Reintjes were supervisors and section chiefs. There was a chain of command and responsibility. Abbate had been at the top of it in Detroit. He might not have known Billy, but a CHS had disappeared in Russia on his watch. Abbate bore some responsibility.

I began outlining Billy's case, but I didn't get far. Abbate interrupted me. "I heard about the story you're working on," he said.

This set me back. I had never met Abbate. In his position, he contended with a ceaseless flow of information. I didn't fathom how he could have been aware of an article that had yet to publish about an obscure three-year-old case. Then I remembered how Tim Waters had pleaded with the Reillys to do their best to impede me. I reasoned that Waters had been carrying out orders from above.

I wanted to make sure I'd understood Abbate. "The Reilly case?" I asked.

"I know it," he quickly replied.

Abbate leaned in toward me and lowered his voice. "Can we speak off the record?" he asked. He had fielded my query with such dexterity that it felt as though he'd been expecting it.

We spoke for a while, but Abbate revealed nothing, confirmed nothing. He was polite and engaging, and I realized how foolish my hope had been. Like everyone else at this DOJ banquet, Abbate had spent years building a career and maneuvering his way toward power. Billy Reilly was threatening to people like Abbate, who had much to lose.[13]

Three years later, in 2021, Paul Abbate would advance further in his career and oversee all domestic and international Bureau investigations and intelligence. With the promotion came a new title, deputy director, the FBI's second in command.[14]

I left the DOJ building and walked all the way home. Abbate hadn't provided new leads, but he had given me something. He had proven that Billy's case, far from the void that the FBI had maintained it to be, was dangerous enough for the Bureau's third-highest official to have it top of mind.

CHAPTER FORTY-THREE

Fused Together

A year into my reporting, I had no resolution for the Reillys. Billy's story continued to consume me. At night in bed, unable to clear it from my mind, I would visualize what might have happened in the hours after Billy's final calls and messages.

"Change in plans," he had told his parents in 2015, after they had pulled their bikes to the side of the Polly Ann Trail in Oxford. "I'm really excited."

What were these new plans, and how had he pursued them? Had he gone over the border and into Donbas, as Bronya and Korshunov maintained? How had he gone from being excited about the new plans to disappearing within hours?

I often thought of Terry and Bill and their emotional suffering. September 2018 had come and gone, and with it Billy's thirty-second birthday. It was hard to imagine him progressing toward forty, and I knew that his parents thought endlessly about these lost years. Bill Reilly told me that he was trying to "balance complete despair and complete rage, being the same emotion, fused together."

One early morning in late 2018, my eyes opened. I was in my place in Washington, lying in bed. I felt disoriented. It was dark on the street outside, and through the windows I heard a faint rainfall. The bedroom was glowing.

Light flooded the ceiling, projecting from a phone screen. The phone was vibrating against the surface of the nightstand. I realized that the sound had awoken me.

I grabbed the phone. The time on it read 5:30 a.m.

The screen displayed several text messages. There had been a flurry of activity while I was sleeping. I strained to understand what was happening.

The phone showed that Nastya Mikhailovskaya had been calling from Russia. My thoughts ran to Billy. There was a text message from Mikhailovskaya. "You have to call Valery," she had written. "He has been trying to reach you."

Mikhailovskaya had never urged me to call Valery Prikhodko. This had to be important. I sat up in bed and prepared to dial him.

But I stopped. Prikhodko had sent me a text message of his own. It consisted of a single word, its five Cyrillic letters burning with magnitude: *Нашел*—"Found."

CHAPTER FORTY-FOUR

Found

I called Valery Prikhodko in Russia. He told me that when I had given him the prints from Billy's Michigan gun-license application, staffers in his organization had begun searching a Russian fingerprint database. Prikhodko said that his people had found a match for the Michigan prints. It was a set from an unidentified body.[1]

I was dubious. The odds were too long. It felt like finding a needle in the haystack of the Donbas war. It was possible that Prikhodko's information was flawed or fabricated. He could have doctored a set of documents. I still didn't know what his motive was, how he and Mikhailovskaya fit into this game. Maybe there was indeed a body, but it was hard to believe that it was Billy's.

Prikhodko sent me the Russian set of prints. They were contained on a standard fingerprint sheet, the paper sectioned into squares, with Russian text at the top. There were only eight fingerprints, with the remaining two squares blank.[2]

I told Prikhodko that I would commission an independent test to confirm the match that he said he'd made. If I found a match, he said he would send me one more document, an autopsy report.

Things were happening too fast. Billy had been gone for three and a half years. Suddenly there was a print match and an autopsy report?

My thoughts turned to Bill and Terry and the terrible information I knew I now might possess. What if the prints were another smoke screen? But what if they were genuine?

I decided to keep this news from the Reillys. I didn't want to inflict emotional distress on them, not until I had commissioned the test and received its results. I understood how Terry's emotions could whipsaw. I wasn't going to tell her that her son was gone, only to inform her later that our lab results were different than Prikhodko's. I needed to be sure.

If the independent test revealed a match, I would have to review the autopsy report, in case it contained details contradictory to Billy's physical characteristics, such as tattoos or piercings or simple height and weight, that would render the fingerprint finding ambiguous.

Paul Beckett and I agreed that if the materials proved accurate, I would fly to Detroit, drive up to Oxford, and tell the Reillys in person. They deserved that.

The American Academy of Forensic Sciences referred me to a lab in Collinsville, Mississippi, Ron Smith and Associates. I phoned Ron Smith's director of laboratory services, a man named Jon Byrd. He held a degree in forensic science and had previously worked for the Colorado Bureau of Investigation. I told Byrd what I wanted to achieve, the comparison of the Michigan and Russian prints, and sent him the two sets. Byrd said it would take about a week to conduct the deep analysis we required.[3]

A week later, Byrd sent his report. It contained plenty of data, and my eye raced to its final page and Byrd's conclusion: "The known fingerprints submitted in Exhibit #1 and the known fingerprints submitted in Exhibit #2, were found to have originated from the same person."[4]

The writing was plain. A single sentence, it said much more. Billy was gone.

There it was, somehow indisputable. But I wouldn't be credulous, and I phoned Byrd straight away with a question.

Couldn't Prikhodko or his associates in Russia have used the prints I had supplied from Billy's Michigan gun-license application to create a duplicate set on a forged fingerprint card? That seemed obvious. The Russian set of prints could have been faked in order to conceal what had truly happened to Billy or where he might be.

Byrd told me that this was impossible. He said that there was greater surface area to the prints on the fingerprint card that Prikhodko had provided. Byrd said that the Russian prints were larger than the Michigan prints, containing more information. Confident in his finding, Byrd said that these were two different sets of prints from the same person taken at different times.[5]

I told Prikhodko the news of Byrd's finding. He sent me the autopsy report.

The report, filed from a morgue in a Donbas town called Shakhtersk, described the body of a John Doe near thirty that had been discovered wrapped in multiple layers of plastic tarp. The report spoke of rigor mortis. It said the body was "cold to the touch." I leafed through the report but couldn't continue. How was I going to tell Terry and Bill?[6]

Beckett and I agreed that there was no time to waste. I had to get to Oxford. I booked a flight to Detroit.

I was at my desk in the *Journal*'s Washington office, in the very chair in which I had been sitting when Bob Foresman had phoned me a year earlier to tell me about Billy Reilly. The autopsy report was on my laptop screen. I stared at it, fearful of what more it contained.

My phone buzzed. There was a text message from Terry Reilly: "Really important. Please call."

*   *   *

After I'd shared the findings of the fingerprint analysis with Valery Prikhodko, he or someone else had leaked the information to a reporter in Donbas.

Russell Bentley, the Texan in Donbas, read an article in the local press. It said that Billy Reilly, an American fighter, had been killed. Bentley sent the article link to the Reillys.[7]

I didn't know this yet. All I knew, from the tone of Terry's text message, was that something had happened. I steeled myself for what came next.

Carrying a secret, I walked through the *Journal* newsroom past my colleagues who were busy at their keyboards. At the back of the office, I found the room that reporters often used to place confidential phone calls. The room was small and had a couch and a desk and chair. I closed the door.

I dialed Terry's number. The phone at my ear, I listened to the ring on the line.

Found. What had Billy found in Russia? Had its discovery been remotely worth the price he had paid? I remembered Dmitri Tyurin, the Russian private eye, and the lunch we had shared along the Krymskaya Embankment. I had the receipt, "Walden" scrawled across it, in a box under my desk. I thought of Siberia's many lakes and rivers and how Billy loved to fish, plumbing the subsurface for activity. Why hadn't Billy gone there? Why hadn't he just come home? Why had he gone to Russia in the first place?

Terry answered my call. She said hello. Her voice was quavering. She placed her phone on speaker mode. Bill and I exchanged greetings.

Terry was eager to tell me what she'd heard with Bentley's help. "We read those news reports from Russia," she said. She was nearly whispering, as though she wanted me to cut in and dismiss them. "Do you, um, know anything about this?" Her voice rose in a plea on the final syllable.

"I do, yes," I said.

I remembered the first conversation I'd had with the Reillys a year before, when Terry had assumed I was about to relay devastating news. I remembered the weather in Michigan that February, when I'd met the Reillys for the first time, at the house in Oxford, then stepped into the slanting rain carrying a mother's confidence.

My mind returned to the phone call. I told Bill and Terry that Valery Prikhodko had contacted me from Russia.

"Uh-huh," Terry said.

I said that Prikhodko had shared a set of fingerprints taken from a John Doe. I explained how I had sent both this set of prints and that of Billy's gun-license application to a forensic expert to perform a comparison. "The analyst called me yesterday with the results," I said.

Bill and Terry gasped.

I searched for the right words. There weren't any. There was only what I knew. "It's a match," I said.

An instant is not a long time, but everything that's dear to you can be held within it. There was an instant of silence on the line. It was all Terry and Bill needed to understand that all was lost.

Terry shrieked: "Oh, God, no! No! Oh, no! Good God!"

Bill cried out incoherently.

"No, God!" Terry exclaimed. "Not my Billy!"

"I don't know what to say or even do," Bill said.

Terry wailed: "I want my Billy's body back."

Bill yelled, "Billy!"

"Oh God, why did they do this to us? God, why?" Terry sobbed, and she screamed, and the line cut.

CHAPTER FORTY-FIVE

Eleven Days

I flew to Detroit the next morning. I drove to Ann Arbor, to the medical school on the university's north campus. This was where the underwear bomber had recuperated in 2009, before receiving a life sentence.

I waited in the lobby of an academic building, and before long a man with a goatee and salt-and-pepper hair joined me. Dr. Jeffrey Jentzen was the director of autopsy in the department of pathology at the University of Michigan Medical School. He had previously served for twenty-one years as the chief medical examiner for Milwaukee County, where he had performed more than 6,000 autopsies. Amid the furor of the 1992 Jeffrey Dahmer murder trial, Jentzen's examinations of some of Dahmer's victims had aided the prosecution in decoding the crimes.[1]

Valery Prikhodko had texted me what he said was a postmortem photo of the John Doe from which the Russian set of fingerprints had been taken. Sitting with Jentzen, I called up the picture on one of my phones, which I handed to him. The image depicted the face of a man of apparent European descent. The man had dark hair and a beard. It was impossible for me to tell if this was Billy, given that there had been decay.

On another phone, I called up a photo of Billy that Elena Gorbacheva had taken on the train platform in Moscow in May 2015. For comparison, I handed this second phone to Jentzen. This was no scientific exercise, but it was all I had. Jentzen said he could not assess identity without access to the body. Nevertheless, he did take note of the beard patterns, noses, and foreheads of the faces in the two photos. "The facial characteristics are consistent," he said.

Jentzen took a concentrated look at the postmortem picture. "This is a typical decomposed body," he said. "If you assume normal temperatures, he would have been dead three to five days, or longer. It looks like he was in the water."[2]

The autopsy report stated that the John Doe had indeed been recovered from a body of water, a reservoir. It was located not in Russia but in Donbas. Billy had made it into Donbas after all, or been transported there.

The village of Dibrivka lies just over the border from Russia into Ukraine and roughly twenty-five miles southwest of another town, Darivka. This is the place where Mikhail Korshunov said he had seen Billy at the volunteer-fighter roundup.

The fingerprint card Prikhodko had provided stated that the John Doe was discovered in Dibrivka on July 10, 2015. This was roughly sixteen days after Billy's final contact with his parents.

This data allowed for a simple equation. If, as Dr. Jentzen assessed, the John Doe had expired, at most, five days before discovery, Billy's apparent date of death was roughly July 5, 2015.

I knew I was edging into speculation but pursued the exercise nonetheless. If this body was indeed Billy's, and if the information contained on the fingerprint card and autopsy was accurate, this meant that Billy had been alive for roughly eleven days after his parents had lost touch with him.

I was still skeptical of Prikhodko's documents, guarding against the possible effort, from the Russian side, to craft a narrative. But these emerging details allowed me to connect facts that had previously been isolated. Eleven days. Had Billy been alive during this span? If he had been, this put the FBI in the dock.

Tim Reintjes's first visit to Oxford suggested he had known that something had disrupted the course of Billy's life in Rostov. The FBI and the US government had no free hand in Russia, but they did have a presence. At the very moment when Billy had most needed aid from the government he had served, Reintjes was instead prevaricating with Billy's parents at the house in Oxford. When he might have helped Billy in some way, Reintjes was instead containing blowback on the Bureau. This was precisely the behavior the FBI had taught its agents in the aftershock of the Whitey Bulger revelations. Once a CHS deviated, an agent had to cut the CHS loose. I wanted to test these deductions with the man who had helped formulate the policy.

It was fifteen miles northeast on Route 14 from Ann Arbor to Plymouth. I met Andy Arena at a bagel shop there. He had been involved in the Bulger aftermath and later led the FBI's Detroit office. He had told me on one of our calls that the FBI might have misfired with Billy. Yet now that it appeared Billy had died in Russia or Ukraine, Arena seemed to have had a change of heart.

"This type of guy, we would dissuade from doing this," he said. "I can't believe this office, with the way it's run, would have sent this guy over there with a wink and a nod."

I reminded Arena of the Reintjes text messages and home visit. Arena shook his head. He allowed that this evidence didn't favor the FBI. Still, he resisted the idea of conspiracy.

"You go to great pains to make sure this person knows he's not an employee of the FBI, that he's not an FBI agent," he said. "'If you do it, you're on your own.' After Whitey Bulger, there was painstaking preparation to make sure this person knows what his role is."

Arena said that, over the years, a few Detroit CHSs had traveled to tricky international destinations despite FBI counsel. "We told them, 'Are you out of your mind?' They said, 'We have to go. My sister is sick.'"

Arena shrugged. "When you operate sources, you do your best. Sometimes these guys go rogue."[3]

Billy was an adult, responsible for his own course of action. This was easy to forget amid the love that Terry and Bill showered on him. He was their son, but he was also a man. He had made his own choices.

I drove to Ypsilanti, an eastern satellite of Ann Arbor, where Catie and Mohammed Cherri had recently moved. Catie was still logging long hours at a clinic. Mohammed had taken up beekeeping. They'd had another son, and he and his brother played in the living room.

I explained the fingerprint analysis and shared some details from the autopsy report. Catie asked few questions and offered little commentary. She kept her eyes focused on the floor and safeguarded her skepticism, unprepared, it seemed, to credit my conclusions.[4]

I then drove to Oxford. The Reillys met me at their front door. I took a seat on the parlor couch for the visit none of us had ever wanted to have.

Terry and Bill looked spent. They had little to say. I knew that my stay would be brief. I handed over copies of the death certificate, the autopsy report, and the fingerprint card that Prikhodko had shared.

The Chief Medical Examiner's Office in the Shakhtersk District of the Donetsk People's Republic had filed the death certificate. The report was signed by a woman named Olga Yermishkina, identified as a forensic medical examiner. I later traded social media messages with Yermishkina. She said she had traveled to Dibrivka and been present when the John Doe had been retrieved from the reservoir.[5]

The certificate described an unknown male, aged thirty to thirty-five years old, and listed the cause of death as "assault with intent of murder or injury." The document stated that death occurred owing to "attack using a sharp object." The "illness" that caused the death was "exsanguination," or loss of blood, and "penetrating stab wounds to the chest bones on the right side followed by an injury of the right lung." It appeared that Billy had been stabbed to death.

Writing in the death certificate, Yermishkina stated that the body she examined had suffered seven stab wounds. One of these wounds had penetrated more deeply than the others and been the principal reason for the massive loss of blood. If this body was indeed Billy's, then this information showed that he hadn't died in battle from a gunshot or shrapnel or a concussive blast, but in an intimate way.

The report stated that the body was discovered without clothes and wrapped in several layers of plastic tarp. Cinderblocks were attached by rope to the legs and head, as though to sink the body. But the body instead floated on the reservoir's surface, allowing for discovery.

I hinted at this information but didn't discuss it with Bill and Terry. It was too much to share. I had translated these Russian-language documents into English, and the Reillys could read them if they wanted to do so.

Terry focused on the fingerprints, as I had done. Were they real? Were they Billy's? She asked if the prints could have been taken from someone who was still alive. She speculated that Billy was locked away in prison in Russia, that these documents were a ruse to conceal his captivity.

Terry's hope still lived. As we turned over the evidence, looking at it one way and another, she reformulated this question, unwilling, like her daughter, to give up Billy.[6]

I didn't have the answer to Terry's question, but I knew where we could find it. Prikhodko had said there was a grave.[7]

CHAPTER FORTY-SIX

Final Miles

Flowers garlanded the headstones of Shakhtarsk's Central Cemetery, laid there by those whose fathers and brothers and wives and children had died in the Donbas war. A single grave, a rump of earth, held no blossoms. Marking the site was a cross made of two pieces of wood joined with a nail, two words scrawled upon it: "Unknown Man."

It was May 7, 2019, at the margin of a Donbas miner's village. A sedan approached the cemetery. There was a chill in the air when Terry and Bill stepped from the car. Bill walked with difficulty but was determined not to let his artificial hips hold him back. Terry, in a T-shirt and faded jeans, approached the grave. She knelt down and spoke to the ground. "We're here to take you home," she said.

The gravediggers began their work. Spades chunked into the turf, scraping against stones packed in the soil, the sound skimming through the graveyard. Bill and Terry watched earth pile by the hole widening in the ground. The diggers set down their shovels. Two of the men eased into the grave.

A box emerged, a John Doe's plywood carton. Dirt fell from the box as the gravediggers passed it up to the surface. The pieces that composed the casket came unfastened. The coffin fell apart, revealing to Terry and Bill what was inside of it, a black plastic bag containing their son's remains.[1]

*   *   *

Riding in a van along with Russell Bentley, the Reillys escorted the remains out of Ukraine, over the Russian border, and into Rostov-on-Don. With the help of State Department employees at the US embassy in Moscow, they began filing the paperwork they would need to bring Billy back to the United States. There was something still more important to do, a DNA test.

Terry submitted a cheek swab to a forensics lab at the Ministry of Health's Rostov office, which took teeth from the Shakhtersk remains and judged them to be a match with 99.99 percent probability. Terry and Bill planned to conduct another DNA test in the US.

In Rostov, they hired an undertaker who arrived at their initial meeting wearing a T-shirt with a large human skull silk-screened on its front. He chaperoned the Reillys to the medical examiner's office, where they waited while seated beneath a velvet portrait of two tigers leaping over a reposing nude woman. The absurdities of their experiences made barely an impression. Their grief made them weary.[2]

I joined the Reillys in Rostov. I suggested we take a road trip while they waited for government offices to approve their documents. I had arranged a meeting with Valery Prikhodko.

The Reillys and I retraced the drive I'd taken north on the M4 from Rostov-on-Don to see Bronya Kalmyk the year before. Terry, Bill, and I stopped at a café along the way and drank *kvas* from plastic cups. Terry lifted hers for a toast. "Here's to finding Billy's murderer," she said.

In the city of Kamensk-Shakhtinsky, ninety miles north of Rostov, we took a table at a restaurant with large chandeliers. Before long, Prikhodko arrived. He and I had spoken often by phone, but this was the first time I had seen him. He was middle-aged with a salt-and-pepper brush cut and a medium build. When Prikhodko tilted his wrist to light a cigarette, he revealed the faded tattoo of a spider running along his inner left forearm.

Terry and Bill expressed their gratitude to Prikhodko for making the fingerprint match that allowed for the recovery of their son's remains. Prikhodko surprised us all when he declared, "We know who's responsible."

He said that he and his associates had identified a group of people whom they believed had been involved in Billy's murder. "We know first and last names," he said. "We'll give them a polygraph. Whoever is still alive, we'll get them. We have eyes on these guys right now."

The Reillys hadn't conceived of getting justice for Billy so quickly.

Prikhodko told us he had heard about Billy's disappearance in 2015. "But I didn't know anyone was interested," he said. "No one was looking for him." If true, this suggested that no US officials had ever made an effort.

I tried several ways but couldn't pry loose information about Prikhodko's suspects. Instead, I asked him about motive. "We heard about the FBI angle," Prikhodko said, "and we started working under this assumption. But if it had been connected to that, they would have come to us." I knew what he meant by *they:* the FSB. "And no one did. This was a simple robbery. Maybe there was a dispute. Maybe they were drunk."

Prikhodko didn't provide more that afternoon, and I returned to Kamensk-Shakhtinsky a few days later on my own, hoping to keep him talking. We met at a biker bar called Legends of the USSR, which was near a Soviet nostalgia museum and overlooked the M4. The traffic passed by, and Prikhodko smoked Russian cigarettes one after another. Across the highway was a motel, its parking lot arrayed with old artillery pieces alongside a T-34 tank.[3]

I tried to feel out Prikhodko, to get a sense for his connections and abilities. He said he had been an officer with the federal border guards in Rostov. He explained that his Moscow superiors had ordered him to establish his anti-extremist organization before the Donbas war had begun. "Maybe they were getting ready for something," he said.

He showed me an automatic pistol. I said I thought he ran a humanitarian organization, and he winked. "Yeah, sure," he said.

Prikhodko said he couldn't share details of Billy's alleged killers until their apprehension. I was hopeful but cautious. What would it cost him to string along the Reillys?

I asked if Billy's death was connected to any state body. Prikhodko grimaced. "There would have been no point in them killing him," he said. "They would have first talked to him. They would have tried to flip him. But kill him? There would have been no point in that."

We watched trucks rumble past on the way north to Moscow.[4]

*   *   *

Vyacheslav Korshunov stood in the road, grinning, the sunlight catching one of his gold teeth. Terry, Bill, and I had driven to the village of Krasny Sulin, north of Rostov-on-Don, to see the man who said he had spoken with Billy in 2015 at the volunteer-fighter roundup in Darivka. We wanted to test the story he'd told.

Korshunov was in his forties and stood roughly five-foot-three. His hair was a militiaman's stubble. He carried himself in the agitated manner of someone who has recently seen combat.

Korshunov's house was a slanting, one-story wooden construction with a grooved metal roof. There was an outhouse in the yard, along with a high-hanging spigot, which must have served as a shower. A mottled sleeve for an MC Hammer album, *Please Hammer Don't Hurt 'Em*, leaned against the side of the house.

Inside were small, dark rooms. Korshunov's wife, Natalia, was a slight woman with auburn hair that she wore in a bun. She looked at us with large eyes. "We've never had an American in our home," she said. Korshunov flashed a look at her, and she lowered her voice and cast her glance downward. "I don't think there's ever been one in Krasny Sulin," she said.

Terry and Bill took seats at the kitchen table, and I joined them. A tabby cat leapt onto a ledge behind us and toyed with Bill's ponytail. Korshunov poured a round of vodka shots and raised his glass and toasted Billy.

Natalia served large bowls of soup, *ukha* with carp. The soup was brackish, fish bones breaking its muddy surface. Terry looked pleadingly from the bowl to Bill.

On social media, as I had seen, Korshunov had posted dozens of front-line photos. In them, he wore fatigues and held an automatic rifle, posturing alongside men who were similarly arrayed. These were stock poses, and I'd often encountered their type, the nonprofessional soldier memorializing his break from society.

Korshunov poured a second round of shots, and this felt like the time to ask him what he remembered of Billy, probing for gaps in the account.

It was July 2015, Korshunov said, when a hundred or so men milled about in a clearing in the summer heat. Battalion commanders discussed how best to apportion them. It was there that Korshunov said he had encountered Billy.

"I was so impressed that someone would come all that way, across the ocean, to fight with us," Korshunov said. "For me, he was a warrior. He was a brother." Korshunov lifted his glass.

I asked how he had come to give testimony to the Rostov Investigative

Committee. "An investigator went to the ataman of the Rome battalion and asked if any of his guys had ever seen William," Korshunov said. "I said I did."

The details of Korshunov's story puzzled me. After four years and the confusions of the war in which he had served, how could he so distinctly remember a single brief encounter with a stranger? I pressed him on these points. He apologized, saying that his memory had begun to fail him, which attested to my point. His memory was good enough for the details contained within his testimony, yet not for any others.

Korshunov tried to explain. "You know how you have a cake," he said. "And then you put a little statue on the top. Like a wedding cake. And that really stands out. That was how William was."

How oddly descriptive, Billy in that clearing, standing apart, captive to fate. Billy was the ornament, a trophy. "In that kind of group," Korshunov said, "you notice someone who is weak."

Korshunov poured another round of vodka. This was the third toast, and we did not touch glasses. "To those who have fallen," Korshunov said.[5]

*   *   *

The Northern Cemetery in Rostov was a sprawling territory, nearly a thousand acres, the largest necropolis in European Russia, with more than a half million graves.[6]

Near the main entrance stood a tan building, a place for embalming. The building served an additional purpose, made plain by the black smoke and deathly odor that spilled from its chimney, as Terry, Bill, and I arrived.

It had taken several weeks, and the Reillys' paperwork was now in order. A mortician and a carpenter were preparing a coffin to transport Billy's remains on a flight home. The Reillys' undertaker arrived wearing his human-skull T-shirt. He escorted me into the crematorium, a foreboding chamber, and pointed out the oven.

I followed him into a room where an embalmer worked on a corpse that was laid out on a slab. The embalmer wore a black apron and held an artist's palette in one hand. With a brush, he mixed paints on the back of one hand. The body in front of him was dressed in a Russian colonel's uniform, and the embalmer painted dark lines on the man's forehead.

The embalmer said he had been the one to receive Billy's remains when the Reillys had brought them from Donbas weeks before. He had opened the coffin and viewed its contents. "There wasn't much left," he said. "A skull. Some bones. That's all that was left."[7]

I stepped away to find the undertaker showing Bill and Terry into a refrigerator. I followed them.

It was a large white-tiled room that might have gone well in the pantry of a steakhouse. The air was cool and dry. On the floor laid the body of an elderly woman in a housedress. She looked like she might be having a nap. Nearby was the corpse of an old man, his jaw hanging open like Marley's ghost. A thin turquoise blanket was pulled to the shoulders, as though the room's low temperature had induced a chill. These were the bodies one expected to encounter in such a place, the remains of people who had lived lengthy lives. This was the order of things. Dying young was the tragedy. Billy's life was composed of all the things he'd never do.

In a corner of the refrigerated room was an aluminum box, prepared for international shipment. Inside were Billy's remains. The Reillys edged toward it. They laid their hands on it. Terry fell to her knees and took in the box's smooth metal. "They packed him up like he's a piece of machinery," she wailed. "I never thought we'd be taking you home like this."

"At least we're taking him home," Bill whispered.

Terry collapsed atop the box. She spread her arms across it, pressed her body against it, as though she were giving Billy a last embrace. Terry's wailing reverberated in the tiled room, while Bill stroked her back. "He's not in there," he said quietly. "His soul is gone."

The days counted down to departure, but there was one final errand. Bill, Terry, and I found a tattoo parlor in central Rostov-on-Don. I put a Johnny Cash record on the turntable, and Bill and Terry sat in turn as a tattoo artist articulated a needle over their arms. He inscribed "Billy" within an infinity loop on the inside of their right wrists. These were the first tattoos for the Reillys since their courtship in Detroit, a way to have Billy with them always.

Afterward, we drove out in a cab through the traffic of the afternoon. We parked at a bar and stepped from the car. "I can't believe it," Bill said, taking in the place. The name of the bar was painted in large Roman letters along an exterior wall. The bar was called, of all things, Billy. The Reillys and I sat facing the road and drank beer in tall mugs.[8]

*　　*　　*

On June 14, 2019, nearly four years to the day they had lost contact with Billy, Terry and Bill landed in Detroit with his remains in the cargo hold of a Delta Airlines A320.

"I remember dropping him off here and saying goodbye," Terry said as she stepped off the airplane. "And how many times he told me, 'Don't worry.'"

She and Bill staggered through the airport concourse, struck by a feeling of finality. "It's surreal being back," Terry said. Their Russian ordeal was behind them but would now always be with them. Their effort to bring Billy home was nearly complete.

Billy's Aunt Kathie and Uncle Jim were waiting at a Delta Cargo hangar north of the airport's passenger terminals, a white airliner painted on the building's facade. Catie and Mohammad Cherri were there, too. Catie's belly was swollen with a third child. She would soon give birth to a son and name him Bilal, honoring her lost brother.[9]

A man from a funeral home in Lake Orion, up north near Oxford, stood by the hangar wearing a dark suit and tie. An airplane took flight from a runway on the other side of an airport road. As the plane rose into the sky, its engines made the sound of tearing paper.[10]

A freight handler wheeled out the metal box that had flown all the way from Rostov-on-Don. The box was scuffed and dented. Bill and Terry had endured all of this before, but for the others, this was the first time they'd seen evidence that Billy had passed away. At the sight of her brother's coffin, Catie howled.

Billy's relatives watched the undertaker roll the casket toward a black mini-van. He pushed it through the rear hatch and into the car and shut the door. The six members of the family joined in an unrehearsed embrace. Their arms flung around one another as they issued oaths and sobs.

The undertaker eased the van out of the parking lot and toward I-94, ferrying Billy the final miles home.

EPILOGUE

In the summer of 2019, Bill and Terry Reilly contracted Universal Forensics in Clarkston, Michigan, a dozen miles southwest of Oxford, to perform a DNA comparison. Technicians swabbed the inside of Terry's mouth and harvested a segment of bone from the mortal remains that the Reillys had transported from Donbas.

In August 2019, Universal Forensics delivered the results: "The alleged mother cannot be excluded as the biological mother of the child. The probability of maternity is 99.9%."[1]

For me, this established the near-absolute certainty of the identity of the remains that the Reillys had brought home. Billy Reilly had perished, and his parents had recovered his corporeal remnant. I accepted this as fact. But this did not mark the end of my effort.

On October 11, 2019, the *Journal* published the article about Billy Reilly.[2]

His parents read the story, and Terry said that it "told it like it was." Yet she and Bill were distressed, the article causing them to relive the terrible events. The Reillys had chosen to expose themselves and their story in exchange for the light that the paper would shine on the mystery of their son's disappearance. Now was the time for that exposure to pay off.

I had faith in the *Journal's* reach. Somewhere, someone had information we still needed about the truth of Billy's trip to Russia and his fate there. A stream of readers contacted me by email, including one from Kansas City, Missouri, who had known agent Tim Reintjes for years. This contact fizzled, but another opportunity arose.

LOST SON

Three days after publication, on October 14, 2019, the man who had proven elusive to me and to Bill and Terry finally weighed in on Billy's case. Inadvertently, Mikhail Polynkov would reveal the nature of Billy's demise.

*   *   *

Reading the *Journal* article prompted Polynkov to write on his LiveJournal account that in Rostov-on-Don, Billy had been "popular. Or rather, not him, but his wallet. One of the volunteer fighters even arranged a small excursion for him around Russia. They went to Ulyanovsk and somewhere else."[3]

Polynkov published screenshots of VKontakte direct-message exchanges, including several with an account named Vasya the Foreigner. These were the messages that Bill, Terry, and Mohammed had read when they'd accessed Billy's account after his disappearance. The screenshots lent credence to Polynkov's LiveJournal posting. They caused me to consider additional possibilities.

VKontakte had become fundamental to the lives of many Russian speakers. Many of the men who volunteered to fight in Donbas posted pictures of themselves on the platform and corresponded via its messaging service. These fighters could be undisciplined with their communications and sometimes shared sensitive information over the platform. I believed that there might be a way to uncover additional, relevant VKontakte exchanges.

*   *   *

Since before 2014, and especially after the start of the Donbas war, Russia and Ukraine had been waging cyber warfare against one another. A hacker group known as the Ukrainian Cyber Alliance[4] had penetrated Russian Ministry of Defense servers. An affiliate outfit, RUH8, had targeted the VKontakte accounts of people fighting for Russian interests in Ukraine. After reading Mikhail Polynkov's LiveJournal post about Billy, I learned from sources in Ukraine that RUH8 hackers had breached his VKontakte account, seizing years' worth of messages.[5]

The RUH8 hackers compiled a database, VK Leaks, combining Polynkov's messages with those taken from other accounts. RUH8 hosted the cache on a public website. I believed that the conversations between Polynkov and others in the Novorossiya movement could provide a retrospective picture of their intentions and behavior. But when I searched for the database, I discovered that it was gone.

The RUH8 collective was tied up in a court case, and agents from the Ukrainian cyber police had raided the group's offices in February 2020, confiscated its hard drives, and deleted the VK Leaks database from its Internet host.[6] However, traces of the database remained online.

I was initially skeptical of the database. US or Ukrainian intelligence officers could have fabricated VK Leaks, or parts of it, in order to buttress versions of events favorable to their causes in Donbas. But as I searched the partial database, I came to believe in it. Within the cache, I discovered the messages in which Billy and Polynkov had planned their meeting at one of Moscow's airports, which Polynkov himself had posted on LiveJournal.

* * *

My confidence in the partial database only grew when I found messages between Polynkov and Elena Gorbacheva, the photographer who had taken photos of Billy at the train station. "When's the interrogation of the Texas separatist?)," Gorbacheva wrote to Polynkov on May 14, 2015, the day before Billy's arrival in Russia. She appeared to be confusing Billy with Russell Bentley, the man from Dallas who fought on the Russian side and later helped Terry and Bill.

"It's not the American I mentioned," Polynkov replied. "It may be some kind of spy)."

Polynkov's message threw me. A spy?

"We need to find a place to torture him and get rid of him)," Polynkov wrote to Gorbacheva the following morning. "Do you have any kind of torture basement in mind with implements?)."

These lines were jarring, considering Billy's fate, but I presumed that Polynkov had intended to amuse Gorbacheva. His usage of a parenthesis at the end of each sentence implied a grin. Was this gallows humor or the expression of intent?

* * *

In the database, there were messages from Andrey Demchuk, the Russian fighter known as Pirate who had accompanied Billy on his Volga sojourn. On May 22, 2015, Billy was in the midst of that trip when Demchuk wrote to Polynkov: "Hello from the American." Demchuk included a snapshot of Billy in a black t-shirt, sitting on a bench outdoors on a sunny day, his hair tousled.

"Pirate?))," Polynkov asked.

"He's dying to get to Donetsk," Demchuk wrote. "Very persistently." And the following day: "He's starting to annoy me. Where. When. What am I, your hostage."

"Well, bro, you should've thought about this when you took him hostage," Polynkov replied.

"He is already stressing out because he wants to get involved in political issues in Donetsk))))," Demchuk wrote. "He's killing my brain." The correspondence then took a turn. "Do you know that the American works for the police in the counterterrorism department. At home there. And desperately trying to get to Donetsk."

"Yes," Polynkov replied. "He talked about it. Don't worry. We'll take care of it."

The mention of law enforcement and counterterrorism was bewildering. A VK Leaks exchange between Polynkov and another user weeks before Billy's arrival in Moscow appeared to provide an explanation.

"An obvious fake is writing to us," the user wrote on April 1, 2015, "supposedly an American from the FBI and all that."

How had this user known of Billy's connection to the Bureau? Pairing this message with Demchuk's, I could conclude only that Billy himself had mentioned his FBI affiliation. Why? Didn't he understand how people in Russian nationalist circles perceived the Bureau? I considered these messages in the context of Billy's previous FBI work. For years, he had been contacting targets, eliciting invitations, penetrating seemingly impenetrable networks. He might well have been doing the same with Polynkov and his circle on behalf of a US agency. Nevertheless, Billy's disclosure was an inexplicable stroke of candor, and it appeared to have compromised him before his arrival in Russia.

"What to do with him?" the VKontakte user asked Polynkov. "Maybe we'll play a game with him and ask him to come to us? :) At the same time, maybe we'll get medals for catching a spy? :)."

"Let's do it)))," Polynkov replied.

"Ok, I'll give him something and ask him to come to Moscow)," the user wrote. This called to mind Catie Cherri's discovery of the printout at her parents' house, which Billy said indicated that people in Russia were "interested in me going there."

The VKontakte user continued: "The funniest thing is how this guy from the FBI presented himself—the name Vasily the Ukrainian)))."

"Yeah, the Ukrainians are probably making some kind of joke," Polynkov wrote. "Let's totally do this." Polynkov and his associates lured Billy to Russia.

As Billy's arrival drew near, Polynkov wrote in a VKontakte group chat: "What should I do with the spy? I'm moving forward."

Another user asked: "the one from the FBI?"

"Yes, someone was bound to come from America from the FBI or wherever he's from there," a third user wrote.

"Understood," Polynkov replied. "Okay, I'll improvise."

Days later, as Billy arrived by train to Rostov-on-Don, where his nationality and demeanor baffled people at the camp, a VKontakte user wrote in a group chat: "He doesn't need to look like a super soldier. I have a suspicion he is a super spy. First of all, he needs to be sent to SMERSH, to check."

SMERSH was a counterintelligence agency established during World War II to eliminate anti-Soviet Nazi infiltrators. It was said that Joseph Stalin himself had coined the term, a portmanteau of the Russian words *smert shpionam*, or death to spies. Stalin disbanded the group after the war, bringing its duties into the main security apparatus, but it remained an amusing term for those in Russia who dealt in counterintelligence or enjoyed imagining that they did. SMERSH served as a convenient villain in the early James Bond books.

Taking in this reference to SMERSH, I recalled my steakhouse lunch with the former CIA officer and our discussion of nonofficial cover, or NOC. I couldn't conceive of the CIA recruiting Billy to work as a NOC in Russia while also directing him to disclose his FBI affiliation in VKontakte chats with Russian nationalists. Billy had walked into a trap.

"He needs to be checked out," a VKontakte user wrote to Polynkov. "I bet they sent him as a Trojan horse."

"Where can I get the address of SMERSH?" Polynkov asked.

"Send me in a personal message everything that's known about this guy and everything that he wrote," another VKontakte user wrote. "Suddenly and truly this is a really interesting character."

* * *

In a May 20, 2015 message, Mikhail Polynkov told Elena Gorbacheva that he had sent Billy "with the guys from the GRU DNR on a trip around Russia)." Polynkov's mention of the GRU, military intelligence, drew Andrey Demchuk, the fighter known as Pirate, into sharper focus.

Demchuk had appeared in social media photos wearing the uniform of the DNR Republican Guard, which had grown out of the so-called republic's military intelligence agency. While Billy was exercising his passions for history and travel during his Volga sojourn, he had been under the watch of the shared counterintelligence apparatus of Russia and Donbas.

During the Volga trip, on May 22, 2015, Polynkov contacted Demchuk via VKontakte, employing a widely used colloquialism for the FSB, *kontor*, or "office." "Talk to the office," Polynkov wrote. "They will tell you what to do."

Simultaneously, Polynkov was engaged in conversation with another VKontakte user. "My people from the Ulyanovsk branch of the fisibi [FSB] will be able to pick him up," the user wrote. "Now this issue is being decided!" The messages revealed that the FSB, in addition to the GRU, was conducting surveillance on Billy.

"This Vasisualia still has stuff at the base," Polynkov wrote, referencing Billy's Russian alias, Vasily.

"He'll get prison clothes anyway," the other user wrote. "Why does he need his stuff))))...There are some interesting plans for him. I will share them later if everything is approved))."

* * *

For years, I had been wondering why Billy had remained at the Rostov base camp while others quickly and routinely filtered through it to Donbas. The VKontakte messages and Polynkov's subsequent social media postings finally illuminated the delays.

On June 3, 2015, Billy wrote Polynkov via VKontakte: "They say that I will be a soldier, but I thought and wanted to make a film. I have no experience as a soldier." Polynkov assured Billy that he wouldn't be forced to fight and that a decision about his next moves was imminent.

"We weren't sure that Vasya was actually an agent of the US intelligence services," Polynkov wrote in his 2019 LiveJournal post. "But there were already serious suspicions. For a while, we just marinated 'Vasya' at the base."

A message from Bronya Kalmyk to Polynkov on June 18, 2015, less than a week before Billy's disappearance, indicated that Russian counterintelligence was deciding his fate. "They said to be patient while the American is here to see how they can close it," Bronya wrote. "They can continue to work, they'll even help."

*   *   *

AN AGENT CHAIN

Just when I believed I had made a breakthrough with the help of the VKontakte texts, there were no more of them. None of the publicly available messages advanced the timeline beyond Bronya's communication.

Searching the partial VK Leaks cache for further context, I noted a September 10, 2015, exchange between Elena Gorbacheva and Polynkov. "Did you say that Vasya was put under surveillance so that he would lead us to his main contacts?)" she asked.

This reference to Billy's "main contacts" aligned with a version of the story that Polynkov had shared in his LiveJournal post. He'd written that "the uncles from the FSB came to the base and took Vasya away. Subsequently, they said that through Vasya, they established an agent chain." Polynkov appeared to be saying that while in the custody of the FSB, Billy had revealed the identities of US-connected agents, officers, or sources operating in Russia.

"He was actually detained by our special services on suspicion of espionage," Polynkov wrote. "According to my information, a chain of his contacts with the CIA was revealed... He came to Russia and then Donbas on their specific assignment. As far as I understand, he actually worked for the CIA and the FBI was supposed to tie up the loose ends."

311

Polynkov's posting explained his mention of the CIA in messages to Bill Reilly in 2015. As provocative as these statements were, however, Polynkov was unlikely to possess reliable evidence, as he wasn't a confirming, direct source for Billy's supposed CIA affiliation or the FBI's alleged role in his trip. Still, it was hard to ignore Polynkov's account.

"Basically, there were many Ukrainians who very persistently tried to infiltrate us," he wrote. "This is not the only spy exposed by (our group), but the first from the United States."

*　　*　　*

INVASION

On February 24, 2022, Russia launched a full-scale invasion of Ukraine. The first bombs fell that early morning and woke me at the Hyatt Hotel in Kiev. I couldn't fathom that Putin had made such a reckless move. The invasion was the fulfillment of the policies he had laid down in his 2007 Munich speech. It had taken fifteen years, but Putin had held onto power all that time and marched his country into an unprovoked war. I knew the woe it would bring to Ukraine.[7]

I spent the following months writing about the war in various Ukrainian cities and towns, speaking with soldiers and government officials and ordinary people. I witnessed the results of Russia's attacks on civilian targets. In early April 2022, I drove into Bucha, outside Kiev, as the local militia retook the town. Two militiamen were reinstalling the Ukrainian flag to the local administration building. For hours that day, and for a week afterward, I saw the corpses of many of the hundreds of civilians that Russia's soldiers had murdered and left strewn around town, some of them dismembered, burned, and decaying.[8]

Unlike the millions of Ukrainians who were dead or displaced or fighting the Russian military, I had the privilege of leaving the war behind. I returned to the United States and thought over what I had seen. I'd spent twenty years making friendships in Russia and Ukraine. Now one country was trying to erase the other. I realized how I had fooled myself over the years about Russian intentions. I learned that history was more than just for reading.

Epilogue

The war released many emotions. It shook loose something of more practical concern.

In the summer, I received a text message from my contact with RUH8, the Ukrainian hacker group that had compiled the VK Leaks database. After Russia had invaded in 2022, officials in the Ukrainian security services solicited RUH8's help in penetrating Russian servers and accounts. My contact told me that the authorities had returned the VK Leaks hard drives. He sent me a link. After two years of searching, I finally had the full database in hand.

I discovered that I already possessed much of the material I'd needed, the direct-message subtext that illuminated Billy's perils in Russia in 2015. Hidden among the messages, however, was an exchange of perhaps greater value.

On July 8, 2015, roughly two weeks after Billy's disappearance, Mikhail Polynkov texted a group of VKontakte recipients to relay a message from Bronya, the manager of the Rostov fighter camp. "He received a call from counterintelligence officer Denis, who picked Vasya up," Polynkov wrote. "He says it's a serious matter."

Vasya was Billy's Russian alias, but who was Denis?

The timing of the phone call that Polynkov mentioned was highly suggestive. The call had come just two days before the July 10 discovery, in the reservoir in Donbas, of the body of the John Doe that fingerprints and DNA tests would later identify as Billy's.

Polynkov wrote again to the group to say he had spoken with Denis.

"[Denis] said it had everything to do with that black crossing attempt," Polynkov wrote, referencing the unofficial corridor that periodically opened on the Russia-Ukraine border. "He said we have to connect with his bosses. This is Rostov counterintelligence."

Polynkov told the group that Russian counterintelligence agents had elicited information from Billy. "[He] confessed and handed over those who were supposed to pull him out." I imagined Billy restrained in a cell, beaten, saying whatever he could to make the pain stop.

Those in the VKontakte message group realized that the Russian security services were ordering them to shutter the Rostov volunteer-fighter base. "That's your thanks for capturing a spy," one user wrote.

These messages filled in missing pieces of the puzzle. Denis, a Russian counterintelligence officer, had arrested Billy at the base on June 25, 2015, local time. This event had caused the suspension of Billy's communications with his parents. Over the next two weeks, with Billy in the custody of the Russian security services, something had gone awry. On July 8, 2015, Denis instructed Bronya to dissolve the Rostov base, the last place Billy had been, perhaps to cover the FSB's tracks. Two days later, Billy's body was discovered in Ukraine.

The timeline didn't lie. Events held together. The security services had taken Billy into custody. He was dead within a dozen days. I needed to know who had set the timeline in motion.

*　　*　　*

In the VKontakte group chat, Mikhail Polynkov, remarkably, had shared a phone number for Denis, the security-services officer.

This allowed for directed research, the keying of Denis's phone number into a database of other numbers compiled from a caller-ID application.

Users installed such caller-ID apps on their phones to identify the numbers of incoming calls that were unknown to them. The apps worked by uploading the contact lists of the people who installed the software. This enabled the apps to crowdsource numbers that had names assigned to them. The apps then collected these numbers and names in massive, ever-growing databases.

The caller-ID database contained the phone number for Denis, along with a complete name. This allowed for cross-referencing.

Online, there was also a database of usernames and phone numbers hacked from Yandex. A Russian approximate of Uber, the taxicab company, Yandex also provided a food-delivery service. Simply by ordering a meal from Yandex, Denis had revealed his identity.

The number Mikhail Polynkov had shared in the VKontakte group chat on July 8, 2015, had the same name assigned to it in both the caller-ID app and the Yandex food-delivery database.

The Russian counterintelligence officer who had apparently arrested Billy at the volunteer-fighter camp in Rostov-on-Don on June 25, 2015, causing his disappearance, was named Denis Aleksandrovich Palyeny.

The following year, Palyeny appeared in a Russian magazine titled *Обзор*, or *Review*. This was a publication of an organization named the National Information Center for the Counteraction of Terrorism and Extremism in the Educational Environment and the Internet. (The name approximated that of the group led by Valery Prikhodko, who had made the initial fingerprint match.) An article in *Обзор*'s December 2016 issue listed D. A. Palyeny among a group of "representatives of the Federal Security Service of the Rostov Region."[9] If *Обзор* was correct, then Denis Palyeny worked for the FSB, Russia's main intelligence agency. Mikhail Polynkov had said as much in social media.

The evidence in sum appeared to show that an organ of the Russian government, the FSB, had liquidated Billy. His death had not been the result of a crime or a drunken passion but meant much more.

* * *

The eleven-day gap between the suspension of Billy's communications in Russia and the discovery of his body in Donbas had been a mystery. But that mystery now fell away. Denis Palyeny had taken Billy into custody. Russia's counterintelligence service had held Billy captive. The autopsy report illustrated what happened next.

Billy had been stabbed and was bleeding. His body was stripped and wrapped in layers of plastic tarp, perhaps to prevent blood from soiling the floor of a vehicle that might have transported him over the border into Ukraine. Weights were fastened to Billy's body in order to sink it. He was then pitched into the reservoir outside the Ukrainian village of Darivka.

Billy's end should have been tidy: an unidentifiable body decomposing at the bottom of a pool of water in Donbas. Billy was meant to dissolve into the abyss of the war. But someone had bungled the job. The weights had come loose. Only by luck had Billy been discovered.

After September 11, the FBI's transformation into an international intelligence agency was no secret to countries hostile to the United States. FBI agents and their operatives around the world were no longer glorified policemen. Other countries considered them infiltrators, provocateurs, and spies out of uniform, NOCs, fair game for rough handling.

The VKontakte messages and Polynkov's own postings strongly suggested that in June 2015 the Russian security services had decided to eliminate an American intelligence operative, no matter if Billy Reilly truly was one of those. The operation had been a calculated risk, resting on the assumption that there would be no reprisal for Billy's liquidation. By the time of Billy's death, with agent Tim Reintjes visiting the Reillys but shielding the truth, the US government had already discarded one more CHS.

I remembered a morning in the summer of 2018. I was sitting at a table on the veranda at the Petrovsky Prichal hotel in Rostov-on-Don with Nastya Mikhailovskaya. I asked her what she thought might have happened to the American lost in Russia. "Someone would have tortured Billy for information and dumped him in LNR or DNR," she said. At the time, this sounded like just another theory. I now realized that Mikhailovskaya, given her contacts and experience, understood the way certain problems were handled.

If this was indeed what had transpired, I needed to know whether or not Billy, stewing at the Rostov base in the summer of 2015, intent on his goal while scanning the Don River, was aware that his life was in the balance. In the late afternoon of June 23, 2015, shortly before disappearing, Billy wrote to Polynkov via VKontakte: "I need to talk to you. I don't know what's going on here."

"I spoke to Bronya," Polynkov replied. "He said that you will go with a humanitarian convoy."

"Do you know when I'll go?" Billy asked.

"This week."

By now, after a month of empty promises, Billy knew that something was wrong. The time stamps on the direct messages in the VK Leaks database showed that five minutes passed before he responded to Polynkov's text. This was time enough to articulate a rising fear.

Billy wrote: "Some people here say that I am a spy."

* * *

A FINAL SEARCH

Holy Sepulchre Cemetery in Southfield, Michigan, between Oxford and Detroit, is a rolling property of 350 acres, and it is finely kept. Along grassy grounds and lanes that wind amid oak and pine trees, nearly 40,000 souls have found their final rest.[10]

A Catholic cemetery, Holy Sepulchre is the place where Billy helped lay down his grandfather Marvin. Along an open path, I drove past the graves for Marvin O'Kray and his wife Irene, Terry Reilly's mother. I saw the flowers, fresh still, that I supposed the Reillys had laid there.

I proceeded farther through the trees' foliage and past imperious headstones and walk-in mausoleums, by the humble grave of Jay Sebring, a victim of the Tate-LaBianca massacres. Like Billy, Sebring had died far away and for no reason and early, and had been brought back home to Michigan. How many other lives among these markers had run an abbreviated term?

I knew that Bill and Terry were meditating over what they'd lost. They hoped for an arrest in Russia or a revelation from the FBI, but their yearning had corroded to scorn. There was no justice for Billy, only excuses and denials.

I phoned the Reillys each year on Billy's birthday and at other times, too. Terry and I would run through what she and Bill had endured, and the experiences we'd had. Sometimes we'd laugh at the curiosities we'd encountered on the way to the discovery we had never wanted to make. I knew that we shared something that was difficult to explain to other people, and often to ourselves.

Since 2017, I had been so intent on uncovering Billy's path that I'd failed to consider whether it was better not to have sought it. The first time I saw Terry, she'd said she was certain that I would find her son. In the end, I was the one who discovered that Billy was no more.

There comes a point in our calls when Terry grows quiet. She says that she and Bill visit Billy's grave each week. They lay flowers there. Terry says she's compensating for the four years that Billy's grave in Donbas had lain neglected, the only plot without flowers or family in a cemetery on a remote piece of land. "It's great having him home," Terry says, and it's only then that she sounds glad. Once I asked if they wouldn't rather still be ignorant of their son's cruel end, and Bill told me, "It's better knowing."

I parked the car along a lane that adjoined a section of graves at the rear limit of Holy Sepulchre's territory. Beyond it was a fence and a public road with light traffic. Rain was coming down.

With a bouquet of flowers in hand, I walked the field of gravestones. They were small and rectangular and affixed flush to the turf. Many were overlaid with grass or pooled in rainwater. Stepping carefully, I read the markers one by one along a patch of land the size of a shopping-mall parking lot. It felt like I was searching for Billy all over again.

I made out an object at the far edge of the burial field, a single headstone.

The marker rose three feet from the ground and was considerable in size. It was in the approximate shape of an anvil, with a thick slab of stone set level across its top. The surname "REILLY" was written in large logo type along the slab's facing edge.

I took in the headstone's inscription:

"No Farewell Words Were Spoken, No Time to Say Goodbye. You Were Gone Before We Knew It, And Only God Knows Why."

Near the grave rested a large, level stone. I sat on the stone to gather my thoughts. Billy had been an adult. He had made his own choices. Had the FBI or another agency sent him to Russia, as the VK Leaks messages suggested? Had Billy truly sympathized with the Russian nationals, or had he simply been pursuing his fascination for the ways the world changes?

A stand of trees clustered nearby, reaching high toward the sky. I imagined that on a pleasant day, with sunlight coming down, the trees would shade Billy's grave. There was solace even in the rain. Flowers resting on the headstone were purple, fresh, and the raindrops tickled their petals.

Terry and Bill had given their son a moving memorial. I thought they might often sit on this stone and try to remember how Billy would smile or talk, and what he would say. They might hear his voice and imagine they are with him. I knew there would be no real consolation. "It just doesn't ever get any better," Terry had said on one of our calls. "I thought, with time, it would. But it just doesn't."

I took the steps to the grave. Crouching, I placed my bouquet atop a stone, flush with the earth, that marked the years of Billy's life. Terry and Bill would soon be here. They might notice the flowers and understand that someone had cared enough to visit.

I stood and turned to go, walking into the rain.

When we are young, we seek our fates. We find we have no great destiny, only lives.

Afterword

After the *Journal* article published in 2019, Michigan senators Peters and Stabenow joined Rep. Elissa Slotkin (who had won Mike Bishop's House seat the year before) in calling for an investigation into the Reilly case. The three wrote a letter to the Department of Justice's inspector general, which read, in part:

We are concerned about the lack of candor and contradictory information provided by the FBI regarding its knowledge of Billy's travel and subsequent disappearance in Russia. To date, the FBI has not been forthcoming in answering questions about Billy's disappearance and death despite their repeated requests for information and engagement from multiple congressional offices.

The letter continued:

We are therefore requesting that your office thoroughly investigate these outstanding questions... The investigation should also address whether the FBI is withholding information about his disappearance and death and whether it followed all protocols and procedures... We believe that an independent investigation is critical. We ask that you give this matter your immediate attention.

I'd been hoping for such a development since the beginning of my report-ing. I had filed numerous Freedom of Information Act requests with DOJ, the FBI, and the CIA. Each petition had elicited an empty response. A *Journal* lawyer and I had gone round and round with DOJ but made no progress. These federal agencies and departments were by law required to conduct only a "reasonable search" for information in response to a FOIA request, acting themselves as judges of reason.

A letter from Capitol Hill was of a higher order. It placed public and institutional pressure on DOJ and the FBI.

Months passed with no result, however. A year went by. Staffers for Peters, Slotkin, and Stabenow told me that the DOJ's inspector general hadn't replied to their 2019 letter.

I filed another FOIA request, this time with the DOJ's inspector general directly, and in Spring 2021, I received a forty-page file. Much of the file contained documents I'd already seen. There was also a series of emails.

"Worth discussing," a DOJ inspector general staffer wrote in a November 15, 2019, email, the day after the Michigan congressional delegation had sent its letter requesting an investigation. "We have the capacity."

There was an email exchange from nearly three months later, beginning on February 4, 2020. "Will you have time over the next few days to set me up with some documents in the SCIF?" one DOJ inspector general staffer wrote to another. "I have them on a disc."

I never learned the contents of the disc mentioned in the emails. But I knew that a SCIF, which is shorthand for sensitive compartmented information facility, is a room in which people with governmental security clearances can securely view classified documents. I concluded that something related to Billy's case had been classified, again upending the FBI's claim of Billy's insignificance.

In the fall of 2022, I contacted the offices of Peters, Slotkin, and Stabenow and learned that three years after they had requested a DOJ investigation into Billy's case, the government had still yet to respond to it.

I tried the FBI once more, disclosing the fact of this forthcoming book and requesting a meeting at headquarters to share my updated findings. The FBI declined.

In 2021, after years of searching, I located Amera Lomangcolob. She was listed in Filipino voting roles as having voted in a presidential election while abroad, via a consulate in Saudi Arabia. I made contact with Lomangcolob through a friend of hers who worked as a domestic there. Via this channel, Lomangcolob told me she had read the 2019 *Journal* article about Billy. She said she wanted to leave all that in the past.

"She has a quiet life now," the friend wrote in a text message. "She was a victim too. She was blinded because she was young then. She has now learned her lesson the hard way. Don't drag her into their chaotic world. She no longer wants to be involved with any of them and she has a new life and family now. Let her be to live a happy life."

In November 2022, I learned that Aws Naser, the Michigan man of Iraqi heritage whom Billy had contacted on behalf of the FBI, was facing new charges. In a case investigated by a JTTF, federal prosecutors in Michigan charged Naser with attempting to provide material support to ISIS from 2011 to 2017 and for being a felon in possession of a destructive device. He faced thirty-five years in prison. Commenting on the Naser charges, James A. Tarasca, who was named the special agent in charge of the FBI's Detroit office after Tim Waters retired in late 2021, said that "the FBI will make every effort to protect Americans at home and abroad."

Dmitri Tyurin, the Moscow private investigator who had worked for the Reillys, doubted the facts of Billy's death. When Tyurin and I spoke in late 2022, he discounted the fingerprint and DNA matches, saying that the remains that Terry and Bill had exhumed in Donbas had been "some homeless, dead body," likely part of an intelligence scheme to install Billy as an operative under deep cover. Tyurin spoke of Billy as a "wonderful agent living somewhere in Russia, with a totally clean background and a new identity." Tyurin predicted that Billy would reappear ten or fifteen years hence amid a US intelligence operation.

Valery Prikhodko, the man who had made the initial fingerprint match, continued to maintain that Billy's death was the result of a banal, even accidental event, rather than connected to the Russian security services. He asked me to persuade Bill and Terry to forget agitating for justice in Russia.

I reached out to Denis Palyeny, the man identified in the hacked VKontakte messages as the security officer who had arrested Billy at the Rostov camp in June 2015. The phone number listed for Palyeny in the VKontakte messages never rang through. By then, in the summer and fall of 2022, the war in Ukraine was at full tilt, and such connections were harder to make. When I emailed Palyeny in early 2023 at an address linked to his phone number, informing him of the book and my discoveries, I received no reply.

Mikhail Polynkov, the volunteer-fighter recruiter, finally spoke about Billy Reilly, by phone, in September 2022. Polynkov confirmed the breach of his VKontakte account and the public release of his messages, which had enabled me to piece together how Polynkov and others in Russia and Donbas had manipulated Billy. "They are real, of course," Polynkov said of the messages. "I have nothing to hide. All is as it is."

Like Tyurin, Polynkov discounted the fingerprint and DNA results. "I know for sure that [Billy] was let go," he said. "Maybe he then tried his own way [to cross the border]. Our people didn't need [Billy's murder]. They were more interested in him alive."

Acknowledgements

Terry and Bill Reilly deserve my lasting gratitude. The Reillys are private people, yet they agreed to share their ordeal, placing their confidence in me, a stranger. Over our countless phone calls and through many meetings and messages, their willingness remained, despite the emotional strain, as they helped me peel the layers of Billy's mystery. In their straits, some families surrender. The Reillys never did.

Catie and Mohammed Cherri also accommodated my numberless requests, opening their lives to help me understand Billy. I thank them for their patience and for their deeply thoughtful contributions to Billy's story.

Paul Beckett, the Washington bureau chief of the *Wall Street Journal*, was the driver of this project at the newspaper. He saw, as I had seen, the narrative potential that lay within Billy's case. Paul encouraged my reporting, walked alongside me through the story's unfolding intricacies, and guided the article's edits. I give him my gratitude.

Robert Ourlian was the national security editor at the *Journal* during the reporting and writing of the article, and he gave me the time and support to achieve results. Sam Enriquez, of the *Journal*'s page-one edit staff, collaborated in constructing and refining the article's published version, with Matthew Rose overseeing; I am thankful to them both. Jathon Sapsford, a deputy Washington bureau chief for the *Journal*, provided timely and critical support. And I thank Jeanne Cummings, also a *Journal* deputy Washington bureau chief, for her ready counsel and for her selfless preparation of prize submissions.

Also at the *Journal*, Lisa Schwartz delivered valuable leads and research, as

Acknowledgements

did Jared Malsin and Jude Marfil. Thank you to Nathan Puffer, the strategic security chief at Dow Jones, and the unit in Princeton for watching my movements in Russia.

I thank my *Journal* colleague and friend Alan Cullison for his reporting support and for his sagacity and avuncularity.

Thank you to Michael Siconolfi and Christopher Stewart, of the *Journal's* investigative unit, for encouraging me to join the paper years ago.

David Granger is the agent I'd long hoped I might find. He was an inventive partner in helping to craft the proposal for this book and stage-managed the process by which we found its home. As the book has marched into existence, David has been a steadfast comrade.

I thank Vanessa Mobley, formerly of Little, Brown, for her potent enthusiasm for the project and for her editorial guidance through the book's initial versions. Pronoy Sarkar became deeply committed to the project, applying his talent for narrative, enriching the book's humanity, and serving as an invaluable resource and advocate. Thank you to Pronoy, and also to Maria Espinosa, for her reads and support.

I thank Michael Noon and Mike Fleming, also at Little, Brown, for their work in production and copyediting, and Chris Nolan for the legal read. My appreciation also goes to Alyssa Persons, Katherine Akey, Gianella Rojas, and Sarah Maymi in the publisher's marketing and publicity departments for enlightening readers to our work and the importance of Billy's story.

A book like this one can be composed only with the selfless contributions of people who have worked in intelligence and law enforcement. Andy Arena, Carlos Fernandez, Kenny Leahman, Don Robinson, John Sipher, and many other former agents and officers from the CIA, FBI, and other US agencies patiently fielded my questions over numerous calls and coffees. They have helped me understand an environment that is designed to resist the grasp of outsiders.

Thank you to Jim O'Kray and Kathy O'Kray for sharing their thoughts of their nephew. Thank you also to Guy Schlachter, Chaz Laflamme, Drew Robertoy, Kathy Lewis, others who knew Billy in high school, and former editor of the *Oxford Leader* C. J. Carnacchio. Walt Power and Shardul Shah were obliging in explaining life in the Detroit area among various ethnic communities. Thank you to Ambassador John Beyrle and former Rep. Mike Bishop.

Acknowledgements

This book benefitted from the toil and creativity of several researchers, principally Michael Sheldon, whose understanding of Russia's volunteer battalions and events in Donbas, along with his digital skills and resourcefulness, were essential to decoding key parts of the mystery. Helena Jensen, Zoe Best, Daria X., and Ksenia K. also provided important research. Florin Safner surpassed my hopes in creating maps that illustrate Billy's range.

Tom Colligan and Milana Mazaeva fact-checked the manuscript and assisted with the compilation of end notes, providing a critical backstop, considering the book's breadth of topics and information. I thank them.

Thank you to Bob Foresman for sharing Billy's case with me and for trading periodic thoughts about US and Russian attitudes to the disappearance. Anthony Scaramucci explained relevant inner workings of the Trump administration.

Robert Koenig deserves my gratitude for his assistance in Ukraine and for his backing and encouragement over the years. Thank you to David Friend for his wisdom and his committed friendship.

Thanks to Angus Roven, Stefan Wathne, and Arthur and Lesya McCallum, who led me down this road years ago. Alex Lareneg, Andrey Shestopalov, and Dmitri Tyurin provided important support and insight in Russia. The ultimate results achieved in the investigation of this case are linked to the efforts of Anastasia Mikhailovskaya and Valery Prikhodko.

I extend gratitude to Charley Dane for his early read of the manuscript and for his faithful friendship of many years. For various assistance, my thanks go also to Paul Pelletier, Mika "Iceman" Immonen, Natalie Gryvnyak, Alexander Sulla, Natalka Pisnya, Elena Postnikova, Alexander Ulanov, Preston Mendenhall, Vyacheslav Konstantinovsky, Zamir Gotta, Shimeng Zhang, Alexander Toulbou, Anna Dyachenko, Serhiy Bosak, Suratni, Dr. Jeffrey Jentzen, Darko Skulsky, Michael Perry, Mark Parekh, Mark Halaway, Leon Beker, Mark O'Keefe, Jess Randall, Caleb Santana, and OJ Lima.

Warm thanks to Brian Best for our talks about Ukraine, and to him and Natasha for the London stay. My gratefulness goes also to Craig, Ulrica, and the kids for the same out West, when this book was a blank page.

*   *   *

Acknowledgements

Note on spellings: The spellings of place names in Ukraine is an emotional subject for some people. In this book, in most instances, I have included geographical spellings as they appear in the *Wall Street Journal*, with a notable exception. I've used the long-accepted exonym of Ukraine's capital city, Kiev, which is the transliteration of the Russian-language spelling of the name, rather than its Ukrainian version, Kyiv. I make no political statement with this choice but a decision of function. To me, Kiev is not a Russian spelling but, for native English speakers, a more pronounceable one.

Bibliography

Trevor Aaronson, *The Terror Factory: Inside the FBI's Manufactured War on Terrorism* (New York: Ig Publishing, 2018)

Michael Beschloss, *Mayday: Eisenhower, Khrushchev, and the U-2 Affair* (New York: Harper and Row, 1988)

Victor Cherkashin and Gregory Feifer, *Spy Handler: Memoir of a KGB Officer—The True Story of the Man Who Recruited Robert Hanssen and Aldrich Ames* (New York: Basic Books, 2005)

Louis J. Freeh, *My FBI: Bringing Down the Mafia, Investigating Bill Clinton, and Fighting the War on Terror* (New York: St. Martin's Griffin; first edition, 2006)

Mark Galeotti, *Armies of Russia's War in Ukraine*, illustrated edition (Oxford, UK: Osprey Publishing, 2019)

Mike German, *Disrupt, Discredit and Divide: How the New FBI Damages Democracy* (New York: The New Press, 2019)

Garrett M. Graff, *The Threat Matrix: Inside Robert Mueller's FBI and the War on Global Terror* (New York: Little, Brown, 2011)

Paul Klebnikov, *Godfather of the Kremlin: The Decline of Russia in the Age of Gangster Capitalism* (New York: Harper Paperbacks, 2001)

Dick Lehr and Gerard O'Neill, *Black Mass: Whitey Bulger, the FBI, and a Devil's Deal* (New York: PublicAffairs, 2012)

Andrew G. McCabe, *The Threat: How the FBI Protects America in the Age of Terror and Trump* (New York: St. Martin's Press, 2019)

Barry Meier, *Missing Man: The American Spy Who Vanished in Iran* (New York: Farrar, Straus and Giroux, 2016)

Nestor the Chronicler, *The Primary Chronicle*, Laurentian text, trans. Samuel Hazzard Cross and Olgerd P. Sherbowitz-Wetzor (The Medieval Academy of America, 1953)

Serhii Plokhy, *The Gates of Europe: A History of Ukraine* (New York: Basic Books, 2017)

Michael Pullara, *The Spy Who Was Left Behind: Russia, the United States, and the True Story of the Betrayal and Assassination of a CIA Agent* (New York: Scribner, 2018)

Mikhail Sholokhov, *And Quiet Flows the Don* (Moscow: Oktyabr, 1928–1940)

Tim Shorrock, *Spies for Hire: The Secret World of Intelligence Outsourcing* (New York: Simon & Schuster; first edition, 2009)

Bibliography

Timothy Snyder, *Bloodlands: Europe Between Hitler and Stalin*, (New York: Basic Books, 2010)

Aleksandr Solzhenitsyn, *Gulag Archipelago: An Experience in Literary Investigation* (New York: Harper & Row, 1974)

Thomas J. Sugrue, *The Origins of the Urban Crisis: Race and Inequality in Postwar Detroit* (Princeton, NJ: Princeton University Press, 1996)

William Taubman, *Khrushchev: The Man and His Era* (New York: W. W. Norton, 2003)

Tim Weiner, *Enemies: A History of the FBI* (New York: Random House, 2012)

Lawrence Wright, *The Looming Tower: Al-Qaeda and the Road to 9/11* (New York: Vintage; first edition, 2006)

9/11 Commission, *The 9/11 Commission Report: Final Report of the National Commission on Terrorist Attacks Upon the United States* (New York: Hill & Wang, 2004)

Notes

CHAPTER 1: THE STATION

1   Elena Gorbacheva, interviews with author, 2018.
2   Patrick Jackson, "Ukraine War Pulls in Foreign Fighters," BBC News, September 1, 2014, https:www.bbc.com/news/world-europe-28951324.
    Mikela Yakkarino, "International Brigades," *Novoe Vremya*, March 23, 2015, https:newtimes.ru/articles/detail/96255.
    Mark Galeotti, *Armies of Russia's War in Ukraine*, illustrated edition (Oxford, UK: Osprey Publishing, 2019).
3   "Three Station Square," Russian Ministry of Culture, https:www.culture.ru/institutes/12243/ploshad-trekh-vokzalov.
    David Kramer, "Russian Style in Architecture as a Search for the National Soul," *Moskvich*, April 28, 2021, https:moskvichmag.ru/gorod/russkij-stil-v-arhitekture-kak-poisk-natsionalnoj-dushi/.
    "A Snake Zilant That Disappeared from the Main Tower of the Kazan Railway Station in Moscow Has Been Found," *Moskovskaya Gazeta*, https:mskgazeta.ru/obshchestvo/najden-zmej-zilant-ischeznuvshij-s-glavnoj-bashni-kazanskogo-vokzala-v-moskve-7799.html.
    "Construction of the Kazan Railway Station in Engravings by Vadim Dmitrievich Falileev and Drawings by Nikifor Yakovlevich Tamonkin," Our Heritage, Russian Federal Agency for Press and Mass Communications, no. 74, 2005, http:www.nasledie-rus.ru/podshivka/7403.php.
4   Elena Gorbacheva and Mikhail Polynkov, VKontakte messages.
    Gorbacheva, interviews.
5   Mikhail Polynkov, *A Soldier's Truth: Military-Political Blog, LiveJournal*, postings, https:polynkov.livejournal.com.
    Mikhail Polynkov, VKontakte account, https:vk.com/polynkov?t2fs=43da76e4b16c3d5844_2.
    Anastasiya Mikhailovskaya, interviews with author, 2018.
    Mikhail Polynkov, interview, 2022.

Notes

6 Elena Gorbacheva, photographs, 2015.

7 Gorbacheva, interviews.

8 "Quiet Don," Avia-Mir, https:avia-mir.ru/poezda/poezd_tihiyi_don/.

9 "Highland Park," Ford company website, https:corporate.ford.com/articles/history/highland-park.html.

Peter Behr, "Silence on the Line at Dodge Main (1914–1980)," *Washington Post*, July 13, 1980, https:www.washingtonpost.com/archive/business/1980/07/13/silence-on-the-line-at-dodge-main-1914-1980/a757ab4a-3609-423a-a054-90ad4eb7fd7a.

10 C. J. Carnacchio, former editor, *Oxford Leader*, interview with author, 2021.

Thaddeus De Witt Seeley, *History of Oakland County Michigan: A Narrative Account of Its Historic Progress, Its People, Its Principal Interests*, vol. 1 (Chicago: Lewis, 1912), 242–50, https:www.google.com/books/edition/History_of_Oakland_County_Michigan/vtzsq71gpFAC?hl=en&gbpv=0.

11 Terry and Bill Reilly, interviews with author, 2017–22.

12 Catie Cherri, interviews with author, 2018–22.

13 Terry and Bill Reilly, interviews.

CHAPTER 2: WINGING IT

1 Jim O'Kray, interviews with author, 2018–22.

Terry and Bill Reilly, interviews.

2 *Polish Americans in Michigan, Subject Guide,* Bentley Historical Library, University of Michigan, https:bentley.umich.edu/wp-content/uploads/2014/09/Polish_Americans_in_Michigan_Subject_Guide.pdf.

3 Walt Power, Detroit resident, interview with author, 2022.

4 Nathan Bomey and John Gallagher, "How Detroit Went Broke," *Detroit Free Press*, September 15, 2013, https:www.freep.com/story/news/local/michigan/detroit/2013/09/15/how-detroit-went-broke-the-answers-may-surprise-you-and/77152028/

Thomas J. Sugrue, *The Origins of the Urban Crisis: Race and Inequality in Postwar Detroit* (Princeton, NJ: Princeton University Press, 1996).

5 Terry and Bill Reilly, interviews.

6 Terry and Bill Reilly, interviews.

7 Willis F. Dunbar, George S. May, *Michigan: A History of the Wolverine State* (Grand Rapids, MI: Eerdmans, 1995), https:www.google.com/books/edition/Michigan/HqGWEAnByeMC?hl=en.

Carnacchio, interview with author, 2021.

Thaddeus De Witt Seeley, *History of Oakland County Michigan: A Narrative Account of Its Historic Progress, Its People, Its Principal Interests*, vol. 1 (Chicago: Lewis, 1912), 242–50, https:www.google.com/books/edition/History_of_Oakland_County_Michigan/vtzsq71gpFAC?hl=en&gbpv=0.

8 "Polly Ann Trail History," Welcome to the Polly Ann Trail, http:pollyanntrailway.org/index.php/about-our-trail/polly-ann-trail-history.

9 Terry and Billy Reilly, interviews.

10 Christopher Singleton, "Auto Industry Jobs in the 1980s: A Decade of Transition," *Monthly Labor Review*, February 1992, https:www.bls.gov/opub/mlr/1992/02/art2full.pdf.

James Risen, "GM to Close 11 Midwest Plants, Cut 29,000 Jobs," *Los Angeles Times,* November, 7, 1986, https:www.latimes.com/archives/la-xpm-1986 -11-07-mn-15593-story.html.

11 Terry and Bill Reilly, interviews.
12 "Michigan," Arab America Foundation, https:www.arabamerica.com/michigan.
James Risen, "Thousands of Lebanese Fleeing Warfare Flood into U.S., Particularly Detroit Area," *Los Angeles Times,* September 23, 1989, https:www.latimes.com /archives/la-xpm-1989-09-23-mn-605-story.html.
13 JoEllen McNergney Vinyard, *For Faith and Fortune: The Education of Catholic Immigrants in Detroit, 1805–1925* (Champaign: University of Illinois Press, 1998), 182, https:archive.org/details/forfaithfortunee0000viny.
14 Power, interview.

CHAPTER 3: DISAFFECTION

1 Certification of Military Service, National Archives and Records Administration, Given at St. Louis, MO, on June 3, 2021.
Archives, Sons of Liberty Museum, Dallas, TX.
2 Terry and Bill Reilly, interviews.
3 Terry and Bill Reilly, interviews. Catie Cherri, interviews.
4 "Regarding Reverends Patrick Casey, Lawrence Ventline and Neil Kalina, PIME," Archdiocese of Detroit, https:protect.aod.org/regarding-reverends-patrick-casey -lawrence-ventline-and-neil-kalina-pime; State of Michigan Department of Licensing and Regulatory Affairs, Bureau of Professional Licensing, Board of Counseling, Disciplinary Subcommittee, Order of Summary Suspension, In the Matter of Lawrence M. Ventline, May 5, 2019, https:www.bishop-accountability.org/wp-content /uploads/2021/12/complaints-administrative-and-order-2019-05-15-and-16-Nessel -MI-AG-re-Ventline.pdf
5 Catie Cherri, interviews.
6 Catie Cherri, interviews.
7 Terry and Bill Reilly, interviews. Catie Cherri, interviews.
8 Billy Reilly, Illinois Institute of Technology, application, June 2014.
9 Terry and Bill Reilly, interviews.
10 Terry and Bill Reilly, interviews.
Kathy Lewis, Our Lady of the Lakes Parish School, teacher, interview with author, 2018.
11 Guy Schlachter, interviews with author, 2018–21.

CHAPTER 4: CATACLYSM

1 Jeanne Cummings and David Rogers, "Bush Demands bin Laden Be Turned Over, Tells U.S. Military 'The Hour Is Coming,'" *Wall Street Journal,* September 20, 2001, https:www.wsj.com/articles/SB1000993322479443320?mod=ig_911archives.
2 Toby Harnden, *First Casualty: The Untold Story of the CIA Mission to Avenge 9/11* (Boston: Little, Brown, 2021).
Henry A. Crumpton, "The CIA in Afghanistan 2001–2002," CIA Directorate of Operations, Archives.gov, https:www.archives.gov/files/declassification/iscap/pdf /2012-041-doc01.pdf

3   Terry and Bill Reilly, interviews.
     Catie Cherri, interviews.
4   Catie Cherri, interviews.
5   Terry and Bill Reilly, interviews.
     Catie Cherri, interviews.
6   College application essay, MS in Computer Science, Reilly hard drives, file: bstate-ment.pdf.
7   Chaz Laflamme, interviews with author, 2018.
     Drew Robertoy, interview with author, 2018.
     Schlachter, interviews.
8   Schlachter, interviews.
     Laflamme, interviews.
9   Catie Cherri, interviews.
10   Reza Aslan, *No God but God* (New York: Random House, 2005).
     Karen Armstrong, *Muhammad: A Prophet for Our Time* (New York: HarperCollins, 2006).
11   Catie Cherri, interviews.
12   Robertoy, interviews.

CHAPTER 5: CONVERSION

1   Catie Cherri, interviews.
2   "President's Remarks in Pontiac, Michigan," Transcript, The White House, October 27, 2004, https:georgewbush-whitehouse.archives.gov/news/releases/2004/10/2004 1027-15.html.
3   "Iraq War Illegal, Says Annan," BBC News, September 16, 2004, http:news .bbc.co.uk/2/hi/middle_east/3661134.stm.
4   Terry and Bill Reilly, interviews.
     Catie Cherri, interviews.
5   Schlachter, interviews.
     Laflamme, interviews.
     Robertoy, interviews.
6   Mohammed Cherri, interviews.
     Catie Cherri, interviews.
7   Terry and Bill Reilly interviews.
     Catie Cherri, interviews.
8   William Reilly, Our Lady of the Lakes Parish School, academic transcript, printed on October 2, 2019.
9   Terry and Bill Reilly, interviews.
10   William Reilly, academic transcript.
11   William Reilly, Oakland University, academic transcript, office of the registrar, issued May 8, 2012.
     Terry and Bill Reilly, interviews.
12   Terry and Bill Reilly interviews.
     Catie Cherri, interviews.
13   Catie Cherri, interviews.
14   Terry and Bill Reilly, interviews.
     Catie Cherri, interviews.

15 Catie Cherri, interviews.
16 Terry and Bill Reilly, interviews.
   Catie Cherri, interviews.
17 Catie Cherri, interviews.
18 Criminal Complaint, *US v. Luqman Ameen Abdullah, et al.*, US District Court, Eastern District of Michigan, Case: 2:09-mj-30436, filed October 27, 2009.
   Niraj Warikoo, "FBI's Killing of Detroit Muslim Leader 10 Years Ago Haunts Communities," *Detroit Free Press*, October 28, 2019, https:www.freep.com/story/news/local/michigan/2019/10/28/ten-years-fbi-imam-luqman-abdullah-death-dearborn/2451750001/.
   "Eleven Members/Associates of Ummah Charged with Federal Violations," FBI archives, October 28, 2009, https:archives.fbi.gov/archives/detroit/press-releases/2009/de102809.htm.
19 Catie Cherri, interviews.
   Mohammed Cherri, interviews.
20 Catie Cherri, interviews.
21 Catie Cherri, interviews.

CHAPTER 6: SIEGE

1 "FBI Files on Umar Farouk Abdulmutallab," *New York Times*, February 22, 2017, https:www.nytimes.com/interactive/2017/02/22/world/document-Umar-Farouk-Abdulmutallab-Documents.html.
2 Andy Arena, interviews with author, 2018–21.
3 Andrew G. McCabe, *The Threat: How the FBI Protects America in the Age of Terror and Trump* (New York: St. Martin's Press, 2019), 104–5, 111–14.
4 "Committee Study of Central Intelligence Agency's Detention and Interrogation Program," Report of the Senate Select Committee on Intelligence, Chair D. Feinstein, 2014, https:www.intelligence.senate.gov/sites/default/files/publications/CRPT-113srpt288.pdf.
   Shane O'Mara, *Why Torture Doesn't Work: The Neuroscience of Interrogation* (Cambridge, MA: Harvard University Press, 2015).
5 McCabe, *The Threat*, 105, 111.
   Tim Weiner, *Enemies: A History of the FBI* (New York: Random House, 2012), 447.
6 McCabe, *The Threat*, 112–13.
7 McCabe, *The Threat*, 112–13, 119.
   Scott Shane, "Inside Al Qaeda's Plot to Blow Up an American Airliner," *New York Times*, February 22, 2017, https:www.nytimes.com/2017/02/22/us/politics/anwar-awlaki-underwear-bomber-abdulmutallab.html.
8 *9/11 Commission Report*, 352.
9 Former FBI special agents, interviews with author, 2018–22.
   McCabe, *The Threat*, 60–61.
10 Paul Pelletier, former US federal prosecutor, interviews with author, 2018–22.
   McCabe, *The Threat*, 58.
11 Weiner, *Enemies*, 11–12.
12 "Palmer Raids," FBI.gov, https:www.fbi.gov/history/famous-cases/palmer-raids.
   Weiner, *Enemies*, 20–22.
13 "FBI's Compliance with the Attorney General's Investigative Guidelines (Redacted),"

Office of the Inspector General, 2005, chap. 2, "Historical Background of the Attorney General's Investigative Guidelines," https:oig.justice.gov/sites/default/files /archive/special/0509/chapter2.htm.

Weiner, *Enemies*, 74, 95–96.

14 Ryan Grim and Jon Schwarz, "A Short History of US Law Enforcement Infiltrating Protests," *The Intercept*, June 2, 2020, https:theintercept.com/2020/06/02/history -united-states-government-infiltration-protests/.

15 "FBI's Compliance," chap. 3: "Attorney General's Guidelines Regarding the Use of Confidential Informants," https:oig.justice.gov/sites/default/files/archive/special /0509/chapter3.htm.

16 Arena, interviews.

17 "Everything Secret Degenerates: The FBI's Use of Murderers as Informants," House Government Reform Committee, US House of Representatives, February 3, 2004, https:www.congress.gov/congressional-report/108th-congress/house -report/414/2.

Dick Lehr and Gerard O'Neill, *Black Mass: Whitey Bulger, the FBI, and a Devil's Deal* (New York: PublicAffairs, 2012).

18 Arena, interviews.

19 Weiner, *Enemies*, 335.

Hearings before the Subcommittee on Civil and Constitutional Rights, House Judiciary Committee, 94th Congress, 1976, https:www.ojp.gov/pdffiles1/Digitization /40551NCJRS.pdf.

Impact of Attorney General's Guidelines for Domestic Security Investigations ("The Levi Guidelines"), Senate Judiciary Committee, 98th Congress, NCJ Number 94098, 1984, https:www.ojp.gov/ncjrs/virtual-library/abstracts/impact -attorney-generals-guidelines-domestic-security.

9/11 Commission Report, 75.

20 Press Briefing by Attorney General William French Smith on the Cabinet Council Meeting on Drug Enforcement Matters, White House Office of the Press Secretary, August 30, 1984, https:www.reaganlibrary.gov/public/digitallibrary/smof/counsel /roberts/box-019/40-485-6908381-019-006-2017.pdf.

Pelletier, interviews.

Jim McGee, "The Rise of the FBI," *Washington Post*, July 20, 1997, https:www. washingtonpost.com/archive/lifestyle/magazine/1997/07/20/the-rise-of-the-fbi/07c00 9a3-ddb0-4e6a-81bd-91bc0aa3c996/.

21 "Attorney General Reno's Confidential Informant Guidelines," Department of Justice, January 8, 2001, https:www.justice.gov/archives/ag/attorney-general-renos -confidential-informant-guidelines-january-8-2001.

22 "Everything Secret Degenerates."

23 "Uniting and Strengthening America by Providing Appropriate Tools Required to Intercept and Obstruct Terrorism (USA Patriot Act) of 2001," Section 201, US Congress, https:www.congress.gov/107/plaws/publ56/PLAW-107publ56.pdf.

Weiner, *Enemies*, 437.

24 Neil Lewis, "Traces of Terror: The Inquiry: Aschcroft Permits F.B.I. to Monitor Internet and Public Activities," *New York Times*, May 31, 2002, https:www.nytimes.com /2002/05/31/us/traces-terror-inquiry-ashcroft-permits-fbi-monitor-internet-public -activities.html.

25   Robert S. Mueller III, biography, Fbi.gov, https:www.fbi.gov/history/directors /robert-s-mueller-iii.

26   9/11 Commission Report, 423.

27   Ibid., 424.

28   Ibid., 424.

29   Andy Arena, interviews.

30   Janet Reitman, "'I Helped Destroy People,'" *New York Times Magazine*, September 1, 2021, https:www.nytimes.com/2021/09/01/magazine/fbi-terrorism-terry -albury.html.
     Yassir Fazaga et al. v. Federal Bureau of Investigation et al., Declarations of Craig Monteilh, US District Court for the Central District of California, Case No. SA CV 11-00301 CJC (VBKx), April 23, 2010– October 12, 2011, https:www.supremecourt.gov/DocketPDF/20/20-828/185460 /20210730194627462_20-828ja.pdf.

31   Arena, interviews.

32   Arena, interviews.

33   Dan Eggen, "FBI Agents Still Lacking Arabic Skills 33 of 12,000 Have Some Proficiency," *Washington Post*, October 11, 2006, https:www.washingtonpost.com /archive/politics/2006/10/11/fbi-agents-still-lacking-arabic-skills-span-classbankhead 33-of-12000-have-some-proficiencyspan/ef10018e-6224-4b0f-bffe-ab6d67f6ba15/.

34   Paul Vitello and Kirk Semple, "Muslims Say FBI Tactics Sow Anger and Fear." *New York Times*, December 17, 2009, https:www.nytimes.com/2009/12/18/us/18mus lims.html.
     9/11 Commission Report, 77.
     Dana Millbank, "FBI Budget Squeezed after 9/11," *Washington Post*, March 22, 2004, https:www.washingtonpost.com/archive/politics/2004/03/22/fbi-budget -squeezed-after-911/169ac386-cab7-4c93-bcda-9801b5d5969d/.
     "Preventing and Combating Terrorism Including Counterterrorism and Intelligence: +227.3 Million in Counterterrorism and Intelligence Enhancements," Department of Justice, Budget Fact Sheet, FY 2008, https:www.justice.gov/archive/jmd/2008fact sheets/pdf/0801_ct_intel.pdf.

35   Reitman, "'I Helped Destroy People.'"
     Paul Vitello and Kirk Semple, "Muslims Say FBI Tactics Sow Anger and Fear."

36   Audit of the Department of Justice's Use of Immigration Sponsorship Programs, Office of the Inspector General, June 2019, 7, https:oig.justice.gov/reports/2019 /a1932.pdf.
     FBI special agents, interviews.

37   FBI special agents, interviews.

CHAPTER 7: FACTOTUM

1   Billy Reilly, Oakland University academic transcript, issued May 8, 2012.
    Terry and Bill Reilly, interviews.
    Catie Cherri, interviews.

2   Reilly hard drives, College application essay, Master's program in Computer Science, file name: bstatement.pdf.

3   Terry and Bill Reilly, interviews.

4   Terry and Bill Reilly, interviews.

5   Terry and Bill Reilly, interviews.
    David Kotal–Terry Reilly, messages.
6   FBI special agents, interviews.
    "Sensitive Site Exploitation Guide," US Department of Defense, https:media
    .defense.gov/2021/Mar/11/2002598879/-1/-1/1/SENSITIVE%20SITE%20EXPL
    OITATION%20GUIDE.PDF.
    Adam Goldman and Julie Tate, "Inside the FBI's Secret Relationship with the Military's
    Special Operations," *Washington Post*, April 10, 2014, https:www.washingtonpost.com
    /world/national-security/inside-the-fbis-secret-relationship-with-the-militarys-special-ope
    rations/2014/04/10/dcca3460-be84-11e3-b195-dd0c1174052c_story.html.
7   Reitman, "'I Helped Destroy People.'"
    Mike German, "Rethinking Intelligence: Interview with John Mueller and Mark
    G. Stewart," Brennan Center for Justice, March 31, 2016, https:www.brennancenter.org
    /our-work/research-reports/rethinking-intelligence-interview-john-mueller-and-mark
    -g-stewart.
8   Lawrence Wright, *The Looming Tower: Al-Qaeda and the Road to 9/11* (New York:
    Knopf, 2006), 395–96.
    "FBI Was Warned about Flight Schools," CBS News, May 15, 2002, https:www
    .cbsnews.com/news/fbi-was-warned-about-flight-schools/.
9   Reitman, "'I Helped Destroy People.'"
10 FBI special agents, interviews.
    McCabe, *The Threat*, 67.
11 McCabe, *The Threat*, 70.
12 FBI special agents, interviews.
13 Terry and Bill Reilly, interviews.
14 Ibid.
15 Ibid.
16 Talal Ansari and Siraj Datoo, "Welcome to America—Now Spy on Your Friends,"
    BuzzFeed News, January 28, 2016, https:www.buzzfeednews.com/article/talalansari
    /welcome-to-america-now-spy-on-your-friends#.ni9wgoxnL.
    Trevor Aaronson, "When Informants Are No Longer Useful, the FBI Can Help
    Deport Them," *The Intercept*, January 31, 2017,
    https:theintercept.com/2017/01/31/when-informants-are-no-longer-useful-the-fbi
    -can-help-deport-them/.
    FBI special agents, interviews.
17 Terry and Bill Reilly, interviews.
    Catie Cherri, interviews.
18 "CHS Assessing," FBI Anchorage, Program Aids, CHS Recruiting Series, derived
    from: FBI NSISCG, Record: 800A-AN-14809, October 6, 2011, 8, https:archive
    .org/stream/ConfidentialHumanSourceAssessmentAid/Confidential%20Human%
    20Source%20Assessment%20Aid_djvu.txt.
19 Terry and Bill Reilly, interviews.
20 Wayne M. Murphy, Assistant Director, Directorate of Intelligence, FBI, State-
    ment before the House Judiciary Committee, Subcommittee on Constitution,
    Civil Rights, and Civil Liberties and on Crime, Terrorism, and Homeland Secu-
    rity, July 19, 2007, https:archives.fbi.gov/archives/news/testimony/improving
    -our-confidential-human-source-program.

21 Confidential Human Source Policy Guide, Federal Bureau of Investigation, Directorate of Intelligence 0836 PG, September 21, 2015, 105.
22 Confidential Human Source Policy Guide, 153–54.
23 FBI special agents, interviews.
24 Trevor Aaronson, "The Informants," *Mother Jones*, September/October 2011, https:www.motherjones.com/politics/2011/07/fbi-terrorist-informants/.
    FBI special agents, interviews.
    Arena, interviews.
25 Confidential Human Source Policy Guide, 12.
26 Reilly hard drive files.
    Billy Reilly–Tim Reintjes, text messages.
27 Billy Reilly–Tim Reintjes, text messages.
    Terry and Bill Reilly, interviews.
    FBI special agents, interviews.
28 FBI Anchorage, "CHS Assessing," CHS Recruiting Series, CHS-Assessing-Aid .pdf, 7.

CHAPTER 8: FALCON

1 Louis J. Freeh, *My FBI: Bringing Down the Mafia, Investigating Bill Clinton, and Fighting the War on Terror* (New York: St. Martin's Griffin; first edition, 2006), 50.
    Weiner, *Enemies*, 103.
2 Weiner, *Enemies*, 134, 137–38.
3 *9/11 Commission Report*, 89.
4 Ibid., 91.
    Weiner, *Enemies*, 226, 343, 360.
5 Confidential Human Source Policy Guide.
6 FBI special agents, interviews.
    CIA officers, interviews.
7 CIA officers, interviews.
8 FBI special agents, interviews.
9 Don Robinson, interviews.
    Department of Justice memorandum, "Authority of the Federal Bureau of Investigation to override international law in extraterritorial law enforcement activities," June 21, 1989, https:irp.fas.org/agency/doj/fbi/olc_override.pdf
    D. F. Martell, "FBI's Expanding Role in International Terrorism Investigations," FBI Law Enforcement Bulletin, vol. 56, no. 11, October 1987, https:www.ojp.gov/pdffiles1/Digitization/107706NCJRS.pdf.
    Federation of American Scientists, "Authority of the Federal Bureau of Investigation to Override International Law in Extraterritorial Law Enforcement Activities," Intelligence Resource Program memorandum, July 21, 1989, https:irp.fas.org/agency/doj/fbi/olc_override.pdf.
10 Wright, *The Looming Tower*, 352.
    9/11 Commission Report, 266.
    US Department of Justice, Office of the Inspector General, "A Review of the FBI's Handling of Intelligence Information Prior to the September 11 Attacks," special report, November 2004, https:oig.justice.gov/sites/default/files/archive/special/0506/chapter5.htm.

11 *9/11 Commission Report*, chap. 13.

12 "CIA Director George Tenet Resigns," *PBS NewsHour*, June 3, 2004, https:www.pbs.org/newshour/politics/politics-jan-june04-tenet_06-03.

13 *9/11 Commission Report*, 411.

14 US Department of Justice, Office of the Inspector General, Oversight and Review Division, "A Review of the FBI's Involvement in and Observations of Detainee Interrogations in Guantanamo Bay, Afghanistan, and Iraq," October 2009, 22, https:www.oversight.gov/sites/default/files/oig-reports/s0910.pdf.

15 *9/11 Commission Report*, 365, or, more broadly, chap. 12.

16 Robert S. Mueller III, Testimony Before the House Appropriations Committee, June 3, 2004, https:archives.fbi.gov/archives/news/testimony/creating-an-intelligence-service-within-the-fbi-1.
    "Intelligence," FBI.gov, https:www.fbi.gov/about/leadership-and-structure/intelligence-branch.

17 CIA officers, interviews.

18 "Model Partnership: New York Joint Terrorism Task Force Celebrates 35 Years," FBI.gov, December 8, 2015, https:www.fbi.gov/news/stories/new-york-jttf-celebrates-35-years.
    9/11 Commission Report, 402.

19 Robinson, interviews.

20 FBI special agents, interviews.

21 Robinson, interviews.
    FBI special agents, interviews.

22 Office of the Inspector General, "A Review of the FBI's Handling of Intelligence Information Prior to the September 11 Attacks," special report, November 2004 (released publicly June 2005), chap. 5, https:oig.justice.gov/sites/default/files/archive/special/0506/chapter5.htm.
    Department of Justice, "Report to the National Commission on Terrorist Attacks upon the United States: The FBI's Counterterrorism Program Since September 2001," April 14, 2004, 44, https:www.ojp.gov/ncjrs/virtual-library/abstracts/report-national-commission-terrorist-attacks-upon-united-states.

23 Jeff Stein, "The Biggest Little CIA Shop You've Never Heard Of," *Newsweek*, November 14, 2013, https:www.newsweek.com/2013/11/15/biggest-little-cia-shop-youve-never-heard-243964.html.
    Dana Priest, "CIA Is Expanding Domestic Operations," *Washington Post*, October 23, 2002, https:www.washingtonpost.com/archive/politics/2002/10/23/cia-is-expanding-domestic-operations/7e62ab9b-8c1c-4202-b7bd-44b3fb6931c0/.

24 FBI special agents, interviews.

25 FBI special agents, interviews.
    Robinson, interviews.

26 FBI special agents, interviews.

27 Zachary Laub, "Syria's Civil War: The Descent into Horror," Council on Foreign Relations, March 17, 2021, https:www.cfr.org/article/syrias-civil-war.

28 Reilly hard drive files.

29 Billy Reilly–Tim Reintjes, messages.

30 Reilly hard drive files.

31 Rockhurst High School, Kansas City, MO, https:www.rockhursths.edu/#/.

Larry Freeman, Rockhurst High School, alumni affairs, interview with author, 2019.
Rockhurst High School, *More Than Just a Name* (yearbook), 1996, https:www
.classmates.com/yearbooks/rockhurst-high-school/4182844225?page=200.
Registrar's office, Villanova University.

32 Terry and Bill Reilly, interviews.
Catie Cherri, interviews.
Billy Reilly–Tim Reintjes, messages.

33 Terry and Bill Reilly, interviews.

34 Terry and Bill Reilly, interviews.

35 Terry and Bill Reilly, interviews.
FBI property slip.

CHAPTER 9: OPERATIONAL

1 Zillow, property assessment, 29712 Warren Rd, Westland, MI 48185, https:www
.zillow.com/homedetails/29712-Warren-Rd-Westland-MI-48185/88308836_zpid/.

2 Michigan Department of Corrections, Aws Naser, biographical information,
https:mdocweb.state.mi.us/OTIS2/otis2profile.aspx?mdocNumber=895010.

3 Dar al Salam website, https:www.daicwestland.org.

4 Aws Naser, interviews with author, 2018.

5 Naser, interviews.

6 L3 spokeswoman, interview with author, 2018.

7 Naser, interviews.

8 Naser, interviews.

9 Weiner, *Enemies*, 428, 432.

10 ACLU, "Unleashed and Unaccountable: The FBI's Unchecked Abuse of Authority,"
September 2013, 37, https:www.aclu.org/sites/default/files/assets/unleashed-and
-unaccountable-fbi-report.pdf.
"Radicalization: From Conversion to Jihad," FBI intelligence report, 2006.

11 *9/11 Commission Report*, 423.

12 Naser, interviews.

13 Trevor Aaronson, "An American ISIS Fighter Describes the Caliphate's Final
Days—and His Own" (podcast), *The Intercept*, 2021, https:theintercept.com/2021
/07/15/american-isis-podcast.

14 Naser, interviews.

15 Aaronson, "An American Isis Fighter Describes the Caliphate's Final Days—and His
Own."

16 Naser, interviews.

17 "Becoming an Agent: An Inside Look at What It Takes, Part One: The First Week,"
FBI.gov, July 18, 2017, https:www.fbi.gov/news/stories/becoming-an-agent-part-1.
"Becoming an Agent: An Inside Look at What It Takes, Part Three: Preparing for
the Field," FBI.gov, August 3, 2017, https:www.fbi.gov/news/stories/becoming-an
-agent-part-3.
Basic Field Training Course, FBI, https:www.fbijobs.gov/sites/default/files/fbi-guide
-bftc.pdf.

18 Former FBI special agents, interviews with author, 2018–22.

19 Ibid.

20 Naser, interviews.

21 *State of Michigan v. Aws W. Naser*, State of Michigan Court of Appeals, LC No. 2013-244672-FC, October 13, 2015.
22 *State of Michigan v. Aws W. Naser*.
   Naser, interviews.
23 Naser, interviews.
   Gil McRipley, interviews with author, 2018.
24 McRipley, interviews.
   Terry and Bill Reilly, interviews.
25 Terry and Bill Reilly, interviews.
26 Terry and Bill Reilly, interviews.

CHAPTER 10: THE SECRET

1 Catie Cherri, interviews.
2 Nargis Rahman, "Tracked and Traced: How Thousands of American Muslims Ended Up on the Terrorist Watch List," WDET, January 19, 2022, https:wdet.org/2022/01/19/tracked-and-traced-how-thousands-of-american-muslims-ended-up-on-the-terrorist-watch-list/.
   Reitman, "'I Helped Destroy People.'"
   "Federal Civil Rights Engagement with Arab and Muslim American Communities Post 9/11," US Commission on Civil Rights, September 2014, https:www.usccr.gov/files/pubs/docs/ARAB_MUSLIM_9-30-14.pdf.
3 Catie Cherri, interviews.
4 "FBI HUMINT Initiative at Logan Airport," August 13, 2012, https:www.documentcloud.org/documents/3123376-HUMINT-Initiaive-at-Logan-Airport.html.
5 Transportation Security Administration, No-Fly List, https:www.tsa.gov/travel/passenger-support/travel-redress-program.
   Terrorist Screening Center, FBI.gov, https:www.fbi.gov/investigate/terrorism/tsc.
6 Charlie Savage, "FBI Casts Wide Net under Relaxed Rules for Terror Inquires, Data Show," *New York Times*, March 26, 2011, https:www.nytimes.com/2011/03/27/us/27fbi.html.
   FBI Domestic Investigations and Operations Guide, December 2008, https:vault.fbi.gov/FBI%20Domestic%20Investigations%20and%20Operations%20Guide%20(DIOG).
   Reitman, "'I Helped Destroy People.'"
7 FBI special agent interviews.
8 Mohammed Cherri, interviews.
9 *Abdulrahman Cherri, Wissam Charafeddine, Ali Suleman Ali, and Kheireddine Bouzid v. Robert S. Mueller III, et al.*, US District Court Eastern District of Michigan, 2:12-cv-11656-AC-LJM, April 13, 2012.
10 Terry and Bill Reilly, interviews.
   Catie Cherri, interviews.
11 Mohammed Cherri, interviews.
   Catie Cherri, interviews.
12 Catie Cherri, interviews.
13 Mohammed Cherri, interviews.
14 Oakland Community College, academic transcript, July 16, 2014.
15 Walsh College, Add/Drop Form, December 1, 2014.

16 Montana Technological University, Reference for Graduate School, March 31, 2014.

17 Billy Reilly, bstatement.pdf, application essay for Master's of Science degree in Computer Science, August 1, 2013.

18 Catie Cherri, interviews.

19 Alan Cullison, Paul Sonne, and Jennifer Levitz, "Life in America Unraveled for Brothers," *Wall Street Journal*, April 20, 2013, https:www.wsj.com/articles /SB10001424127887323809304578432501435232278.

20 Greg Miller, "Anti-Terror Task Force Was Warned of Tamerlan Tsarnaev's Long Trip to Russia," *Washington Post*, April 26, 2013, https:www.washingtonpost.com/world /national-security/anti-terror-task-force-was-warned-of-tamerlan-tsarnaevs-long-trip -to-russia/2013/04/25/0ed426de-addb-11e2-8bf6-e70cb6ae066e_story.html.
Timothy Heritage, "Boston Suspect Was under FBI Surveillance, Mother Says," Reuters, April 20, 2013, https:www.reuters.com/article/us-usa-explosions-boston -mother-idUKBRE93J0AE20130420.

21 Josh Dawsey, Evan Perez, Devlin Barrett, and Jennifer Lefitz, "Manhunt Ends with Capture of Boston Bombing Suspect," *Wall Street Journal*, May 8, 2013, http: online.wsj.com/article/SB10001424127887324493704578432030609754740.html?reflink=desktopwebshare_permalink.
Ann O'Neill, "Tsarnaev Trial: Timeline of the Bombings, Manhunt and Aftermath," CNN, May 15, 2015, https:www.cnn.com/2015/03/04/us/tsarnaev-trial-timeline /index.html.

22 Robinson, interviews.
9/11 Commission Report, 76.

23 Robinson, interviews.

24 Dmitri Trenin, "The Forgotten War: Chechnya and Russia's Future," Carnegie Endowment for International Peace, November 2003, https:carnegieendowment.org /files/Policybrief28.pdf.
Department of State Diplomatic Security, "Chechen Female Suicide Bombers: The New Face of Terrorism in Moscow," https:www.hsdl.org/?view&did=14112.
Human Rights Watch, "Into Harm's Way: Forced Return of Displaced People to Chechnya," January 2003, https:www.hrw.org/reports/2003/russia0103/.

25 Terry and Bill Reilly, interviews.

26 McCabe, *The Threat*, 84.

27 Reilly hard drive, file: calirussianbros.docx.

28 McCabe, *The Threat*, 89.

29 Jim O'Kray, interviews.

30 Terry and Bill Reilly, interviews.

31 Arena, interviews.

32 Robinson, interviews.
Arena, interviews.
FBI special agents, interviews.

33 FBI special agents, interviews.

34 Reilly hard drives, file: Reillycoverletter: Re: Intelligence Analyst, GS 7/9 (External), n.d.

Notes

CHAPTER 11: ORIGINS

1   Serhii Plokhy, *The Gates of Europe: A History of Ukraine* (New York: Basic Books, 2017).

Nestor the Chronicler, *The Primary Chronicle*, Laurentian text, trans. Samuel Hazzard Cross and Olgerd P. Sherbowitz-Wetzor (Cambridge, MA: Medieval Academy of America, 1953).

"Scandinavia and Russia: Where Did the Russian Land Come From?," Arzamas, https:arzamas.academy/materials/716.

"People of the North," *Diletant*, https:diletant.media/articles/35026059/.

John Haywood, *North Men: The Viking Saga, AD 793–1241* (New York: Thomas Dunne Books, 2016).

Vilhelm Thomsen, *The Relations between Ancient Russia and Scandinavia, and the Origin of the Russian State*, Taylor Institute, Oxford University, 1877.

2   Par Hansson, ed., *The Rural Viking in Russia and Sweden*, lectures, 1996, http:gnezdovo.com/wp-content/uploads/2020/05/100_Ingmar-Jansson.pdf.

Plokhy, *The Gates of Europe.*

3   Ishaan Tharoor and Gene Thorp, "How Ukraine Became Ukraine in 7 Maps," *Washington Post*, March 9, 2015, https:www.washingtonpost.com/news/worldviews/wp/2015/03/09/maps-how-ukraine-became-ukraine/.

"Vikings at the Court of Yaroslav the Wise," *Diletant*, https:diletant.media/articles/45272160/.

A. V. Nazarenko, *Ancient Russia on International Routes: Interdisciplinary Essays of Cultural, Trade, Political Ties of XII Centuries* (Schaumburg, IL: Book on Demand Ltd., 2018).

4   Brett Forrest, "Russia–Ukraine Conflict Lies in the Bones of an 11th-Century Prince," *Wall Street Journal*, January 1, 2022, https:www.wsj.com/articles/russia-ukraine-conflict-lies-in-the-bones-of-an-11th-century-prince-11641052801.

5   Ekaterina Gudkova, "How Did They Arise and What Is the Historical Meaning of 'Rus,' 'Russian,' 'Russia'?," Russian Ministry of Culture, https:www.culture.ru/s/vopros/rossiya/.

Alexander Pipersky, "Russian, Russian," *Arzamas*, https:arzamas.academy/micro/etnonim/11.

6   Alexander V. Maiorov, "The Mongolian Capture of Kiev: The Two Dates," *Slavonic and East European Review*, October 2016, https:www.jstor.org/stable/10.5699/slaveasteurorev2.94.4.0702.

Charles Halperin, *The Tatar Yoke: The Image of the Mongols in Medieval Russia* (Bloomington, IN: Slavica, 2009).

7   Halperin, *The Tatar Yoke.*

Orlando Figes, *The Story of Russia* (New York: Metropolitan Books, 2022).

8   Plokhy, *The Gates of Europe.*

"Ukraine, Name," Encyclopedia of the History of Ukraine, Institute of History of Ukraine, National Academy of Sciences of Ukraine, http:resource.history.org.ua/cgi-bin/eiu/history.exe&I21DBN=EIU&P21DBN=EIU&S21STN=1&S21REF=10&S21FMT=eiu_all&C21COM=S&S21CNR=20&S21P01=0&S21P02=0&S21P03=TRN=&S21COLORTERMS=0&S21STR=1.%201.

Orest Subtelny, *Ukraine: A History* (Toronto: University of Toronto Press, 2009).

"To the Independence Day of Ukraine: History of Ukraine and State Formation,"

Mykolaiv City Council, 2015, https:mkrada.gov.ua/content/do-dnya-nezalezhnosti
-ukrainiistoriya-ukraini-ta-derzhavotvorennya.htm.

9   Ian Talley and Alan Cullison, "Ukraine Corruption Concerns Stall IMF Bailout,"
    Wall Street Journal, October 31, 2019, https:www.wsj.com/articles/ukraine
    -corruption-concerns-stall-imf-bailout-11572535061.
    Lilia Shevtsova, "The Maidan and Beyond: The Russia Factor," *Journal of Democracy,*
    July 2014, https:www.journalofdemocracy.org/articles/the-maidan-and-beyond-the
    -russia-factor/.
    Vladimir Putin, "Vladimir Putin's Article 'On the Historical Unity of Russians
    and Ukrainians,'" Kremlin website, July 12, 2021, http:kremlin.ru/events/president
    /news/66181.

10 Boris Shramko, "Antiquity of the Seversky Donets," Kharkiv State University, 1962,
    http:dalizovut.narod.ru/hramko/hramko.htm

11 Galeotti, *Armies of Russia's War in Ukraine.*
    "Ukraine Crisis: Timeline," BBC, November 13, 2014, https:www.bbc.com/news
    /world-middle-east-26248275.

12 Billy Reilly–Mikhail Polynkov, text messages.

13 Jon Ostrower, Alexander Kolyandr, Margaret Coker and Paul Sonne, "Map of a Trag-
    edy: How MH17 Came Apart over Ukraine," *Wall Street Journal,* http:
    graphics.wsj.com/mh17-crash-map/.
    "MH17 Incident," Government of the Netherlands, https:www.government.nl
    /topics/mh17-incident.

14 Reilly hard drive file: ukrplane.docx.
    "#BBCtrending: How It Trended—The MH17 Blame Game," BBC, July 18, 2014,
    https:www.bbc.com/news/blogs-trending-28371461.

15 Galeotti, *Armies of Russia's War in Ukraine.*
    "Where Are They Now?" *Meduza,* May 31, 2019, https:meduza.io/en/feature/2019
    /06/01/where-are-they-now.

16 "Video: Rebel Shoot-Down of Ukrainian Military Plane," *Wall Street Journal,* July
    18, 2014, https:www.wsj.com/video/video-rebel-shoot-down-of-ukrainian-military
    -plane/CD20477D-B677-4212-A3AD-43C620CFED11.html.
    "Ukraine Crisis: Military Plane Shot Down in Luhansk," BBC, June 14, 2014,
    https:www.bbc.com/news/world-europe-27845313.

17 Nick Shchetko, "Ukraine Forces Repel Two Fresh Assaults on Donetsk's Airport,"
    Wall Street Journal, September 30, 2014, https:www.wsj.com/articles/ukraine-forces
    -repel-two-fresh-assaults-on-donetsks-airport-1412081687.

18 "Marvin Paul O'Kray," Lewis E. Wint and Son Funeral Home, https:www.wintfun
    eralhome.com/obituary/4846041.

19 Catie Cherri, interviews.

20 Terry and Bill Reilly, interviews.
    Catie Cherri, interviews.

21 Reilly hard drives, funeral videos and photos.

CHAPTER 12: ENTANGLEMENT

1   CIA officers, interviews with author, 2018–19.

2   Reilly hard drive files.
    Billy Reilly–Tim Reintjes, messages.

Notes

3   Paul Harris, "The Ex-FBI Informant with a Change of Heart: 'There Is No Real Hunt. It's Fixed,'" *The Guardian*, March 20, 2012, https:www.theguardian.com /world/2012/mar/20/fbi-informant.

    Leila Rafei, "How the FBI Spied on Orange County Muslims and Attempted to Get Away with It," ACLU.org, November 8, 2021, https:www.aclu.org/news/national-security /how-the-fbi-spied-on-orange-county-muslims-and-attempted-to-get-away-with-it.

4   Tresa Baldas, "FBI Translator in Detroit Secretly Married ISIS Leader," *Detroit Free Press*, May 2, 2017.

5   Jason Burke, "'Gangsta Jihadi' Denis Cuspert Killed Fighting in Syria," *The Guardian*, January 19, 2018, https:www.theguardian.com/world/2018/jan/19/gangsta -jihadi-denis-cuspert-killed-fighting-in-syria.

    Scott Glover, "The FBI Translator Who Went Rogue and Married an ISIS Terrorist," CNN Investigates, May 1, 2017, https:www.cnn.com/2017/05/01/politics /investigates-fbi-syria-greene/index.html.

    Haroon Siddique, "FBI Translator Married Isis Recruiter She Was Meant to Be Investigating," *The Guardian*, May 2, 2017, https:www.theguardian.com/us-news /2017/may/02/fbi-translator-syria-rapper-isis-islamic-state.

6   Paul Abbate, biography, FBI.gov, https:www.fbi.gov/about/leadership-and-structure /fbi-executives/abbate.

7   Reilly hard drives, files.

    Philippines security services, interviews with author, 2018–19.

8   Billy Reilly–Tim Reintjes, messages.

9   Reilly hard drives, pictures.

10   Billy Reilly–Amera Lomangcolob, messages.

    Department of Foreign Affairs, Republic of the Philippines, "Population of Overseas Filipinos in the Middle East and North Africa," https:dfa.gov.ph/dfa-news/dfa-releasesup date/25776-population-of-overseas-filipinos-in-the-middle-east-and-north-africa.

11   Billy Reilly hard drive, pictures.

12   Billy Reilly–Lomangcolob, messages.

13   Billy Reilly–Tim Reintjes, messages.

    Reilly hard drive, itinerary.

14   Billy Reilly–Tim Reintjes, messages.

15   Screenshot of Twitter posting, @bolansang (AMZ Lycn), Billy Reilly hard drive, file name: IMG_0494.PNG, Dec. 28, 2014.

16   Reilly hard drives, files, money transfer receipt, "ML Kwarta Palada."

    Billy Reilly–Amera Lomangcolob correspondence.

17   Suratni, interviews with author, 2018.

18   Reilly hard drives, images.

19   Seventy-seven pictures, Billy Reilly hard drive, February 2–12, 2015.

    James Hookway, "Abu Sayyaf Muslim Rebels Roil Waters of Southern Philippines," *Wall Street Journal*, September 7, 2000, https:www.wsj.com/articles /SB96826689188973238.

    "Abu Sayyaf Leader behind Execution of Foreigners Is Killed, Philippines Says," Reuters, April 12, 2017, https:www.reuters.com/article/us-philippines-militants/abu -sayyaf-leader-behind-execution-of-foreigners-is-killed-philippines-says-idUSKBN 17E0J5.

Notes

CHAPTER 13: THE FALCON FLIES

1 Terry and Bill Reilly, interviews.
2 Terry and Bill Reilly, interview.
3 Billy Reilly–Tim Reintjes, messages.
4 Grand Jury Indictment, United States District Court, District of Massachusetts, *United States of America v. Dzhokhar Tsarnaev*, June 27, 2013, https:www.justice.gov /iso/opa/resources/632013627162038513370.pdf.
5 Reilly hard drive file, Inspire_Issue_13_HQ.pdf, Al-Malahem Media, Issue December 2014, 1, 68–111.
  Transportation Security Administration, Mission Hall Exhibit, "Remembering the Past, Informing the Future, 2007-Present: The Evolution," https:www.tsa.gov/sites /default/files/9003_layout_mission_hall_exhibit_the_evolution.pdf
6 Billy Reilly–Tim Reintjes, messages.
  Reilly hard drives, file.
  "Al-Qaeda in the Arabian Peninsula (AQAP) Releases Issue 13 of Its English-Language Magazine *Inspire*," Middle East Media Research Institute, December 24, 2014, https:www.memri.org/reports/al-qaeda-arabian-peninsula-aqap-releases -issue-13-its-english-language-magazine-inspire.
7 Terry and Bill Reilly, interviews.
8 Terry and Bill Reilly, interviews.
9 Terry and Bill Reilly, interviews.
  Mohammed Cherri, interviews.
10 Catie Cherri, interviews.
11 Gregory L. White, "Russia Sends Aid Convoy to Eastern Ukraine," *Wall Street Journal*, https:www.wsj.com/articles/russian-aid-convoy-leaves-for-ukraine-140782 4191.
12 Catie Cherri, interviews.
13 Terry and Bill Reilly, interviews.
14 Catie Cherri, interviews.
15 Jim O'Kray, interviews.
16 Terry and Bill Reilly, interviews.
17 Reilly hard drive file, amz.odt, May 11, 2015.
18 Catie Cherri, interviews.

CHAPTER 14: THE BASE

1 Reilly family, WhatsApp group chat.
2 Elena Gorbacheva–Mikhail Polynkov, VKontakte messages.
  Gorbacheva, interview.
3 Reilly family, chat.
4 Reilly family, chat.
5 Paul Rekoff, "A Look at the Pro-Russian Separatists," *Wall Street Journal*, July 18, 2014, https:www.wsj.com/articles/BL-DISPATCHB-4075.
  Tatyana Voltskaya and Daisy Sindelar, "Volunteer Now! Russia Makes It Easy to Fight in Ukraine," Radio Free Europe / Radio Liberty, February 3, 2015, https:www.rferl.org /a/russia-ukraine-volunteers-kremlin-easy-to-fight-/26828559.html.
6 Galeotti, *Armies of Russia's War in Ukraine*.

7   Ibid.
     Polynkov, *A Soldier's Truth.*
8   Bronya Kalmyk, Facebook, https:www.facebook.com/profile.php?id=10001173436
     9611.
     Sanal Viktorov, Odnoklassniki, https:ok.ru/profile/540593988467.
     Viktorov Sanal Vladimirovich, *Myrotvorets*, April 28, 2015, https:myrotvorets.center
     /criminal/viktorov-sanal-vladimirovich/.
9   Polynkov, *A Soldier's Truth.*
     Mikhailovskaya, interviews.

CHAPTER 15: VOLGA SOJOURN

1   Billy and Terry Reilly, texts.
2   Janet M. Hartley, *The Volga: A History of Russia's Greatest River* (New Haven, CT: Yale
     University Press, 2021).
     "Russia's Troubled Waters Flow with the Mighty Volga," National Public Radio, No-
     vember 1, 2010, https:www.npr.org/templates/story/story.php?storyId=130837658.
3   "Saratov Plant Completely Liquidated," SaratovBusinessConsulting, August 13,
     2012, https:news.sarbc.ru/main/2012/08/13/125622.html.
4   Ulyanovs' town mansion "V.I. Lenin's House-Museum," Lenin Centre, http:
     leninmemorial.ru/en/muzeynyy-kompleks/dom-muzey-v-i-lenina.html
     Billy and Terry Reilly, texts.
5   Billy and Terry Reilly, texts.
6   Mamayev Kurgan Memorial Complex "To the Heroes of the Battle of Stalingrad,"
     UNESCO World Heritage Convention, https:whc.unesco.org/en/tentativelists
     /5936/.
7   Billy and Terry Reilly, texts.
8   "Ho Chi Minh Monument in Moscow: A symbol of Vietnam–Russia Friendship,"
     Vietnam Television, May 18, 2020, https:english.vtv.vn/news/ho-chi-minh
     -monument-in-moscow-a-symbol-of-vietnam-russia-friendship-20200531234958
     032.htm.
9   Billy and Terry Reilly, texts.
10   Reilly hard drives, files, money transfer receipt, "ML Kwarta Palada."
     Reilly–Lomangcolob correspondence.
11   Terry and Bill Reilly, interviews.
12   Billy and Terry Reilly texts.
     June 29, 2015, Moscow-Doha-Bangkok plane ticket.
     June 30–July 4, Bis Bangkok Riverside hotel booking.
13   Billy and Terry Reilly, texts.
14   Alexandr Rublev, social media postings.
     Galeotti, *Armies of Russia's War in Ukraine.*
15   Billy and Terry Reilly, texts.

CHAPTER 16: BLOOD

1   Billy and Terry Reilly, texts.
2   OSCE Special Monitoring Mission to Ukraine, https:www.osce.org/special
     -monitoring-mission-to-ukraine.

3   Billy and Terry Reilly, texts.
4   Billy and Terry Reilly, texts.
    Terry and Bill Reilly, interviews.

CHAPTER 17: THE COMPUTER

1   Catie Cherri, interviews.
2   Catie Cherri, interviews.
    Mohammed Cherri, interviews.
3   Mohammed Cherri, interviews.
4   Mohammed Cherri, interviews.
5   Catie Cherri, interviews.

CHAPTER 18: AGENTS AGAIN

1   Terry and Bill Reilly, interviews.
2   Terry and Bill Reilly, interviews.
3   Billy Reilly–Tim Reintjes, text messages.

CHAPTER 19: 300

1   Terry and Billy Reilly, interviews.
2   Billy Reilly–Tim Reintjes, text messages.
3   Polynkov, *A Soldier's Truth*.
4   Aleksandr Solzhenitsyn, *The Gulag Archipelago: An Experiment in Literary Investigation* (Paris: Éditions du Seuil, 1973), preface.
5   David J. Nordlander, *Origins of a Gulag Capital: Magadan and Stalinist Control in the Early 1930s* (Cambridge, UK: Cambridge University Press, 2017).
    James O. Jackson, "Soviet Union Gateway to the Gulag," *Time*, April 20, 1987, https:content.time.com/time/subscriber/article/0,33009,964077,00.html.
6   Polynkov, *A Soldier's Truth*.
    David E. Hoffman, *The Oligarchs: Wealth and Power in the New Russia* (New York: PublicAffairs, 2001).
    Glenn E. Curtis, ed., *Russia: A Country Study* (Washington, DC: GPO for the Library of Congress, 1996), http:countrystudies.us/russia/57.htm.
7   Polynkov, *A Soldier's Truth*.
8   Polynkov, *A Soldier's Truth*.
9   Maxim Boycko, Andrei Shleifer, and Robert W. Vishny, "Privatizing Russia," Brookings Papers on Economic Activity, no. 2, 1993, https:scholar.harvard.edu/files/shleifer/files/privatizing_russia.pdf.
    Congressional Research Service, "The Russian Financial Crisis of 1998: An Analysis of Trends, Causes, and Implications," 1999, https:www.everycrsreport.com/files/19990218_98-578_353c595b8980dfeaab66aa782deab2898c3b6889.pdf.
10 Polynkov, *A Soldier's Truth*.
11 Masha Gessen, *The Man Without a Face: The Unlikely Rise of Vladimir Putin* (London: Penguin, 2012).
    Catherine Belton, *Putin's People: How the KGB Took Back Russia and Then Took On the West* (New York: Farrar, Straus and Giroux, 2020).

12 Vladimir Putin, "Speech and the Following Discussion at the Munich Conference on Security Policy," Kremlin website, February 10, 2007, http:en.kremlin.ru/events /president/transcripts/copy/24034.

13 "Text of Putin's Speech at NATO Summit (Bucharest, April 2, 2008)," Ukrainian Independent Information Agency of News, April 18, 2008, https:www.unian.info /world/111033-text-of-putin-s-speech-at-nato-summit-bucharest-april-2-2008.html. "President Vladimir Putin Addressed a Meeting of the Russia–NATO Council," Kremlin.ru, April 4, 2008, http:en.kremlin.ru/events/president/news/44078.

14 Marc Champion, Andrew Osborn, and John D. McKinnon, "Russia Widens Attacks on Georgia," *Wall Street Journal*, August 11, 2008, https:www.wsj.com/articles /SB121834170757727521.

15 "Putin's Speech at NATO Summit."

16 Former senior State Department officials, interviews with author.

17 Polynkov, *A Soldier's Truth*.

18 Adrian A. Basora and Aleksandr Fisher, "Putin's 'Greater Novorossiya'—The Dismemberment of Ukraine," Foreign Policy Research Institute, May 2, 2014, https:www.fpri.org/article/2014/05/putins-greater-novorossiya-the-dismemberment -of-ukraine/.

19 Polynkov, *A Soldier's Truth*.

20 Terry and Bill Reilly, interviews.
Polynkov, *A Soldier's Truth*.

21 Bill Reilly and Mikhail Polynkov social media messages, eleven screenshots provided by Reilly family, August 5–September 23, 2015.

22 Billy Reilly, phone bill.

23 "Ukraine Crisis: Russian 'Cargo 200' Crossed Border—OSCE," BBC.com, November 13, 2014, https:www.bbc.com/news/world-europe-30039004.
Diana Magnay, "Ukraine Invasion: Why the Phrase 'Cargo 200' Ignites Terror among the Mothers of Russian Soldiers," Sky.com, March 1, 2022, https:news.sky.com /story/ukraine-invasion-how-hearing-the-phrase-cargo-200-leaves-relatives-of-russian -soldiers-fighting-in-ukraine-distraught-12554715.

24 Terry and Bill Reilly, interviews.
Interpreter, interview with author, 2018.

25 Galeotti, *Armies of Russia's War in Ukraine*.

26 Bill Reilly and Mikhail Polynkov, messages.

CHAPTER 20: BEOWULF

1 Dmitri Tyurin, interviews with author, 2018–22.

2 Graeme Smith, "In the Stolen-Data Trade, Moscow Is the Wild East," *Globe and Mail*, July 2, 2005, https:www.theglobeandmail.com/news/world/in-the-stolen -data-trade-moscow-is-the-wild-east/article18240345/.
Charles Clover, "Goldmine of Black Market in Russian Data," *Financial Times*, November 24, 2009, https:www.ft.com/content/07dedd34-d921-11de -b2d5-00144feabdc0.

3 Tyurin, interviews.
Terry and Bill Reilly, interviews.

4 Tyurin, interviews.

5 Office of the Historian, US State Department, "U-2 Overflights and the Capture of

Francis Gary Powers, 1960," https:history.state.gov/milestones/1953-1960/u2 -incident.

Michael Beschloss, *Mayday: Eisenhower, Khrushchev, and the U-2 Affair* (New York: Harper and Row, 1988).

6   Dmitri Tyurin, investigative reports filed to Reilly family, 2015–16.

7   Galeotti, *Armies of Russia's War in Ukraine*, 36.

Henry Foy, "Vladislav Surkov: 'An Overdose of Freedom Is Lethal to a State,'" *Financial Times*, June 18, 2021, https:www.ft.com/content/1324acbb-f475-47ab -a914-4a96a9d14bac.

Amy Mackinnon and Reid Standish, "Putin Fires His Puppet Master," *Foreign Policy*, February 21, 2020, https:foreignpolicy.com/2020/02/21/putin-fires-vladislav -surkov-puppet-master-russia-ukraine-rebels/.

8   Dmitri Tyurin and Bill Reilly correspondence, 2015–22.

9   Terry and Bill Reilly, interviews.

10   Terry and Bill Reilly, interviews.

CHAPTER 21: DNR

1   Federal Law of 28.12.2010 N 403-FZ (ed. of 01.04.2022), "On the Investigative Committee of the Russian Federation," Ministry of the Russian Federation for Press, Television and Radio Broadcasting and Mass Communications, http:www .consultant.ru/document/cons_doc_LAW_108565/019eea665257980aca04050c9f 33da30f551c857/.

2   Tyurin, interviews.

Tyurin, reports.

3   Tyurin, interviews.

Tyurin, reports.

4   Simon Ostrovsky, "The Only American Fighting for Ukraine Dies in Battle," *Vice*, August 20, 2014, https:www.vice.com/en/article/j544vy/the-only-american -fighting-for-ukraine-dies-in-battle.

"American OSCE Monitor Killed in Ukraine Identified as Joseph Stone," Voice of America, April 24, 2017, https:www.voanews.com/a/joseph-stone-american-osce -monitor-killed-ukraine/3823304.html.

5   Ministry of State Security of the Donetsk People's Republic, http:mgbdnr.ru/.

6   Aleksandar Vasovic, "Ex-electrician Backed by Putin Helps Unite Ukraine Rebels," Reuters, February 10, 2015, https:www.reuters.com/article/uk-ukraine-crisis -zakharchenko/ex-electrician-backed-by-putin-helps-unite-ukraine-rebels-idUKKB N0LE1DZ20150210.

Marc Bennetts, "Rebel Leader Alexander Zakharchenko Killed in Explosion in Ukraine," *The Guardian*, August 31, 2018, https:www.theguardian.com/world/2018 /aug/31/rebel-leader-alexander-zakharchenko-killed-in-explosion-in-ukraine.

7   "Chronology of Prisoner Exchanges: 2014–2020, Justice for Peace in Donbas, https:jfp.org.ua/blog/blog/blog_articles/58?locale=en.

Stanislav Aseyev and Andreas Umland, "Prisoners as Political Commodities in the Occupied Areas of the Donbas," The Swedish Institute of International Affairs, Feb-ruary 2021, https:www.ui.se/forskning/centrum-for-osteuropastudier/sceeus-report /no-2-prisoners-as-political-commodities-in-the-occupied-areas-of-the-donbas/.

8   Tyurin, interviews.

Notes

Tyurin, reports.
Tyurin-Reilly correspondence.
9   Terry and Bill Reilly, interviews.
Sen. Stabenow, Sen. Peters, Rep. Bishop staffers, interviews with author, 2018–19.
10 Tyurin–Reilly correspondence.
11 Tyurin, interviews.
Tyurin, reports.
12 Tyurin, interviews.
Tyurin, reports.

CHAPTER 22: THE LIST

1   Freeh, *My FBI*, 183–84, 282.
2   James O. Finckenauer and Elin J. Waring, *Russian Mafia in America: Immigration, Culture, and Crime* (Boston: Northeastern University Press, 1998).
Robert I. Friedman, *Red Mafiya: How the Russian Mob Has Invaded America* (Boston: Little, Brown, 2000), 119–39.
Robert Mueller, remarks to Citizens Crime Commission of New York, January 27, 2011, https:archives.fbi.gov/archives/news/speeches/the-evolving-organized-crime-threat.
FBI special agents, interviews.
3   "Russian Pilot Sentenced in Manhattan Federal Court to 20 Years in Prison . . . ," United States Attorney Southern District of New York, September 7, 2011, https:www.justice.gov/archive/usao/nys/pressreleases/September11/yaroshenkokonstantinsentencingpr.pdf.
Aleksey Tarasov, Yaroshenko lawyer, interviews with author, 2019–22.
4   TASS, "The Case of Konstantin Yaroshenko: How and Why the US Imprisoned a Russian Pilot," April 27, 2022, https:tass.com/society/1444277.
5   "Russia Prepares Documents for Extradition of Bout, Yaroshenko-Lavrov," TASS, September 8, 2012, https:tass.com/archive/681604.
6   "Russian Pilot Sentenced in Manhattan Federal Court."
Lee Ferran and Patrick Reevell, "The Twisted Tale of the Alleged Russian Smuggler Floated as a Potential Prisoner Swap," ABC News, January, 17, 2019, https:abcnews.go.com/International/twisted-tale-alleged-russian-smuggler-floated-potential-prisoner/story?id=60420220.
7   Arshad Mohammed, "U.S. Blames Fax for Diplomatic Gaffe over Russian," Reuters, July 22, 2010, https:www.reuters.com/article/us-russia-usa-apology/u-s-blames-fax-for-diplomatic-gaffe-over-russian-idUSTRE66L5ZA20100722.
8   James Hookway, "Thailand Sends Russian to U.S. for Terror Trial," *Wall Street Journal*, November 16, 2010, https:www.wsj.com/articles/SB10001424052748703326204575617622684681424.
Chad Bray, "Suspected Russian Arms Dealer Sentenced to 25 Years," *Wall Street Journal*, April 5, 2012, https:www.wsj.com/articles/SB10001424052702303302504577326183705420436.
9   Owen Matthews, "Viktor Bout's Secrets Frighten the Kremlin," *Newsweek*, September 2, 2010, https:www.newsweek.com/viktor-bouts-secrets-frighten-kremlin-72249.
10 Samuel Rubenfeld, "Magnitsky Act Compliance Is Straightforward, Experts Say,"

Wall Street Journal, December 22, 2017, https:www.wsj.com/articles/magnitsky-act -compliance-is-straightforward-experts-say-1513941016.

William Browder, *Red Notice: A True Story of High Finance, Murder, and One Man's Fight for Justice* (New York: Simon and Schuster, 2015).

11 US Department of the Treasury, Specially Designated Nationals List Update, April 12, 2012, https:home.treasury.gov/policy-issues/financial-sanctions/recent-actions /20130412.

"Sergei Magnitsky Rule of Law Accountability Act of 2012," Public Law 112-208, December 14, 2012, https:www.govinfo.gov/content/pkg/PLAW-112publ208/pdf /PLAW-112publ208.pdf.

12 Robinson, interviews.

13 Ibid.

CHAPTER 23: INDUCEMENT

1 Tyurin–Reilly correspondence.

2 Reilly hard drive file, FSB.jpg, October 27, 2015.
Terry and Bill Reilly, interviews.

3 Tyurin, interviews.

4 Jeff Stein, "In Russian Hacks of Democrats, a Ghost of the Soviet Past," *Newsweek*, October 9, 2016, https:www.newsweek.com/russian-hacks-democrats-ghost-soviet -past-508094.

Davis Lauter, "Now KGB Has Cause to Fear," *Los Angeles Times*, August 23, 1991, https:www.latimes.com/archives/la-xpm-1991-08-23-mn-974-story.html.

"The History of the Special Services Since 1917," FSB website, https:fsb.dossier .center/history/.

5 "History of the Monument to Dzerzhinsky," *Kommersant*, February 17, 2021, https:www.kommersant.ru/doc/4694171.

"Monument to Dzerzhinsky in Moscow. Dossier," TASS, June 24, 2015, https:tass.ru /info/2067571?utm_source=google.com&utm_medium=organic&utm_campaign =google.com&utm_referrer=google.com.

6 Ralph Boulton, "WITNESS—The 'Naughty Schoolboys' Who Plotted 1991 Soviet Coup," Reuters, August 17, 2011, https:www.reuters.com/article/idINIndia-588 27320110817.

Claire Bigg, "Could the KGB Founder Again Find a Place in Central Moscow?," Radio Free Europe / Radio Liberty, October 14, 2013, https:www.rferl.org/a/statue -dzerzhinsky-moscow/25136577.html.

7 Tyurin, interviews.

8 Tyurin, reports.
Tyurin–Reilly correspondence.

9 Tyurin, reports.
Tyurin–Reilly correspondence.
Tyurin, interviews.
Terry and Bill Reilly, interviews.

10 Barry Meier, *Missing Man: The American Spy Who Vanished in Iran* (New York: Farrar, Straus and Giroux, 2016).

11 McCabe, *The Threat*, 131–32.

12 "Disappearance of Robert A. Levinson (Kish Island, Iran March 9, 2007)," US De-

partment of State Rewards Justice Program, https:rewardsforjustice.net/rewards
/disappearance-of-robert-a-levinson/.

"FBI Washington Field Office Statement on Robert A. Levinson and the Department of State Rewards for Justice Announcement," FBI Washington Public Affairs,
November 4, 2019, https:www.fbi.gov/contact-us/field-offices/washingtondc/news
/press-releases/fbi-washington-field-office-statement-on-robert-a-levinson-and-the
-department-of-state-rewards-for-justice-announcement.

13 Andrew Higgins, "Our Man in Tblisi," *Wall Street Journal*, October 18, 2008,
https:www.wsj.com/articles/SB122428609504746507.

Michael Pullara, *The Spy Who Was Left Behind: Russia, the United States, and the True
Story of the Betrayal and Assassination of a CIA Agent* (New York: Scribner, 2018).

14 "Hostage Recovery Fusion Cell Marks Third Anniversary," FBI.gov, June 29, 2018,
https:www.fbi.gov/news/stories/hostage-recovery-fusion-cell-062918.

15 Brian Michael Jenkins, "Does the U.S. No-Concessions Policy Deter Kidnappings of
Americans?," RAND Corporation, 2018, https:www.rand.org/content/dam/rand
/pubs/perspectives/PE200/PE277/RAND_PE277.pdf.

16 Kevin Cirilli, "Jackson Returns with Freed Prisoners," *Politico*, September 20, 2012,
https:www.politico.com/story/2012/09/jackson-returns-with-released-prisoners-081
475.

Carla Anne Robbins, Betsy McKay, and Stephen J. Glain, "U.S. Soldiers Freed
to Jackson as NATO Vows to Press On," *Wall Street Journal*, May 3, 1999,
https:www.wsj.com/articles/SB925622788976195854.

17 "Hostage Recovery Fusion Cell Marks Third Anniversary," FBI.gov, June 29, 2018,
https:www.fbi.gov/news/stories/hostage-recovery-fusion-cell-062918.

18 Hostage Recovery Fusion official, interview with author, 2018.

19 Terry and Bill Reilly, interviews.

CHAPTER 24: "MR. TRUMP!"

1 Terry and Bill Reilly, interviews.

2 Kathleen Gray, "Donald Trump Speaks to Crowd in Novi," *Detroit Free Press*,
September 30, 2016, https:www.freep.com/story/news/politics/2016/09/30/donald
-trump-opponents-rev-up-before-novi-rally/91314042/.

"Full Event: Donald Trump MASSIVE Rally in Novi, MI 9/30/16," Right
Side Broadcasting Network, YouTube, https:www.youtube.com/watch?v=uBIj1x
-OZb0.

3 Photos of T-shirts, provided by Terry and Billy Reilly.

4 Terry and Bill Reilly, interviews.

5 Tom McCarthy, "Inside Trump Tower, Where the Transition Plays Out in Plain
Sight," *The Guardian*, December 7, 2016, https:www.theguardian.com/us-news
/2016/dec/07/trump-tower-new-york-city-president-house.

6 "Assessing Russian Activities and Intentions in Recent US Elections," Intelligence
Community Assessment, Office of the Director of National Intelligence, January 6,
2017, https:www.dni.gov/files/documents/ICA_2017_01.pdf.

Ken Bensinger, Miriam Elder, and Mark Schoofs, "These Reports Allege Trump
Has Deep Ties to Russia," *Buzzfeed News*, January 10, 2017, https:www.buzzfeed
news.com/article/kenbensinger/these-reports-allege-trump-has-deep-ties-to-russia.

Anna Nemtsova, "Amid Hacking Blowback and 'Golden Showers,' Moscow Fears

Losing Trump," *Daily Beast*, January 11, 2017, https:www.thedailybeast.com/amid -hacking-blowback-and-golden-showers-moscow-fears-losing-trump.

7   Paul Sonne and Michael C. Bender, "Donald Trump Offers Michael Flynn Role as National Security Adviser," *Wall Street Journal*, November 18, 2016, https:www.wsj.com/articles/michael-flynn-offered-role-as-donald-trumps-national -security-adviser-1479442042.

8   Anthony Scaramucci, interviews with author, 2018.

9   "Bob Foresman," EastWest Institute, https:www.eastwest.ngo/profile/bob-foresman. Securities and Exchange Commission, Twelve Seas Investment Company II filing, November 18, 2021, https:www.sec.gov/Archives/edgar/data/1819498 /000121390021061964/ea151356-8k_twelveseas2.htm.

10 Ted Man and James Grimaldi, "Trump Didn't Know of Flynn's Work for Turkey before Security-Post Nomination," *Wall Street Journal*, March 10, 2017, https:www.wsj.com/articles/trump-didnt-know-of-flynns-work-for-turkey-before -security-post-nomination-1489187449.
Dion Nissenbaum, "Mike Flynn's Pro-Turkey Work: An Unfinished Documentary to Boost Country's Image," *Wall Street Journal*, May 30, 2017, https:www.wsj.com/articles/mike-flynns-pro-turkey-work-an-unfinished -documentary-to-boost-countrys-image-1496183276.

11 Ivan Grek, interview with Alexander Voloshin, SMU Dedman College of Humanities & Sciences, Center for Presidential History, February 8, 2022, https: www.smu.edu/Dedman/Research/Institutes-and-Centers/Center-for-Presidential -History/CMP/US-Russian-Relations-under-Bush-and-Putin/Alexander-Voloshin.

12 Bob Foresman, interviews.

13 Del Quentin Wilber and Aruna Viswanatha, "Former FBI Director Robert Mueller Named Special Counsel for Russia Probe," *Wall Street Journal*, May 17, 2017, https:www.wsj.com/articles/former-fbi-director-robert-mueller-named-special-counsel -for-russia-probe-1495058494.

14 Rebecca Ballhaus, Michael C. Bender, and Del Quentin Wilber, "Before James Comey's Dismissal, a Growing Frustration at White House," *Wall Street Journal*, May 9, 2017, https:www.wsj.com/articles/before-comeys-dismissal-a-growing-frustration -at-white-house-1494385212.
James Comey, *A Higher Loyalty: Truth, Lies, and Leadership* (New York: Flatiron Books, 2018).

15 "Appointment of Special Counsel," Department of Justice website, May 17, 2017, https:www.justice.gov/opa/pr/appointment-special-counsel.

16 Maegan Vazquez, "Trump Slams DOJ and FBI in Weekend Tweetstorm," CNN.com, December 4, 2017, https:www.cnn.com/2017/12/03/politics/trump -flynn-twitter-rant.
Adam Serwer, "Trump Escalates His Attacks against FBI Officials," *The Atlantic*, December 23, 2017, https:www.theatlantic.com/politics/archive/2017/12/trump -escalates-his-attacks-against-fbi-officials/549164/.

17 Terry and Bill Reilly, interviews.

18 "Factbox—The 11 Candidates Being Considered for FBI Director," Reuters, May 12, 2017, https:www.reuters.com/article/uk-usa-trump-fbi-candidates-factbox -idAFKBN1882YN.

19 McCabe, *The Threat*, 227, 257–58.

20 "Paul Abbate, Deputy Director," FBI.gov, https:www.fbi.gov/about/leadership-and
-structure/fbi-executives/abbate.
21 Terry and Bill Reilly, travel itinerary.

CHAPTER 25: IN HIS FOOTSTEPS

1 Sonia Smith, "War of Words: Meet the Texan Trolling for Putin," *Texas Monthly*,
April 2018, https:www.texasmonthly.com/articles/son-wealthy-businessman-foot
-soldier-vladimir-putin-russia-hacking/.
Tim Dickinson, "The Bizarre Story of How a Hardcore Texas Leftist Became a Frontline
Putin Propagandist," *Rolling Stone*, March 3, 2022, https:www.rollingstone.com/politics
/politics-features/russell-texas-bentley-putin-propaganda-ukraine-interview-1315433/.
2 Terry and Bill Reilly, interviews.
Russell Bentley–Terry and Bill Reilly correspondence, 2018–19.
3 Terry and Bill Reilly, interviews.
4 "Rostov Arena: All You Need to Know," FIFA.com, February 9, 2018, https:
www.fifa.com/tournaments/mens/worldcup/2018russia/news/rostov-arena-all-you
-need-to-know-2929294.
5 Terry and Bill Reilly, interviews.
Rostov-on-Don, Investigative Committee, William Reilly investigative file.
6 Terry and Bill Reilly, interviews.
Billy and Terry Reilly, messages.

CHAPTER 26: CONTACT

1 "Reporter Daniel Pearl Is Dead, Killed by His Captors in Pakistan," *Wall Street Journal*,
February 24, 2002, https:www.wsj.com/public/resources/documents/pearl
-022102.htm.
2 Terry and Bill Reilly, interviews.
3 Catie Cherri, interviews.
4 Terry and Bill Reilly, interviews.

CHAPTER 27: RETICENCE

1 Stefan A. Pluta, FBI Special Agent, "Affidavit in Support of Criminal Complaint,
Arrest Warrant and Search Warrants," FBI.gov, February 2001, https:www.fbi.gov
/file-repository/hanssen-affidavit.pdf/view.
2 "Aldrich Ames," FBI.gov, https:www.fbi.gov/history/famous-cases/aldrich-ames.
"Robert Hanssen," FBI.gov, https:www.fbi.gov/history/famous-cases/robert
-hanssen.
Tim Weiner, *Betrayal: The Story of Aldrich Ames, an American Spy* (New York:
Random House, 1995).
"Secrets, Lies, and Atomic Spies," *Nova*, PBS, January 2002, https:www.pbs.org
/wgbh/nova/venona/dece_ames.html.
Victor Cherkashin and Gregory Feifer, *Spy Handler: Memoir of a KGB Officer—The
True Story of the Man Who Recruited Robert Hanssen and Aldrich Ames* (New York:
Basic Books, 2005).
Viktor Cherkashin, interviews with author, 2002.

3 Andrei Soldatov and Irina Borogan, *The New Nobility: The Restoration of Russia's Security State and the Enduring Legacy of the KGB* (New York: PublicAffairs, 2011).

Katie Cella, "Famous KGB Spies: Where Are They Now?," *Foreign Policy*, June 18, 2012, https:foreignpolicy.com/2012/06/18/famous-kgb-spies-where-are-they-now/.

4 Vladimir Putin, biography, Kremlin website, http:putin.kremlin.ru/bio/page-4.

5 Gregory L. White and Jeanne Whalen, "Arrest of Yukos Chairman Imperils Russia's Revival," *Wall Street Journal*, October 27, 2003, https:www.wsj.com/articles /SB1067081861267708 00.

Paul Sonne, Anton Troianovski, and Bertrand Benoit, "Russia Frees Mikhail Khodorkovsky," *Wall Street Journal*, December 20, 2013, https:www.wsj.com /articles/SB10001424052702304773104579269582372351584.

6 Soldatov and Borogan, *The New Nobility*.

Andrei Illarionov, "Reading Russia: The Siloviki in Charge," *Journal of Democracy*, April 2009, https:www.journalofdemocracy.org/articles/reading-russia-the-siloviki -in-charge/.

7 Cherkashin, interviews.

8 Brett Forrest, "The Sleazy Life and Nasty Death of Russia's Spam King," *Wired*, August 2006, https:www.wired.com/2006/08/spamking/.

9 Amit Kachhia-Patel, FBI Special Agent, sealed complaint, "United States of America v. Anna Chapman and Mikhail Semenko," June 27, 2010, https:www.justice.gov /sites/default/files/opa/legacy/2010/06/28/062810complaint1.pdf.

Maria L. Ricci, FBI Special Agent, sealed complaint, "United States of America v. Defendants 1–8, Vicky Pelaez," June 25, 2010, https:www.justice.gov/sites/default /files/opa/legacy/2010/06/28/062810complaint2.pdf.

"Ten Alleged Secret Agents Arrested in the United States," US Department of Justice press release, June 28, 2010, https:www.justice.gov/opa/pr/ten-alleged-secret-agents -arrested-united-states.

10 "Russian Spies Receive Top Honours," *The Guardian*, October 19, 2010, https:www.theguardian.com/world/2010/oct/19/russian-spies-receive-top-honours.

Gregory L. White, "Where Spies Go Undercovered," *Wall Street Journal*, July 2, 2010, https:www.wsj.com/articles/SB10001424052748704178004575351033461486698.

11 Brett Forrest, "The Big Russian Life of Anna Chapman, Ex-Spy," *Politico*, January 4, 2012, https:www.politico.com/states/new-york/albany/story/2012/01/the-big-russian -life-of-anna-chapman-ex-spy-069297.

12 Evan Perez, Michael Rothfeld, Chad Bray, and Gregory L. White, "U.S., Russia to Swap Agents," *Wall Street Journal*, July 8, 2010, https:www.wsj.com/articles /SB10001424052748704111704575354863581918490.

Gus Russo and Eric Dezenhall, *Best of Enemies: The Last Great Spy Story of the Cold War* (New York: Grand Central Publishing, 2018).

Adam LeBor, "Two Spies, Two Opposing Sides, One Fast Friendship," *New York Times*, November 16, 2018.

Gennady Vasilenko, interviews with author, 2018.

13 Shaun Assael and Brett Forrest, "The FBI vs. FIFA," *ESPN The Magazine*, February 16, 2016, https:www.espn.com/espn/feature/story/_/id/14767250/the-exclusive -story-how-feds-took-fifa.

14   Brett Forrest, "How the World's Biggest Bookie Was Snared at Last Year's WSOP—and Walked a Free Man," ESPN.com, November 12, 2015, https:www.espn.com/chalk/story/_/id/14095257/how-world-biggest-bookie-paul -phua-was-snared-fbi-last-year-world-series-poker-walked-away-free-man.

15   Dareh Gregorian, "Who Is Robert Mueller, the Man behind the Report on Trump?" NBC News, March 23, 2019, https:www.nbcnews.com/politics/justice-department /who-robert-mueller-man-behind-report-trump-n974296.
      Cullen Couch, "Robert S. Mueller III '73 On the Front Lines Again," *UVA Lawyer*, Fall 2002, https:www.law.virginia.edu/static/uvalawyer/html/alumni/uvalawyer/f02 /mueller.htm.

16   Del Quentin Wilber and Aruna Viswanatha, "Former FBI Director Robert Mueller Named Special Counsel for Russia Probe," *Wall Street Journal*, May 17, 2017, https:www.wsj.com/articles/former-fbi-director-robert-mueller-named -special-counsel-for-russia-probe-1495058494.
      Brett Forrest, "Q&A with Former FBI Director," *Alumni Horae* 95, no. 3 (Spring 2015), http:mediafiles01.myschoolcdn.com/ftpimages/36/misc/misc_118096.pdf.

17   Weiner, *Enemies*, 418.

18   Robert Mueller, interview with author, 2015.

CHAPTER 29: EASY MARK

1   Billy and Terry Reilly, messages.

2   Chase bank statement, account activity May 20–24, 2015; Chase online account activity June 6–14, 2015; Citibank statement, account activity May 16–June 11, 2015; Citibank online account information June 14, 2015.

3   "Demchuk Andrej Vladimirovich," *Myrotvorets*, May 9, 2015, https:myrotvorets .center/criminal/demchuk-andrej-vladimirovich/.
    "Andrej Sheremetov," *Myrotvorets*, March 18, 2016, https:myrotvorets.center /criminal/sheremetev-andrej/.
    Andrey Demchuk, Odnoklassniki profile, https:ok.ru/profile/119556600256.

4   Luke Harding, "Ukraine Extends Lease for Russia's Black Sea Fleet," *The Guardian*, April 21, 2010, https:www.theguardian.com/world/2010/apr/21/ukraine-black-sea -fleet-russia.
    Spencer Kimball, "Bound by Treaty: Russia, Ukraine, and Crimea," *Deutsche Welle*, March 11, 2014, https:www.dw.com/en/bound-by-treaty-russia-ukraine-and -crimea/a-17487632.
    "Ukraine Announced Russia's Obligation to Pay Rent for the Black Sea Fleet," June 23, 2020, https:www.rbc.ru/politics/23/06/2020/5ef209e39a7947555dc 02f31.

5   Stephen Fidler, "In Crimea, a Long History of Russian Power Struggles," *Wall Street Journal*, February 27, 2014, https:www.wsj.com/articles/SB10001424052702 303801304579408322329678800.
    Mark Kramer, "Why Did Russia Give Away Crimea Sixty Years Ago?," Wilson Center, https:www.wilsoncenter.org/publication/why-did-russia-give-away -crimea-sixty-years-ago.

6   Neil Kent, *Crimea: A History* (London: Hurst, 2016).

7   Leo Tolstoy, *The Sevastopol Sketches* (1855; repr. & trans., London: Penguin, 1986).

"Crimean War," National Army Museum, London, https:www.nam.ac.uk/explore /crimean-war.

8   Andrey Demchuk–Mikhail Polynkov, VKontakte message.
"Demchuk Andrej Vladimirovich," *Myrotvorets*.
Sheremetov Andrej, *Myrotvorets*.
Andrey Demchuk, Odnoklassniki profile.

9   Demchuk–Mikhail Polynkov, VKontakte message.

10 Andrey Kiselev, VKontakte account, https:vk.com/id8052246.
Andrey Kiselev, VKontakte, photo with Billy Reilly, https:vk.com/id80522 46?z=photo8052246_367517890%2Fphotos8052246.

11 Demchuk–Polynkov, messages.
Bill and Terry Reilly, messages.

12 Demchuk–Polynkov, messages.

13 Anastasiya Mikhailovskaya, interviews.

14 Dmitry Tikhonov, "Minister of Defense of the Donetsk People's Republic Igor Strelkov Resigned," *Kommersant*, August 14, 2014, https:www.kommersant.ru/doc /2544960.

15 Bronya Kalmyk–Mikhail Polynkov, VKontakte messages, 2015.

16 Billy Reilly–Mikhail Polynkov, VKontakte messages, 2015.

17 Chase bank statement; Chase and Citibank online account information.

18 Billy Reilly, credit card statements.

CHAPTER 30: CONSPIRACY

1   Billy Reilly–Tim Reintjes, messages.

2   "Biographical Information," Michigan Department of Corrections, https:mdocweb .state.mi.us/OTIS2/otis2profile.aspx?mdocNumber=895010.

3   Aws Naser, interview with author, 2018.

4   "U.S. Policy in Ukraine: Countering Russia and Driving Reform," Senate Hearing 114-77, Committee on Foreign Relations, March 10, 2015, https:www.govinfo.gov /content/pkg/CHRG-114shrg96831/html/CHRG-114shrg96831.htm.
Mark Galeotti, "Russian Intelligence Is at (Political) War," *Nato Review*, May 12, 2017, https:www.nato.int/docu/review/articles/2017/05/12/russian-intelligence -is-at-political-war/index.html.

5   David George-Cosh and Alistair MacDonald, "Driver Who Killed Canadian Soldier Had Been Questioned on Terrorist Links," *Wall Street Journal*, October 21, 2014, https:www.wsj.com/articles/canadian-soldier-dies-in-hit-and-run-1413892193.

6   "October 22, 2014: House of Commons Incident Response Summary," House of Commons, Canada, June 3, 2015, https:www.ourcommons.ca/Content/Newsroom /Articles/2015-06-03-Summary-e.pdf.

7   Reilly hard drive file, Анкета Добровольца, January 16, 2015.

8   Billy Reilly–Mikhail Polynkov, VKontakte messages.

9   Billy Reilly–Reintjes, messages, November 14.

10 Reilly hard drive.

11 Reilly hard drive.

12 Tim Reintjes, phone call with author, 2018.

Notes

CHAPTER 31: A DANGEROUS CHALLENGE

1   Billy and Terry Reilly, messages.
2   Source, interview with author, 2018.

CHAPTER 32: MOSCOW

1   "December Armed Uprising in Moscow (1905)," *RIA Novosti*, December 22, 2015, https:ria.ru/20151222/1346331334.html.
    Will Englund, "Moscow Police Raid New Protest Site," *Washington Post*, May 16, 2012, https:www.washingtonpost.com/world/europe/moscow-police-clear -occupied-park/2012/05/16/gIQADpAHTU_story.html.
2   Terry and Billy Reilly, interviews.
3   Tyurin, interviews.
4   Gregory L. White and Guy Chazan, "American Editor of Forbes Russia Is Shot and Killed," *Wall Street Journal*, July 12, 2004, https:www.wsj.com/articles /SB108940332526259954.
    Guy Chazan, "Russians Mourn Slain Journalist; Putin Ends Silence," *Wall Street Journal*, October 11, 2006, https:www.wsj.com/articles/SB116052753110088814.
    "New investigation into murder of 'Novaya Gazeta' journalist," Human Rights House Foundation, January 22, 2009, https:humanrightshouse.org/articles/new -investigation-into-murder-of-novaya-gazeta-journalist/.
5   "A Glance at Russian Journalists Attacked or Killed," Associated Press, May 30, 2018, https:apnews.com/article/cfbe9fb70d4943e1881be5157b221cca.
    "Journalists in Russia, 1993 to 2009—Deaths and Disappearances," International Federation of Journalists, https:web.archive.org/web/20090709092723 /http:www.journalists-in-russia.org/.

CHAPTER 33: RED SQUARE

1   David Owen and David O. Robinson, "Russia Rebounds," International Monetary Fund, September 9, 2003, https:www.imf.org/external/pubs/nft/2003/russia /index.htm.
2   "President Putin Visit," The White House, President George W. Bush, November 14, 2001, https:georgewbush-whitehouse.archives.gov/president/putin-visit/04 .html.
    Jeanne Cummings, "Bush, Putin Make Progress on Some Goals But Summit Ends without Major Accords," *Wall Street Journal*, November 16, 2001, https:www.wsj.com/articles/SB1005868207330521200.
3   Marc Champion, Andrew Osborn, and John D. McKinnon, "Russia Widens Attacks on Georgia," *Wall Street Journal*, August 11, 2008, https:www.wsj.com/articles /SB121834170757727521.
    "2008 Georgia–Russia Conflict Fast Facts," CNN, April 5, 2022, https:www.cnn.com /2014/03/13/world/europe/2008-georgia-russia-conflict/index.html.
4   Paul Sonne, "Russia Says 2018 World Cup Preparations On Track," *Wall Street Journal*, June 3, 2015, https:www.wsj.com/articles/russia-says-2018-world-cup -preparations-on-track-1433356004.

Notes

CHAPTER 35: A REACTION

1 Polynkov, *A Soldier's Truth.*
2 Viktorov Sanal Vladimirovich, *Myrotvorets.*
3 Elena Gorbacheva, interview with author, 2018.
4 Tyurin, interviews.

CHAPTER 36: WITH THOSE GUYS NOW

1 Brett Forrest, "Midnight in Moscow," *Vanity Fair*, July 2006, https:www.vanityfair
.com/news/2006/07/moscow-society-nightlife.
2 Anastasiya Mikhailovskaya, interviews with author, 2018–22.

CHAPTER 37: BLACK HOLE

1 "Ukraine Sends Force to Stem Unrest in East," *New York Times*, April 15, 2014,
https:www.nytimes.com/2014/04/16/world/europe/ukraine-russia.html.
Daniel Sandford, "Ukraine Says Donetsk 'Anti-Terror Operation' Under Way," BBC,
April 15, 2014, https:www.bbc.com/news/av/world-europe-27031318.
2 "Leonid Derkach Appointed Head of SBU," *Den*, November 13, 2012,
https:m.day.kyiv.ua/en/article/day-after-day/leonid-derkach-appointed-head-sbu.
"Former head of the SBU Leonid Derkach has died," Interfax-Ukraine, January 14,
2022, https:interfax.com.ua/news/general/791684.html.
Ekaterina Malyuga, "Former Head of the SBU Leonid Derkach Has Died," Unian
News Agency, January 14, 2022, https:www.unian.net/politics/umer-leonid-derkach
-eks-glava-sluzhby-bezopasnosti-ukrainy-novosti-ukraina-11672131.html.
3 Simon Shuster, "How an Accused Russian Agent Worked with Rudy Giuliani in a
Plot against the 2020 Election," *Time*, June 3, 2021, https:time.com/6052302
/andriy-derkach-profile/.
"Treasury Sanctions Russia-Linked Election Interference Actors," US Department of
Treasury website, September 10, 2020, https:home.treasury.gov/news/press-releases
/sm1118.
4 Derkach, interviews with author, 2018.
5 Andrew Roth, "Who Is Viktor Medvedchuk and Why Does His Arrest Matter to the
Kremlin?," *The Guardian*, April 13, 2022, https:www.theguardian.com/world/2022
/apr/13/viktor-medvedchuk-arrest-matter-to-kremlin.
Oleg Babanin, interview with author, 2018.
6 Richard Brooks, dir., *The Brothers Karamazov*, 1958, Turner Classic Movies,
https:prod-www.tcm.com/tcmdb/title/640/the-brothers-karamazov#overview.
7 "Two Russian Organized Crime Figures Charged in Plot to Murder Businessmen,"
US Department of Justice website, March 24, 2006, https:www.justice.gov/archive
/usao/nye/pr/2006/2006mar24.html.
8 Slava Konstantinovsky, interview with author, 2018.

CHAPTER 38: COSSACKS

1 Evgeny, Rostov-on-Don historian/guide, interviews with author, 2018.
G. H. Chalkhushyan, "History of the City of Rostov-on-Don," *Donskoy Vremennik*,
no. 7, 1998, 111–13, http:donvrem.dspl.ru/Files/article/m1/22/art.aspx?art_id=67.

Notes

2 "Cossacks—Who Are They?," *Meduza*, August 30, 2019, https:meduza.io/feature /2019/08/30/kazaki-eto-voobsche-kto-takie-i-pochemu-oni-hodyat-v-forme-i-byut -nagaykami-https:eupress.ru/uploads/files/H-133_pages.pdfprotestuyuschih.

Evgraf Saveliev, *History of Cossacks from Ancient Times to the End of the XVIII Century* (Novocherkassk: Donskoy, 1915), http:passion-don.org/history-1/chapter-2.html.

3 Serhii Plokhy, "The Ghosts of Pereyaslav: Russo-Ukrainian Historical Debates in the Post-Soviet Era," *Europe-Asia Studies*, May 2001, https:www.jstor.org/stable/826545.

Serhii Plokhy, *The Cossack Myth: History and Nationhood in the Age of Empires* (Cambridge, UK: Cambridge University Press, 2012).

Philip Longworth, *The Cossacks* (New York: Holt, Rinehart and Winston, 1970).

4 Brian Boeck, *Stalin's Scribe: Literature, Ambition, and Survival: The Life of Mikhail Sholokhov* (New York: Pegasus Books, 2019).

"Sholokhov, Biographical," Nobel Prize, https:www.nobelprize.org/prizes/literature /1965/sholokhov/biographical.

5 Christina Winkler, "The Holocaust on Soviet Territory—Forgotten Story? Individual and Official Memorialization of the Holocaust in Rostov-on-Don," Cambridge University Press, October 6, 2020, https:www.cambridge.org/core/books/abs /beyond-the-pale/holocaust-on-soviet-territoryforgotten-story-individual-and-official -memorialization-of-the-holocaust-in-rostovondon/8EA05E46699852ACD98FC7D 5D11F4950.

Samuel J. Newland, *Cossacks in the German Army 1941–1945* (Milton Park, UK: Routledge, 1991).

6 "Tank T-34: Eight Facts from the History of the Legend," *Rostec*, December 17, 2021, https:rostec.ru/news/tank-t-34-vosem-faktov-iz-istorii-legendy/.

"Miracle of the XX Century," Museum and Historical Complex, https:museum -t-34.ru/чудо-хх-века/.

Timothy Snyder, *Bloodlands: Europe Between Hitler and Stalin* (New York: Basic Books, 2010).

7 Nikolai Tolstoy, *Stalin's Vengeance: The Final Truth about the Forced Return of Cossacks After World War II* (Washington, DC: Academia Press, 2021).

8 Galeotti, *Armies of Russia's War in Ukraine*.

9 Petrovsky Prichal Hotel & Spa, https:hotel-petrovsky-prichal-luxury-hotel-spa -rostov-on-don.booked.net.

10 Byron Tau, "Maria Butina Pleads Guilty to Conspiracy to Influence U.S. Politics," *Wall Street Journal*, December 13, 2018, https:www.wsj.com/articles/maria-butina -pleads-guilty-to-conspiracy-to-influence-u-s-politics-11544719313.

11 Alec Luhn, "Ukraine: Murdered Council Member Vladimir Rybak Buried," *The Guardian*, April 24, 2014, https:www.theguardian.com/world/2014/apr/24/ukraine -murdered-council-member-vladimir-rybak-buried.

Halya Coynash, "Horrifically Tortured and Murdered, or Imprisoned in Crimea and Donbas for the Ukrainian Flag," Kharkiv Human Rights Protection Group, August 4, 2017, https:khpg.org/en/1503486891.

"Families of Murdered Hostages Demand Proper Investigation," Kharkiv Human Rights Protection Group, August 22, 2014, https:khpg.org/en/1408542900.

12 "Rostov Arena: All You Need to Know," FIFA.com.

13 Mikhailovskaya, interviews.

14 Galeotti, *Armies of Russia's War in Ukraine*, 38.

15 "Russia's Brutal Mercenaries Probably Won't Matter Much in Ukraine," *The Economist*, April 9, 2022, https:www.economist.com/international/2022/04/09/russias -brutal-mercenaries-probably-wont-matter-much-in-ukraine.
"Russian Mercenaries in Syria," Warsaw Institute, April 22, 2017, https:warsawinsti tute.org/russian-mercenaries-in-syria/.
Vitaly Shevchenko, "'Little Green Men' or 'Russian invaders'?," BBC, March 11, 2014, https:www.bbc.com/news/world-europe-26532154.

16 "Syria War: Who Are Russia's Shadowy Wagner Mercenaries?," BBC, February 23, 2018, https:www.bbc.com/news/world-europe-43167697.
"Russian Mercenaries in Syria."

17 Terry and Bill Reilly, interviews.

18 Mikhailovskaya, interviews.

CHAPTER 39: A DIFFERENT COUNTRY

1 Sergey Shvetsov, interviews with author, 2018.

2 Alexander Ganus, interview with author, 2018.

3 Terry and Bill Reilly, interviews.

4 Rostov-on-Don Investigative Committee, William Reilly Investigative File.

5 "Donetsk Airport: Ukraine's Coveted Prize," BBC.com, January 22, 2015, https:www.bbc.com/news/world-europe-30931105.

6 Vyacheslav Korshunov, Interview, Rostov-on-Don Investigative Committee, "Explanation," Krasny Sulin, Rostov Administrative Region, October 28, 2017.

CHAPTER 40: A DRIVE

1 "Sholokhov, Biographical," Nobel Prize.

2 Wendy Sloane, "Report Says Solzhenitsyn Target of 1971 KGB Poisoning Attempt," Associated Press, April 20, 1992, https:apnews.com/article/8a513d7f1f54bfe0 6759caa8df9f12b7.
David Remnick, "KGB Plot to Assassinate Solzhenitsyn Reported," April 21, 1992, *Washington Post*, https:www.washingtonpost.com/archive/lifestyle/1992/04/21/kgb -plot-to-assassinate-solzhenitsyn-reported/aa5de1cd-efa2-4953-ba6a-2a42f93e33b1/.

3 Sanal Viktorov, interview with author, 2018.

CHAPTER 41: WASHINGTON

1 House of Representatives, press staff, interviews with author.
"Behind-the-Scenes," US House of Representatives, Office of History, Art & Archives, https:history.house.gov/Education/Capitol-Tour/Behind-the-Scenes-Tour/.
Edward Kachinske, US House of Representatives Press Gallery, interview with author, 2021.

2 "Bishop, Michael Dean, 1967–," Biographical Directory of the US Congress, https:bioguide.congress.gov/search/bio/B001293.
Member Spotlight: Rep. Mike Bishop, Press Release, House of Representatives Judiciary Committee, February 2, 2015, https:republicans-judiciary.house.gov/press -release/member-spotlight-rep-mike-bishop/.

3 Char Adams, "Hippo Kills Michigan Grandmother during African Safari: She Was

an 'Absolute Treasure,'" *People*, August 11, 2017, https:people.com/human-interest
/grandmother-dies-hippo-attack-africa/.

4   Mike Bishop, interviews with author, 2018.
Mike Bishop staff, interview with author, 2018.
5   Arena, interviews.
6   FBI special agents, interviews with author.
7   Former CIA officer, interviews with author, 2018.
8   FBI Confidential Human Source Policy Guide, 2015, 151.
9   Reilly–Reintjes, messages.
10   Catie Cherri, interviews.
11   FBI Confidential Human Source Policy Guide, 151.
12   Interregional Public Organization, "Center for Assistance to the State in Counteracting Extremist Activities," https:www.csgped.ru/.
13   Valery Prikhodko, interviews with author, 2018–22.
14   Michigan State Police, interviews with author, 2018.
15   Michigan fingerprint file, file name: NA11001605P, Impressions taken by Reeves,
Agency Submitting Card MI3300600, June 28, 2011.
16   Don Robinson, interviews with author.
17   John Beyrle, interview with author, 2018.
Jon Huntsman, interview with author, 2019.
18   John Tefft, emails with author, 2018.
19   Hostage Recovery Fusion Cell official, interviews with author, 2018.
20   "History of FBI Headquarters," FBI.gov, https:www.fbi.gov/history/history-of-fbi
-headquarters.

CHAPTER 42: OUTREACH

1   Terry and Bill Reilly, interviews.
2   McCabe, *The Threat*.
3   "Timothy Waters Named Special Agent in Charge of the Detroit Field Office," FBI
National Press Office, December 11, 2020, https:www.fbi.gov/news/press-releases
/press-releases/timothy-waters-named-special-agent-in-charge-of-the-detroit-field
-office.
Kim Kozlowski, "Detroit's FBI Special Agent in Charge Retires," *Detroit News*,
December 31, 2021, https:www.detroitnews.com/story/news/local/detroit-city/2021
/12/31/detroits-fbi-special-agent-charge-retires/9062415002/.
4   Terry and Bill Reilly, interviews.
5   Terry and Bill Reilly, interviews.
6   Philip Mason, "Transportation in Michigan History," 1987, https:web.archive.org
/web/20220422210759/https:www.michigan.gov/documents/mdot/RR668ADMIN
_8_539527_7.pdf.
7   US General Services Administration, Patrick V. McNamara Federal Building,
https:www.gsa.gov/about-us/regions/welcome-to-the-great-lakes-region-5/buildings
-and-facilities/michigan/patrick-v-mcnamara-federal-building.
8   Terry and Bill Reilly, interviews.
9   Terry and Bill Reilly, interviews.
10   Terry and Bill Reilly, interviews.
11   US Department of Justice, "National Security Division Names New Chief of Coun-

terterrorism Section," April 17, 2007, https:www.justice.gov/archive/opa/pr/2007 /April/07_nsd_257.html.

"Lexpat Welcomes Former DOJ Counterterrorism Chief Mike Mullaney," Lexpat Global Services, July 27, 2020, https:www.lexpatglobal.com/2020/07/lexpat -welcomes-former-doj-counterterrorism-chief-mike-mullaney/.

12 "The Pearl Project: The Truth Left Behind: Inside the Kidnapping and Murder of Daniel Pearl," International Consortium of Investigative Journalists, Center for Public Integrity, 2011, https:cloudfront-files-1.publicintegrity.org/documents/pdfs /The_Pearl_Project.pdf.

Asif Shahzad, "Pakistan Court Orders Release from Prison of Mastermind in Daniel Pearl Case," Reuters, February 2, 2021, https:www.reuters.com/article/pakistan -usa-danielpearl-int/pakistan-court-orders-release-from-prison-of-mastermind-in -daniel-pearl-case-idUSKBN2A20TI.

13 Paul Abbate, interview with author, 2018.

14 Paul Abbate, FBI biography, https:www.fbi.gov/about/leadership-and-structure/fbi -executives/abbate.

CHAPTER 44: FOUND

1 Valery Prikhodko, interviews.

2 Дактокарта, July 10, 2015.

3 Ron Smith and Associates, Inc., https:www.ronsmithandassociates.com.

4 Jon S. Byrd, "Latent Print Examination Report," Ron Smith and Associates, Inc., November 29, 2018.

5 Jon S. Byrd, interviews with author, 2018.

6 Autopsy report: Act of the forensic medical research of the corpse No. 221. Research started July 11, 2015, completed August 18, 2015.

7 Terry and Bill Reilly, interviews.

CHAPTER 45: ELEVEN DAYS

1 Jeffrey Mitchell Jentzen, biography, University of Michigan Health, https:www .uofmhealth.org/profile/1216/jeffrey-mitchell-jentzen-md-phd.

J. Jentzen, G. Palermo, L. T. Johnson, K. C. Ho, K. A. Stormo, and J. Teggatz, "Destructive Hostility: The Jeffrey Dahmer Case. A Psychiatric and Forensic Study of a Serial Killer," *American Journal of Forensic Medicine and Pathology* 4 (December 15, 1994): 283–94, PMID: 7879770, https:pubmed.ncbi.nlm.nih.gov/7879770.

2 Jeffrey Jentzen, interview with author, 2018.

3 Arena, interviews.

4 Catie Cherri, interviews.

Mohammed Cherri, interviews.

5 Death certificate: Medical certificate of death no. 240, July 11, 2015.

Olga Yermishkina, text messages with author, 2021.

6 Terry and Bill Reilly, interviews.

7 Prikhodko, interviews.

Notes

CHAPTER 46: FINAL MILES

1   Terry and Bill Reilly, interviews.
2   Terry and Bill Reilly, interviews.
3   Bike Hotel, http:bike-hotel.ru.
    Hotel Museum, "Legends of the USSR," http:sssr-hotel.ru.
    Park Hotel Patriot, http:www.park-hotel-patriot.ru.
4   Prikhodko, interviews.
5   Vyacheslav Korshunov, interview with author, 2019.
6   "Europe's Largest Rostov Cemetery 'Captured' More Than 170 Hectares of Land," *RIA Novosti*, June 21, 2013, https:ria.ru/20130621/944926058.html.
7   Vladimir, undertaker, interview with author, 2019.
8   Billy's Bar, Facebook, https:www.facebook.com/profile.php?id=100080057755292.
9   Catie Cherri, interviews.
10 Modetz Funeral Homes, Lake Orion, https:www.modetzfuneralhomes.com/contact/orion.

EPILOGUE

1   DNA Test Report, Universal Forensics Corporation, signed by Zach Gaskin, chief scientific officer, August 29, 2019.
2   Brett Forrest, "The FBI Lost Our Son," *Wall Street Journal*, October 11, 2019, https:www.wsj.com/articles/the-fbi-lost-our-son-11570806358.
3   Polynkov, *A Soldier's Truth*, October 14, 2019.
4   Ukrainian Cyber Alliance, https:www.facebook.com/UkrainianCyberAlliance.
5   RUH8 member, interviews with author, 2020–22.
6   "Odessa Police Searched Activists of the Ukrainian Cyber Alliance Group," February 25, 2020, *Biznes Tsenzor*, https:biz.censor.net/news/3177755/odesskaya_politsiya_prishla_s_obyskami_k_aktivistam_gruppy_ukrainskiyi_kiberalyans.
    "'Ukrainian Cyber Alliance' Is Being Searched," UA.news, https:ua.news/ru/ukraine/v-ukrainskom-kiberalyanse-prohodyat-obyski.
    @UkrainianCyberAlliance, Facebook, February 25, 2020, https:www.facebook.com/UkrainianCyberAlliance/posts/2418252768486438.
    Odessa criminal case file.
    RUH8 member, interviews.
7   Yaroslav Trofimov, Alan Cullison, Brett Forrest, and Ann Simmons, "Russia Begins Military Operation in Ukraine," *Wall Street Journal*, February 24, 2022, https:www.wsj.com/articles/ukraine-shifts-to-war-footing-tells-citizens-to-leave-russia-11645616181.
8   Brett Forrest, "In Ukraine, New Reports of War Crimes Emerge as Russians Retreat from Kyiv Area," *Wall Street Journal*, April 3, 2022, https:www.wsj.com/articles/ukrainians-count-dead-dig-mass-graves-clear-land-mines-after-russian-pullback-11648970003.
9   Indira Sultanovna Sapozhnikova, "Prevention of extremism and the ideology of terrorism in educational organizations of the city of Rostov-on-Don," *Обзор.НЦПТИ*, 68, December 2016, https:ncpti.su/obzor/katalog-zhurnalsor.
10 Holy Sepulchre Cemetery, Catholic Funeral & Cemetery Services, https:www.cfcsdetroit.org/location/holy-sepulchre/.

Index

References to Billy Reilly in subheads are indicated by BR.

Index

About the Author

BRET T FORREST is a national-security reporter for the *Wall Street Journal*, where his investigative work focuses on the former Soviet Union. In the Russo-Ukrainian war, Forrest was the first reporter to reach the town of Bucha and uncover evidence of atrocities. He is the author of *The Big Fix*, an international bestseller, and *Long Bomb*. Forrest shared a National Magazine Award at ESPN, where he co-directed the true-crime documentary Pin Kings, an Emmy nominee. His international-affairs reporting has appeared in the *New York Times Magazine, Vanity Fair, The Atlantic*, and *National Geographic*. He has lived and worked in Russia, Ukraine, Brazil, and other countries.